THE GOWER HANDBOOK
OF LOGISTICS AND
DISTRIBUTION MANAGEMENT

The Gower Handbook of Logistics and Distribution Management

Fourth Edition

Edited by

John Gattorna

Gattorna Strategy Consultants, Sydney, Australia

Assistant Editors

Gretchel Trost
Andrew Kerr

GOWER

© Gower Publishing Company 1990

Published by
Gower Publishing Company Limited
Gower House
Croft Road
Aldershot
Hants GU11 3HR
England

Gower Publishing Company
Old Post Road
Brookfield
Vermont 05036
USA

Reprinted 1992

British Library Cataloguing in Publication Data
The Gower Handbook of logistics and distribution management. –
    4th ed.
    1. Retail trades. Goods. Physical distribution. Management
    I. Gattorna, John II. Handbook of physical distribution management
    658.788

ISBN 0 566 09009 0

Printed in Great Britain by
Bookcraft (Bath) Ltd.

Contents

Notes on contributors

Philip C. Alling (Corporate Profitability and Logistics) was appointed Director, Transportation of CIBA-CEIGY Corporation in 1988. Prior to joining CIBA-CEIGY, he held the position of Project Manager with Drake Sheahan/Stewart Dougall, Inc. and previously held a number of transportation positions with Westvaco Corporation and Firestone Tire and Rubber Company. Mr. Alling is a registered Interstate Commerce Commission practitioner, and a member of the Association of Transportation Practitioners. He is a past member of the Executive Committee of the Council of Logistics Management, and a co-author of *Corporate Profitability & Logistics*. He is currently a member of the Distribution Committee of the Chemical Manufacturers Association and Chairman of the Transportation Safety Work Group. He has a BSc in Business Administration and an MBA degree in International Business.

Andrew Aschner (Managing and Controlling Logistics Inventories) holds the position of Senior Industry Consultant with Fact Australia. In recent years he has successfully conducted consulting and marketing assignments achieving the introduction of state of the art technologies and significant operational improvements. Prior to joining Fact, he was Industry Consultant with Hewlett Packard working in the logistics area with major international corporations. He conducts seminars in Australia and New Zealand and has taught production and inventory management for a variety of organizations. Mr. Aschner is a qualified Industrial Engineer and holds the APICS Certificate of Production and Inventory Management. He is the immediate past Chairman and Director of the Australasian Production and Inventory Society with memberships in the Logistics Management Association of Australia and the Society of Manufacturing Engineering.

Dr Paul Bender (Development of Optimum Logistics Strategies) has over 17 years of combined experience as a management consultant, with 8 years as a high level executive with International Paper

Company, Blue Bell (Wrangler Apparel) Inc. and IT&T. His work focuses on the development and application of quantitative techniques, automation technology, and behavioural sciences to the solution of management problems. He specializes in logistics management and has developed original methods and techniques for application in this area. Dr Bender has degrees in Mathematics, Engineering, Operations Research and Information Science. He regularly lectures at Universities, Colleges, and seminars in the USA, London, Stockholm, Japan and Australia. He has written and co-authored many books and articles.

Keith Campbell (Managing Logistics Facilities) is a member of the Grace Brothers Management Board, and was responsible for all the functions of the Distribution Centre – distribution channel management, traffic and transportation, operations systems, company loss prevention, fleet management and in-house functions. He worked with Grace Brothers, a chain of 45 department stores, for 19 years and was involved in the initial planning and establishment of the 54,000 square metre Distribution Centre. He held several management positions, the most recent being as Group General Manager, Operations and Personnel. Mr. Campbell is President and Director of the Logistics Management Associations of Australia (NSW Division) and National Vice-President of the LMA.

Dr Norman Chorn (The Human Resource Factor in Logistics; The New Logistics Organization) is a Director of Gattorna Strategy, and specializes in the areas of organizational effectiveness and organization culture change. He uses various techniques he has developed to measure culture, in order to assess the organization's capability to implement strategies. Prior to joining Gattorna Strategy, he lectured in South Africa, was a management consultant and held positions with Chloride SA Ltd, and with Andcor Construction Company. He has a BA, a Higher Dip. Pers Mgmt, an MBA and a Ph.D.

Professor Martin Christopher (Developing Strategic & Operational Plans for Logistics, Developing Customer Service Strategies) is Professor of Marketing & Logistics and Chairman of the Marketing Group at the Cranfield School of Management, one of Europe's leading business schools. For many years he has been responsible for developing executive programmes in marketing and logistics management at Cranfield and elsewhere. He is widely recognized as a leading authority in the field of logistics in Europe, and is actively involved with current problems in marketing and logistics in Europe and overseas. He is a frequent contributor to management programmes in Europe, North America and Australasia. In addition he is Joint Editor of The International Journal of Business Logistics and the author of many books including *The Strategy of Distribution Management* and *Effective Logistics Management*. From 1971 to 1987 he served as Editor of *International Journal of Physical Distribution and Materials Management*. For several years Professor Christopher has been a member of the Council of the Institute of Logistics and Distribution Management and is the recipient of the Institute's 1988 Award for Excellence. He holds a Ph.D., an MSc, a BA and is a FCIM.

Professor Gary Davies (The Role Logistics can Play in International Competitiveness) is currently MFI Professor of Retail Marketing at Manchester Polytechnic. Gary has written or edited six texts and monographs on physical distribution including *Purchasing International Freight Services* with Richard Gray, published by Gower Press. He has consultancy experience with manfacturing and transport companies in the management and marketing of freight services. He is now specializing in retail distribution, and has a BSc, PhD, ARSM, DIC.

Dr Grahame Dowling (Strategic Partnership Marketing) is a Senior Lecturer in Marketing at the Australian Graduate School of Management, University of NSW, Australia. He has expertise in the areas of consumer behaviour, marketing audits and research, corporate image and advertising. He has consulted to financial institutions, telecommunications, engineering, chemical and paper companies and sporting teams. Dr. Dowling has a B.Comm, a Dip Business Studs, an M.Commerce and a Ph.D.

Stig Ehnbom (Personalizing Customer Service) is Chairman of TMI (Time Manager International Pty Limited) in Australia – a member of the Danish Time Manager International Group, which develops professional and personal time based skills. Before forming his own management consulting practice in 1974, he gained professional experience in senior management positions in subsidiaries of large multinational corporations. As a Chief Executive of a declining business, he was responsible for rebuilding the company through product development, production rationalization and aggressive marketing and sales activities worldwide. Time Manager International developed and has conducted Customer Service programmes for over 1,000,000 people over the last 15 years in such well known organizations as British Airways, Scandinavian Airlines, Audi Volkswagen, Telecom New Zealand, American Express and Japan Airlines.

Professor Dag Ericsson (Business Resource Management – a Framework for Strategic Management of the Materials Flow) is Professor Industrial Logistics at Chalmers University of Technology in Gottenburg, Sweden. He is also head of the consulting company Business Resource Management, and has written several books and articles in logistics, purchasing, marketing and organization development.

Professor David Farmer (In-coming Materials Management: a Case of Reverse Distribution) is Professor of Management Studies at Henley, the Administrative Staff College. Prior to becoming a management teacher he had 15 years industrial purchasing and marketing experience in four industries. He is the co-author of five texts, including the best selling European book *Purchasing Principles and Techniques* Pitman, (3rd edn.) He has lectured in every Western European country, Eastern Europe, Australasia and the United States, and was the first European to attain a doctorate in a topic associated with purchasing. He recently became the first European to have a Professorship conferred as a result of his work in the purchasing field.

Dr John Gattorna (General Editor, Adding Value through Managing the Logistics Chain, Managing Logistics in a Changing Environment, Developing a Channels Strategy, Auditing Internal Logistics Performance, The Logistics Interface with Marketing) is Chairman of Gattorna Strategy Consultants in Sydney, Australia. He is a Visiting Fellow in Marketing at the Australia Graduate School of Management, University of NSW, International Professor in Marketing Planning and Logistics at the International Management Centres, UK, Editor-in-Chief of the *Asia Pacific International Journal of Business Logistics*, Regional Editor of the *International Journal of Physical Distribution and Materials Management* and Director of the Effective Logistics Management programme at the University of NSW. Dr Gattorna is author of hundreds of books, monographs and articles and is considered a world authority in the areas of distribution, logistics, customer service, marketing planning, retailing and corporate strategy. He has developed a number of "corporate revitalization" techniques which he uses in his strategy consulting work and in the

100 or more public and in-house programmes he contributes to each year. He has a BE, an MBA and a Ph.D.

Garry Greenhalgh (Logistics Interface with Manufacturing) is a Senior Consultant in the Division of PA Consulting Group concerned with capital intensive and manufacturing industries. From a background in the food and pharmaceutical industries, he has worked during his 2 years with PA in the areas of manufacturing and logistics for organizations in the steel, electronics, timber, and electrical equipment industries, as well as statutory authorities. His specific areas of competence include: manufacturing strategy development, logistics strategy development, physical distribution management, production management and short term performance improvement.

Gerry Hatton (Designing a Warehouse or Distribution Centre, Materials Handling, Storing the Inventory, Order Picking, Building Design & Layout) is founder and Managing Director of Colby Handling Systems, which is the market leader in Design, Manufacture and Installation of sophisticated warehousing systems in Australasia. He is also founder and Managing Director of Technics Pacific Consultants Group which is the largest and most advanced Materials Handling System Design Group in Australia. Colby/Technics Systems has won twice as many awards in the last 5 years as all other consultant and manufacturing companies combined. Colby won "Exporter of the Year", Enterprise Australia and other Business and Management Awards. In 1987 he purchased Creswick Industries, a major innovative designer and manufacturer of smart packaging and filling systems.

Phil Heenan (The Path of Successful Implementation of DRP) offers experience based assistance on project planning, education, human and organizational needs. He is an instructor in Oliver Wight classes in Maufacturing Resource Planning in Australia and New Zealand and Managing Director of his own consultancy firm. Prior to founding his consulting firm, he worked for successful companies such as: Stafford Ellinson, Red Tulip, Beatrice and Cadbury. With the Red Tulip group he was Logistics Manager responsible for Planning, Supply, Customs, Stores and Distribution areas. As MRP II Project Manager at Cadbury, he managed all MRP II education and implementation activities. Mr. Heenan is a member of the Victorian and New South Wales Chapters of APICS and obtained a CPIM in 1982.

He is a frequent and popular speaker and a regular contributor to conferences and journals. He has a Grad Dip in Log Mgmt.

Andrew Kerr Assistant Editor, (The Logistics Interface with Marketing, The Impact of Technology on Delivered Costs) is Managing Director of Griffin Corporate Services, a Sydney based consultancy specializing in the fields of business planning and logistics with particular emphasis on service operations management. His involvement with logistics began in the late 1960s when he served in a number of line and staff appointments with various Australian Army Supply units within Australia and overseas. Prior to becoming a consultant, he held senior logistics positions with Myer, GEC, Digital Equipment and Sperry. Mr Kerr is a Visiting Lecturer at the School of Business, University of Western Sydney. He is a member of the Australian Institute of Management and the Logistics Management Association of Australia and is actively involved in that Association's Education Committee. He holds an MBA from Macquarie University.

Professor Richard A. Lancioni (Reverse Logistics: The New Distribution Structure for the 1990s and Beyond) is Professor of Marketing and Logistics and Director of Logistics Programmes at Temple University. He holds a BA in Government Administration from Lasalle College, an MBA in Marketing from Ohio University and a Ph.D. in Logistics from the Ohio State University. He has spent 6 years in industry with Standard Tank and Sea as Controller and with Alcoa Aluminium as a Distribution and Marketing Analyst. Professor Lancioni taught marketing and economics at Ohio State University. He has published articles in all the major marketing and logistics journals.

Kees De Leeuw (Management Support System for Logistics including EDI) joined Philips Industries in Holland in 1965 and was involved in several large projects concerning the development of Management Information Systems for production and stock control, and later managed a number of pilot projects concerning logistic strategies for Philips in Europe. In 1979 he was transferred to Philips Australia and in 1981 was appointed National Physical Distribution Manager. He joined Colby Engineering in 1984 as Manager of the Systems Implementation Group and in 1987, joined Digital Equipment Corporation in the role of Logistics Consultant. His main tasks include providing technical sales support, assisting in the developing of business solutions and advising about appropriate software solutions. He holds a M.Ec from Erasmus University, Rotterdam.

Martin Mitchelson (Materials Management in Capital Intensive Industries) is a Divisional General Manager with PA Consulting Group, responsible for PA's work in the manufacturing and public sectors throughout the Asia Pacific zone. In his 12 years with PA he has worked in heavy industry around the world and has specialized in materials management in oil and gas, utilities, steel and shipbuilding. He is currently advising a number of major Australian corporations on their future logistics strategies.

Chris Robinson (Strategic Partnership Marketing) is Managing Director of Gattorna Strategy Consultants. He has expertise in the areas of buying, marketing, importing and distribution of general merchandise, issues management, retail customer segmentation, strategic retail marketing planning, strategic partnering and supplier audits. He is regarded as one of the most experienced importers of general merchandise from China. Prior to joining Gattorna Strategy, he held senior positions up to Associate Director with the Woolworths chain of retail stores for 18 years.

Alan Slater (Choice of the Transport Mode) is a management consultant at Price Waterhouse in Manchester where he is responsible for the logistics consulting group. The majority of his recent work has been with rapidly growing businesses in areas as diverse as food and drink, fashion, electronics, consumer products, engineering and the distribution service sector. He has been a management consultant since 1982 after industrial experience including managerial responsibility for distribution operations with Sony, British Oxygen, Rank and Plessey. He is a regular speaker at conferences, has published over thirty articles on specific distribution issues, and is the author of *"A Handbook of Physical Distribution Software"*.

Gene R. Tyndall (Corporate Profitability and Logistics) was appointed Partner in Charge of the United States Transportation and Logistics Management Consulting Group of Ernst & Whinney in 1982. He has directed specialized consulting services to manufacturing, merchandizing, distribution, and transportation companies, in business strategy, logistics and distribution, marketing, and information systems. Previously, Mr Tyndall developed and applied computer-based analyses to problems in logistics and transportation for private companies with another consulting firm. In the late 1960s, he was a logistics analyst for General Research Corporation and before that, he served at the Pentagon, where he worked on strategic mobility analysis and defense logistics. Mr. Tyndall is currently expert logistics columnist for *Marketing News*, and for the *Journal of Cost Management*. He has a Bachelor of Science degree in Industrial Engineering; a Master's in Business Administration, and has completed all pre-dissertation requirements for his doctorate in Business Management.

Figures

Tables

Abbreviations

AGV	automatic guided vehicle
ANSI	American National Standards Institute
AS/RS	automatic storage and retrieval
BRM	business resource management
CAD	computer-aided design
CAPS	computer-aided picking system
CASE	computer-aided software engineering
CEO	chief executive officer
CID	computer-integrated distribution
CIM	computer-integrated manufacturing
CIP	cost, insurance and freight
CL	carload
CRM	capital resource management
DC	distribution centre
DCP	cost and freight
DDP	delivered duty paid
DPP	direct product profitability
DRP	distribution resource planning
DRP II	distribution requirements planning
EDI	electronic data interchange
EFT	electronic funds transfer
EOQ	economic order quantities
ESS	electronic spreadsheet
EXW	ex-works
FIFO	first in-first out
FOB	free-on-board
GMA	Grocery Manufacturers' Association (US)
HRM	human resources management
IRM	Information resources management
ISO	International Standards Organization
LTL	less-than-truckload
MPS	master production schedule
MRM	materials resource management

MRP	materials requirement planning
MRPII	manufacturing resource planning
OR	operational research
P&D	pick-up and delivery
PDM	physical distribution management
PLC	product life cycle
PSC	programmable sort controller
ROA	rate of return on assets
ROMI	return on management investment
SAD	Single Administrative Document
SAS	Scandinavian Airlines System
SIRATAC	a computer-based tactical crop management system
SKU	Stock-keeping unit
TL	truckload
TQC	total quality control
VAN	value-added network
VMS	vertical marketing system

Foreword

For many enterprises it is axiomatic that the 1990s will see the global market continue to reduce in size through technological, social, and political change. The implications to remain competitive are significant.

Successful logistics management will need to consider strategic alliances in purchasing and manufacturing; the rationalization and co-ordination of manufacturing facilities to reduce costs and maximise asset utilization; sophisticated warehousing; transport through longer distribution channels that will span national boundaries; computer integrated manufacturing and logistics, and maximum use of order information technology to improve customer service.

I am delighted that this 4th edition of the Handbook of Logistics and Distribution Management addresses these topics. Dr Gattorna has assembled the research and expertise of leading international logistics practitioners and the handbook will be a valuable reference for all students and managers.

Peter T. Bartels
Chief Executive
Elders Brewing Group
Melbourne, 1990

Preface to the Fourth Edition

Jack Welch, CEO of General Electric in the US is reported to have said "Control your own destiny or someone else will". Sound advice indeed in today's turbulent times, but easier said than done! Practitioners and users of this book anywhere in the world will find insights which go at least some of the way towards achievement of this goal, by bringing together in one place the most comprehensive up-to-date treatment of the corporate logistics activity.

This book is designed to take a general management rather than a specialist perspective of logistics. It suggests that the degree of "alignment" between the operating environment, logistics strategy, and the human and organizational factors will in the end determine what service performance is actually delivered.

The logistics manager of the 1990s, for whom this edition is written, will find it an invaluable aid in making the transition from functional specialist to general manager of the firm's not inconsiderable investment in logistics resources.

This book attempts to shepherd the GM Logistics safely through the many paradoxes he/she faces, eg. the pressure to drive costs down – and at the same time increase the "value" of our product/service as perceived by customers. No policy manual can handle such apparent conflict.

So it's high time we sorted out the confusion and found a way through the maze of data, competitive action, government regulation, etc. The challenge for readers therefore, is to take the templates offered herein and use them to gain extra insights which translate into bottom-line results. Indeed, the old Chinese proverb, "What you see of the [logistics] mountain depends on where you stand", is a good description of this book.

The perspectives offered here on the environment, service, distribution channels systems, hardware/software, and implementation are at the leading edge of good practice in the best companies worldwide. We exhort the reader to use these ideas as the vehicle for change – before you have no choice.

My thanks to all the contributing authors, many of whom are long standing personal friends and leaders in their own fields. Special recognition is due to Gretchel Trost and Andrew Kerr for their unwavering support and infinite patience with the demanding editorial role – their contribution has ensured that the "vision" became the reality. Finally, my appreciation to the publisher, Gower Press, whose confidence in the project has never wavered. In bringing this body of knowledge to a worldwide audience, Gower too is also a major influencer of change.

Dr John L. Gattorna
Sydney, 1990

Part I
STRATEGIC ISSUES IN LOGISTICS

Overview to Part I

During the latter half of the 1980s, logistics has been accorded greater recognition as evidenced by the number of logistics departments appearing on organization charts. Yet, despite this hierarchical elevation, many logistics managers have failed to capitalize on this newly acquired status. In essence they have failed to convince their Chief Executive Officers (CEOs) of the added value which logistics can bring to both operational effectiveness and bottom-line profitability.

In Chapter 1 Gattorna suggests that logistics managers must remove their narrow operational blinkers and adopt a strategic perspective of logistics and its role in achieving corporate profitability. The main focus is on logistics adding value to the organization's products and services as they move through the channel towards the final consumer. The successful logistics managers of the 1990s are profiled as possessing a broad understanding of the strategic issues facing their organizations, coupled with an ability to identify the value-added activities and effectively direct the organization's logistics resources in pursuit of corporate goals.

The concept of strategic perspective is further developed in Chapter 2 which suggests that logistics managers capable of coping with an ever more rapidly changing environment, will play a leading role in managing the organizational inter-relationships which effect the flow of goods and services to customers. In introducing the notion of strategic planning, a methodology for planning and managing in turbulent times is outlined, and it is suggested that survival is dependent upon an organization's ability to adapt continually to its changing environment.

Chapter 3 details the findings of a major study of US organizations successfully utilizing logistics as a strategic resource. Alling and Tyndall describe the 10 principles of logistics excellence common to all organizations striving to achieve the full profit potential from their logistics operations. This incisive study highlights many of the issues covered in depth elsewhere in this handbook, and stresses the importance of logistics in the organization's strategic planning process.

Finally, in Chapter 4, Martin Christopher examines what is involved in developing strategic and operational plans for logistics. He graphically depicts the processes and the interdependencies involved in developing effective plans and highlights the value of

3

decision support systems to assess the likely impact of proposed strategies.

1 Adding Value through Managing the Logistics Chain

John Gattorna

Introduction

Today, logistics departments appear on the organization charts of many large European, UK and US organizations alongside marketing, manufacturing and finance. Yet, despite this apparent growth in organizational importance, many senior managers and chief executives still perceive the role of logistics as nothing more than getting the right product to the right place at the right time for the least cost.

It is not surprising that chief executives have such a limited view of logistics. Logistics practitioners have been far too obsessed with their own professionalism and the inner workings of their own departments to worry about how their business decisions impact profitability and add value to their organizations' products and services.

Successful logistics managers in the 1990s will need to develop a wider perspective of their role within the organization and begin to think strategically. They will need to convince their chief executives that logistics – defined as the process of strategically managing the acquisition, movement and storage of materials, parts and finished inventory (and related information flows) through an organization and its marketing channels to fulfil orders most cost-effectively – does add value and can play a vital part in organizational profitability.

Only by linking all logistics activities directly to the organization's strategic plan can logistics managers work effectively to support their organizations' strategy for achieving competitive advantage.

5

Value added

Value is the amount a customer is willing to pay for the products or services provided by an organization. Value added is the difference between what the customer pays and the cost to the organization of providing that product or service. Organizations attempting to isolate the costs associated with providing products and services must address two key concepts of channel management:

1   How much *value is being added* to the product as it moves down the channel from supplier to consumer?
2   How much does it *cost* the supplier to have such value added (at each level)?

Figure 1.1 depicts the activities as a product moves from procurement of raw materials through to purchase by the consumer and poses the question: who provides the service and what does each party do? Logistics managers must seek to identify those activities where they can add value and thereby help to differentiate their organizations' products from those of their competitors.

Differentiation and competitive advantage

Many organizations are capable of incrementally differentiating their products or services from those offered by their competitors. With the complexities of modern products it is easier to make a product slightly different, but it is often difficult for the customer to discern that the difference exists. Unless the customer perceives the difference, it does not exist in the marketplace and any anticipated advantage is lost.

Successful organizations tend to be significantly different in one or more ways that are important to their customers. Often intangibles such as the organization's reputation for support, quality or service are the only perceived advantages. Clearly, many opportunities exist for logistics to focus on those differences valued by customers and thus help gain a competitive advantage.

The cost of information was one of the few business costs to reduce during the 1980s. The revolution in information technology (see Chapter 27) provides the opportunity for logistics to utilize transaction-based and decision support systems as a source of competitive differentiation and increased market share. For example, manage-

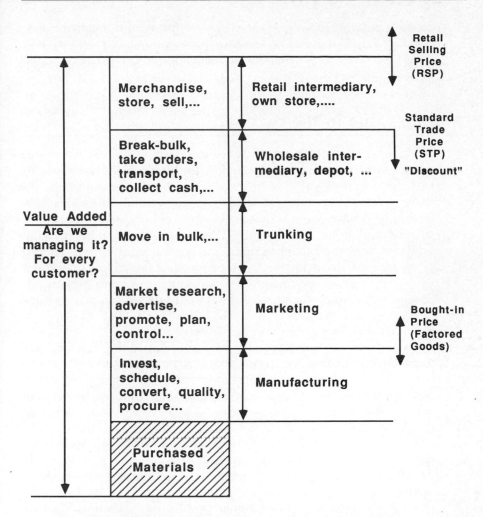

WHO PROVIDES SERVICE - WHAT DOES EACH DO?

Figure 1.1 Adding value in the logistics chain

ment of inbound raw materials utilizing electronic data interchange (EDI) between the organization and key suppliers can provide substantial cost savings. Similarly, the use of EDI between manufacturer and customer can provide inventory and order cycle time savings for the customer that enhance the customer's competitive position. Sharing the value-added benefit throughout the distribution channel helps to foster a spirit of partnership, and creates high switching costs for customers and effective entry barriers against competitors.

Adding value in the channel

Products reach customers in many different ways, often through distributors and other intermediaries. In these cases, customers are frequently more loyal to their distributors than their suppliers. For example, one US general line distributor took the decision to hold in inventory a comprehensive range of marine closures (ships portholes, hatches and doors and so on). These items were normally only available from their manufacturers on special order with a delay of between four to seven weeks depending upon factory workload. Customers valued the immediate availability and were prepared to pay a substantial premium. As a result of this decision, the distributor now profitably services a nationwide market whilst its suppliers benefit from a more uniform level of demand.

Given that distributors can be powerful differentiators and influencers, organizations must learn how to bias the distributor network in their favour. Distributors who feel that they are in partnership with their suppliers can influence customers to purchase one supplier's product over another. In short, distributors can make the product different.

In some instances, the brand image of a product is so strong that a distributor has no option but to supply what the customer demands. At other times the product demanded is unique, one-of-a-kind. Frequently, however, the customer will be influenced by the service given in the past and the relationship with the distributor. In these cases, the distributor provides the value added by promoting one supplier's product over another.

Logistics departments often have more frequent contact with distributors than sales or marketing departments. Through their interaction with distributors and other intermediaries, they have a unique opportunity to provide those services valued by the distributor, thereby strengthening the sense of partnership between the two organizations. Activities such as those depicted in Figure 1.2 must be considered for their potential impact on distributors and customers. Scarce logistics resources must be directed towards those activities

At EACH STAGE in distribution consider:

1. Who makes replenishment decision? Size, frequency, timing, and who administers it.

2. What product range is carried/handled?

3. Schedule, receive and handle deliveries.

4. Store products:
   - available from stock.
   - Scarcity, stock rotation, condition.
   - Seasonal stocking.

5. Closeness to market; coverage of potential market.

6. Breaking bulk.

7. Order receipt and order processing.

8. Pick, pack and load.

9. Delivery; scheduling/frequency/routing.

10. Administer orders; invoices, statements.

11. Credit control: credit worthiness of customer (non-recourse); credit limits; terms of credit/financing credit; cash collection and incentives.

12. Pricing administration: change notices, volume discounts, lead time factors.

13. Merchandising, P.O.S. activity and materials, promotions management, promotional activity, representation and sales canvassing.

14. Customer relations:
    - Representation.
    - Warranty administration.
    - Changes to product, pricing.
    - Product performance.
    - Technical support - people and material.

15. Market information:
    - Competitor action.
    - Industry and sales/stockholding/availability. performance.
    - Product and user reports.
    - New opportunity.

16. What discounts/mark-ups do they work within? Are these typical for industry? Are they performing the service we expect? Should they/could they be doing more?

17. How important is our product to them? How important are they to us?

Figure 1.2   Who adds value?

valued by the customers, since it is the value added by these activities that gives the organization its competitive advantage.

Conclusion

Successful logistics managers in the 1990s will be characterized by their broad understanding of their organizations' strategic plan and the role of logistics in bringing that plan to fruition. No longer content to be merely a subject-matter specialist, logistics managers will work with marketing. manufacturing, and finance to identify those activities that add value to their organizations' products and services.

The challenges for logistics in the 1990s will be many and varied. One thing, however, is certain: logistics will play a significant strategic role in those organizations which gain a sustainable competitive advantage in the global marketplace. To meet these challenges logistics managers must develop a new range of skills, convince their chief executives of the value of logistics and provide a level of service that is valued by their customers.

2 Managing Logistics in a Changing Environment

John Gattorna

Darwin's great theory of the evolution of the species rested on his idea about survival. By survival of the fittest he did not mean, as some assume, survival of the strongest. It was a matter of evolving – in other words, the ability of an animal to adapt to its environment.

Faced with a rapidly changing environment and an increasingly uncertain future, many organizations have been forced to rethink their traditional assumptions. Revolutionary changes in technology, continued government deregulation, the shortening of product life cycles, proliferation of product lines and shifts in traditional manufacturer–retailer relationships, have replaced the continuing expansion, soft markets, comfortable margins and good returns of little more than a decade ago.

The last year of certainty was probably 1972. In 1971 the United States took the dollar off the gold standard. Exchange rates fluctuated for a while, briefly became fixed, and then were allowed to float again in 1972. In August 1973 the price of oil tripled. By the end of 1974 it had quadrupled. Inflation soared, investment plummeted, and unemployment began its alarming, and still largely unchecked, rise.

The oil 'crisis', whether real or imagined, orchestrated or spontaneous, was probably the single most significant change in the past 15 years. That single ingredient changed forever the face of industry, politics, economics and consumerism.

Coping with change

It is not hard to look around the business community and identify those organizations which do not know how to cope with change. They are the ones which tend to reorganize with monotonous

11

regularity, assuming that they are catering for change by changing themselves. They make the mistake of not *planning* for change, not realizing that the nature of today's environment is change itself. Reactive organizations that fail to adapt to changes in their environment are the endangered species of the corporate evolutionary process. The difference between these *reactive* organizations and other *proactive* organizations is the difference between tactics and strategy. Not long ago, many people made the mistake of thinking of logistics as simply another name tag for 'finished goods distribution' – the front end of manufacturing. This view ignored the 'materials management' role of logistics concerned with the inward flow of raw materials, sub-assemblies, proprietary items, manufactured parts and packaging materials. It is this summation of the materials management activities at the back end of production, and the finished goods distribution activities at the front end, which together constitute the totality of logistics and logistics management. Accompanying this physical flow is the two-way flow of information which is the amalgam in which the whole logistics function is set.

Logistics and change

Increasingly, proactive organizations are recognizing that logistics, far from being just another operational variable, is uniquely placed within the organization to manage the interrelationship of all the factors which affect the flow of both information and goods necessary to fill orders. This flow begins when the customer decides to place an order and ends when the order is fulfilled and monies collected.

Organizations which believe that *the single output of any organization is customer service* understand the strategic significance of logistics in this process. They know that, to succeed in today's environment, they must adopt a disciplined and systematic approach to the market, create carefully considered priorities, allocate resources in the strictest possible manner and make often difficult trade-off decisions.

It is not yet common for the logistics manager to be involved with the initial phases of an organization's strategic planning. However, the size of the corporate profit slice which logistics affects is sufficiently large to suggest that the logistics manager *should* be a key figure at the strategy formulation stage.

The strategic process

In describing strategic planning as the process of formulating plans which ensures the long-term profitability of an organization, we earlier referred to actions taken in anticipation of customer needs. The logistics manager is the only person in the organization charged solely with managing *all* flows of information and materials in the conception to consumption chain, and their interactions. It is this unique position that provides the logistics manager with an appreciation of the organization's capacity to respond to expectations.

Strategic planning forces management to reconcile two almost contradictory tasks: long-term (visionary) planning with short-term responsiveness to customers. To achieve this seemingly impossible balance we must focus on the 'strategic' side of planning and not consider strategy to be just another word for 'long-term'.

Strategic planning covers three steps:

- vision statements (what we stand for);
- aims (directions we want to go in);
- objectives (specific quantified targets).

The chief executive is in the best position to understand the expectations of 'stakeholders' (shareholders and employees) and the organization's long-term goals. Accordingly, he (or she) must be the one to articulate the vision statement.

The difference between aims and objectives is the difference between quantitative and qualitative analysis. Aims are the qualitative statements, the expression of desires and goals. Objectives are quantitative and therefore must be measurable. It is not enough to set an objective as 'increasing sales' because there is no way to determine if the objective has been met. Increasing sales may be the aim, but increasing sales by 3 per cent within six months is the objective. This gives a finishing point and a specific target. Once the aims and objectives are established, operational plans can follow.

Proper procedures for implementation, control and evaluation are needed to translate plans from mere words on paper to actions on the ground. This is where the effectiveness of the logistics manager will determine the success or failure of the whole planning effort.

The creation of a strategic plan does not provide a guarantee of success, rather it provides a frame of reference against which changes in the environment external to the organization can be evaluated. In this way the organization can respond to both anticipated and unexpected changes in the external environment in a planned manner. It is this ability to evolve and adapt that distinguishes the strategically oriented organization from its endangered counterpart.

Understanding the environment

It has been suggested that all organizations are directly affected by six environments: the market; government; suppliers of materials and services; the labour market; and the finance market. Four other environments either directly or indirectly affect the organization: the economy; the community; the nation's resource base; and the world environment.

Organizations can effect changes in their environment, although these changes are usually limited to its own environment – that is, to its internal environment. Strategically oriented organizations realize that successfully coping with rapid change necessitates a new stance towards the future.

Many executives find that making the transition to thinking and acting strategically requires a radical change to their way of operating. For the organization to make this transition successfully, a top-down cultural change needs to be promoted and supported by the chief executive. Without this level of support, individual efforts are doomed to failure. This process of change is neither easy nor comfortable. However, there are clear guidelines to help structure the work required:

1   establish a disciplined framework (or logic) for undertaking the planning process;
2   underpin this framework with a visible marketing intelligence function;
3   take the necessary steps to convert plans into strategic behaviour on the ground.

Scanning the environment

The first stage for an organization making the transition to a strategic orientation is the analysis of the underlying social forces and trends in the external environment. This is necessary because organizations depend for survival upon exchanges with the external environment, which is changing at an accelerating rate and increasing turbulence and uncertainty.

An awareness of these changes enables organizations to anticipate them and assess, to the extent possible, their strength, timing, and potential impact. Scanning, as part of a strategic orientation, creates an atmosphere in which the boundary between the organization's internal and external environment is seen as highly permeable.

A strategic planning approach seeks to answer four key questions:

1   Where are we now?
2   Where do we want to be?
3   How do we get there?
4   How do we know when we have arrived?

To determine 'where we are now?', logistics managers should audit their logistics performance regularly. This process begins by conducting a customer perceptions audit, where customers are asked about how the organization's delivery performance compares with that of competitors. This often highlights critical areas where improvement is needed.

The logistics manager must first convince senior management that the logistics area plays a significant role in the organization's long-term growth, success and future profitability. Then, the output of the logistics audit, described in detail in Chapter 10 of this Handbook, will assist in answering the first of the four key strategic questions: 'Where are we now?'. The output from the audit, when related to the total strategic plan, will help determine the answer to the second question: 'Where do we want to be?'. The actions of the logistics manager will be the means of fulfilling the central aim: 'How do we get there?' and will provide the answer to the fourth question: 'How do we know when we have arrived?'. Having a plan does not guarantee a problem-free future. The environment is always changing. How then does the organization cope in a changing environment?

Managing issues

Creating sound strategic plans is not incompatible with responding to environmental changes or issues as they occur. In fact the ability to do this is precisely the objective of what we call 'issue management'.

An issue is something, either a condition or a pressure, which may affect an organization's performance, aims, or future. By its very nature an issue is almost always controversial, as different people tend to have different views on the size or implications of the issue. Whatever the issue, a strategic response is demanded.

Issue management is a focused way of defining those issues to be addressed via the strategic planning process. In this way, it is effectively the springboard for ultimate actions and considered responses rather than ill-considered reactions.

Effective scanning of the environment will provide the intelligence from which the organization can identify issues. Staff must be shown how to monitor and remain aware of both internal and external factors which are subject to change. Different areas of the organization can be charged with the responsibility for monitoring the environment and thus feel commitment to the strategic process.

An issue might be a competitor's new product line or a government regulation concerning trade. It might be the emergence of a strong 'animal rights' league campaigning against the poultry industry, or an exposé on the harmful effects of nitrates in food.

We must expect that, occasionally, issues will occur suddenly, with little or no warning. These must be dealt with in keeping with the corporate plan, or organizations run the risk of becoming simply reactive and unmanaged. When an issue is detected, senior line management must be informed. Ideally, senior management should form a task force charged with the responsibility for analysing issues. There are two important reasons why this task force should comprise senior management:

1   Senior management can best judge the significance and potential impact of an issue.
2   Senior management involvement means that action can be taken, not simply recommended. This is particularly important when thinking about those issues requiring urgent and immediate action.

In determining an appropriate response to an issue, senior management must evaluate the potential impact of the issue in terms of the organization's critical success factors, established as part of the strategic planning process. Depending upon the potential impact of the issue and the degree of immediacy, issues can be allocated a priority and resources allocated accordingly. In this way, scarce resources are not wasted and critical issues receive the priority attention they deserve.

The vital keys to successful issue management can be summarized as:

- an in-house system which can respond to the strength and complexity of emerging issues;
- action appropriate to the resources available to the organization.

The benefits of issue management are twofold:

1 The organization is not the victim of environmental changes, but anticipates and manages the impact of those changes.
2 Employees are a part of the response and are not left to feel that they, and the organization, are without defence. This is very important in terms of morale and participation.

As part of the strategic planning process, scanning and issue management point the way forward for organizations which aim to be progressive and proactive in the years ahead. Logistics, and the role of the logistics manager, are being recognized by strategically oriented organizations as key ingredients in successfully meeting the challenges of these increasingly turbulent times. Logistics managers must adopt a strategic approach if they are to be equal to the challenges that await them in the future.

3 Corporate Profitability and Logistics

Philip C. Alling and Gene R. Tyndall

Introduction

The corporate activity known as logistics has undergone a quiet revolution during the past 10 years. The fundamental nature of the discipline has changed, and so has the role that the logistics activity plays in the strategies of successful corporations.

Reducing the cost of producing and distributing products, while improving quality and service to customers, is a goal of most corporate executives. Tangible improvements in cost, quality, and service are critical in modern competitive markets. In today's increasingly global economy, such improvements often determine a business unit's survival.

The sense of urgency brought on by this 'survival of the fittest' environment is prompting more and more companies to examine, restructure, and reposition their operations to gain competitive advantage. Logistics, sometimes overlooked in this process, can be vital in implementing the integration and differentiation strategies designed to produce this advantage.

This chapter draws heavily on the findings of a multi-year industry research project in which the authors were involved. The three-phase study, jointly sponsored by the Council of Logistics Management and the National Association of Accountants in the United States, culminated in late 1987 with the publication of the book *Corporate Profitability and Logistics*.[1]

More and more senior executives now realize the importance of logistics to the success of their corporate strategies. In the companies studied for this project, we found that logistics excellence enables them to turn an activity traditionally considered a 'service function' into a strategic resource contributing measurably to market share and profitability.

Myriad factors make a logistics operation 'world class'. Each company follows a different approach to making the most of logistics operations. Underlying these tactics, however, are 10 basic principles which we identified as common to all excellent logistics departments, and which we describe later. When taken together, these principles create the foundation for logistics excellence by allowing companies to achieve the function's full profit potential.

Few executives are completely satisfied with the state of logistics development in their companies. In every case, they feel there are one or more principles needing additional attention. (That continual quest for improvement in itself is a characteristic that differentiates the 'winners' from the other 'players' in the logistics arena.)

The role of logistics in profitable companies

With major changes occurring in industry, the perception of logistics in executive offices has failed to evolve in concert, principally due to continual changes in logistics terminology. Nevertheless, business executives are increasingly questioning the distribution/logistics potential for contributing to overall profitability. These questions are typified by the following comment from a chief executive of a leading *Fortune* 200 company:

> . . . I now know what physical distribution can do to save money. Tell me what it can do to improve my profits, to increase my share of the market, to improve my cash flow, to open new territories, to introduce new products, and to get the stockholders and board of directors off my back . . .

Notice that the chief executive asks if logistics can do anything important for profitability, and if so, what? Logistics must make this profitability contribution if it is to expand its role in the company.

The value chain concept
In *Competitive Advantage: Creating and Sustaining Superior Performance*,[2] Michael Porter describes how a company can (and does) put generic strategies (cost leadership, differentiation, and focus) into practice. More specifically, he addresses such questions as: How does a firm gain a sustainable cost advantage? How can it differentiate itself from competitors? How does a company choose a market segment so that

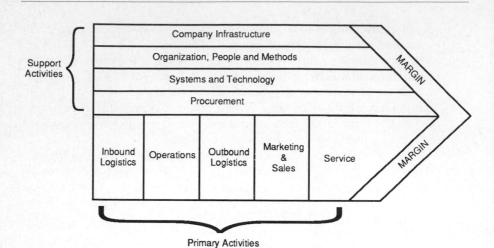

Figure 3.1   The value chain

competitive advantage grows out of a focus-based strategy? When and how can a firm gain competitive advantage from competing with a coordinated strategy in related industries? How is uncertainty introduced into the pursuit of competitive advantage?

How can a firm defend its competitive position? Porter asserts that competitive advantage derives from the value a company creates for its buyers. This value may take the form of selling equivalent product at below-competitor prices. Or, value can manifest itself in the provision of unique benefits that offset a premium price. Porter uses a tool called 'the value chain' to separate buyers, suppliers and a firm into the discrete, but interrelated, activities from which value stems. The value chain concept may be used to identify and understand the specific sources of competitive advantage, and how they relate to buyer value. In developing the value chain concept, Porter provides a systematic way of examining the activities a company performs and how they interact. The value chain is, indeed, a concept, but it also is a proven and practical tool for determining how to sustain competitive advantage in an increasingly competitive marketplace.

Why does the value chain theory help us to determine the role of logistics in profitable companies? First, the concept recognizes how the logistics function fits into the business pipeline. In Figure 3.1, which we adapted slightly from Porter, note that logistics represents two of the five primary business activities that add value to a product (or service). We believe that Porter is the first leading business scholar/practitioner to acknowledge this process and link it specifically to competitive advantage.

It is useful to review how Porter defines the five categories of primary activities involved in competing in any industry:

- *Inbound logistics.*   Activities associated with receiving, storing, and disseminating inputs to the product, such as materials handling, warehousing, inventory control, vehicle scheduling, and returns to suppliers.
- *Operations.*   Activities associated with transforming inputs into the final product form, such as machining, packaging, assembly, equipment maintenance, testing, printing, and facility operations.
- *Outbound Logistics.*   Activities associated with collecting, storing, and physically distributing the product to buyers, such as finished goods distribution, warehousing, materials handling, delivery vehicle operation, order processing, and scheduling.
- *Marketing and Sales.*   Activities associated with providing a means by which buyers can purchase the product and inducing them to do so, such as advertising, promotion, sales force management, quoting, channel selection, channel relations, and pricing.
- *Service.*   Activities associated with providing service to enhance or maintain the value of the product, such as installation, repair, training, parts supply, and product adjustment.

While interviewing dozens of executives in leading corporations during the past several years, we looked for innovative activities within inbound or outbound logistics that create value and competitive advantage for those firms. The value chain concept provides a useful framework for seeking this information and positioning it within the business units. This approach detects and exposes 'linkages' between the way one value activity is performed and the cost or performance of another, thereby reflecting 'trade-offs' which can yield competitive advantage.

The role of logistics in today's and tomorrow's profitable companies will change as the value of products changes, and also as the value that buyers or customers ascribe to products changes. This statement represents a new concept for many logistics managers, who were trained in transportation, warehousing, and other such functions to conduct their activities based on least-cost or other hard-measure priorities. Modern logistics managers must find innovative ways to help their companies improve profits, increase market share, improve cash flow, open new territories, introduce new products, and get the stockholders and board of directors 'off the president's back'. This is a major challenge for logistics managers, but one that is helped by the principles and examples in this section.

The principles of logistics excellence

The principles introduced

Recognizing the role of logistics in profitable companies helps us to understand how the function fits into the overall scheme of business. One must go beyond this recognition, however, to identify precisely what makes logistics operations successful.

To explore logistics' impact on corporate profitability, our research focused on senior logistics executives known for improving corporate profits through logistics decisions. We delved into how their business decisions impact on profitability and add value to their companies' products and services.

Our research also focused on pinpointing exactly what principles determine the success of a logistics operation. Naturally, every logistics organization is unique in many respects. However, successful logistics organizations adhere to a handful of essential principles that transcend industry, company type or geographic location. These principles of logistics excellence, as we call them, are neither startling nor revolutionary; in fact, some consider them obvious or mundane. We think of them as 'uncommon sense' – that is, practices that most executives regard as common sense, but overlook so often that they are not part of their companies' routines. In fact, the intensity with which world-class companies view them is a key contributor to their excellence and profitability.

We know that applying these principles and thereby achieving excellence in logistics improves corporate profitability. Where logistics operations follow the principles by conducting activities linked to business objectives, quantitative improvements occur in measures such as:

- compound asset growth
- compound equity growth
- market to book (wealth creation)
- return to total capital
- return on equity
- return on sales

- return on management investment
- economic value added
- market share

The 10 principles
1   Link logistics to corporate strategy

All aspects of logistics operations must be directly linked to the corporate strategic plan. This is the first and most important rule in achieving the profit improvement potential of logistics.

Many executives share a common goal. They manage the logistics functions to support their company's strategy for achieving competitive advantage, be it through cost leadership, service differentiation, or both. These logistics heads operate under the premise that their department or division performs a value-added activity.

Because of historical deficiencies in logistics, too many companies settle for a logistics operation that is a neutral element within the company. Top management in these firms views logistics as a 'necessary evil'. Unfortunately, this outdated attitude is present in all too many executive suites. Pioneering logistics executives have, however, altered that view among their top management. They make certain the chief executive understands the true magnitude of costs controlled or influenced by logistics. This is not necessarily because of the structure provided by the value chain, rather it is the ability of the approach to detect and expose 'linkages', or relationships between the way one value activity is performed and the cost or performance of another.

The linkages exposed through value chain analysis reflect the 'trade-offs' made among activities to achieve competitive advantage. They also reflect the need to coordinate different functions. For example, on-time delivery – a goal of most companies – requires coordination of activities in operations, outbound logistics, service and sales/marketing. Because the same task can be accomplished in different ways, with different costs and performance, assessing activities and their linkages is crucial to understanding how logistics can impact on corporate profitability.

In industries such as bulk commodities or automotives, where logistics represents a large percentage of total cost, an efficient, low-cost logistics operation is an important source of competitive advantage. Cost-effective logistics also impacts on companies' standing in highly competitive areas such as consumer products, where even a small cost advantage is crucial. For example, several grocery manufacturers give top priority to improving logistics productivity. Their approaches differ, but their objectives are similar: to effect major cost reductions that allow more competitive prices, add directly to the bottom line, or both.

One of the most popular approaches to gaining competitive advantage today is for firms to establish themselves as the superior service supplier in their markets. Recent emphases on 'getting close to customers' and striving for quality in all aspects of operations seem responsible for this trend. One consumer goods manufacturer, for example, uses a team of sales and distribution personnel to 'sell' superior service in presentations customized to individual customers' needs. The team highlights the specific customer service measures and operational approaches they use to deliver the promised levels of service.

Related to cost leadership and service differentiation is logistics innovation. Some companies prefer to develop new approaches rather than rely on being the best at performing the traditional ones. Once these new approaches succeed, management uses them as a source of competitive advantage. For instance, one consumer goods manufacturer felt it had market logistics cost advantages in certain areas. The firm embarked on a multi-year programme to popularize an approach to direct product profitability (DPP) that emphasized the cost areas in which it excelled. Perseverance paid off. Today, the industry-standard DPP model favours their operation over those of competitors. This fact helps the company portray its products as the most profitable for retailers to carry.

Ideally, the successful linking of logistics with the corporate business strategy follows a process like the one illustrated in Figure 3.2. Each 'box' in the process represents a linkage step – forward and backward – that allows logistics operations to be driven by, and contribute to, the corporate business strategy. We developed this framework as a result of our work with several leading logistics departments.

The linkage principle is the best example of how the 10 principles of logistics excellence represent 'uncommon sense'. It may seem surprising that so few companies have succeeded in linking logistics directly to the corporate strategy. Nevertheless, the fact remains that logistics, like manufacturing, has lagged behind the more glamorous company functions of marketing, finance, and mergers and acquisitions in providing strategic or competitive advantage.

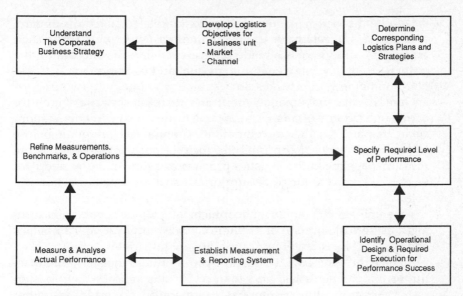

Figure 3.2 Framework for strategy-focused operations

What factor has the greatest influence on a company's ability to retain its customer franchise? Is the company's strategic objective to remain or become the low-cost producer? To meet customers' needs for consistent service quality? To be the new products innovator? The operational answers to these questions have been neglected for too long. However, they provide the basis for differentiating the company from its competitors. More than ever, top management understands that this differentiation is critical to a firm's survival.

2 Organize comprehensively

The second principle of excellence calls for a comprehensive logistics organization that controls all corporate logistics functions under a single business unit. Materials management, transportation, warehousing, distribution, inbound logistics – whatever functions are relevant – should be unified under an appropriate mix of centralized and decentralized management.

Providing appropriate logistics service levels requires close coordination of operations with the business strategy. Low-cost logistics involves continual trade-offs (for example, greater transportation spending for lower inventory and warehouse costs). Good decisions in both areas are easier to make if a single executive is responsible for all closely related logistics functions.

Despite the logic in grouping all logistics-related functions under a single umbrella, relatively few companies structure their activities in this manner. Industry has made progress toward this end during the past five years, but movement is gradual and evolutionary.

Encouragingly, companies are beginning to integrate two important areas – materials management and distribution. The search for better utilization of transportation and warehouse assets is responsible, in part, for this development. Companies' adoption of the 'value chain' concept confirms the logic of such integration. These firms manage the entire logistics pipeline as a single, integrated flow using the complete range of supporting structures and assets available.

To eliminate the kinds of 'conflicts of interest' that arise from logistics' broad sphere of influence, most innovative companies address the logistics organization in an integrated context. They recognize the essential interrelationships between logistics, manufacturing, marketing, sales, and finance. In this process they seek to foster *joint* goal-setting to emphasize synergistic opportunities rather than simply to minimize conflicts of interest. This means the firm identifies what functions or activities comprise logistics and pinpoints how they are best integrated and managed to support and enhance the combined efforts of all company activities.

If logistics functions are unified under a single control, what mix of centralized and decentralized management works best? We find the best place to address the centralization/decentralization issue is at the activity level, rather than at the broader function level. Selecting the appropriate carrier for an individual shipment, for example, is a decision often best made at the field level. On the other hand, deciding issues of national or global scope is most effectively carried out by headquarters personnel.

Most companies' distribution operations which were centralized in the 1970s are decentralized today, reverting to more field-based logistics decision-making. Increased use of computer-based systems, discussed below, has accelerated this shift.

3 Use the power of information

Successful logistics departments take full advantage of information and information-processing technology. These departments view both transaction-based and decision support systems as essential resources for realizing the profit potential of logistics. Electronic data interchange links with customers, for example, can be a source of

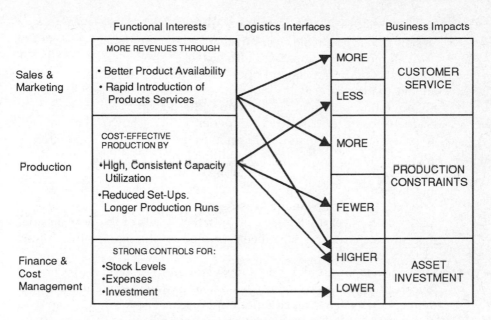

Figure 3.3 Functional interests and impacts: conflict management

competitive differentiation and increased market share even in international markets. Creative use of computer-based models can yield cost–service improvements which also bolster competitive advantage.

Information is one of the few business resources that has declined markedly in cost over the last decade. As a result, companies increasingly consider investments in information management systems as an alternative to expenditures for more conventional logistics assets. One manufacturer we studied reduced raw material inventory levels at a key plant from a four-day to a four-hour supply, largely by installing an improved data system linking manufacturing, logistics, suppliers, and carriers.

In the past, most computerized systems devoted to logistics focused on transaction processing (for example, order processing, purchasing, inventory and so on). This situation is changing rapidly. Many companies are developing versions of these systems that use the speed and expanded capabilities of the new generation computer and telecommunications hardware.

Some executives are looking beyond speed/capacity enhancements to systems that offer decision support capabilities. During the next decade, these decision support networks will evolve into 'expert systems' that play major roles in logistics decision-making.

A number of companies already use sophisticated computer models to aid in tactical and operational decision-making. One such model analyses specific product mixes in orders, and decides where to locate transportation equipment at the dock in order to minimize warehouse travel distances. Experience has shown that system development and enhancement are most effective when conducted as an evolutionary, rather than revolutionary, process. The large data-base management complexities alone create growth problems. Many businesses now avoid the 'big bang' approach to systems overhaul, whereby they implement a single, massive, multi-year project designed to meet the logistics information needs of the next decade. Logistics departments have been 'burned' in the past by this 'all-or-nothing' approach.

By developing 'quick and dirty' systems prototypes (often in a microcomputer environment), a company can experiment with, and refine, new systems development approaches. As a result, it can reap the benefits of the new application immediately. One company designed a microcomputer system to budget and control over US $75 million in transportation costs. It recovered the system development expense during the first quarter of use, and expects first-year savings to pay for the mainframe version of the software. Companies are just beginning to exploit the considerable opportunities that information systems offer. Management is still in the first stages of learning to handle information as a business asset. Corporate culture in this area is changing fast, however, and we expect the pace of innovation and implementation to pick up.

Given this scenario, logistics executives must nevertheless continue to focus on the real business purpose of information technology. A logistics vice president of a large manufacturer succinctly defined this purpose: 'Our goal, similar to the logistics objectives with our products, is to get the right information to the right person at the right time, so that the right decision can be made for the right reason – to beat our competitors'.

It is interesting to note that, for over 20 years, the logistics profession has been trying to get the right product to the right place at the right time. Now, in the 1990s, we strive for excellence (and competitive advantage) by 'substituting information for inventory'. The companies which learn to do this well, while also getting the right products distributed properly, will be the winners in tomorrow's marketplace.

4   Emphasize human resources

Enlightened human resource management is vital to achieving logistics excellence. Logistics excellence flourishes in an environment that recognizes people as the department's most important resource. Recruiting, education, training, and job enrichment are standard practice. Management acknowledges individuals for productivity gains, and, in some cases, sets up incentive programmes to foster excellence within the logistics function.

Senior logistics executives understand that experienced, well-trained managers are critical to the success of their strategies and plans. Today's logistics departments, however, demand a new breed of logistics manager, and finding these innovators can be a worrisome job for logistics operations heads. One executive at a major manufacturer considers recruiting so critical that he and his chief assistants spend significant amounts of time meeting with professors and students.

In a related development, these same executives are increasingly concerned about their suppliers' human resource management efforts. As more corporations form long-term strategic alliances with outside vendors, human resource management becomes a shared concern. One logistics executive organized meetings between outside personnel experts and senior management at his company's key carriers to ensure that these firms have adequate staff depth to provide stable operations.

Quality and human resources are inextricably linked. If you do not instil a quality orientation into your people, nothing else will be really successful in achieving quality products and services. The most profitable companies manage their logistics people in such a way as to make quality a daily priority. One company that sustains such quality in logistics is retailer L. L. Bean of Freeport, Maine, USA. The company employs some 1,800 permanent, and 200 temporary, workers. Most come from the Maine area and enjoy the outdoor life, the company's merchandise and serving customers. All newly hired employees go through an extensive training/retraining programme, designed to educate them as to the firm's quality standards. Workers soon learn that these standards motivate, support and reward high-quality performance. Thus, the company derives its success not only from the products it sells, but from the people who deliver them.

Pillsbury Company, the grocery products giant, is another example of a company that has successfully linked quality performance standards to operations. Pillsbury implemented a warehouse productivity measurement system that aids operations planning and scheduling as well as monitoring labour performance. A central feature of Pillsbury's approach is the ability to identify, by activity, where employees are performing well and where they need help. Top performers of key activities are recognized and encouraged to help the other employees adopt their effective techniques. This approach has fostered better team work and has significantly improved the quality of warehouse operations and responsiveness to customers. The additional business and reduced costs that have resulted have made a marked contribution to Pillsbury's profitability.

In the training area, management no longer views on-the-job training as a sufficient guarantee of a successful logistics operation. Many corporations send logistics managers and staff to formal training programmes aimed at upgrading skills and introducing new concepts and techniques. In some cases, such outside training is essential in subsequent implementation of new management approaches and systems. For example, one consumer products manufacturer embarked on a major quality effort in its manufacturing and logistics operations. As part of that programme, the company enrolled several hundred employees in a training course covering a broad range of quality techniques. In addition, the manufacturer offered the training to key suppliers and carriers.

All in all, world-class corporations view personnel investments in a new light today. These firms have reaped the cost reductions and service enhancements available from operational improvements and are turning to human resource development as an untapped opportunity for savings. The annual plans of a number of companies now include fully-fledged programmes to buy or develop specific technical and management skills.

In this vein, a number of companies are discovering that a renewed emphasis on labour productivity can yield cost savings and service improvements. Elimination of unnecessary or redundant procedures saves time and money while also improving employee morale and motivation. Following a major labour productivity overhaul, one grocery manufacturer's distribution centre now handles more volume in less time, with half the people it had four years ago. It accomplished these improvements without major expenditures for automation.

5   Form strategic alliances

A fifth principle of logistics excellence calls for companies to form close partnerships with other participants in the product chain or channel.

Stiff competition from Japanese manufacturers has forced the American business community to take a hard look at the way firms in the two countries do business. A study of Japanese business practices reveals several intriguing contrasts. At the top of this list is the fact that the Japanese don't 'do' business with their supply/demand-chain partners. Rather, they commit to a business partner relationship that is presumed to be long-lasting, if not permanent. No matter how good the supplier's products or services are, or how low the price, the involved parties have no relationship until they commit to a binding business partnership.

These 'win–win' partnerships do not arise simply for cultural reasons. Rather, they generate the kind of strategic and operational value that produces long-term gains for both parties. Successful operating practices, such as 'just-in-time' manufacturing, have evolved from these partnerships.

World-class companies that do well in Japan – Coca-Cola, Johnson & Johnson, Schick, Hewlett-Packard, and Xerox – are those that form effective partnerships. These partnerships are based, first and foremost, on shared corporate values and strategic goals. In addition, they rely on close communication and coordination of plans and activities, to the point of sharing plans for new products or market expansions.

Overall, companies are changing the way they view their business alliances. No longer do they consider these relationships short-term, cost-control efforts. Instead, they are cultivating strategic alliances with suppliers, customers, and carriers – even including them in early planning for new ventures.

These partnerships cannot succeed without open and timely exchange of information. Companies need to share financial and operational data, as well as forecasting, planning, and scheduling information. Major manufacturers are providing suppliers with 'frozen' production schedules a week or two in advance of target shipment dates. Taking advantage of these increased lead times, the suppliers improve service levels. At the same time, the manufacturers reduce raw material inventory levels.

Planning and executing effective alliances is not simple, particularly for multinational companies. It requires careful thought, coordination with customers and suppliers, and the support and education of all personnel. It also may require expenditures to prepare and sustain the operational changes. And it certainly requires the commitment of the senior management team. The pay-offs, however, can be significant. Some companies are realizing cost savings from process improvements, and market share growth from becoming preferred suppliers to their customers. A most successful company said that its strategic alliances helped it achieve market share growth of eight points – clearly an attractive achievement.

Like other principles of logistics excellence, formation of strategic alliances offers virtually unlimited opportunities for profit. Leading transportation companies are demonstrating how they can be full partners with manufacturers and merchandisers in the logistics chain. Similarly, innovative public warehouse companies are formulating strong alliances, providing third-party storage and handling services.

As industry faces increasingly complex and competitive markets, logistics will play a larger role in serving customers. Those firms that best cultivate their strategic alliances with selected suppliers, carriers, distributors and customers will achieve profit contributions beyond those that operate business as usual.

6   Focus on financial performance

The logistics function should use return on assets, economic value added, cost and operating standards, or similar financial indicators as measures of performance. Additionally, our research shows that functions such as transportation, warehousing, and customer service are best managed as cost or profit centres. In this way, the company encourages entrepreneurial attitudes among logistics managers.

As emphasized in Principle 1, linking logistics strategy to corporate strategy is one key to logistics excellence. Proper financial management of logistics functions is critical to that process. Knowing the financial consequences of logistics activities is essential to forward planning. And operations management, based on their broad financial effects, is necessary for achieving performance that is consistent with strategic objectives and plans.

This focus on logistics financial management has evolved to the point where several major companies appointed managers with financial backgrounds to head up their logistics operations. Notable among these firms are Gillette, Thomas J. Lipton, and Baxter Travenol Laboratories. In these cases, logistics performance has improved as a direct result of the new financial orientation.

One of the firms reaping the reward of emphasizing financial performance in logistics is Xerox Corporation. Xerox reduces costs and tailors service levels to the needs of its manufacturing units by creating logistics profit centres which provide the kinds of services its manufacturing executives demand and pay for.

In recent years, world-class corporations have adopted rate of return on assets (ROA) as the most important financial measure of profitability – shifting away from using the net income yardstick. In line with this shift, some companies are beginning to calculate return on logistics assets, rather than absolute cost levels, as the measure of logistics performance. In addition, these firms find that non-traditional measures such as return on management investment (ROMI) can be useful indicators of logistics performance.

As a direct result of the ROA focus, more companies are using third-party suppliers of logistics service as a means to reduce high logistics asset investment. According to our research, the motivating factor behind this trend is a reduction in asset levels and improvement in ROA. The recent decline in private truck fleets is directly related to this emphasis on ROA. Similarly, more and more corporations are using public warehousing. A few years ago, those same firms shunned that option.

Financial management expertise has not been a priority of logistics managers because of the way in which each function's performance has traditionally been measured. Specifically, the practice of measuring costs such as freight, labour, and warehouse rates, which are readily attributed to the logistics managers, causes companies to adopt them as measures of logistics financial performance. This narrow focus ignores the most important factors influencing costs of logistics, which relate directly to the overall business strategy. The measurement of key logistics success factors that relate to strategic business plans can positively affect corporate profitability. Fortunately, more logistics and financial managers are becoming comfortable with the concept of 'total logistics system costs', or total product cost from raw material to customer delivery. The more this approach is used, the more logistics value-added services will contribute to corporate profitability.

7   Target optimum service levels

Companies that target optimum service levels improve their profitability. Targeting optimum service levels, therefore, should be one of the main elements of a company's logistics strategy. To do this, businesses must quantify the incremental revenue gained from providing excellent customer service, and measure the revenue/cost trade-offs for setting graded service levels. This involves understanding their customers' service needs and expectations and the levels of service they are willing to buy. In other words, companies need to calculate their 'optimum' service levels, and pinpoint the costs associated with sustaining those levels. This may lead, for example, to 'tiered pricing', wherein different levels of service are priced according to the different costs in reaching them (for example, delivery times).

Most world-class firms recognize the competitive importance of customer service. They have established service parameters and closely monitor how well they meet service commitments. Relatively few companies, however, analyse the service requirements of their major markets in sufficient detail to set unique standards appropriate to the competitive requirements of these markets. Such fine-tuning of service parameters helps maximize profitability as illustrated by the major distributor that increased market share by 2 per cent (US $440 million in sales) over a three-year period by making selective adjustments to service levels for key product lines in important markets.

As noted above, an increasing number of corporations combine both distribution and materials management functions under the umbrella of the logistics department. One of the major responsibilities of these combined departments is serving the needs of manufacturing. This department manages the direct sourcing/delivery of materials, parts, and supplies to manufacturing plants, and handles logistics support for parts and supplies used or sold by field service organizations.

These integrated operations require the same level of effort in targeting service level as that expended on external customer service. A case in point is the major distributor who solved an after-sales service problem that was eroding market share. The company revamped its service parts distribution strategy using the same modelling software it used to fine-tune the product distribution network. In another example, the logistics group of a major electronics manufacturer 'contracts' with each of the company's manufacturing divisions for the level of service desired by the division. Through use of a sophisticated transfer-pricing mechanism, the logistics group charges the divisions for whatever levels of service they request.

Increasingly, the specialized expertise of logistics professionals proves critical in achieving and maintaining smooth operations. The part-time attention given materials management issues when they fall under the control of manufacturing personnel is 'too expensive' for many companies.

8   Manage the details

Streamlining operations and procedures is important to profitability, but attention to details can mean real savings. The best logistics operations always have the fundamental issues under control, and are constantly resolving seemingly 'minor' problems. Collectively, these solutions add up to smooth performance. Here again, one needs to link the details with the business strategy in order to manage the 'right details'. Obviously, corporate logistics policies that dictate the wrong operating practices for customer needs can result in lost sales through seemingly minor inconveniences.

A major supplier to the health care industry has been setting cost/service improvement goals for many years, even though it already enjoys a reputation as a highly cost-effective supplier. When asked when the firm will achieve all the improvement possible, management replied, 'We don't know. There seems to be no limit to the creativity of our employees.' Management attributes many of the recent improvements to paying attention to details. No aspect of the operations is considered unimportant.

When it comes to improving operations, simple solutions work best. As one logistics vice president commented when discussing his approach to identifying operational improvements, 'If any activity is complicated, there's a better way to do it . . . and in all likelihood the better way is simpler.'

Logistics executives who meet the challenge of integrated logistics realize that complex operations do not have to be complicated – indeed, they should not be. At its Buick City automobile plant, General Motors achieved extremely close coordination of its manufacturing operations with the operations of major suppliers and carriers. This interwoven chain of activities would not work had GM not streamlined its entire materials pipeline.

One key to streamlining and simplifying logistics operations is harnessing the knowledge, experience and creativity of line employees and first-level managers. Many productivity break-throughs cited by companies are attributable to involved employees.

In one food-processing firm, a distribution centre staffed with self-acknowledged 'losers' was transformed into the lowest-cost, highest-quality operation in the company after an enlightened manager successfully convinced workers in the company they could be the 'best'. Of course, intensive training was an integral part of this success story. The factor that made the difference, however, was the manager's ability to harness the workers' knowledge of the operation and of changes that were possible in the facility. The goal of this approach is to ingrain a strategic focus and quality orientation in every employee. This goes well beyond worrying about 'details' only when required to satisfy customer needs. It extends to the very 'heart and soul' of the organization. It involved workers at a distribution centre who had won a monetary award for the detailed operating improvements their quality circle team suggested. They used their award to buy a tree and a plaque. They planted the tree at the customer entrance to their distribution centre.

Several companies are now leaders in quality, productivity and profitability, but most attribute their success in part to making sure the 'little things' are done right. As soon as these firms committed themselves to improving quality, other problems disappeared. They reduced costs, eliminated errors, and improved product/service performance. These achievements, in turn, contributed positively to the firms' net profits.

Of course, managing the details is not the only path to quality and profitability. Without effective control of hourly, daily, or weekly 'minor' problems, however, other efforts are wasted. When we see a smooth-running logistics operation in which the details are under control, we invariably find high-quality service and healthy profits.

Effective detail management also produces consistency. In today's companies, where multiple personnel, customers, departments and disciplines interact across geographic regions, consistency can be a scarce commodity. Consistency of purpose, objectives, image, and information to customers are all important. It is the logistics executive's job to manage the distribution process to ensure consistency. This means attending to the basics and rewarding employees for doing the right thing. It also means creating common procedures and functions to simplify the job of handling details.

9 Leveraging logistics volumes

Our ninth logistics principle specifies that successful logistics operations consolidate shipment volumes, inventories and the like to gain operating and financial leverage. These consolidations pay off handsomely in terms of improved service and cost performance. To take advantage of these leveraging opportunities, however, management has to analyse every logistics choice and trade-off creatively, looking for new approaches to handling products, markets, modes, carriers and customers.

In company after company, regardless of its particular logistics mission and organization, distribution managers have a clear grasp of how much they paid for freight services last period, how much inventory was stored at company-owned warehouses during a given time period, and how many outbound shipments moved last quarter. Beyond these basics, however, these same managers consistently have less-than-adequate knowledge about factors that generate real leverage in materials handling and transportation, and with carriers, suppliers, customers, and markets.

Freight consolidation is one of the more popular leveraging methods. A new generation of software applications is making dynamic consolidation of shipments an operating reality. Indeed, one computer manufacturer reduced its transportation costs by more than 20 per cent using such software, even though it already had a manually operated consolidation programme in place.

Reducing the number of carriers used can be an effective way to consolidate volumes. One company pared its outbound carrier pool from several dozen to five, and negotiated strategic alliances with those five carriers on a regional basis. Interestingly, during the whittling-down process, the manufacturers played an instrumental role in mergers among several of the previous carriers. Those mergers proved beneficial to all parties.

As integrated logistics departments evolve, there is increased coordination of inbound and outbound shipment volumes, which usually produces sizeable transportation savings. Once again, real-time information systems make this coordination manageable.

One of the immediate benefits of managing inbound and outbound volumes collectively is improved equipment and driver utilization for private truck fleets. In fact, the significant boost it gives ROA is often the most persuasive argument in favour of implementing such a programme.

Excellent logistics operations find that broad-based coordination of all logistics activities, including intra-company transportation, warehousing and order servicing, can be well worth the trouble. These companies report improvements in customer service and financial performance. One major consumer goods manufacturer embarked on a multi-year programme to distribute several divisions' projects through corporate distribution centres. Implementing the programme was complicated, but management is realizing the kinds of benefits that prove the wisdom of its approach.

For several years we in logistics have been saying, 'It's time to think international', and few would argue that we now do business in a 'global' economy. Indeed, it is increasingly difficult for a firm of any size to avoid involvement (or at least interest) in foreign or offshore supply, production or finished goods distribution. With international logistics, however, comes international problems – problems of customs regulations, entry requirements, packaging standards, tariffs, currency translation, price controls, political constraints, and more. It may be years before these barriers are resolved sufficiently to permit the smooth flow of goods across international borders. Until that time, companies which trade internationally must find ways to cope with such barriers. Several companies have done just that – developed innovative logistics arrangements that set them apart from their competitors. These corporations use 'logistics leverage' to create competitive advantage in world markets.

One common way to gain international advantage is by entering into joint ventures and other types of strategic alliances. Proliferation of such alliances makes it more difficult to tell where a product is manufactured. For example, Mitsubishi makes Caterpillar equipment in Japan, and IBM manufactures communications equipment for Nippon Telegraph and Telephone. In fact, US and Japanese companies enter into dozens of cooperative business deals each year in industries such as steel, automobiles, computers, pharmaceuticals, telecommunications and consumer electronics.

The concept of 'third-party' or 'contract' logistics has recently gained popularity. It is already a common practice in Europe, where manufacturing companies often contract with outside parties for services such as transportation, warehousing and other distribution functions, and particularly appeals to those companies that view logistics as a necessary business expense rather than as a competitive weapon. This is not to suggest that contract logistics is simply a money-saving option. Outside service vendors, such as public warehouses, often can provide a better, more cost-effective, logistics service than the manufacturing firm.

Whether the logistics function is performed in-house or by an outside contractor, one fact remains clear. The practice of leveraging logistics volumes and flows will proliferate. Why? Because our increasingly global economy demands that companies constantly plan and evaluate logistics operations to stay competitive. Also, top management will continue to step up the pressure for logistics performance – especially return on assets.

Excellent logistics departments strive to understand, measure and monitor all logistics volumes that are ordered, transported, stored and handled throughout the corporation as a whole. They collect this information for every product group from the entire logistics value chain – supplier to customer – regardless of organizational boundaries. Once managers acquire this information, and have ready access to it, opportunities to gain leverage or implement creative options will surface. Whether in freight consolidation, carrier or supplier management, inbound/outbound coordination, logistics investments, inventory turns, third-party support or joint ventures, the ability to leverage logistics volumes will produce cost savings, improved profitability, and competitive advantage far into the future.

10 Measure and react to performance

Once achieved, logistics excellence must be sustained or gains will be short-lived. Companies must measure their logistics performance and react to the results in an on-going dynamic fashion.

The most effective logistics operations are those linking their operating procedures directly to their overall logistics strategy. That logistics strategy is, in turn, linked to the corporate strategy. The corporate strategic goals form the basis for management identification of the level of performance necessary for success, and how best to measure that performance. This approach guarantees that logistics activities mesh with marketing and manufacturing initiatives. More than one company has learned the value of coordinating logistics, marketing and manufacturing strategies the hard way. These companies reduced the number of warehouses to cut inventories and improve ROA, only to discover the resulting market share losses wiped out any cost savings.

Without constant attention and fine-tuning, performance measurements soon decay into oblivion. Although every company is quick to acknowledge that logistics is a very dynamic function, few reflect this dynamic environment in their monitoring of the adequacy of their performance measures.

World-class corporations view logistics as a strategic tool, rather than as a cost-incurring function, and logistics coordinates its activities with production, sales, marketing, research and development, and other operating functions of the business. For logistics to perform in this manner, management must design its performance measures to monitor 'how it is doing' in meeting the company's strategic goals. Additionally, logistics managers should be ready to take appropriate corrective action whenever logistics is not progressing appropriately toward achieving its strategic objectives.

When discussing performance measurement with logistics managers, there are two common complaints. 'Sure, we know what our logistics functions should be doing', these managers say, 'but we just don't know how to get timely, reliable and comprehensive information about how well we're doing.' Or, these same executives comment, 'We measure our operating performance pretty well, we think, but our measures are not meaningful for our customers.'

These two complaints embody the main thrust behind our principles of logistics excellence. They address two broad and essential goals: positioning logistics within the corporate strategy so that it fully supports the business goals, and helps meet them profitably; and focusing logistics on effective service to the firm's customers in order to gain optimal profit from alternative service strategies.

The importance of measuring how well logistics meets these two challenges cannot be overstated. We recommend that logistics and other operating executives treat the measurement of logistics performance with the same care and attention they devote to measuring operations, systems or personnel performance. This means the logistics executive should challenge existing measures, work to improve how performance is reported, and *innovate, innovate, innovate*. It also means the managers should focus on what the customers need, and how well the department meets those needs. Above all, a logistics executive should never accept yesterday's measures of performance as adequate for tomorrow.

Putting it all together: world-class logistics and projects

Many companies throughout the world today are increasingly concerned about 'competitiveness', or the ability to compete domestically and against growing foreign competition. Is logistics innovation just another hopeful remedy? Do these innovative practices really give companies competitive advantage over their domestic and foreign competitors? Can achieving the 10 principles of logistics excellence really improve profitability?

Undoubtedly, readers and any manager seeking solutions to corporate problems or competitive threats, will ask these questions. We should reflect on the context in which excellence in logistics – as one corporate function – provides a measurable contribution to profitability (and, indeed, to survival). We close this chapter with the full knowledge that improving logistics activities is not a panacea for corporate ills. Certainly in most companies, production (operations), sales and marketing and service – the other three key value-added activities in a company's value chain – together represent substantially more resources and work processes and therefore can offer a combined greater impact on profitability than logistics. Nevertheless, logistics excellence can be an important weapon in the corporate competitive arsenal.

All businesses – regardless of location, size, product, or industry – should, we believe, focus constantly on unrelenting fundamentals, which include the following:

- new product development
- improved productivity
- superior quality
- new technology
- commitment to human resources
- solid value offerings
- aggressive sales and merchandising programmes
- effective product distribution and logistics
- second-to-none customer service.

These last two factors – distribution and logistics and customer service – form the essence of this chapter.

Regardless of its source – foreign or domestic – intensified competition is a fact of today's business life. All companies, therefore, should devote their energies and resources to understanding and prospering within their increasingly competitive markets. Good products and sales, while still essential, are not enough. Companies must emphasize 'total business management', and develop the ability to approach products, costs, markets, and even volume, more critically than in the past. And they must develop a concise strategy to conduct it over time.

Today, the traditional product lines of most companies are firmly positioned. The challenge is to manage the business properly and to turn these core businesses into solid assets, earning a respectable return on the investments they represent.

Formulating and renewing strategies for competing in today's markets tie in nicely with the principles on striving for logistics excellence. In meeting the objectives reflected in the 10 principles of logistics excellence, companies will be well on their way toward implementing 'total business management'. A world-class logistics function, because of its positive interrelationship with virtually every corporate activity, can stimulate the kinds of tangible, operations-based improvements that can make all the difference in competing in world markets.

Conclusion

In both the current and future competitive business environments, it is inadequate for any company to develop and execute strategy that merely fulfils a marketing plan at lowest total cost. Logistics holds an increasingly important place in the corporation today, interfacing with manufacturing, merchandising, sales and marketing and service. The challenge facing companies is to take full advantage of logistics as a powerful competitive weapon. By organizing, focusing, and advancing logistics to excellence, it will make its real contributions to corporate profitability.

References

1. *Corporate Profitability & Logistics: Innovative Guidelines For Executives*; Prepared by Ernst & Whinney for the Council of Logistics Managers. Oak Brook, Illinois, 1987.
2. Porter, M; *Competitive Advantage: Creating and Sustaining Superior Performance*; New York, The Free Press, and London; Collier Macmillan Publishers, 1985.

4 Developing Strategic and Operational Plans for Logistics*

Martin Christopher

Introduction

Increasingly, many companies have recognized the need to develop more formal approaches to planning. The uncertainties of the market environment and the increased complexity of business decisions have provided an incentive to these organisations to seek ways in which corporate resources can be better allocated and contingencies provided for. Nevertheless, formal business planning still tends to be confined to the larger companies, and often those that are involved in so-called fastmoving markets. Thus the Unilevers and Procter and Gambles of the world are using highly sophisticated planning techniques, but many other companies still lag behind. This is due not so much to a lack of resources to commit to the planning function, but more often to a lack of appreciation of the necessity for planning.

Planning enables the business to anticipate change rather than to react to it. It also assists in the identification of risk and enables the costs and benefits of alternative strategies to be more precisely assessed. Without a planning orientation, the organization is simply carried along by the tide of events rather than actually influencing their shape.

In this chapter we are concerned primarily with distribution planning, but it is important to recognise its relationship to the other planning activities of the business. Figure 4.1 depicts the hierarchy of planning concepts, showing how the distribution plan is a subset of

---

* This chapter is based upon the author's book, *The Strategy of Distribution*, Aldershot: Gower, 1984.

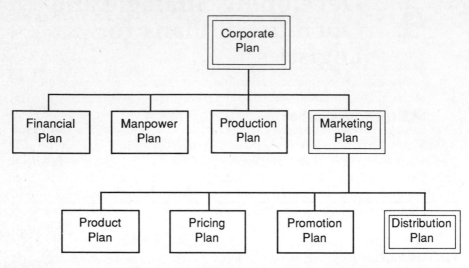

Figure 4.1   The hierarchy of planning systems

the marketing planning function, which is itself given direction by the corporate plan.

The corporate plan is essentially a statement of the overall business strategy, detailing the definition of the business, the global corporate missions, the directions for future development and resource allocation and the specification of financial objectives for the firm. Once these overall business objectives are determined, the way becomes clearer for the development of the marketing plan, specifying how those corporate requirements will be achieved through the sale of products (or services) into markets. As Figure 4.1 suggests, the marketing plan itself comprises four major components – each reflecting the key elements of the marketing mix. The aspect of the marketing plan on which we focus here is the distribution plan, but it must be recognized that no one element of the marketing mix can be considered in isolation. Hence, in developing the distribution plan, constant cross-reference must be made to its interrelationship with the other marketing mix elements.

Distribution planning horizons

Distribution planning has to work both at the short-term and long-term levels. Short-term planning which will normally extend for a budget or calendar year is essentially 'Operational planning'. On the other hand, the need exists to take a longer-term view, perhaps with a horizon of five or more years and this we might term 'Strategic' or 'Resource' planning.

Operational planning, as its title suggests, is concerned with the planning of appropiate responses to events whilst resources are fixed to all intents and purposes. It is in reality the planning of the day-to-day management of the system. In operational planning, we are concerned with such issues as vehicle scheduling, lead-times, inventory replenishment, warehouse utilization and so on. Often, in the past, this has been the area of 'seat of the pants' management, usually followed by 'fire-fighting'. Now, with the advent of more systematic management and planning concepts, a greater discipline is being exerted in this area. Later, we shall discuss the impact that decision support systems can have on the development of better operational planning.

Strategic planning is concerned with the longer-term allocation of resources and adopts a time-frame where all resources are variable. Thus, issues such as the numbers and location of depots, changes in transport mode, new channels of distribution and so on are the type of decisions to be impacted on at this level of planning. The strategic role of distribution is often neglected and yet the ability to respond effectively to market and environmental changes is just as necessary in distribution as it is elsewhere in the business. The penalties for neglecting the strategic component of the distribution task are usually expensive – for example, a depot network unsuited to current market requirements and current cost profiles or commitment to distribution modes that do not meet changed criteria for cost-effectiveness.

The Distribution planning framework

At its most simple the tasks to be encompassed within the distribution planning framework of the business can be depicted as in Figure 4.2.

The first task is to gain a detailed understanding of the present position. This is the distribution audit to provide a picture of current performance. Without this comprehensive picture of the present operating characteristics and capabilities of the business it is not possible to move to the second step – the setting of distribution missions and objectives. The definition of missions and objectives is a vital step; in the words of the old saying, 'if we don't know where

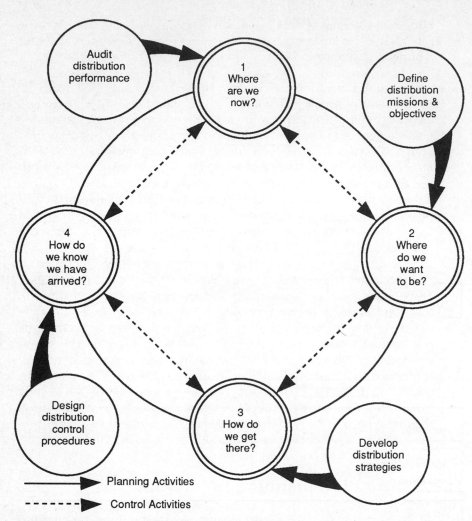

Figure 4.2   The distribution planning tasks

we're going, any road will take us there!' The concept of the distribution mission can be described as 'a set of goals to be achieved by the system within a specific product/market context'.

Missions can be defined in terms of the type of channels and outlets served and by the products that are sold to them within the constraints of specified levels of cost and service. Figure 4.3 highlights some of the factors that could be relevant in the definition of distribution missions.

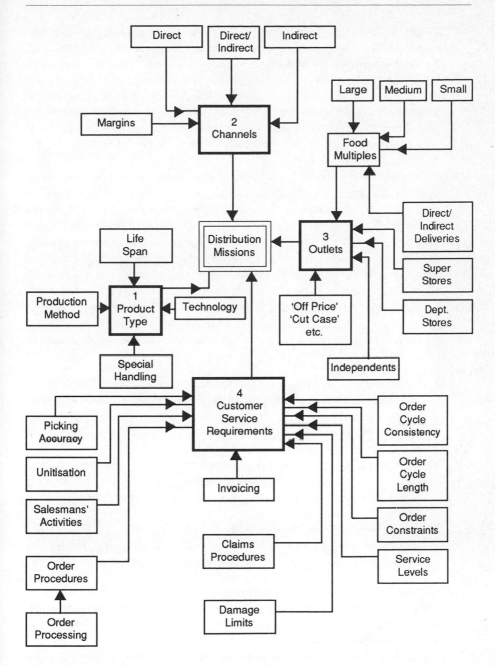

Figure 4.3   Defining distribution missions

The importance of this stage of the process is that it provides the focus for subsequent decisions. Naturally the precise definition of distribution missions and the specific objectives that flow from the definition will need to be based on marketing and operational requirements and hence the need for the fullest co-ordination at the planning level between these different areas. As a result of the careful specification of missions and objectives, the next stage in the planning sequence can follow logically – that is the development of distribution strategies.

Strategies are the means whereby objectives are to be achieved – the 'route to the goal'. Normally there will be alternative strategic options available to the business in its pursuit of objectives and one of the tasks of planning is to identify and evaluate these alternatives. In the case of distribution strategy, the planner will be concerned to examine options in terms of cost-effectiveness. This can either mean seeking strategies that will achieve required customer service objectives at least cost, or alternatively working within a given distribution budget and attempting to maximize service. Whilst the former may be the more desired approach, the latter is often adopted for pragmatic reasons.

Murray[1] has summarized the distribution planning process as follows:

1   Developing a thorough understanding and appreciation of business strategies and marketing plans. This understanding is essential for providing sound strategic planning recommendations and for moving toward a distribution system that balances cost and service effectiveness.
2   Evaluating customer service requirements to determine what elements are viewed as key – how service is measured, what levels of performance are expected and how the business measures up against its competition.
3   Analysing the distribution system and total costs of production and distribution to identify the lowest cost network that meets business marketing and customer requirements.

Thus the basis for the development of viable distribution strategies rests on the recognition of customer service requirements and the costs of providing that service combined with an understanding of global corporate goals.

Based on these principles, we can construct a simple model of the distribution planning process which indicates the linkages from

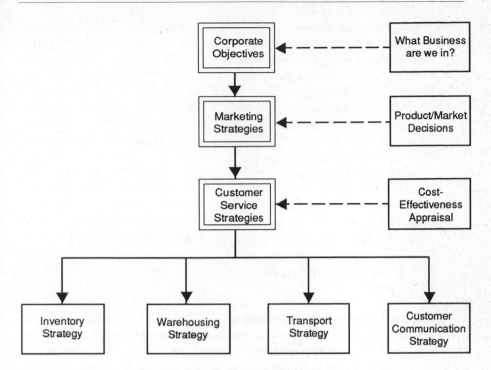

Figure 4.4   From corporate objectives to distribution strategy

corporate objectives down to the specific components of distribution strategy (see Figure 4.4).

Thus the distribution plan, as a formal written document, should include sections on corporate objectives, marketing strategies and customer service strategies as well as the specific detail on inventory, warehousing, transport and customer communications strategy. These latter aspects represent the core of the distribution plan, both at the strategic and the operational level, and the plan should cover at least the following:

1   Inventory strategy
   - service level policy
   - replenishment strategy
   - differential deployment (ABC concept)
   - stock-turn targets
   - stock location
2   Warehousing strategy
   - number of stock-holding points

- location of depots
- use of public warehouses
- warehouse design and layout
- materials handling methods

3 Transport strategy
   - Own account/third party split
   - Lease/buy decisions
   - Customer pick-up/direct delivery/other options
   - Vehicle utilization targets
   - Routing flexibility
   - Modal split

4 Customer Communications Strategy
   - Order cycle time policy
   - Differential customer response strategies
   - Order processing systems
   - Damages/claims/returns strategy
   - Order status reporting.

The final planning task depicted in figure 4.2 was the development of monitoring and control procedures. It will be obvious that planning and implementation will come to nothing without an efficient means of monitoring and controlling the 'actual' against the 'plan'.

A suitable focus for such a monitoring system is customer service, both from the view of performance and the costs of its provision. Setting up the service monitor should be a systematic procedure. Heskett *et al.*[2] suggest a sequence which, slightly modified, would be:

1 Identify all important logistics cost categories along with other inputs of effort which the organization incurs in providing customer service.
2 Institute systems and procedures for the collection of this cost data.
3 Identify and collect output data.
4 Prepare a set of desired measures by which the logistics activities within the organization might be evaluated.
5 Set up a mechanism for the regular presentation of status reports.

This procedure begins with the recognition that customer service costs, wherever they occur, should be flushed out and brought together. Typically, traditional accounting systems will not be capable of providing the data in the form in which it is required. Many customer service costs will be lost in the 'general overheads' of the business, such as order processing costs. Designing the procedures for the collection of this data is therefore no easy task.

Identifying and collecting output data may also be problematic. Output data in the customer service context are concerned with revenue, thus the problem becomes one of pinpointing the extent to which the service package has resulted in the generation of revenue. Obviously, this is not possible and so, assuming a relationship between revenue generation and service level, we use the latter as a surrogate measure. Hence measures such as order cycle time, percentage of back-orders, consistency of delivery lead-times and so on have to be used. Fairly simple recording and reporting systems will normally be sufficient to generate the required data. For example, regular samples can be taken of individual customer orders to check on order cycle lead-times, likewise for the percentage of orders met from stock and so on.

Measuring performance within the logistics organization involves the collection, on the same regular basis, of such data as warehouse costs (handling, storage) and utilisation, transportation costs and utilisation, inventory costs, order processing costs and so on. This data is often conveniently presented in the form of ratios – for example, cost per case, cost per ton-mile, etc.

Information such as this should be compared with the performance standards previously set. As far as cost standards are concerned, some care is necessary in setting these standards. In most cases it will be advantageous to adopt a *flexible* budgeting system where account is taken of the changed level of activity or volume and the effects of these changes is separated from other variances. At the same time performance standards should also reflect the highest level of efficient working rather than being based on past achievement, it being possible that past performance was itself less than perfect.

The means of providing distribution management with feedback on the performance of the plan must also be considered. As yet, however, too many organizations supply their distribution managers with only rudimentary information through regular performance reports.

The planning tasks described above follow a logical sequence from the audit through to monitoring and control. Indeed the whole process should ideally be viewed as a cycle (see Figure 4.5) whereby the distribution plan becomes a continuing activity, guiding the direction taken and providing a firm base for the allocation of resources.

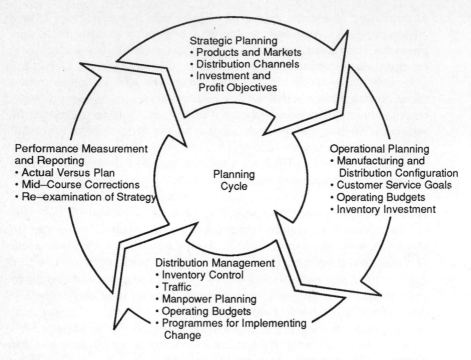

Source: Moore, J., 'Strategic Considerations in Measuring and Reporting Performance for Physical Distribution Management', NCPDM *Annual Meeting Proceedings*, 1977.

Figure 4.5   The distribution planning cycle

Decision support systems in distribution planning

The discipline imposed on the distribution function by the planning process has led to the search for aids to the management of this task. In recent years, developments in computer-based modelling and simulation techniques have made possible the creation of so-called 'decision support systems'.

With the assistance of these systems managers can quickly compare trade-offs among a variety of strategic and operational options to identify optimum, or improved, solutions to logistics problems. In its simplest form, a decision support system is a computer-based model that describes the process to be managed (for example, the distribution system) combined with a data-base which contains actual data on the operating characteristics of the system (for example, costs, demand and so on). The computer can then be instructed to answer a vast number of 'what if?' type questions. Examples might be: what if this depot was to be closed? What if inventory coverage on these items was to be reduced? What if order cycle time was to be reduced by one day? The answer to these 'what if?' questions would detail the effects of such changes on service levels, total system costs and other operating characteristics.

A recent study[3] on the use of decision support systems in logistics management reported a number of typical applications:

- Agrico, a chemical company, through co-operation between corporate and outside management science consultants, has implemented an integrated computer-based production, distribution and inventory management system. This system, which is used exclusively to evaluate the cost – benefit impact of alternative capital investments, has, according to Agrico management, already saved over US $40 million;
- International Paper, under the direction of the corporate operational research (OR) group, has developed a general purpose decision support system to help make resource allocation decisions. The scope includes operational, tactical and strategic planning from the woodlands, through all the intermediate processing, and the distribution of finished primary and by-products. The system has identified significant cost improvement opportunities. In addition, the system has been quoted as substantially reducing the level of contention surrounding resource allocation decisions, and
- The R and G Sloane Manufacturing Company, a leading manufacturer of plastic pipes and fittings for the building and chemical industries, utilized a management support system to aid in production and sales planning. The system is credited with an increase of 13 per cent in generating profits during a recent year.

Whilst it is beyond the scope of this chapter to discuss the technical aspects of model-building and simulation in great detail, it is neverthless now becoming such an important management concern and, as the above examples demonstrate, a practical device for improving profitability that a brief review of the field would be appropriate.

Model building and simulation

A 'model' is a representation of relationships within a system. At the simplest level, these relationships may be expressed in verbal terms such as 'an increase in service levels will improve our market share'. At a more sophisticated level, such relationships would be quantified and made more specific; for example, 'given no change in competitive actions and general economic conditions a change from 95 per cent in-stock availability to 97 per cent on Product X will result in an increase in market share from 23 per cent to 26 per cent'. Frequently the more complex models will consist of a number of such statements, each connected to the other, so that the model is in effect a set of interrelated, quantified relationships. Models need not be designed to be 'predictive', their primary use may be for explanation. This is particularly the case where models of market behaviour are to be constructed.

Indeed there is a whole 'family' of models, and the choice of the appropriate type will depend on the use to which it is to be put. Increasingly the emphasis in model-building is not so much the construction of 'optimizing' models – that is, models which will generate a unique solution that cannot be bettered – rather there is a recognition that the complexity of real-world relationships is such that such optima, if they exist at all, may not be attainable. Instead it is frequently more realistic to seek to identify outcomes which are the 'best currently available' or the 'best yet identified'. It is here that *simulation* as a technique comes into its own. Simulation is not an optimizing technique but an approach to evaluating alternative options using models of the system under consideration. Thus, in the same way a car designer would use wind tunnel tests to identify improved body designs to reduce drag, so too can the logistics planner use simulation to identify solutions which give better results than others.

One of the problems with simulation, at least until recently, has been that the construction of the model to represent the system is often a time-consuming and complex task. However there are now a number of widely available computer software packages which enable any organization's logistics system to be adequately represented. There still remains, however, the need to generate an adequate database using actual data from the recent past: for example, daily demand; item by item; vehicle capacity; transport costs; labour rates, and so on. Once this is to hand, the system can be simulated using actual data (see Figure 4.6) to ascertain the extent to which it reproduces actual outcomes, such as customer service levels. This is a validation procedure necessary to ensure the accuracy of the system representation. Given that a high degree of validity is established, management can now begin to use the model as a decision support system. In other words, 'what if?' questions can be asked and answered. This is the real power of simulation and, in a sense, it is one of the most important management techniques available to the distribution planner. It will, in all probability, revolutionize distribution planning and strategy formulation in the years to come.

Industrial dynamics

Often considerable insights can be gained into the 'dynamics' of a logistics system though the use of simulation. This is because in most logistics systems there will be 'leads and lags' – in other words, the response to an input or a change in the system may be delayed. For example, the presence of a warehouse or a stock-holding intermediary in the distribution channel can cause a substantial distortion in demand at the factory. This is due to the 'acceleration effect' which can cause self-generated fluctuations in the operating characteristics of a system.

Taking the example of a manufacturing company that sells its output to a wholesaler, who then sells it to retailers, it is possible to illustrate the effect of accelerated relationships (Figure 4.7).

The company has a service policy which requires it to keep the equivalent of eight weeks' stock as a buffer; the wholesaler keeps 12 weeks' stock and the retailer three weeks' stock. Now, for some reason, say, a promotion, final consumer demand increases in the month by 10 per cent over the previous month. If the retailer wishes to maintain his previous service level, he will increase his order to the wholesaler not by 10 per cent but by 11 per cent (that is 10 per cent + 10 per cent (3/52)) in order to maintain three weeks' safety stock. Now the wholesaler is faced with an increase in demand of 11 per cent which, if he readjusts his stock levels, will result in an increase in his monthly order to the manufacturer of 13 per cent (that is, 11 per cent + 11 per cent (12/52)). Similarly, the manufacturer producing for stock and wishing to maintain eight weeks' safety stock increases production by 15 per cent (that is, 13 per cent + 13 per cent (8/52)). Thus, an initial increase in consumer demand of 10 per cent has resulted in an eventual increase in production of 15 per cent. If final

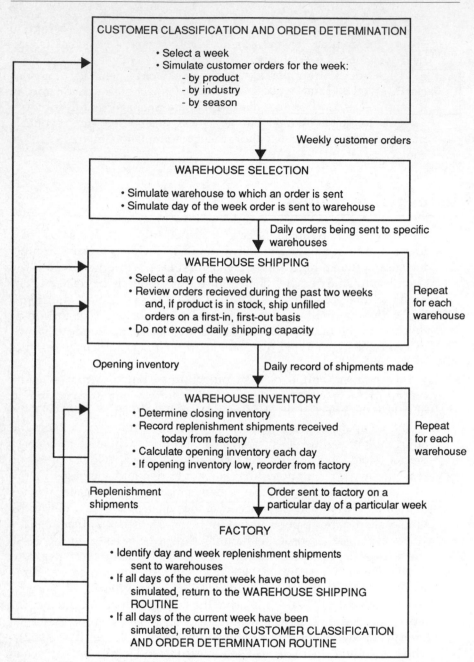

Figure 4.6   Distribution system simulation

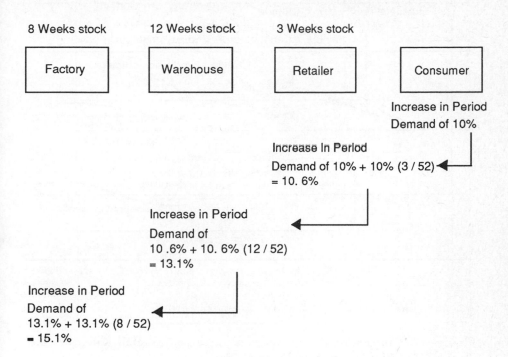

Figure 4.7   The acceleration effect

demand were to fall back in the next period, the same process in reverse would be experienced.

Taking concepts such as the acceleration effect and the interrelationships within complex business systems, Forrester has developed the notion of 'Industrial Dynamics'[5] which he defined as:

The study of the information feedback characteristics of industrial activity to show how organisational structure, amplification (in policies) and time delays (in decisions and actions) interact to influence the success of the enterprise. It treats the interactions between the flows of information, money, orders, materials, personnel and capital equipment in a company, an industry or a national economy.

Industrial dynamics provides a single framework for integrating the functional areas of management – marketing, production, accounting, research and development and capital investment.

Using a specially developed computer simulation language,

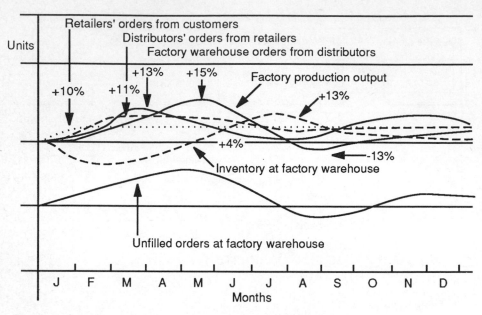

Units

Retailers' orders from customers
Distributors' orders from retailers
Factory warehouse orders from distributors

+13%   +15%   Factory production output
+10%   +11%   +13%

+4%   -13%

Inventory at factory warehouse

Unfilled orders at factory warehouse

J   F   M   A   M   J   J   A   S   O   N   D
Months

Adapted from: J. Forrester, *Industrial Dynamics*, MIT Press, 1961

Figure 4.8   Impact of an unexpected increase in retail sales on the distribution system

DYNAMO, Forrester built a model of a production – distribution system involving three levels in the distribution channel: a retailer's inventory, a distributor's inventory and a factory inventory. Each level was interconnected through information flows and flows of goods. The model used real-world relationships and data and included parameters such as order transmission times, order processing times, factory lead-times and shipment delivery times. Management could then examine the effects on the total system of, say, a change in retail sales or the impact of changing production patterns or any other policy change or combination of changes.

If we apply the industrial dynamics logic to the earlier example of the manufacturer – wholesaler – retailer stock adjustment effect, we can see quite clearly the disturbance that is caused throughout the system with the resultant effect on service levels (see Figure 4.8).

Using simulation in this way can thus help both to explain the reasons for fluctuations in a system as well as providing a guide to management action to overcome these effects[6].

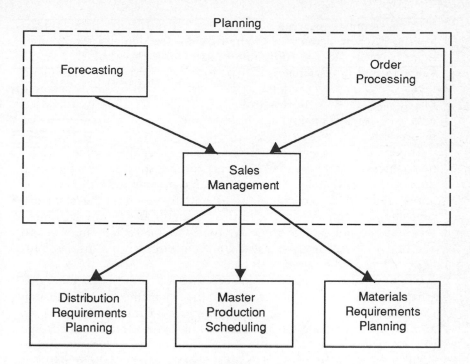

Figure 4.9   Demand management

Demand management and the distribution plan

Recently, a new area of management concern has arisen, partly through the discipline brought about through the use of distribution requirements planning (DRP), which has come to be termed 'demand management'.

The concept of demand management is a combination of the sales forecasting, order processing and sales management tasks. Whilst the sales forecast anticipates demand and the order processing system enters that demand, sales management takes decisions, where necessary, relating to that demand – for example, product substitution, product upgrade, order rotation, partial shipment, split shipment or back-ordering. Thus demand management 'generates information on sales forecasts by item, customer satisfaction, demand vs. shipment, capacity vs. demand and deployment of existing inventory'[7]. Figure 4.9 shows the relationship of this view of demand management to the planning task.

In distribution requirements planning, the only items to be forecast are those where demand is independent – the demand for all other items is calculated. One of the problems is that the number of stock-keeping units (SKUs) that need to be forecast as independent demand items can often be very high, particularly as DRP requires separate forecasts from each stock location. DRP also requires time-phased forecasts, so seasonality, cyclicality, and so on, also need to be incorporated in any forecast.

There are many forecasting techniques available, some simple, many highly complicated[8]. However, for the short-term forecasting of SKU demand it is really only 'statisical' methods that will be appropriate. These techniques are essentially based on the 'statistical projection of the past into the future', to quote R. G. Brown[9], one of the major exponents of these methods. Whilst there may be no alternative to using past sales data to forecast the future, this approach should be used with care.

One source of potential error in such forecasts is the assumption that what happened in the past will be repeated in the future, and that trends and patterns presently discernible will continue. Often such an approach is acceptable for the short term, but not for extended time periods. This is because the marketing environment is dynamic and so factors can intervene to negate the effects of past and current trends. For example, the entrance of an overseas competitor into a market would quite clearly upset the sales forecasts of existing companies if they have been based on past and current data. Similarly, changes in consumer tastes, the development of substitute technologies, government inter-vention and changes in the national economy can have severe effects on the accuracy of forecasts based on extrapolation.

Thus for longer-term strategic planning, other, more qualitative forecasts may provide a better guide. One technique that has been used with success in this connection is the 'Delphi Forecast'. This is a method whereby the opinions of a panel of experts are combined through a series of questionnaires. To avoid bias and to provide anonymity, the panel do not know the identity of the other members. The results of each questionnaire are used to design the next questionnaire so that convergence of the expert opinion is obtained.

Whatever techniques are adopted, the role of demand management is to integrate the resulting forecasts into the distribution plan. This will often mean that forecasts need to be adjusted in the light of managerial judgments; that demand data which is inputted to the forecast is corrected to take account of back orders, product substitutions and so on, and that the effects of systems dynamics can be factored into the final forecast. Essentially, therefore, demand management can be seen as a crucial component of the distribution planning task, mediating between data, statistical technique, customer contact and the order processing system.

Attention paid to improving demand management can have substantial rewards; in the words of one writer:

How many companies could benefit from a system where marketing was selling the same thing that manufacturing was making, that inventory was replenishing, that finance was budgeting and that customer service was promising?[10]

References

1 Murray, R. E., 'Strategic Distribution Planning: Structuring the Plan', Proceedings of the Eighteenth Annual Conference of the National Council of Physical Distribution Management, (NCPDM, Chicago), October 1980.
2 Hesket, J *et al.*, *Business Logistics*, Ronald Press, 1973.
3 Closs, D. J. and Helferich, O.K., 'Logistics Decision Support System: An Integration of Information, Data Base and Modelling Systems to Aid the Logistics Practitioner', *Journal of Business Logistics*, vol. 3, no. 2, 1982.
4 Waller, A., "Computer Systems for Distribution Planning", *International Journal of Physical Distribution and Materials Management*, vol.13, no.7, 1983.
5 Forrester. J. W., *Industrial Dynamics*, MIT Press, 1961.
6 Coyle, R. G., *Management System Dynamics*, John Wiley and Sons, 1977.
7 Muir, J. W., 'Manufacturing Resource Planning and Demand Management' in *Components of Manufacturing Resource Planning*, Auerbach Publishers Inc., 1981.
8 Wheelwright, S. C. and Makridakis, S., *Forecasting Methods for Management* (3rd edn.), Wiley Interscience, 1980.
9 Brown, R. G., *Statistical Forecasting for Inventory Control*, McGraw-Hill, 1959.
10 Muir, J. W. and Newberry, T. L., 'Management's Role in a Forecasting System', American Production and Inventory Control Society 24th Annual Conference Procedings, Boston, US, 1981.

Part II

CUSTOMER SERVICE: THE DRIVING FORCE

Overview to Part II

Martin Christopher raises the value-added concept again in Chapter 5, this time in the context of developing customer service strategies. He examines various customer service strategies and suggests that customer service must form part of the organization's overall philosophy – in other words, form part of the total quality package offered to customers. Christopher argues that with shorter product life cycles, and more sophisticated customers, organizations must develop customer service strategies that meet customers' perceptions whilst supporting overall corporate goals. This, he suggests, is achieved by first adopting an appropriate strategic position and only then concentrating on operational efficiency.

In Chapter 6 Ehnbom looks at customer service from the customer's perspective and argues convincingly that employees in contact with the customer can make or break a company's customer service strategy. Ehnbom stresses that management must focus on outcomes rather than activities, with front-line contact staff being encouraged to use their initiative and take responsibility for achieving customer service satisfaction. According to Ehnbom, management's role is to empower, support and motivate front-line contact staff ensuring that employees at all levels know, relate to, and fully understand the organization's customer service strategy and their vital role in its effective implementation. The importance of customer service to long-term organizational viability is, Ehnbom argues, self-evident, yet finding and experiencing really good customer service is still a rarity today.

5 Developing Customer Service Strategies

Martin Christopher

What is customer service?

Customer service is concerned with making the product available to the customer. Put another way, there is no value in a product or service until it is in the hands of the customer. But 'availability' in itself is a complex concept, impacted upon by many factors which might include delivery frequency and reliability, stock levels and order cycle time. Ultimately customer service is determined by the interaction of all those factors that affect the process of making products and services available to the buyer.

Clearly there are many aspects of customer service but amongst the most important are:

- Order cycle time – How long from the receipt of the order to delivery?
- Consistency and reliability of delivery – Is the delivery on time, every time?
- Inventory availability – Is the product ordered available from stock?
- Order-size constraints – Is there a minimum quantity or value on the order?
- Ordering convenience – How easy is it for the customer to do business with us?
- Delivery times and flexibility – Can we deliver at the customer's convenience?
- Invoicing procedures and accuracy – Is the invoice correct and easy to process?
- Claims procedures – How do we handle complaints and claims?

- Condition of Goods – What is our record on quality of goods on arrival?
- Visits by sales people – Do our sales representatives act as 'service ambassadors'?
- Order status information – How well do we communicate with our customers about their orders?

Of course, in any particular product or service and market situation, some of these elements will be more important than others and there may be factors other than those listed above which have a significance in a specific market.

Not only is customer service concerned with many different aspects of the business operation, it also takes place at different stages in relation to the actual purchase of a product or service. It has been suggested that customer service should be examined under three headings:

1   pre-transaction elements;
2   transaction elements;
3   post-transaction elements.

Pre-transaction elements relate to corporate policies or programmes, for example, written statements of service policy, adequacy of organizational structure and system flexibility. The transaction elements are those variables directly involved in performing the physical distribution function; for example, product availability, order cycle time, order status information and delivery reliability. The post-transaction elements are generally supportive of the product in use, for instance, product warranty, parts and repair service, procedures for customer complaints and product replacement.

Considering customer service in this way again reminds us of the wide range of aspects of the business involved. It also emphasizes the importance of customer service from the initial customer interest in our product or service through to the eventual replacement purchase at the end of the life of that item. It also influences any other potential transactions that the customer may make for other products or services in our range. Studies on customer service have shown that, whilst a satisfied customer will tell only three people of a good experience, a dissatisfied customer will tell 11 people of a bad experience.

Customer service and total quality

In recent years there has been an upsurge in interest in 'excellence' generally which has heightened the consciousness and awareness of customer service. It has been recognized that a crucial source of competitive advantage can be achieved through superior marketplace service. Although customer service is only one of the elements in the quest for total quality, its importance and impact on the customer can be demonstrated in the description of how a major Italian fashion company, Benetton, have incorporated marketing and distribution management to obtain a cost advantage whilst also giving the customer excellent service. Benetton are now a major international company having grown rapidly from a small family business.

Benetton's order system is 'just-in-time' as production runs are not started until orders have been received. A key aspect of its system is the dyeing of knitted goods after production rather than dyeing yarn prior to knitting. This allows Benetton outlets to delay commitment to particular colours until later in the production cycle. Since each selling season typically begins with about 10 alternative colours with only about three usually resulting in high demand, the delay in colour choice affords Benetton an opportunity to respond directly to market demand. The retail system itself provides valuable information to Benetton for production planning via daily orders. These feed production with current demand, on which replenishment schedules for designs and colours may be based. The timeliness of this order data is crucial since popular colours will often sell out in the first 10 days of a new season. This rapid response system gives Benetton retailers a competitive edge over their less responsive competitors. The order information is digested and fed back to those customers whose orders appear to be out of line with others in their area. Further, Benetton uses CAD (Computer-aided design) for design and cutting in order to respond to dynamic demand as rapidly as possible. Finally, the company's marketing strategy promotes simple colour fashion with heavy advertising support, which in turn maximizes the benefits from the delayed dyeing production process.

This example well illustrates the incorporation of customer service into the total quality package that the customer is offered. But, of course, good customer service in isolation from the other elements of the marketing mix will never lead to success. A weak product with good customer service is unlikely to succeed, although a strong product with poor customer service may survive but never reach its full market potential. Benetton not only offers good customer service, impacting on availability, reaction speed to demand and so on, it also offers products that are appropriate to its target market in terms of quality, style, price, designs and in outlets with the right image and appeal to support its products.

American Express provides another example of the integration of customer service into their total company philosophy. Replacement cards are provided within 24 hours to more than 1.5 million customers per year anywhere in the world, at a cost of US $5 million dollars. Although this service is costly, if the customer does not have his card then he cannot use it, hence the desire to get it back to him as quickly as possible. A decrease in the time taken to process new applications from 32 days to 15 days and signing on new outlets in nine days instead of 25 days, results in 17 days' more revenue and 16 more days' commissions. Customers are continually researched to find their opinions on new and existing services. This has allowed American Express to cut its advertising expense and to target new markets. At the same time customers are given an opportunity to voice any dissatisfactions with the company and its services.

Again, the American Express example shows the integration of customer service into the entire way of thinking and operating. Although these examples are from large international companies, what lessons do they afford the small business? Essentially, whatever the size of the organization, customer service should be viewed as an integral part of the total quality package offered to the customer. In the examples of successful companies given, the recognition of customer service is a part of the company philosophy. In setting up a business, it is easier to instil the idea of customer service early on and let the concept develop rather than attempt to transplant the idea into a medium sized company later in its development.

Customer service and distribution strategy

One of the most important influences on customer service is the company's distribution policy. Traditionally, distribution has been viewed by many as a source of cost – admittedly a necessary cost, but a cost nevertheless. Inevitably such a viewpoint leads to a search for improvement in operating efficiency and a focus on cost reduction. Thus improving vehicle utilization, warehouse throughput times, materials handling methods and so on are the constant concern of many distribution managers.

Whilst not wishing to diminish the importance of cost containment, it can be argued that such a concern with efficiency can, on occasion, lead to a failure to recognize the real issue in distribution – that is, how *effective* is our distribution strategy? This distinction between efficiency and effectiveness was most clearly defined by Peter Drucker, who argued that efficiency was a concern with 'doing things right', whilst effectiveness placed the emphasis on 'doing the right things'.

Such a statement could be dismissed as purely a clever play on words yet it has a crucial significance for management. It is saying that operating efficiency often takes precedence over strategy. However, successful companies – those which have developed leadership positions in the market – tend to be those that have recognized that competitive advantage comes, first, from their strategic position and, second, from their operating efficiency. Clearly, a combination of the two is better still.

It must be recognized that the advantage in the marketplace does not always go to the lowest cost producer. Within the car industry, Jaguar has achieved substantial success not so much by cutting costs but by adding value. Much has been said about the new approach to quality at Jaguar and how it has led to major improvements in the final product. However, just as important to its success has been its concentration on improving customer service, especially in North America. A radical overhaul of its US dealer network plus a major emphasis on improving the logistics of spares support has transformed its market position.

Other examples of value-added strategies based around superior service could be cited: companies like DEC and IBM, for example, dominate the segments in which they compete as much through their service package as through their technology. We can see through these examples that two options are open to us if we wish to compete and succeed: we can either aim to win a cost advantage or we can aim to provide superior values and benefits to the customer. In deciding which of these options to pursue, we must also consider the fact that there can, by definition, be only one lowest-cost producer, which may be influenced by new technology or new materials protected by patents and therefore outside of our control or access. However, by researching our markets and identifying customer needs for service within different market segments, providing superior benefits to our customers is a route more readily open to us and can provide us with a unique position against our competitors.

Today, changes in the environment make such a revised orientation even more appropriate. One such change has been the steady transition to 'commodity'-type markets. By this is meant that, increasingly, the power of the 'brand' is diminishing as technologies of competing products converge, thus making the differences less apparent. Faced with such situations the customer may be influenced by price or by 'image' perceptions, but overriding these aspects may well be 'availability': in other words, is the product in stock?

A second change is that customer expectations of service have increased, so that in almost every market the customer is more demanding and more sophisticated then he or she was 30 years ago. Industrial buyers are more professional too, with increasing use made of the formal 'vendor appraisal' system and suppliers now confronted with the need to provide 'just-in-time' delivery performance.

The third change that has had a particularly severe impact in many industries is the trend for product life cycles to become shorter. The product life cycle represents the period of time that a brand or specific model is an effective player in the market. What we have witnessed in many markets is the effect of changes in technology and consumer demand combining to produce more volatile markets where a product can be obsolete almost as soon as it reaches the market. There are many current examples of shortening life cycles, but perhaps the personal computer symbolizes them all. In this particular case we have seen rapid developments in technology which have, first, created markets where none existed before and almost as quickly rendered themselves obsolete as the next generation of product is announced. Such shortening life cycles create substantial problems for logistics management, distribution and, ultimately, customer service.

Developing a Customer Service Strategy

Identifying customer service needs

It is a common fault in marketing to fail to realize that customers do not always attach the same importance to the attributes of our products or services as we do ourselves. Thus, it sometimes happens that products or services are promoted on attributes or features that are less important to the customer in reality than other aspects. A floor cleaner that is sold on its ease of application, for example, will not succeed unless 'ease of application' is a salient benefit sought by the customer. If 'shine' or the need for less frequent cleaning are important to the customer then we might be better advised to feature those aspects on our promotion. The same principle applies to customer service. If a company places emphasis upon stock availability but the customer regards delivery reliability more highly, it may not be allocating its resources in a way likely to maximize sales. Alternatively, a company which realizes that its customers place a higher value on completeness of orders than they do on, say, regular scheduled deliveries could develop this to its advantage.

There is, therefore, a great premium to be placed on gaining an insight into the factors that influence buyer behaviour and, in the context of customer service, which particular elements are seen as most important. The use of market research techniques in customer service has lagged behind their application in such areas as product testing and advertising research, yet the importance of researching the service needs of customers is just as great as, say, the need to understand the market reaction to prices.

How then can we use these standard, proven market research techniques in order to assess the needs of our customers with respect to their service requirements. By working through a formalised four stage process, described below, we can progress through the data collection process to the ultimate development of a competitive service package.

Identifying the key components of customer service
If we are to identify the components of customer service, we must first identify who to ask within our customer's organization. Where are the relative sources of influence on the purchase decision? This is not always an easy question to answer as, in many cases, there will be several people involved. A purchasing manager of a company with whom we deal may only be acting as an agent for others within the company. In other cases, his influence will be considerably greater. If we are manufacturing products for sale through retail outlets, is the decision to stock made centrally by head office or locally by the store manager?

Having identified who to ask, we need to carry out a small-scale research programme, based on personal interviews with a representative sample of buyers. The purpose of this interview is to elicit, in the language of the customers, first the importance they attach to customer service as against that attached to other elements within the marketing mix such as price, product quality, promotion and so on and, second, the specific importance they attach to the individual components of customer service. After a dozen interviews, a pattern of responses is likely to emerge.

A study within a company servicing the grocery market identified senior buyers as being the people responsible for purchasing decisions. Interviews with these buyers resulted in 23 customer service elements being identified, of which six occurred most frequently. The following elements were mentioned:

- Frequency of delivery
- Time from order to delivery*
- Reliability of delivery*
- Emergency deliveries when required
- Stock availability and continuity of supply*
- Orders filled completely
- Advice on non-availability*
- Convenience of placing order
- Acknowledgement of order
- Accuracy of invoices
- Quality of sales representation*
- In-store merchandising support*
- Regular calls by sales representatives
- Manufacturer monitoring of retail stock levels
- Credit terms offered
- Customer query handling
- Quality of outer packaging
- Well-stacked pallets
- Easy-to-read use-by dates on outer packaging
- Quality of inner packaging for in-store handling and display
- Consultation on new product/package development
- Regular reviews of product range
- Coordination between production, distribution and marketing .

*items occurring most frequently

Establishing the relative importance of customer service components

Clearly, customers will have priorities when it comes to service. Certain elements of service will be seen as being of greater importance than others. Thus, in developing a customer service strategy, knowledge of the relative importance of each element of the service mix is a prerequisite.

A variety of devices can be used to assess the importance attached by customers to the service issues previously identified. The most powerful is 'trade-off analysis', a research technique that identifies the 'weights' that individual customers place on each aspect of service. Less complex methods include simple ranking exercises or rating scales.

Whatever method is used, the objective is to identify the key service issues that can then be used as the basis for competitive performance assessment.

Measuring customers' perceptions of service performance

The previous two steps provide the means for the construction of a questionnaire which can be used to measure customers' perception of our service compared to our competitors. This is the idea of competitive 'benchmarking'. Using a rating scale against each of the key service elements, customers are asked to score each of the companies against which we wish to be compared. The resulting service 'profile' can provide a powerful and objective basis for the development of a competitive customer service strategy.

Segmenting the market by service requirements

Most companies recognize the considerable advantages in not treating markets as if they were homogeneous, with customers sharing common characteristics and seeking similar benefits from the products or services on offer. Those companies realize that, within a total market, there will normally be a number of distinct sub-markets or segments, each with distinct characteristics or requirements. Sometimes these differences can be catered for by a strategy of product differentiation – that is, by adjusting the nature of the product or service to meet the specific needs of a segment. However, it may also be possible to target the product or service more specifically at chosen market segments by varying other elements of the marketing mix such as price, promotion or, in this case, customer service.

The underlying philosophy is that it is insufficient to offer a blanket level of service across all market segments or trade sectors. It may be that, for some segments, the service offered is higher than necessary to achieve the sale and, for other segments, it may be too low. Equally, some segments may respond more to one aspect of service than another. Whilst it is not suggested that every customer's particular requirement should be specifically catered for, it is important to attempt to isolate major groupings in the total market and recognize the service factors which have greatest impact upon them.

Developing a competitive service package

To compete effectively in any market requires the ability to develop some differential advantage over competing companies and their products or services. Sometimes this differential advantage may be in terms of distinctive product attributes or related benefits as perceived by the customer. In just the same way, customer service can be used to develop a differential advantage and, indeed, there can be a major benefit to the company using customer service in this way. For example, in competitive markets where real product differentiation may be difficult to establish, and where to compete on price would only lead to profit erosion, it makes sense to switch the marketing emphasis to customer service.

Earlier it was stressed that it is important to establish those components of the total customer service mix which have the greatest impact on the buyer's perception of us as a supplier. This thinking needs to be carried right through into the design of the customer service offering. This offering can best be described as the customer service 'package'. In developing a package, we need to take account of the different needs of different market segments and to make the package as cost-effective as possible. The following steps have been suggested in order to achieve this objective:

1 Determine the customer service practices and policies of competitors for each product and market channel.
2 Identify and measure key elements which lead to becoming a preferred supplier.
3 Measure the impact of each aspect of service on market share and profitability.
4 Assess the performance of the company on each of these service components.
5 Redesign the service package to emphasize effective service expenditures and de-emphasize ineffective ones.

The precise composition of the customer service package for any market segment will depend upon the results of the analysis, as well as by budgetary and cost constraints. If alternative packages can be identified which seem to be equally as acceptable to the buyer, then it obviously makes more sense to choose the least-cost alternative.

Organizing for service management

If the policy that we have defined is to succeed, then it is essential that the customer service goals are based on the strategic objectives of the company as a whole. Customer service policy can not be viewed in isolation but must be viewed as an integral part of the company's marketing strategy. But, whilst many other aspects of the marketing policy are clearly controlled by certain individuals, as we have already seen, customer service affects many different parts of our organization and is implemented by many individuals. For some staff, customer service forms the totality of their specific jobs such as a service engineer or a sales representative. Others, however, are more indirectly involved, such as production managers who would not have direct contact with customers but whose management of scheduling or flexibility of approach may affect availability of products.

A prerequisite for customer service-oriented distribution management is an appropriate organizational structure. Customer service failings are often due to organizational problems. Frequently, as we have identified, responsibility for the different elements is spread around the organization with little attempt to coordinate it. Effective customer service management requires that all those activities involved from the time the order is placed until the goods are delivered are managed in an integrated way. Thus order processing, order status, order assembly, stock management, transport management and even invoicing must all be seen as vital parts of the customer service chain.

6 Personalizing Customer Service Strategies

Stig Ehnbom

Some years ago, I was appointed chief executive of a large, but ailing, company and I asked a group of executives, 'What do we need for a successful business?'

The answer, which came as a surprise to many of them, was *'customers'*.

The aim of any company's strategy must be to add value for the customer. Why? Because experience shows that growth and profit will only come from satisfied customers.

A long-running US market research programme, Profit Impact of Market Strategy, highlights the factors that have a crucial bearing on a company's success. These studies clearly show that an organization giving service and products with perceived quality advantages regularly out-earns other companies. The top one-third of companies in the survey show a return on sales at least twice as great as the bottom one-third and a return on investment that is three times as high.

It is also apparent from this survey that organizations which offer quality service attract customers prepared to pay for that service. By meeting customers' expectations, the organization then meets shareholders' expectations as well.

The message is clear – when you look after the customers, you effectively look after the shareholders.

Service means contact

It is important that we recognize that the service part of a customer service strategy consists of people. However good the strategy, it is people who have to carry it out, and it is the customer's perception of their service that will make or break that strategy.

How many people are able to define their organization's customer service strategy? More important, how many are even aware that such a strategy exists?

An effective strategy only exists if everybody knows it, relates to it and understands it. A good acid test is to ask a recently employed junior person if they know what the customer service strategy is. If they cannot tell you, there is no such strategy.

Product-based companies have traditionally associated customer contact with marketing and sales which can indeed account for some 90% of customer contacts. However, in service-based companies, the percentages may be reversed and the great majority of employees will have customer contact. An airline is a typical example. Staff at the check-in and reservations, the flight crew, cabin and ground staff will all be dealing with the airline's customers. Any one of these staff members can influence a customer's perception of that airline and the service it provides.

Implementing the strategy

Any service strategy must eventually come down to a system and those processes that deliver consistency of service. We can break this system and its processes down into four areas: the system itself; system control; cost control; and quality service control. To make all of them work for the benefit of the customer – and, therefore, the organization – people have to give the personal service needed with both passion and persistence. They have to believe in what they are doing.

Personalizing the customer service strategy means finding the focal point where employees will tend to agree. The point of agreement is, of course, that the customer is paying for the service. That is something that all of us can recognize.

This, however, is not always immediately apparent. In many companies, if you ask the Marketing people what we need to do to sell more, they would answer: 'advertise more, support more, market now.' Ask Research and Development and they would say: 'spend more on research and develop new products.' The Finance people would inevitably say: 'cut costs, reduce the capital employed, cut back on labour.' Those involved in Production would say: 'spend more on updating and modernizing plant.' Management Information Systems would suggest more of the latest computer hardware and software', while the unions would say: 'pay us higher wages. Reward us in exchange for a deal on productivity.' One thing which they all have in common, and which they are all overlooking, is 'What is in it for the customer?'

The customer service strategy has to have a starting-point that defines the value the organization can generate for the customer. The manager who can then turn this into 'What's in it for you', is personalizing the company's service strategy into the major motivational driving force for his or her staff. By personalizing service strategy, management is able to build a solid foundation which will gain the cooperation of staff in putting the strategy in place.

Putting the emphasis on people

The key is commitment. This means that people have to talk about outcomes, not activities. What they do is not important. What they achieve is crucial.

They will achieve the best result only if they know what to do. In order to know what they should do, management needs to clearly spell out what the customer service strategy is. The strategy must identify what is in it for the customer and also what is in it for the individual employee.

We can see a very good example in the experience of the Scandinavian Airlines System, SAS, in the early 1980s. After years of profitability, SAS, like many other airlines, found the oil crisis and increased competition had cut revenue and caused it to suffer losses of US $30 million in 1979 and 1980. The newly appointed President, Jan Carlzon, determined to focus on a perceived gap in the market and to become the 'best airline for the frequent business traveller'. To do that, he concluded that service and the front-line people who delivered it were the key success levers. He shifted the emphasis from aeroplanes and manuals to people and service. He asked his customers, the regular business flyers, what they really wanted and, when he found out what that was, he implemented it. Punctuality, service and efficient luggage-handling ('when we change flights, the bags must go with us') were more important to business travellers than cheap fares or the latest aircraft technology.

With a clear strategy in place, he set about energizing the workforce. To do that, he turned the traditional pyramid of management upside down, encouraging front-line staff to take responsibility and to use their initiative, while redirecting management into a strong supporting and motivating role. As a result, the airline returned to profitability in just one year.

This was not a once-and-for-all exercise but an on-going process of communication and motivation. This process contained many messages for staff to meet the challenges of the frequent business traveller and, at the same time, also told the world who would get preferential treatment. Customers knew what to expect, and their expectations were met.

How do we recognize quality service?

When people think of service they think of specific things – punctuality, function, affordability, the right characteristics of size, weight, colour, and so on. Quality service and quality product are closely associated with all of these.

The motive for a customer to commit to a particular product or service comes from customer expectations which are more to do with feelings – a sense of personal service. These feelings are created by the person dealing with the customer. They concern ethics, commitment, trust, values, beliefs and emotions, none of which show up in a balance sheet.

Personal service deals with people's feelings and expectations which are often perceived as the relative difference in quality between one product and another. Particularly in a highly competitive environment, two products may be physically identical, but the customer will buy from the person whom they feel is offering more. The difference for the customer is in the individual with whom he or she is dealing and whether or not *they care*. That is personal service.

Personal quality service has much to do with caring. So much so that the word 'CARE' should stand for 'Customers Are Really Everything'.

Caring means going out of your way, being prepared to give of yourself. When people learn to do that they will realize that that, in itself, produces a lot of positive response from a customer. That is also when they find that their own jobs become more tolerable.

'The way your employees feel is the way your customers are going to feel' (Karl Albrecht)[1]

The whole method of personalizing a customer service strategy is to make the service job more tolerable for the service employee by making it more rewarding. This is not in a 'take-home pay' sense, but by making them feel less tired and more energetic after a demanding work session. If they feel that they have achieved something, they feel good. Then they have a good evening. After five good days they have a terrific weekend. When they enjoy their weekends they feel good about Monday mornings. Gradually, they start to feel good about what they are doing and to gain a greater sense of commitment. They also feel that they are an important part of the organization and its strategy. When they know they will be missed if they fail to turn up, that is when people feel really needed.

By personalizing the work you are also humanizing the service strategy. Whatever your strategy, it ultimately boils down to what Jan Carlzon calls 'the moment of truth'[2] – the contact between a service giver and a service receiver, either face-to-face or voice-to-voice, which requires 100 per cent concentration and attention by the service giver to the moods and feelings of the customer. That is extremely difficult to do unless the server feels good about him or herself.

The changing role of management or, 'What you stroke, you get' (Eric Berne)[3]

The biggest challenge for management today is to personalize all company strategies (not least customer service strategies) so that employees associate themselves with those strategies on a personal level and feel real empathy with them. When they fully understand the customer service strategy they will act out what they know – even with extremely demanding customers. Service is produced on the spot, and both giver and receiver are part of the process. Personal service is the ability to create rapport. It is not a product that can be kept in a warehouse or on a shelf to be tasted and sampled.

It is relatively easy to formulate a customer service strategy that will appeal to the well-educated and/or experienced senior manager, but the challenge is to obtain commitment from the front-line people making day-to-day customer contact.

Neither does doing the job well always generate positive feedback. It is a well known fact that customer service satisfaction is mute satisfaction. No two customers are the same. Front-line people must use their full potential and ability to make tangible the customer service strategy, and that means spelling out the benefits which are appropriate for each individual customer. To do it well is extremely demanding work.

There is no such thing as an average day. People do unusual things every day as colleagues go off sick, have accidents or have to look after their children. There is always something that calls for that little extra effort in providing quality service. Management needs to be aware of these positive actions and provide positive 'strokes' in reward. A word of thanks or praise for a job well done is worth more than a bonus to most of us.

Helping front-line employees give quality service calls for management commitment at all levels. Management has to visibly support the service strategy by acting out the key elements of how to add value to the customer. It must be seen to do things and to be caring for people in the front line. Management must be accessible.

The most visible way to achieve this is through 'walkabout' management – not to inspect what people are doing but to support, positively and genuinely, the organization's employees. This often involves a fundamental change in management attitudes, since it means looking at employees as volunteers, not as conscripts or, as in the Australian tradition, convicts.

There is a worldwide trend that managers must follow. Every individual must be made to feel that he or she is needed. Indeed, it is much deeper than a trend. It goes to the heart of the problem. People need to feel that they have real jobs in terms of results, not just activities. In order for that to happen they need to know what they should expect to achieve.

Today, job descriptions which set out what people are expected to do are being superseded by job effectiveness descriptions – what people are authorized to achieve. A customer service-based organization requires a management style based on giving information, education and support rather than defining restrictions and limitations with elaborate rules and policies.

People in the front line need to be treated as individuals in order to be able to treat customers as individuals.

'Knowledge itself is power' (Francis Bacon)[4]

'A person without information cannot take responsibility', says Jan Carlzon. 'A person with information cannot avoid taking responsibility'.[5]

Personalizing the customer service strategy is heavily based on continuing, in-depth education of the workforce so that they will act responsibly under pressure to meet the customer's demands, and also under extreme time pressure. To use the airline industry again as an example, it is often said that the moments of truth for the company are the contacts between customer and employee which have an average duration of 15–20 seconds. You can blow your entire customer service strategy in just that amount of time.

On the other hand, if your front-line people have been properly educated they will be 100 per cent alert to these moments. Then the moment of truth can guarantee that the customer will come back to your company for that service again and may bring a friend or two.

It is worth remembering that statistics show it costs five times as much to get a new customer than to retain an existing one – and that really has been proved many times over.

In conclusion, I believe that no service strategy will work unless it is personalized. Ultimately, it must be based on the commitment of the people who carry it out. If they don't feel good about it, they won't carry it out effectively.

It is a basic fact about education that you cannot learn anything that you don't know something about already. A lot of people talk about customer service – and it is self-evident that customer service is the secret of long-term viability of any organization – and yet how many of us have ever experienced really good customer service?

An entirely new approach is therefore required to make 'people education' an integral part of the development and implementation of any customer service strategy. This will require management that is genuinely interested in people, management that is motivated by the challenge of showing people what the service strategy means to them. Most managers are good at telling people management by know-how but customer service strategies require 'leadership by show-how'. The old, traditional military maxim that the officers go to bed last, get up first and eat after the troops have been fed is very apposite.

Motivating management and staff at all levels is the key to

personalizing the customer service strategy. Companies that have understood this have adopted the technique popularly known as 'wall-to-wall' training where all employees attend the same programme in large groups. The success of this method is based on the ability of the instructors to bring out people's own feelings about what they do and to make these inner feelings explicit. This training is often set up as an annual event and should always be part of an on-going process of quality service education.

True customer service also requires that managers at all levels know the business and know the right thing to do because they deal daily with actual customer data and not fiction.

It we look at most managers' in-trays, they are 89 per cent filled with internal memos and reports, 10 per cent external matters and, if we are lucky, 1 per cent reports of customer satisfaction surveys. The secret of a successful customer service strategy is to reverse that ratio.

References

1   Albrecht, Karl, *At America's Service*, Homewood, Illinois, Dow Jones-Irwin, 1988
2   Carlzon, Jan, *Moments of Truth*, Sydney, Harper and Row, 1987
3   Berne, Eric, (*Transactional Analysis*), Games People Play, Sydney, Signet books, 1978, London, Penguin, 1970
4   Bacon, Francis, 'Knowledge is Power', Ante 1620, (English proverb based on Francis Bacon.)
5   Carlzon, Jan, *Moments of Truth*, Sydney, Harper and Row, 1987

Further Reading

Albrecht, K.; Zemke, R., *Service America*, Homewood, Illinois, Dow Jones-Irwin, 1989
Ansett, B.; McManamy J.; Ker, J., *The Customer*
Barry, L. L.; Barnett D. R.; Brown C. W., *Service Quality*, Homewood, Illinois, Dow Jones-Irwin
Blanchard, K.; Peale, N. V., *The Power of Ethical Management* New York, William Morrow and Co. Inc., 1988
Heskett, J. L., *Managing in the Service Economy*, Boston, Harvard Business School Press, 1986

Normann, R., *Service Management*, Chichester, John Wiley and Sons, 1984

Pumpin, C., *Essence of Corporate Strategy*, Aldershot, Gower, 1987

Peters, T., *Thriving on Chaos*, London, Alfred A. Knopf, 1988

Part III
CHANNELS OF DISTRIBUTION

Overview to Part III

The scene is set for Part III with the proposition, in Chapter 7, that developing a channels strategy is probably the most strategically significant issue facing many organizations today. Having defined distribution channels, Gattorna then outlines the activities performed by a distribution channel as well as the determinants of channel structure and the role of intermediaries. In discussing the concept of power in channel relationships, it is suggested that long-held assumptions about control of distribution channels are today less valid, and that conflict between channel members is always at the expense of the most important channel member, the customer. An alternative approach based on interdependence rather than conflict is described, and this concept of channel partnerships is developed more fully in Chapter 8.

In Chapter 8 Dowling and Robinson provide a comprehensive overview of Strategic Partnership Marketing, a technique which emphasizes cooperation as the basis for developing joint competitive advantage for members in a common distribution channel. Strategic partnerships are contrasted with traditional channel strategies, and the authors graphically describe the varying types of mutual coope-ration that can exist between members of a distribution channel. Having outlined the basic ingredients necessary for a successful partnership, Dowling and Robinson introduce a six-step approach for initiating such an arrangement. Whilst extolling the benefits of this approach, the authors conclude by describing some of the reasons preventing wide-scale adoption of the technique in the short to medium term.

7 Developing a Channels Strategy

John Gattorna

Introduction

Developing a channels strategy is probably the most strategically significant issue facing many organizations today. Progressive organizations including airlines, banks and insurance companies are realizing the vital role channels strategy plays in profitably servicing diverse market segments.

Channels have traditionally been defined as 'flows of economic goods and services' with emphasis always on the economics of the flow. For too long organizations were overly concerned with minimizing cost and maximizing efficiency. Important factors such as creating long-term, integrated strategic plans and fostering productive channel relationships, were largely ignored. Channels were often viewed as closed systems, operating as separate static entities. The focus was on behaviour within the organization rather than on behaviour between organizations. As a result, channel relationships were often marked by power struggles and conflict.

Today, organizations operate in an environment characterized by increased product complexity, rapid technological change, and increasing economic, social and political pressures. Strategically-oriented organizations are realising that a key to sustainable long-term profitability is increased interdependence. These proactive organizations understand that this can only be achieved by building and fostering productive and mutually beneficial channel relationships.

Channels are essentially the non-physical commercial arrangements between organizations designed to facilitate the physical flow of goods or the performance of services. The commercial arrangements for facilitating the flow of raw materials and components to production in a manufacturing environment (channels of supply), may differ from those concerned with distribution of finished goods (channels of distribution). This chapter examines the essential elements of channels of distribution.

Distribution channels

The term 'distribution channels' describes the commercial arrangements established to enable a product to flow from the point of production to the point of ultimate consumption. It is important to note that the physical product and its title (that is, the rights of ownership) may not necessarily follow the same route.

The question of whether an organization should itself undertake all of the many activities involved in the distribution function is of extreme importance. Organizations have the option of subcontracting all or part of their distribution activities. Whilst this decision can be likened to a 'make or buy' decision, where all the relevant costs and benefits must be considered, it also has strategic significance. Figure 7.1 depicts the various alternatives (reflecting market segmentation) that are available.

The activities performed by a distribution channel fall into three categories:

1 activities concerned with changes in ownership – that is, negotiation, buying and selling; the trading channel;
2 activities concerned with the physical supply of the product – including transportation and storage; the physical distribution network;
3 activities that are auxilliary to or facilitate either of the above; such as collecting and disseminating information, risk-taking, financing and promotional activity.

Frequently, distribution channels consist of chains of institutions. With the exception of the original supplier and end-user, these institutions are intermediaries. Each intermediary undertakes a number of activities which either directly move a product and/or its title closer to the end-users, or facilitates such a move. Intermediaries involved with trading, such as wholesalers, tend to be renumerated by way of margins whereas non-trading intermediaries, such as distribution service companies, tend to receive a straight payment for services rendered. Figure 7.2 depicts the intermediaries in the distribution channel of a typical international airline operator.

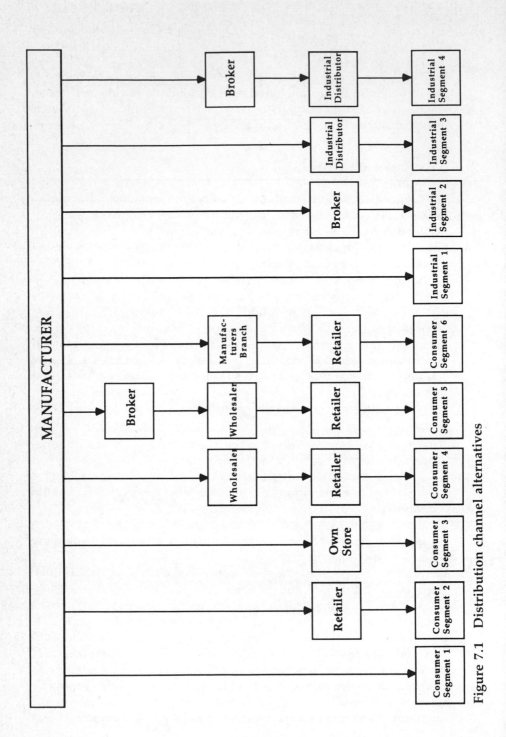

Figure 7.1 Distribution channel alternatives

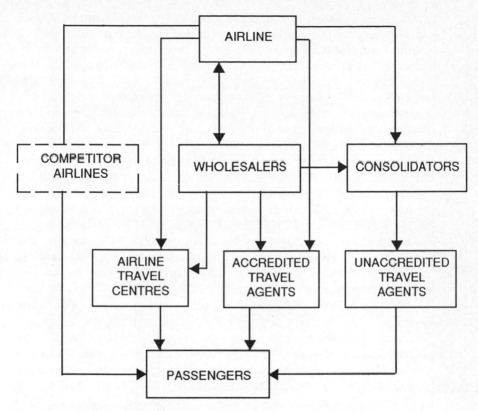

Figure 7.2   An airline distribution channel

Distribution channel structure

There are three main determinants of channel structure:

- the requirements of the final customer, which when aggregated give a grouping of customers with similar requirements – a segment;
- the capabilities of the originating organization;
- the availability and willingness of appropriate intermediaries (if needed) to participate in the channel.

The trading channel is very much a variable in the marketing mix, although it is not often seen as such. It is therefore vital that marketing management takes the lead in channel design and management. The image of the product, the pricing and promotional effort, as well as the physical presentation of the product itself, can all be reinforced or, alternatively, jeopardized by the particular trading channel used. An image of exclusivity would not, for example, be enhanced by selling through a supermarket chain. Disregard for this vital area of marketing means that many opportunities for the profitable development of market potential are passed over.

Channel structures are not static or universal; they can and do change and evolve over time and vary from market to market. Distribution channels serving rural markets, for example, tend to have more intermediaries than channels serving urban markets, since the lower volume demanded in rural areas generally makes direct delivery to retailers less attractive. Other 'rules of thumb' for channel structure are that the lower the gross margin of the product and the higher the frequency with which it is purchased by consumers, the more intermediaries there will be in the channel. Conversely, the longer the time an end-user is willing to spend looking for a product and the lower the frequency with which it is purchased, the shorter the distribution channel.

One area where changes in channel structure have been quite dramatic is in the food and grocery industry. Until the late 1960s distribution of food, drink and tobacco products was largely the responsibility of the supplier. Next we saw groupings of independent retailers serviced by wholesalers. As these groups grew it became economical for wholesalers to effect final delivery, and local depots were opened. Further growth through expansion and acquisition brought ever more distant retailers into the group, increasing transportation costs and creating shortages of warehousing space.

Manufacturers have often tended to establish depots on the assumption that food outlets and population density will follow the same pattern. Changes in the way that retail chains have organized their supply systems have presented problems for the manufacturers, making the subcontracting of all or part of the distribution requirements for an organization an appropriate alternative.

Intermediaries

We suggested earlier that the decision to utilize intermediaries to perform all or part of the organization's distribution activities required careful evaluation of the costs and benefits involved. Figure 7.3 depicts this process.

BENEFITS OFFERED BY INTERMEDIARIES

Lower Selling Costs – More Outlets –
Stock Holding – Lower Costs – Better
Coverage – 'Product Range' Extension –
Customer Appeal – Market Development –
Increased Sales Information –
Improved Market Knowledge –
Customer Finance – Increased Sales

MARGIN
TRADE–OFF

COSTS OF USING INTERMEDIARIES

Loss of Control – Could Reduce Sales –
Loss of 'Central Focus For Product' –
Information could be: Limited, Biased –
Customer Service at Risk

Figure 7.3 Benefits and costs offered by intermediaries

The main reported advantages of using a distribution service company as an intermediary would appear to be:

- ability to meet stringent customer service requirements at reasonable cost;
- reduction in the amount of capital employed in distribution;
- flexibility of capacity;
- increased geographical coverage;
- lower operating costs, both overall and in peripheral areas;
- spreading of the industrial relations risk;
- availability of specialist services;
- ability to redeploy management resources;
- reduction of overall risk.

On the other hand there can sometimes be a number of disadvantages to set against these benefits. Some of these disadvantages are:

* loss of direct control;
* inadequate feedback;
* reduced stock rotation/product control;
* increased costs of stock-holding due to higher stock levels;
* lack of priority consideration;
* problems of establishing accountability, such as for stock losses;
* inability to respond to special demands;
* higher direct costs;
* higher costs due to damage and stock losses;
* communication problems with customers.

Whilst the above list can represent distinct disadvantages, most can be overcome with strong and effective management. Reporting and monitoring systems, combined with an attitude of partnership as described later in this chapter, provide the means.

Distribution channel control

The concept of power in channel relationships has been defined as 'the ability of a channel member to control the decision variables in the marketing strategy of any members in a given channel at a different level of distribution'. In most channels, one member will emerge as the leader. Traditionally it was assumed that the manufacturer, as the most powerful member, was always the channel leader. Currently however, this assumption appears less valid. The power wielded by retailers in the food and grocery industry is a classic example. As more and more merchandise is distributed through fewer and fewer outlets, the balance of power has shifted from the manufacturer to the distributor. Many manufacturers now have little choice but to accede to the demands of the major retail chains. This trend alone, which has continued worldwide for the last decade, dictates the need for cooperation and an end to the 'independent organization' model. Figure 7.4 depicts the differing objectives that might apply in a typical manufacturer – distributor channel relationship.

Distribution channel conflict

Conflict in channel behaviour is most often a result of goal differences. Manufacturers want to make marketable products – products

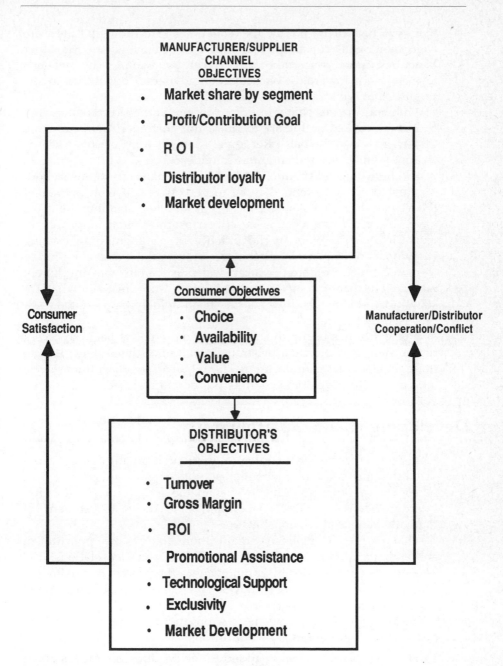

Figure 7.4   The distribution channel

that will be purchased by the consumer. Accordingly, they are concerned with 'consumptive behaviour'. Retailers, on the other hand, are more concerned with 'buyer behaviour'. The retailer's loyalty is not towards a particular brand name, but rather to the product that will draw the customer through their doors.

What both parties share, but often forget, is their common goal of customer service. Both exist to serve the customer; both need the customer to 'pay the bills'. Recognizing this is a major step towards creating joint plans and common activities.

Another source of channel conflict is discrepancy in sophistication. Manufacturers have tended to be more conversant with marketing theory and the value of such concepts as strategic planning. Retailers have suffered from what is described as the '35mm approach to marketing'. This refers to the practice of photographing exciting showrooms or displays in other stores around the world, then trying to mimic several different concepts at once, often with indifferent results. The benefits of strategic planning and creating 'what we stand for' statements has neither been widely appreciated, nor practised by the trade.

This stance has begun to change as some retailers begin to accept the burden, and benefits, of strategic planning themselves. It is to these retailers that manufacturers should begin to attach themselves, with a view to developing channel partnerships.

Developing channel partnerships

Earlier we suggested that strategically-oriented organizations, recognized that increased interdependence, not coercion and conflict, was necessary in order to achieve sustainable long-term profitability. Interdependence implies cooperation and the establishment of mutually beneficial relationships.

What are the incentives for organizations to foresake opportunism and embark upon a cooperative approach to channel relationships? The incentive is provided by adding value – the process of making the product more valuable as it moves down the distribution channel from supplier to consumer.

The concept of adding value to a product as it moves down the distribution channel raises two questions:

1   How much value is being added to the product as it moves down the channel from supplier to consumer?

2   How much does it cost the supplier to have such value added (at each level)?

Transport provides a good example of an answer to the first question. We used to think of transport as a commodity; the best form of transport was one which got the goods to the customer at the lowest cost. Now, industry is beginning to change its view and see transport as a service with a value which changes according to customer and circumstances. That is one explanation for the rapid increase in express freight, when the customer is prepared to pay a premium for fast and dependable service. Public transport is changing for the same reason, with frequency and quality of service adding value for the end-user.

The concept of 'partnership marketing', discussed in detail in Chapter 8, is about improving relationships within the distribution channel. This occurs through *marketing* activities taking place between suppliers and retailers, or between manufacturers and retailers to achieve mutual profit.

A strategy to implement the philosophy of partnership marketing will consist of the following actions:

1   Determine the effectiveness of distribution by conducting regular audits.
2   Review existing channel arrangements.
3   Consider possible changes in channel arrangements.
4   Implement trade marketing practice with selected channel members.

Completing the first two actions will provide answers to the question we posed earlier about how much it costs the supplier to have value added as the product moves through the channel.

Understanding the perspective of other members of the channel is essential if a spirit of mutuality, rather than polarity, is to be established. By combining forces in this way, all channel members can work effectively with a common aim – winning the customers' business. Figure 7.5 depicts this process.

The benefits of partnership

Effective partnerships in the channel create working relationships which emphasize interdependence, rather than dominance and power. The opportunity exists to build joint marketing plans and explore new territory in terms of:

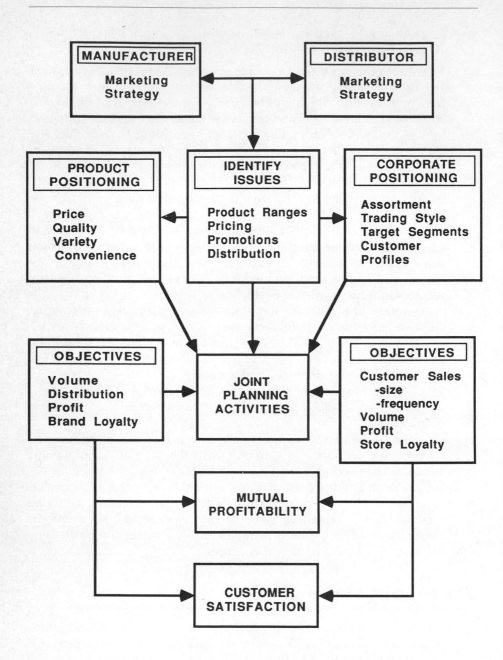

Figure 7.5   Supplier/distributor joint planning activities

- product range mixes;
- ordering procedures;
- delivery schedules;
- enhanced communications (EDI);
- trading terms and credit arrangements;
- packing and handling;
- special packs and pack sizes;
- selling aids and point-of-sale material;
- just-in-time logistics;
- credits, returns, breakages and empties;
- joint product development;
- joint promotion;
- trade-off opportunities.

Partners have common objectives and strategies for achieving them. They also have a common defence against any intrusion into the partnership. They are *allies not adversaries*. This is the way forward for progressive organizations in the 1990s as they seek platforms for long-term prosperity rather than short-term gain which is quickly dissipated.

8 Strategic Partnership Marketing

Grahame R. Dowling and Chris Robinson

Introduction

A scan of the recent academic literature on strategic marketing shows regular attention given to competitive aspects of marketing. Terms such as 'strategic advantage', 'marketing warfare', 'competitive advantage', 'market share', 'power and conflict', 'advertising share of voice', 'price-cutting', 'negotiation', and so on, all imply or reflect competition in the marketplace. The discipline of economics has developed sophisticated theories about competition, and some of the basic principles inherent in these theories have been enshrined in business law. In recent years marketers have turned to the disciplines of game theory and biology to gain further insights into competitive behaviour.

Competition, however, is only one aspect of strategic marketing. By itself it provides an unbalanced view of marketplace behaviour. When one looks closely at many marketing phenomena it is possible to isolate aspects of both competition and cooperation. In an area such as distribution channel management where organizations are dependent on each other for their mutual well-being, cooperation seems to be a more appropriate model of behaviour.

In many scientific disciplines the concept of symbiosis plays an important role. A dictionary definition of symbiosis is the permanent union between organisms each of which depends on the other (*Concise Oxford Dictionary*). The emphasis here is on cooperation and partnership, not competition and conflict. In this chapter we describe a technique called 'strategic partnership marketing' which relies on cooperation as the basis for developing a joint competitive advantage for members of a distribution channel. This approach stresses the development of trust, the sharing of information and the common interest between channel members. These factors are critical in the renewal process for many organizations as they respond to increased competition in the marketplace (Waterman, 1987). Partnership marketing also represents one way to operationalize Porter's (1985) now-famous concepts of value systems, value chain and channel value. As Porter notes 'gaining and sustaining competitive advantage depends on understanding not only a firm's value chain but how the firm fits in the overall value system' (Waterman, 1987: 34)

In the next section a brief review of some of the alternative models used to describe the structure and function of distribution channels is presented. Following this is an outline of strategic partnering and a set of guidelines for operationalizing the technique.

Distribution models

Traditionally, distribution channels have been viewed as closed systems (see Chapter 7) but they can, however, be viewed as open systems where there is shared responsibility for making products and services available to customers, understanding the characteristics of the market, and providing an appropriate level of service.

Distribution involves three main decision areas (McDonald and Gattorna, 1984):

1 how the physical movements of products and services are organized;
2 the choice of channel; and
3 the level of availability of the product/service.

The first decision involves delivering products and services to customers in the most profitable way(s) subject to constraints imposed by geographic factors, transport systems, competitors, and so on. (This is similar to a typical optimization problem and is often modelled using operations research techniques.) From the customer's point of view this value-adding function amounts to the creation of time and access utility for products and/or services. The second and third decisions are more strategic in nature and their impact is reflected in the management of the organization's marketing mix.

Given the diversity of markets and customer needs, it is not surprising that a variety of generic forms of distribution channel have evolved (and are evolving) over time. Lilien and Kotler (1983: 433–4) describe four such typical channel structures:[1]

1   the traditional standard channel (for example, manufacturer – wholesaler – retailer),
2   corporate channels, characterized by successive stages of production and distribution under single ownership;
3   administered channels, where successive stages of production and distribution are coordinated by the (economic) power of one of the parties; and
4   contractual channels, where a group of independent channel members contract to integrate their marketing programmes to achieve more economies and/or market impact (for example, franchising).

The use of (a variant of) one or more of these forms of distribution systems often depends on the marketing strategy of the manufacturer.[2] The historical marketing options have been to either 'push' or 'pull' the product through the distribution channel.[3] With a push strategy the emphasis is on ensuring that channel members perform all the necessary wholesale and retail functions. Coordination of these functions can be achieved in a variety of ways and requires the management of cooperation (for survival) and conflict (due to different economic goals) among channel members. With a pull strategy, the emphasis is on generating customer demand (via, say, branding, advertising and promotions, and so on).[4] Here, cooperation is still necessary and conflict is still likely to be present but, because channel members are 'buying from each other' as opposed to 'selling to each other' (with a push strategy), the characteristics of the cooperation and conflict are likely to differ.

   Distribution systems are dynamic. Bucklin and Schmalensee (1987) outline some of the principal reasons for this evolution. For example, at the retailer level, three main changes have occurred:

a)   increased concentration;
b)   increased managerial sophistication (for example, strong logistics and warehousing capabilities, development of own brands, traffic-building activities, collection of sales and scanner data, direct product profitability analysis, and so on);
c)   better market segmentation and targeting (for example, by tailoring merchandise selection, price and service levels to more homogeneous groups).

Changes are also evident for manufacturers. For instance, more products are in the later stages of their product life cycles, product proliferation has increased, and brand franchises have weakened. This means that manufacturers have to work harder to gain retail coverage and market share.[5] Product line extensions and increased budgets for advertising and promotion are common strategies here. The product line extension strategy however has been criticized as being strategically unsound by Ries and Trout (1981).

The translation of operations research techniques into user-friendly computer software for small computers has provided the opportunity for a more sophisticated analysis of the wholesale and warehousing functions. Quantitative models have now been developed to provide answers to questions concerning the optimization of resources configured as a network (see Chapter 9). As a firm changes its marketing strategy, and/or as parts of the distribution network change in significant ways, it is possible to estimate the impact of these changes on the overall function (cost, profit and product–market fit) of the channel. This is a major advance and is providing the impetus for managers to re-evaluate the role of alternative configurations of physical distribution resources.

Probably the most important impetus for change in distribution channels stems from changes in consumer behaviour. Bucklin and Schmalensee (1987) cite demographic shifts (such as the increase in two-income households for example) and changes in consumer expectations (such as low prices and more variety) as two primary factors. These changes, coupled with a better appreciation of all aspects of marketing by retailers, has seen them move towards becoming 'a buying agent for the consumer' as opposed to a 'selling agent for the manufacturer' (Davidson, 1987). As a consequence of this, customers are becoming more loyal to stores and less loyal to particular brands. This trend can be seen as a modification of the traditional pull strategy.

In a recent conference on the changing consumer goods distribution scene a number of themes were raised which are of critical importance to distribution managers (Bucklin and Schmalensee, 1987):

1 cooperation among channel members (as opposed to the management of conflict);
2 the necessity for manufacturers to develop new and improved products to reclaim brand loyalty;

3　the necessity for manufacturers to segment product, price and service offerings to retailers;
4　the necesssity for manufacturers and retailers to master information technologies;
5　the necessity for manufacturers to improve their delivery systems;
6　the need for manufacturers to help retailers cope with labour shortages and rising wage costs.

These six issues are equally applicable for consumer goods, industrial goods, and not-for-profit channels. The overriding theme linking each issue is cooperation. This can be implemented in a variety of ways from computer-to-computer information exchange to simply trying harder to understand each other party's needs. The technique of partnership marketing outlined in the next section uses the theme of cooperation to show how channels can become more effective marketing assets.

Partnership marketing

Partnership marketing can be thought of as a positive sum (or win-win) two-person game. That is, the aim of the procedures outlined in this section is to enhance the benefits accruing to both parties in a loose coalition. These coalitions involve coordinating or sharing value chains with partners to broaden the effective scope of each individual firm's value chain (Porter, 1985).[6] Figure 8.1 adapts Porter's approach to illustrate this concept for a simple manufacturer–wholesaler–retailer channel. Movement along the horizontal axis represents each channel member's value chain and product, information and service flows. The vertical size of each channel member is used to indicate the relative amount of value that each firm adds to the final value of the buyer. The heavy arrows are used to illustrate primary interchannel linkages, while the dashed arrows signify less important areas for mutual cooperation.

Figure 8.1 is a useful way to sketch the broad areas where strategic partnerships could be developed or strengthened. In this case, it shows some of the activities for a traditional channel where the manufacturer is using a marketing strategy to pull products through the channel. This is represented by the heavy arrow from the manufacturer's marketing activity to the final customer. For example, advertising is used to create a brand image (primary demand) and

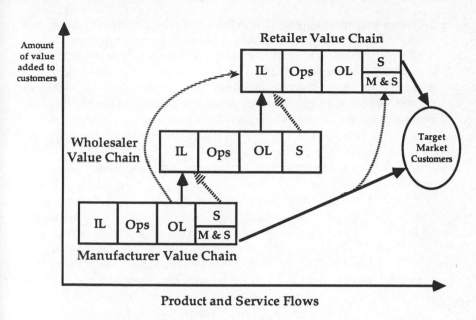

Product and Service Flows

(IL - inbound logistics; Ops = operations; OL - outbound logistics; M - marketing; S-sales
→ primary ; ····|||··· secondary)

Figure 8.1   Representative opportunities for partnership arrangements

some of this has a second-order effect on the retailer (because if they feature the brand they receive some influence from the brand's image on their store image). The manufacturer ships stock to the wholesaler (heavy arrow from OL-manufacturer to IL-wholesaler) and packages it in a way that facilitates its easy storage and use by the retailer (dashed arrow from OL-manufacturer to IL-retailer). The wholesaler supplies the retailer (heavy arrow) and does this on a just-in-time basis (dashed arrow). The retailer provides a custom fitting service to final customers (heavy arrow).

Maps of value-adding activities and their interlinkages are a useful starting-point for any consideration or review of partnership marketing. It is important to all members of the channel to understand the relative contribution each makes to the utility derived from the product or service by the customer. Maps such as Figure 8.1 provide an efficient medium for communicating to individual channel members the role of the distribution channel in the delivery of service to final customers. Also, they can be extended by adding the value provided by marketing service agents (such as an advertising agent) to show how a complete marketing strategy is implemented.

The responsiveness of the primary and secondary flows identified in Figure 8.1 to more expenditure can be also quantified. Traditional input–output cost studies are only one alternative. A different perspective is gained if one uses market research to identify the core benefit that the product delivers to customers and then works backwards through the channel to identify how this benefit can be 'best' delivered. For example, service is an important aspect of the core benefit of many products and it can be accumulated in various ways as a product travels through a channel. The service can be provided by manufacturer's salespeople, wholesalers and/or retailers, and a familiar problem which faces many distribution managers relates to determining the optimum level of service and how it should be delivered. The usual trade-off is to increase service levels directly or to increase margins and/or incentives and expect (hope) that this stimulates better service by downstream channel members. However, knowing customers' expected service requirements enables managers to evaluate the critical interlinkages between channel members' value-adding activities and ensure that upstream firms provide the type and level of service that downstream firms need. In this way each channel member's activities are coordinated to deliver value to the final customer.

What has been described so far in this section is the integration of separate firms' corporate/marketing strategies. Such an approach assumes that each partner understands the other's marketing activities and their strategic orientation. (Our proprietary research shows, however, that this is often not the case.) The approach also implies that one channel member needs to take the initiative to develop partnerships where it is evident that a joint competitive advantage can be secured. The organization which usually assumes this leadership role is the one with the highest level of marketing expertise and/or power in the channel. How this leadership role is executed, however, can have a profound impact on the success of the joint venture. For example, research has shown that the amount of conflict arising from both administrative and product-service issues diminishes if the leader uses a style which emphasizes participation, support and discretion in carrying out these activities (Schul, Pride and Little, 1983).

In Figure 8.2 (a–d) we outline four basic types of mutual cooperation between a supplier and a retailer.[7] Each variation of Figure 8.2

starts by assuming that channel members have a certain level of knowledge about the marketing functions to be performed. The overall level of this understanding and its distribution between the two channel members (in this case) will influence how the leadership role evolves and how the channel will play a part in the overall marketing strategy. (This is summarized in the first enclosed box and the last part of each figure respectively.) Based on this understanding, one or both of the parties will play a leading role in choosing how the market is segmented and which target market(s) are chosen. At this point in each figure we postulate that there will be a latent need for the channel members to cooperate. (This statement is surrounded by a dashed line.) In the following box we indicate how better quality (and sometimes more) cooperation could be achieved. The final section of each figure shows some of the outputs of such cooperation. It is the bottom portions of the figures which illustrate the likelihood of a partnership marketing approach being adopted.

Figure 8.2d reflects a situation which is far removed from a strategic partnership. In our experience many medium and small businesses seem to function in this way. Marketing acumen seems to be little more than applied common sense in these situations. There is a basic need to upgrade marketing skills and to develop cooperative links with other channel members in order to survive and grow. Management consultants have typically been active in this area by providing in-house training and strategic advice. The short-term output is often a more formalized approach to marketing while in the longer term a Type 2 or a Type 3 (Figures 8.2b and 8.2c) situation may arise.

Figures 8.2b and 8.2c reflect situations where there is an asymetric distribution of marketing expertise in the channel. The channel member with the best understanding typically guides the development of an 'overall' marketing strategy based on its perception of customer needs and how these can be most profitably satisfied. This is often implemented by establishing short-term cooperation among the parties and/or by coercive practices. In either case, a set of exclusive arrangements are formed which shape the overall functioning of the channel. Our observation (at least in Australia) indicates that this is a common mode of channel organization. The situations outlined in Figures 8.2b and 8.2c are one step removed from what we consider here as partnership marketing.

Figure 8.2a embodies the essence of strategic partnership marketing. Here there is a highly developed understanding of market behaviour, marketing strategy and tactics, and the role and needs of

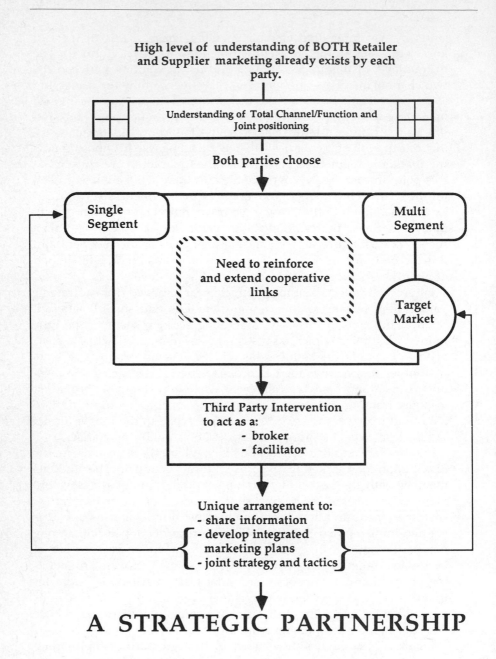

Figure 8.2a   Types of cooperation: Type 1 – mutually-driven

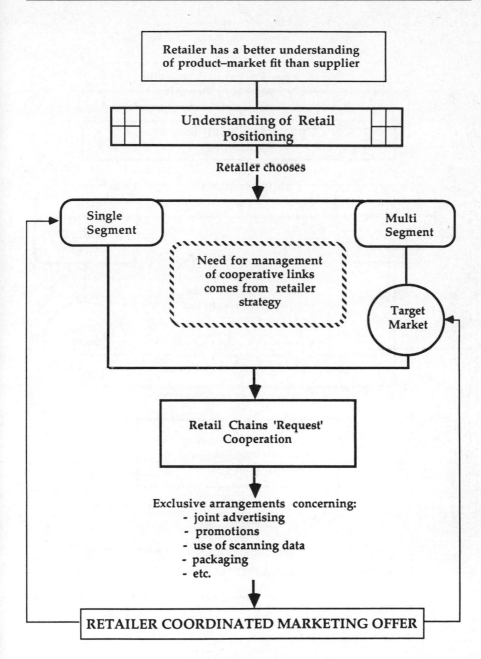

Figure 8.2b   Types of cooperation: Type 2 – retailer-driven

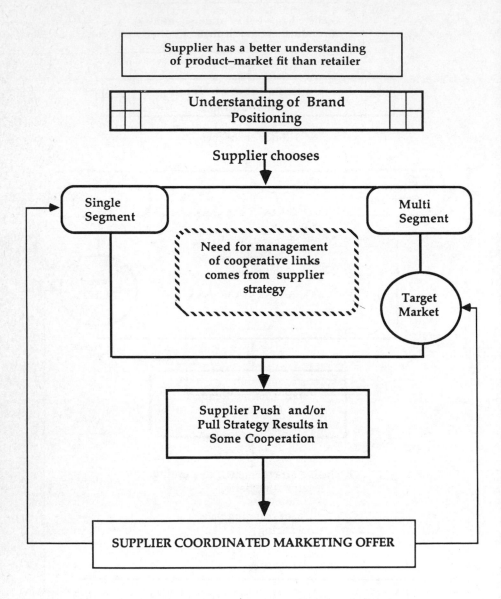

Figure 8.2c   Types of cooperation: Type 3 – supplier-driven

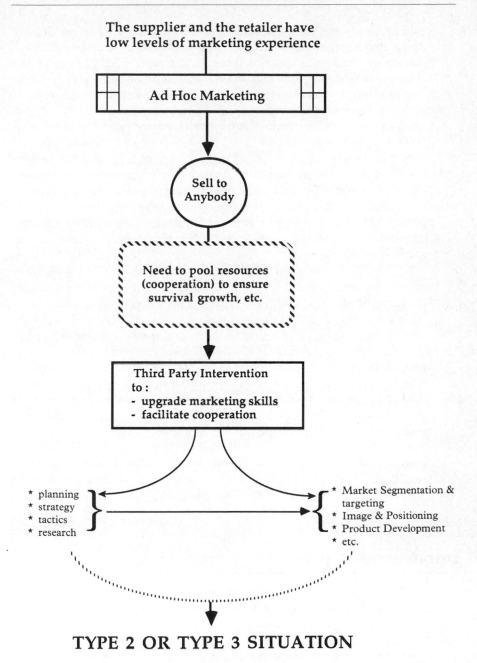

TYPE 2 OR TYPE 3 SITUATION

Figure 8.2d   Types of cooperation: Type 4 – not driven

each channel member. The outgrowth of this is the joint positioning of the channel members' products and services in the minds of target customers. That is, there is a good fit between what is offered (for example product design, and so on), where it is offered (type, image and location of the retailer, and so on), and how it is offered (type of advertising, levels of service, and so on) to customers. The latent need in this type of channel is for the reinforcement of cooperative linkages. (This is in contrast to the needs in Figure 8.2d which are for the development of cooperation and in Figures 8.2b and 8.2c where the need is for the management of linkages.) Our experience shows that this can often be achieved by using a third party to act as a broker or facilitator to help maintain enthusiasm for the cooperative arrangements. Occasionally these people will also be called on to arbitrate disputes between the parties and help to implement changes to existing relationships.

Figure 8.2 indicates that the desired outcome of a partnership marketing arrangement is the development of integrated marketing plans, joint strategy and joint tactics. This should allow more cost-effective service to customers because there is increased scope to allocate the various marketing tasks to the lowest-cost producer (all other things being equal). It is also a logical progression in competitive markets because it helps to transform 'the channel' from a collection of interdependent entities into a unified system where the output (measured by profit and customer satisfaction) adds to more than the sum of the individual parts – a truly competitive marketing asset. However, such cooperative arrangements will involve sharing considerable amounts of confidential information and trusting the integrity of other firms (something which many organizations are reluctant to do and another area where an independent third party can play a facilitating role). The potential gains from sustained cooperation are significant.

Implementing partnership marketing

The development of strategic partnerships is based on establishing *unique*, although not *exclusive*, relationships.[8] For example, suppose that a manufacturer of a range of branded merchandise wanted to maximize the flow-on effects of different retailers' images on the positioning of the brands. Instead of trying to influence each retailer to sell more of the 'standard product range', the manufacturer could work with retail chains to develop unique assortments of products which would better fit the image of both the brand and the retail outlet. Other areas of cooperation could also be explored, for example:

- ordering procedures,
- trading terms and credit arrangements,
- special packs and pack sizes,
- packaging for bulk handling and storage,
- selling aids and point of sale,
- just-in-time logistics,
- joint product development initiatives, and
- joint advertising and promotions.

A partnership marketing strategy is, at the very least, a uniquely beneficial logistics linkage between two (or more) major trading partners. To transcend this, however, it requires a broad understanding of marketing and distribution, the sharing of information between parties and the development of personal rapport between managers at a number of levels in both organizations. These are the basic ingredients necessary for success. Using the following six-step approach they can be mixed into a partnership arrangement:[9]

1 *Setting the environment.* This is a workshop session with key managers in the firm wishing to lead a programme to establish partnership marketing. The aim of the workshop is to foster an appreciation of the concept and to establish realistic objectives for such a programme. External consultants may usefully be used to run such a workshop. They can add legitimacy to the concept and act as an independent 'sounding board' for internal managers to test out the robustness of the concept to their firm. Experienced consultants can also provide case histories of successful partnership ventures.

2 *Selecting partners.* This step starts by selecting 'target' business areas in which to develop strategic partnering initiatives. Managers must then develop specific partnership objectives for each target business area and the inputs required from both parties. A list of potential firms is then proposed. The strengths and weaknesses of each potential partner are evaluated and any obstacles to the development of a coordinated working arrangement highlighted. Using a set of evaluative criteria and/or the help of an external consultant, a shortlist of firms is drawn up.

3 *Making contact.* Sometimes external consultants can act as brokers

to help bring parties together in a non-threatening environment. In other cases it may be more appropriate for the initial contact to be made between CEOs. In either case it is probably better for the concept to be introduced at the top of the potential partner's organization so that it can trickle down to the levels where it will be implemented. The key here is to present the objectives of partnering and the costs and benefits to both parties in a way which stresses the 'win–win' nature of the relationship.

4   *Establishing the relationship.* A joint workshop hosted by an independent third party is a good way to begin this working relationship. Such a workshop would go over much of the ground covered in the workshop outlined in Step 1 and would then proceed to facilitate the development of the joint aspects of a potential relationship. The critical aspect of this step is to allow sufficient time for trust to grow and relationships to develop. (We have found that sometimes a series of short sessions is best.) It is also necessary to ensure that managers who attend this workshop are at equivalent levels from the respective organizations. The aim of this workshop is to get to the stage of 'agreement in principle'.

5   *Making it happen.* One of the major impediments to strategic partnering is that many managers do not trust managers from other organizations. This mistrust may stem from a variety of sources and each will need to be addressed if a joint working arrangement is to be consummated. Another major impediment is that many companies are unable to draft their own marketing plans, so that the task of developing a joint marketing plan is beyond them. Again, marketing consultants can play a vital role here by using their planning skills to help both parties develop this joint plan.

6   *Implementation.* Translating joint plans into reality is never easy. Partnerships can only be driven by mutual self-interest and a joint commitment to succeed. Scheduling regular joint planning meetings helps, and setting up formal procedures for sharing information on a day-to-day or weekly basis can speed up the process. There also needs to be regular personal contact between key managers. In short, this systematization of relationships between partners is a key success factor.

As with all marketing planning, much of the benefit of strategic partnering is to do with the process itself as well as with the final output. Going through the process forces a degree of rigour which is seldom achieved when decision making is unstructured. Constant feedback and realistic goal setting are key success factors in the implementation phase.

Figure 8.3 presents an overview of the joint planning process and the way in which these plans are translated into objectives, strategies, actions, and budgets. The first module involves the preparation of a 'vision' (or mission) statement for both parties. This is a philosophical statement of what both firms stand for and it is sometimes reflected in the corporate image advertising so prominent in business magazines. The process of formulating and comparing vision statements significantly reinforces the need for managers to understand the other party's business. It also prepares the way for identifying and understanding any potential points of conflict between the parties – even though they are serving the same customers.

Module 2 is a standard part of most planning activities. It requires both parties (in this case) to conduct a formal scan of the operating environment in which they function to serve customers. Insights are sought into broad macro-economic and social conditions which will have significant impact on the market in which the partners operate. Descriptive scenarios and long-term forecasts are the types of information which set the broad parameters within which future cooperation will take place. There are usually a number of market research firms in each country which specialize in providing this type of information in a cost-effective format.

The third and fourth stages in the planning process entail identifying and listing issues critical to individual companies and the joint partnership. A critical issue is anything which is, or will, impact on the performance of the organization now or in the future (within a specific time-frame). It may emanate from the organization's internal or external operating environment and may have a positive or negative impact on performance. The definition of these issues is critical to the success of the partnership as they guide the development of the remaining workflow in the planning cycle. Issue definition revolves around separating symptoms from causes of problems and the classification of the issues into strengths, weaknesses, opportunities and threats to the partnership.[10]

Module 5 takes as its starting-point the set of critical issues (usually only 6 to 10) identified in Modules 3 and 4. These are then rated in terms of their potential impact on the partnership's performance and the relative urgency with which they must be addressed. As can be seen from Figure 8.3, if this is done properly there should be a spread of issues throughout the prioritization matrix. (It is highly unlikely

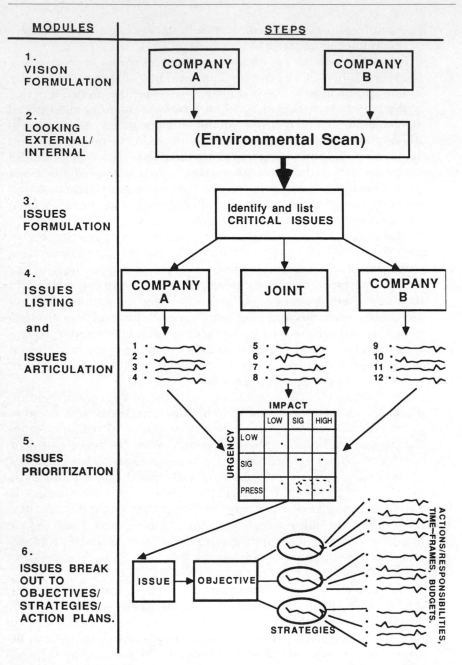

Figure 8.3   Joint planning

that every issue facing a firm will be significant and urgent.) Also, over time, we would expect issues to gravitate from the top of the matrix to the bottom right hand corner. Having rated each issue in terms of its urgency and importance, the framework is now in place to allocate the partnership's available resources to these areas.

The final module outlines a set of activities which are common to many planning frameworks. In this case, for each issue that is selected for immediate response, an objective is formulated and quantified, and strategies developed to achieve the objective. The strategies are translated into required actions, responsibilities, time-frames, budgets and so on, for their attainment. This structure ensures that both groups understand and agree on what is to be achieved and the process for implementation.

Conclusions

Our proprietary research in Australia has indicated that, while some organizations have had considerable success with this concept, it is likely to take some time for the strategic partnering idea to attain widespread adoption. Some of the reasons for this are that:

a)   the strongest emphasis in channel relationships is still placed on measurable performance (in-store display, coupon redemptions, and so on), as opposed to developing long-term cooperation;
b)   the physical movement of products and customer service are currently the only two areas where many firms are focusing their attention;
c)   retailers and wholesalers think that manufacturers' performance needs substantial improvement;
d)   retailers believe that manufacturers don't fully understand their marketing positioning;
e)   there is an asymetric demand for more understanding of other channel members' operations – for example, more retailers want manufacturers to understand their operations better than vice versa; and
f)   those organizations currently practising the concept have tended not to publicize their success.

The theory of the adoption and diffusion of innovations leads us to suspect that many of these artificial barriers will break down as some of the early adopters of this approach are seen to be successful in the marketplace. While this process is occurring, there is substantial scope for more innovative firms to embrace the partnership marketing approach and attempt to secure a joint competitive advantage in the marketplace.

As Stephen Wolf of the giant US retailer Sears Roebuck says, the aim of partnership marketing is better synchronization, dependability of supply, value and efficiency (Wolf, 1987). This will lead to a better fit between customer expectations and the types of products and services offered. It manifests itself at Sears in terms of a 'Partners in Progress' programme which recognizes suppliers for quality, cost, service, and presentation and promotion of merchandise. It also helps to focus attention on the basic question facing many companies regarding the choice of a particular form of channel relationship to develop:

1   owning sources of supply (and tying up capital);
2   purchasing opportunistically (and gaining flexibility but running the risk of jeopardizing long-term strategic planning); or
3   forming a partnership with up- and/or downstream channel members to serve customers.

Notes

1   Direct distribution is not defined here as a channel because the emphasis of this chapter is on the relationship between two or more intermediaries.
2   A particular channel may also be used because it is the only one available (eg., at the time a new product is launched), or the power of a retail chain to organize other channel members may restrict the available options.
3   Paul Farris suggests that push strategies will tend to be more effective for small to moderate levels of distribution while pull strategies are needed to move towards saturation levels of distribution (Farris in Bucklin and Schmalensee, 1987).
4   In consumer goods markets, promotion is also used as a push strategy. Sales promotions are often part of the price for buying shelf space in supermarkets.
5   Paul Farris has found that as distribution coverage increases and nears saturation, market share increases exponentially (Farris in Bucklin and Schmalensee, 1987).

6 A firm's value chain is the collection of activities that are performed to design, produce, market, deliver, and support its products or services. Each of these activities employs purchased inputs, human resources, and some form of technology to perform its function. Each activity also uses and creates information. Value activities are the building blocks of competitive advantage. How they are performed combined with their economics determines the cost position of a firm. This performance also determines the contribution to buyer needs.

7 While there could be many other forms, these are sufficient for illustrative purposes. Also, only a two-organization channel is used to keep the example as simple as possible.

8 If a trading relationship moves from the status of being unique to being exclusive it may well be in contravention of some type of Trade Practices legislation in many countries.

9 This six-step approach is used by Gattorna Strategy Consultants on a regular basis and has been very successful in getting channel members to move towards the formation of strategic partnerships.

10 A practical test for a well defined issue is that it should lead to more than one strategy for its resolution.

References

Bucklin, R. E. and Schmalensee, D. H., 'Viewpoints on the Changing Consumer Goods Distribution Scene: Summary of a Marketing Science Institute Conference', *Marketing Science Institute*, 19–20 May 1987.

Davidson, H., *Offensive Marketing*, Harmondsworth: Penguin, 1987.

Farris, P., 'Why Distribution is So Crucial: The Link Between Distribution and Market Share' in R. E. Bucklin and D. H. Schmalensee (eds), 'Viewpoints on the Changing Consumer Goods Distribution Scene: Summary of a Marketing Science Institute Conference', *Marketing Science Institute*, 19–20 May 1987, pp. 13–15.

Lilien, G. and Kotler, P., *Marketing Decision Making: A Model Building Approach*, New York: Harper & Row, 1983.

McDonald, M. and Gattorna, J., *Marketing Plans*, London: Heinemann, 1984.

Porter, M. E., *Competitive Advantage*, New York: Free Press, 1985.

Ries, A. and Trout, J., *Positioning: The Battle for Your Mind*, New York: McGraw-Hill, 1981.

Schul, P. L., Pride, W. M. and Little, T. L., 'The Impact of Channel Leadership Behaviour on Intrachannel Conflict', *Journal of Marketing*, vol. 47, no. 3, 1983, pp. 21–34.

Waterman, R. H., *The Renewal Factor*, Toronto: Bantam Books, 1987.

Wolf, S. G., 'The Changing General Merchandise Retail Environment' in R. E. Bucklin and D. H. Schmalensee (eds), 'Viewpoints on the Changing Consumer Goods Distribution Scene: Summary of a Marketing Science Institute Conference', *Marketing Science Institute*, 19–20 May, 1987,pp. 26–28.

Part IV
LOGISTICS SYSTEMS

Overview to Part IV

In Chapter 9 Bender outlines a methodology which combines field-tested methods with the most advanced management science and computer technologies to develop optimum logistics strategies designed to maximize an organization's competitiveness. He describes the types of distribution problems facing organizations and then outlines a methodology for optimizing logistics systems design. In describing this approach, Bender highlights the advantages of this proposed methodology whilst exposing the deficiencies of older approaches. It is clear that these new decision support tools will have far reaching ramifications for logistics managers in the 1990s.

In Chapter 10 Gattorna addresses the issue of how organizations must effectively manage their logistics resources if they are to compete successfully in an increasingly turbulent environment. The outlined methodology for conducting a logistics audit provides a systematic basis for examining the physical flows of materials and information through an organization, as well as for reviewing both the internal and external dimensions of the organization's operating environment. Successful completion of a logistics audit will provide any organization with a detailed understanding of its current position, together with clear guidelines for future directions.

The evolution of management support systems is outlined by de Leeuw in Chapter 11. The author highlights the developments in both computer hardware and software over recent years and traces the developments of computer systems for logistics through to today's fully integrated operational support systems. Also described are the various types of decision support systems (DSS) including level 3 systems as described by Bender in Chapter 9. Finally, de Leeuw describes current developments in the area of electronic data interchange, including the push for standards and the opportunities for logistics that such standards herald.

9 Development of Optimum Logistics Strategies

Paul S. Bender

Introduction

This chapter outlines a methodology to develop optimum logistics strategies. The aim of this methodology is to provide strategies that maximize an organization's competitiveness, which is accomplished by blending an approach tested in hundreds of real-life situations with the use of the most advanced management science and computer technologies available today.

The precise statement of the logistics strategy development problem depends on the characteristics of products, customers and marketing channels used by a specific organization. For that reason, we start this outline with a definition of the different types of logistics situations which an organization may confront.

In this outline we leave out some extreme cases, such as those where all material movement is performed through pipelines, and those where there is no need for a logistics network to channel products to the market, as is the case of the aviation industry.

Statement of the basic distribution problem

As illustrated in Figure 9.1, the basic distribution problem is characterized by a flow of finished products between *sources* and *sinks*. Sources are facilities that only originate freight, such as company plants, outside contractor plants, vendor warehouses or co-packers. Sinks are facilities that only receive freight, mainly customer locations, but may also include company plants or warehouses, or public warehouses.

The basic distribution strategy development problem can be stated as follows:

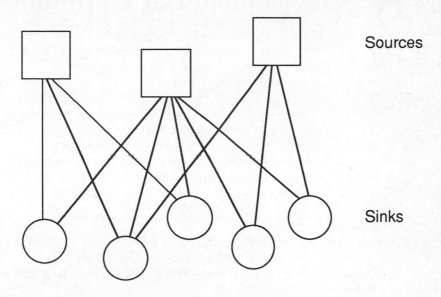

Figure 9.1   The basic distribution network

1   Given:
a)   Sinks, characterized by
  - their locations;
  - their demands by product, as points, ranges, or demand curves relating sales to price and service;
  - Their frequency distribution of demand size, by product.
b)   Sources, characterized by
  - their locations;
  - capacity constraints for each location, including
    - maximum and minimum by product,
    - maximum and minimum for the location;
  - costs associated to each product, to each process within the facility, and to the facility itself;
  - constraints such as maximum inventory investment allowed in the system;
  - customer service requirements, in terms of response time, order completeness, shipment accuracy, and shipment condition;
  - conditions of a technical, legal, or operational nature that must be respected in the solution to ensure its practicality. Those are logical, *non-numerical* restrictions such as

- 'if product x is shipped from a given source, then product y must also be shipped from that source',
- 'if product a is handled through process 1 then product b should also be handled through process 1',
- Transportation flows, including
  - permissible moves, or links, in the system, defined as origin – destination – product – mode combinations,
  - unit cost of each link, including transportation, insurance, in-transit inventorying, and packaging,
  - constraints on flow levels for any link, including minimum and maximum flow levels to be respected by the solution.

2   Determine:
How much of each product should be shipped from each source to each sink, so that the profit contribution of the operation is maximized (or its cost is minimized), while respecting all constraints and conditions established.

The problem stated above is the simplest type of logistic problem, since it involves only direct shipments from sources to sinks. That situation happens in practice when any of the following conditions is present:

a)   the size of most shipments is large enough to guarantee low transportation rates;

b)   the region considered is small enough to enable an acceptable delivery time to customers from a service point of view;

c)   final distribution to customers is effected through forwarders, who become the sinks in the system.

Problems of increasing complexity

The trans-shipment problem

When shipment size is generally less-than-truckload (LTL), and/or service considerations dictate the need to carry inventories between sources and sinks, the logistics strategy development problem takes the form shown in Figure 9.2: an intermediate level of facilities must be introduced, to trans-ship products, and obtain several advantages:

1   *Reduction of transportation cost*, by allowing the movement of large shipments – truckload (TL) or carload (CL) quantities – long

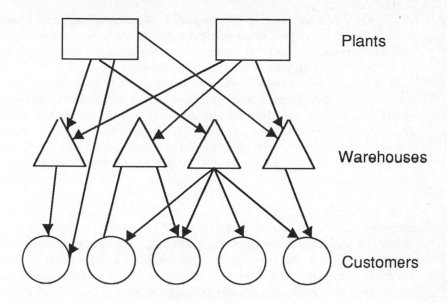

Figure 9.2   Trans-shipment distribution network

distances to intermediate warehouses, at low rates, and from there the movement of LTL shipments to sinks, short distances, at higher rates. Thus, the total transportation cost f.o.b. customers is lower than that incurred with direct shipments from sources.

2 *Improvement of response time*, by placing inventories closer to final demands, thus allowing shorter response time to meet customer service requirements than direct shipments from sources.

3 *Increase in system reliability* by dispersing inventories so that any problem affecting one or more warehouses is not enough to paralyse the system. Such problems may occur because of bad weather, fire, strike, or other unforeseen events.

The potential disadvantages of a trans-shipment system are:

4 *Increase in inventorying costs*, due to higher requirements for in-transit, working, and safety stocks.

5 *Increase in warehousing costs*, because of additional handling, storing, dispensing, and shrinkage at intermediate warehouses. There may also be increases in other costs for operations performed at the warehouses, such as repacking, relabelling, or finishing, due to smaller processing volumes.

The problem is to determine the *optimum* number of intermediate warehouses needed, so that the increases in inventorying and warehousing costs are more than compensated by the decrease in total transportation cost, or so that desired customer service is provided with minimal, or no, reduction in profit contribution.

In the design of trans-shipment systems there may be large shipments worth shipping directly to sinks, without passing through warehouses. They must be included in the analysis because they affect the capacity constraints at the sources. To define that problem, additional data must be developed to describe the characteristics of the intermediate warehouses. Such data is similar to those already described for sources.

The multi-level problem

Sometimes the logistics problem may not be as simple as the trans-shipment problem. There are conditions that require considering two or more levels of distribution facilities. Such conditions apply, for example, when most sources are concentrated in a small region, and sinks are dispersed throughout a large region. Then, reaching a dispersed network of warehouses becomes expensive, slow, or both.

Under such conditions, inventory levels at the warehouses may have to be substantially increased to ensure that larger shipments are sent to them less frequently, but at lower transportation cost. Alternatively, a higher level of warehousing, made up of master warehouses or distribution centres (DCs) is positioned between warehouses and sources. In this case, sources ship goods in TL or CL quantities to DCs, where they are trans-shipped in TL or CL quantities to regional warehouses, or directly to sinks.

This latter type of system, illustrated in Figure 9.3, may also be used when the number of products in inventory is very high but only a small fraction of them is affected by stringent customer service requirements. Then DCs carry a full-line inventory, warehouses carry only fast-moving items, and faster warehouse replenishments are possible from DCs than would be possible from sources directly. Such arrangements are also useful in intercontinental distribution systems, where one level of warehousing feeds a second level, which in turn feeds customers and tertiary levels of warehousing, and so on.

To define this problem, additional data must be developed to describe the characteristics of the intermediate DCs. Such data is similar to that described before for sources.

The advantages of multi-level warehousing systems in distribution are essentially the same as those mentioned for a trans-shipment

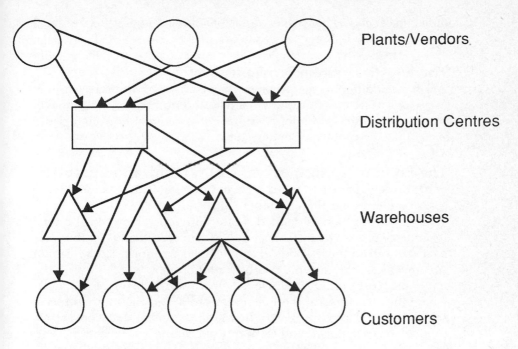

Plants/Vendors

Distribution Centres

Warehouses

Customers

Figure 9.3   Multi-level distribution network

system, plus added reliability in the system. This results from the additional full-line inventories available in the system: if sources are affected by negative conditions, the distribution system can continue to operate without disruption for a while. The disadvantages of multi-level systems are essentially the same as those mentioned for trans-shipment systems, plus the fact that multi-level systems are significantly more complex to manage.

The international problem

In international logistics systems, in addition to the conditions outlined for multi-level systems, there is need to determine simultaneously with the number and location of DCs and warehouses, the best ports of loading and unloading, and the best border customs points. Ports and border crossing points therefore become additional levels in the logistics system and are treated as such in the design process.

Another very important consideration in international logistics systems is that of optimal transfer prices. The logistics network must be designed in such a way that it takes maximum advantage of tax differentials and other national factors in arriving at the optimal structure.

The logistics system problem

When, in addition to the problem characteristics just discussed, it is necessary to determine simultaneously the number and location of plants, and to select vendors, we have the statement of the logistics system design problem (Bender, 1982).

The profit maximization vs. cost minimization problem

In the design of any system, it is always preferable to maximize profit contribution, rather than to minimize cost.

Profit contribution is defined as the difference between the total revenue generated by the sale of goods delivered, minus all the costs incurred to land those goods at the demand locations. Under certain circumstances, the maximum profit solution may be identical to the minimum cost solution. However, there are many circumstances where the structures of the maximum profit and the minimum cost solutions will *always be different*: their facility number, locations, sizes, product mix, supplier and demand allocations, will be different. There are three cases that are of great practical importance to us in the design of logistics and distribution systems:

1 *There are constraints and margin differentials.*
   If any part of the logistics network must respect maximum capacity constraints, such as supply availability, production capacity, warehousing capacity, or transportation capacity, and there are profit margin differentials among different products, then the maximum profit solution will *always* be different from the minimum cost solution.

   Margin differentials may result for many reasons, such as production cost differentials, freight equalization offered to some customers, or differences in prices for a given product in different demand areas, which is a common situation in international logistics systems.

2 *Demands are expressed as ranges*
   If demands are expressed as ranges (minimum/maximum) instead of points (single values), then the maximum profit solution will *always* be different from the minimum cost solution.

3 *Demands are described by demand curves*
   When demands are expressed as functions of price and/or service,

then *the only possible way* to design an optimum logistics network is by maximizing profit while simultaneously calculating the optimal price levels. Under those conditions, cost minimization has no meaning whatsoever.

Since the conditions outlined above occur frequently in practice, the recommended approach is always to structure the problem under consideration as a profit maximization problem.

When problem characteristics preclude profit maximization, as is the case in situations where no revenue function is present, the profit maximization approach ensures that the solution obtained automatically minimizes cost. This result is obtained by setting the objective function as the difference between zero (total revenue), and the total cost: the only way to maximize the difference between zero and the total cost is to minimize total cost.

Logistics and distribution system design methodology

The methodology outlined here is summarized in the flowchart in Figure 9.4 and is explained in detail in Bender (1985a, 1985b). Throughout the application of this methodology, several types of activities are necessary, and these are described below.

Data development

The first step in developing a logistics strategy is to define the specific data requirements to formulate the problem in an efficient and realistic manner. Data requirements include:

- *Data consolidation*, to determine the best groupings of products, customers, and suppliers. Data consolidation is of critical importance in logistics and distribution system design.
- *Sales forecasts* based on mathematical projections of historical data, on market research, on other statistical techniques, such as using analysis by value to forecast new products without history, or econometric analysis, or a combination of the above.
- *Transportation costs*, based on actual data, on retrieval from electronic files, or on rate estimator models.
- *Transportation times*, based on actual data.
- *Warehousing costs*, based on public warehousing cost database, or estimated from construction and labour cost databases.

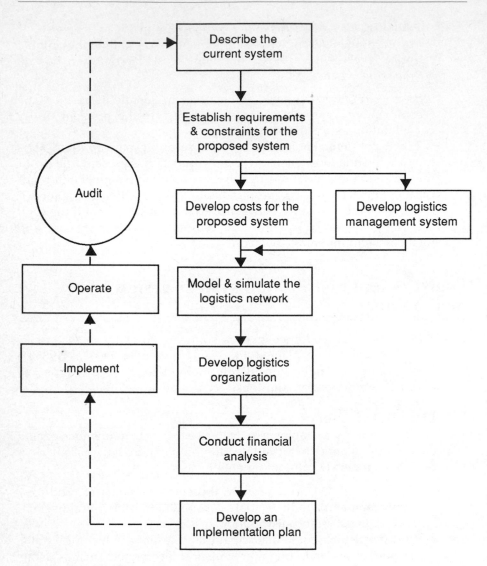

Figure 9.4   Design methodology flowchart

- *Inventorying costs,* expressed as a function of throughput, based on company policies, and statistical relations between inventory activity and turnover ratio.
- *Purchasing costs,* on the basis of historical and projected data.
- *Production costs,* on the basis of historical and projected data.

Modelling and simulation

Once the basic data has been assembled, it must be integrated into a mathematical–logical model, which must faithfully represent all the characteristics of the problem.

The state-of-the-art approach in modelling is to generate automatically a custom-made model of a specific problem, using artificial intelligence techniques. Such techniques, in the form of 'natural languages', enable logistics personnel without training in mathematical modelling or data processing easily to generate and optimally solve any logistics strategy problem.

Development of recommendations

The findings from the optimum simulations must then be compiled into a series of specific, practical recommendations which can be implemented in the real world. The best approach is to organize them in the form of an action plan, showing the recommended implementation sequence, milestones, deadlines and major resource requirements.

Logistics network design is only one of the three dimensions of a logistics system (see Bender, 1985a), the other two being the management system needed to plan, operate and control the functioning of the logistics network and the organization structure needed to perform such functions efficiently.

Advantages of a computerized approach

Use of a computerized, rather than manual, approach, provides many significant advantages including the following:

- It handles uncertainty and complexity in an effective manner, through the use of sensitivity analysis and multiple scenario contingency planning. Computers enable users to find more profitable solutions than manual approaches through the modelling of large-scale, integrated systems, including all relevant trade-offs. Furthermore, they can conduct more in-depth analyses of a situation, enabling the thorough examination of many 'what if?' questions.
- It handles conflicting interests effectively, through the establishment of an optimal solution that constitutes a benchmark and the ability to cost out the penalties of any alternatives proposed.
- It adapts efficiently to changing conditions: when significant

changes take place, it is simple and fast to update an automated model and calculate the new optimal solution.

- It identifies counter-intuitive solutions, providing answers that would be impossible for a human being to fathom without a computer. This is an excellent use of the computer as a skill-transferring device, where an enormous amount of technical skills in mathematical modelling and computers can be put at the command of users with little or no background in those specialities.

Advantages of an optimization approach

An optimization approach to identify the best solution for a given set of conditions solves the major problems associated with empirical approaches, such as determining centres of gravity, or using heuristic models.

The centre of gravity approach became obsolete in the early 1960s, when second-generation computers enabled the use of heuristic models for facility location. In turn, heuristic models became obsolete in the mid-1960s, when third-generation computers enabled the use of linear programming models for facility location. Since then, numerous advances in mathematical programming and model generation techniques have made optimization the preferred approach to locate facilities and, in that context, optimally to allocate all other relevant resources.

Centre of gravity approaches ignore all constraints – capacity, financial, operational, legal and others – and all costs other than transportation. They assume that all transportation costs are directly proportional to distance, and independent of the direction of traffic. Furthermore, they assume arbitrary boundaries within which single facilities must be located, and assume that the centre of gravity of the volumes within each arbitrary region will be a facility location acceptable in practice. Such assumptions are so far removed from the real world that any answers arrived at by using centre of gravity techniques are of no value to profit-minded business people.

Heuristic approaches to facility location problems may use actual transportation costs and may include other costs, such as warehousing. Nevertheless, they have very serious shortcomings. Heuristic approaches cannot handle the effect of constraints, are based on their authors' preconceived ideas about the characteristics of a 'good' solution, rely on trial and error to develop the method to calculate a solution (the method that produces answers most similar to those used in the past is normally selected), and cannot even estimate how far from optimum are the solutions obtained. This lack of optimization capability means that these types of approach cannot provide any meaningful type of sensitivity analysis. Also, they simply replicate manual approaches with computer speeds, thus wasting the computer's capability to transfer skills.

An heuristic approach that is becoming increasingly popular is the use of electronic spread sheets (ESSs), which are useful in conducting limited 'what-if?' analyses. However, their use for sensitivity analysis is based on the flawed premise that when some input values are changed, the *structure* of the solution remains unchanged. That is seldom true in the real world: when input values are changed, the revised optimal solution may have a very different structure than the previous optimum. ESSs do not have the capability to calculate optimal answers; all they do is show what happens to answers previously obtained when input changes do not affect the structure of the solution found.

The use of artificial intelligence languages

The use of artificial intelligence languages, also known as 'natural languages' to generate automatically custom-made models of a logistics situation enables technically unskilled users to create complex models with minimum effort. Such models can be used to calculate the optimum solution given all alternatives. This approach ensures logistics strategies that maximize profitability and, therefore, competitiveness.

To gain a good understanding of the behaviour of a logistics system, it is advisable to make multiple runs of a model. These represent different scenarios, corresponding to various sets of conditions. A typical sequence to perform the runs is:

1 Generate the 'current system' with base year data, to calibrate the model: the solution obtained should be comparable in revenues and costs to actual experience.
2 Generate the model with a minimum of constraints to obtain an initial solution representing the most profitable answer possible under the stated conditions.

3   Make a series of runs progressively increasing the restrictions on the system, to learn the cost impact of new constraints and conditions on the answer.
4   Identify the optimal solution that contains *all* restrictions to be respected to ensure the practicality of the answer.
5   Run user-inspired solutions and compare them against the optimal answer, to assess the penalties involved in adopting a non-optimal solution.
6   Run simpler than optimal solutions to see if a quasi-optimal solution makes sense.
7   Analyse all runs and select the best logistics network configuration.

Advantages of the recommended approach

Our experience indicates that the recommended approach has many important advantages:

- *It is user friendly*. There is no need for users to become expert in data processing or operations research. They can concentrate on the characteristics of the business, and the nature of the problems examined.
- *It is all-encompassing*. The technology recommended can generate and optimally solve models of virtually any size and structure. This provides users with a powerful tool to directly tie in logistics and distribution with marketing, production, finance, and research and development.
- *It has dynamic capabilities*. Users can model multiple time periods and obtain the optimal answer for the entire interval. This enables them to model explicitly the dynamic effects of inventory variations, for example.
- *It enables sensitivity analysis*. This provides users with major advantages in dealing with uncertainty and complexity (see Bender, 1983).
- *Logical conditions can be handled explicitly*. Therefore the optimal solution obtained respects them.
- *It gives data independence*. Since our system generates custom-made models, we can use data in any structure available in the client's files.

Typical questions that can be answered

The approach described here can provide answers simultaneously and in an optimal fashion to a wide variety of questions such as:

- How many warehouses do we need, where should they be located, what areas should they serve, with what products?
- How many levels of warehousing should we have?
- How should each warehouse be supplied?
- Which warehouses should serve each customer on a regular, and on an emergency, basis?
- What transportation modes should be used, where, to move what commodities, in what quantities?
- Which products should be obtained from what sources, in what quantities?
- How much inventory, by product, should be carried at each warehouse?
- How many plants of each type should we have, where should they be located, to produce what products, in what quantities?
- How should plants be supplied, and what recipes should they use to transform raw materials into finished goods?
- Which warehouses and customers should each plant supply, with which products, in what quantities?
- What price should we charge for each product at each demand area?
- What customer service level should be provided for each product, at each demand area?
- Which ports and border crossings should we use, and what transfer prices should be charged, where?

In addition, the recommended approach can answer a variety of solution-related questions, such as:

- What is the maximum profit solution for a given set of demand, cost, and service conditions, subject to given restrictions?
- What are the penalties associated with any non-optimal solution?
- How much can estimated data – such as sales forecasts, and costs projections – change without changing the structure of the optimal answer?
- If there is high seasonality, what are the advantages of a varying network, and how should it vary throughout the year?
- What restrictions could be relaxed slightly to increase profit substantially?

- What would be the impact on the network, and on total profit, of alternative production processes?
- What would be the impact on the network of using alternative warehousing methods, or forwarders, instead of warehouses?
- What is the impact of varying transportation costs on the network configuration?
- What is the optimal network with exactly 'M' warehouses, and 'N' plants?

Typical cost–benefit ratios

Our experience using the recommended methodology and technology to design logistics/distribution systems is documented in Bender (1983). There we show that the total cost of developing data, modelling, simulation, analysis and implementation is typically less than 1 per cent of the benefits obtained by users, when recommendations are implemented and used. This means that for every US $1 users invest on this type of project, they can obtain more than US $100 in benefits.

In addition, users using the recommended technology typically obtain annual profitability improvements averaging 12 per cent, with a range of 5 per cent to over 20 per cent (Bender, 1983).

References

Bender, Paul S., 'Measuring the Value of Automated Decision Support Systems' in Lorin and Goldberg (eds) *The Economics of Information Processing*, New York: John Wiley & Sons, Inc., 1982.

Bender, Paul S., 'Logistic System Design' in National Council of Physical Distribution Management (NCPDM), *Distribution Handbook*, New York: Free Press, 1985a.

Bender, Paul S., 'International Logistics' in National Council of Physical Distribution Management (NCPDM) *Distribution Handbook*, New York: Free Press, 1985b.

Bender, Paul S., *Resource Management: An Alternative View of the Management Process*, New York: John Wiley & Sons, Inc, 1983.

10 Auditing Internal Logistics Performance

John Gattorna

Introduction

Achieving long-term profitability in today's turbulent environment depends to a large degree on an organization's ability to anticipate and adapt to change in a planned manner. To meet this challenge effectively, the organization must creatively manage all its resources to develop and maintain a competitive edge.

Increasingly, organizations are realizing the extent to which the seven key decision areas which comprise the 'logistics mix' affect corporate profitability. These seven elements, depicted in Figure 10.1 are: inventories; facilities; communications; unitization; transport on the finished goods side; and materials management and production scheduling on the input side. Coincidently, the finished goods element of the logistics mix, is also the 'positioning' or 'place' component in the organization's marketing strategy and is therefore especially crucial.

Logistics management's role is to help reduce uncertainty by ensuring that the organization's logistics resources and capabilities are compatible with the demands currently being made, or likely to be made by customers in the future. Achieving this in a cost-effective manner requires both a comprehensive and integrated view of the whole of the logistics function and a clear understanding of the implications where logistics interfaces with other organizational functions.

The logistics audit

Whilst not radically new in content, the logistics audit provides a disciplined systems-based approach for reviewing both the internal

141

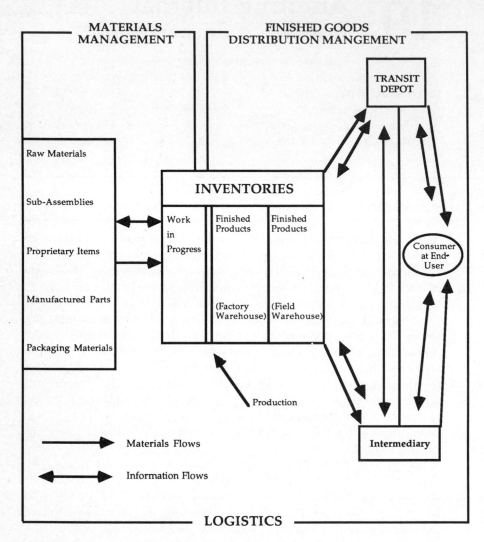

Figure 10.1　The logistics mix

and external dimensions of the organization's operating environment as it impacts on logistics resources. The methodology examines the physical flow of materials, together with the information flows which initiate and support these physical movements right across the organization and for some distance either side. It attempts to answer the questions:

- Where are we at this point in time?
- How cost-effective is our current logistics system?

Figure 10.2 depicts this 'logistics capability' requirement.

The key elements in an appraisal of the external environment are depicted in Figure 10.3 under the headings of source market profile, user market profile, competitive profile, channel profile and government regulation. It is not necessary for the logistics executive to be expert in all these areas. Rather, an awareness of structural changes in the various areas enables the logistics executive to assess the potential impact on the logistics function and thereby assist in the development of appropriate strategies.

The internal change appraisal in Figure 10.4, depicts the items of concern inside the organization. Whilst the logistics executive may have a more detailed knowledge in this area, the real focus in the first instance should be upon reviewing the *existing system capability*, as it is this area where the logistics executive has the potential to make the most direct impact.

The audit is a *systematic* investigation which must be approached objectively and with no preconceptions. Problem definition(s) and the formulation of corresponding solution(s) follow as a result of such research, rather than precede it. Failure to adopt this rigorous approach may result in:

- too many wrong questions asked,
- too many right questions asked of the wrong people, and
- too many 'problems' solved before the real problems are known.

Information
One of the biggest problems when undertaking a logistics audit for the first time is the installation of the necessary information collection system. This need not be sophisticated and, above all, the cost of setting it up should not outweigh the potential savings. It may be useful to tie the information collection responsibility to personnel at different operating levels within the organization.

Standards
Even if the necessary information is available, the next major problem is to derive suitable standards against which to measure system performance. It is acknowledged that appropriate standards are

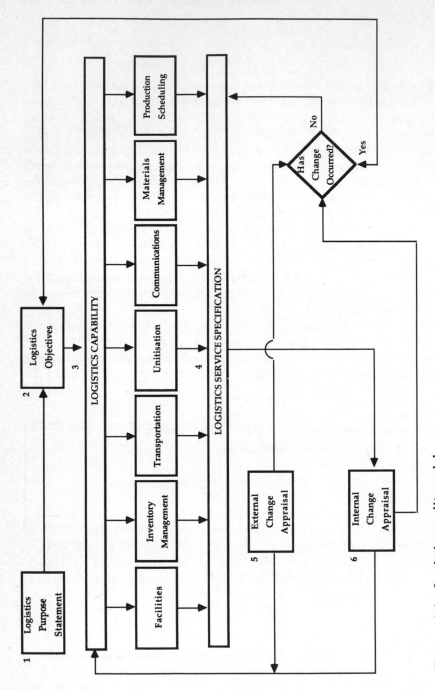

Figure 10.2 Logistics audit model

144

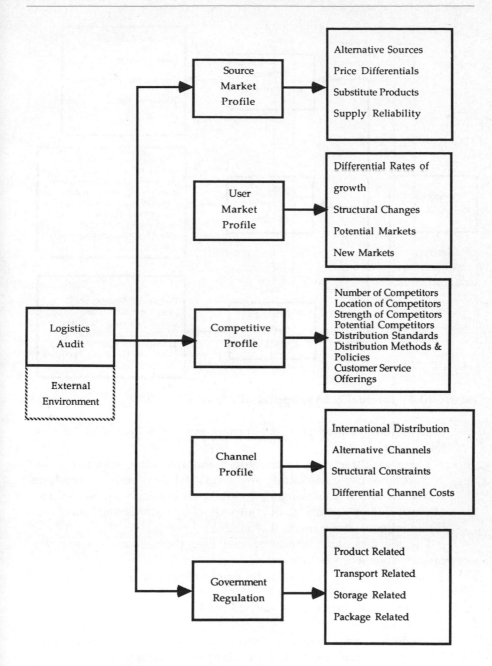

Figure 10.3 External change appraisal

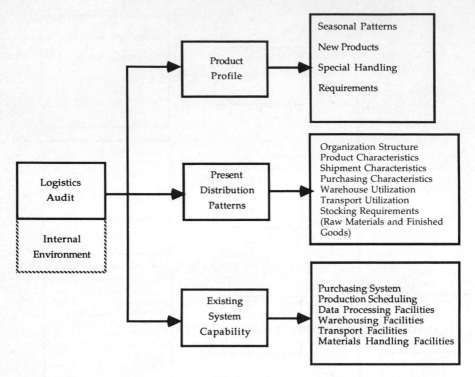

Figure 10.4   Internal change appraisal

difficult to set. However, without them meaningful control is impossible.

There are three ways to develop standards. First, review existing
performance using workstudy and industrial engineering procedures
and then attach values using cost-accounting techniques. Second,
attempt to gain some idea of competitors' standards and, third, use
intercompany comparisons if available.

The logistics audit begins by mapping the logistics system. The
tasks involved are as follows:

1 Define the organization's logistics objectives in the context of
   corporate and marketing objectives.
2 Identify target levels of service and other 'outputs' of logistics
   activities.
3 Flowchart the 'trigger' communications and information flows,
   beginning with the receipt of a customer's orders.
4 Flowchart the corresponding materials flow patterns.

5 Look for discrepancies between materials and information flows.
6 Identify the 'points' at which performance can be measured.
7 Specify the important interdependencies between the logistics function and other areas of the organization.

Perhaps one of the most difficult, and certainly the most detailed, task in undertaking a logistics audit for the first time is developing the composite flowchart from the steps outlined above. However, it can be done and is, in itself, a valuable undertaking. Figure 10.5 is an example of such a flowchart.

With this specification of what the logistics system should be doing, the next step is to determine the extent to which the existing processes are achieving their purpose. At this stage, the task usually divides into five sub-audits: customer service perception audit; competitor audit; channels audit; materials supply audit; and finished goods distribution audit. The rest of this chapter will concentrate on the finished goods distribution audit, and the other audits will be addressed elsewhere in this handbook.

Finished goods distribution audit

The finished goods distribution audit may be carried out as part of an overall logistics audit, or as a separate activity. An evaluation of an organization's distribution system is worthwhile under the following circumstances:

- when the organization makes a significant change in its marketing strategy (for example, going direct versus selling via wholesalers);
- when the size of the organization changes significantly;
- when new businesses or products are added to the distribution system;
- when five to ten years have passed since the last evaluation;
- when any of the signs of maldistribution appear.

Signs of maldistribution may manifest themselves as:

1 *Inventories that turn slowly.* Distribution inventories should turn between six and 12 times per year in most organizations except in unusual product/industry situations. Indeed, you should be aware what the norm is for your own industry. Inventory turns less than the industry average often indicate deeper problems.
2 *Poor customer service.* Inventory investment equal to about two

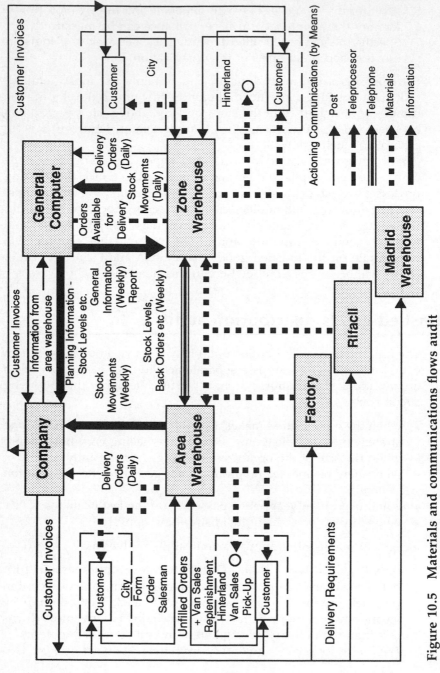

Figure 10.5   Materials and communications flows audit
(Example: Spanish Food Manufacturing Company)

The following text labels appear within the figure:

Customer Invoices

Customer

City

Hinterland

Customer

Actioning Communications (by Means)

Post
Teleprocessor
Telephone
Materials
Information

Delivery Orders (Daily)

General Computer

Orders Available for Delivery

Stock Movements (Daily)

Zone Warehouse

Customer Invoices

Information from area warehouse

Planning Information - Stock Levels etc.

General Information (Weekly) Report

Stock Movements (Weekly)

Stock Levels, Back Orders etc (Weekly)

Company

Area Warehouse

Factory

Rifacil

Madrid Warehouse

Delivery Orders (Daily)

Customer

City Form Order Salesman

Unfilled Orders + Van Sales Replenishment

Hinterland Van Sales Pick-Up

Customer

Delivery Requirements

Customer Invoices

months of sales should provide about 99 per cent service. Investment of half this amount should achieve about 90 per cent service.
Failure to achieve these levels can mean that the inventory is in
the wrong products, the wrong location or both. In any event,
listening to customers in the market-place should be enough to
determine whether or not all is well. Frequent complaints often
signal problems.

3   *Interwarehouse shipments*. Stock transfers between locations within
the distribution system require double-handling, and distribution
managers rarely trans-ship except in emergencies. A significant
volume of interwarehouse transfers is therefore usually a sign of a
system in continual trouble.

4   *Premium freight charges*. A distribution system that relies on
premium freight is in trouble for the same reasons. Cost savings
are usually significant when the problem is corrected. It may also
indicate problems elsewhere in the cycle – such as hold-ups in
order processing – which only manifest themselves in the shipp-
ing/despatch area as managers try to keep faith with promised
delivery dates despite the loss of time earlier in the cycle.

Distribution cost analysis

One of the main reasons for undertaking an audit is to determine the
total cost of running the current distribution system. For this reason
the audit encompasses both assets employed and physical volumes
processed, the ultimate aim being to relate these two streams to each
other. One line of investigation attempts to build up an accurate
picture of total distribution costs, the other an understanding of what
physical performances are being achieved by the system in whatever
units are relevant.

Deciding on an appropriate unit (or units) of work output is vital.
This unit (or units) measures (physical) activity levels within the
organization's distribution system and, when related to costs,
provides further insight into system efficiency.

Key performance measures

To derive any benefit from the audit, it is mandatory to establish the
true total cost of distribution, which then forms part of the 'key
performance ratio'. The concept as depicted in Figure 10.6 uses
distribution costs as a percentage of net sales. However, some
organizations might choose distribution cost as a percentage of gross
margin, or as a percentage of product cost, or all three, whichever is

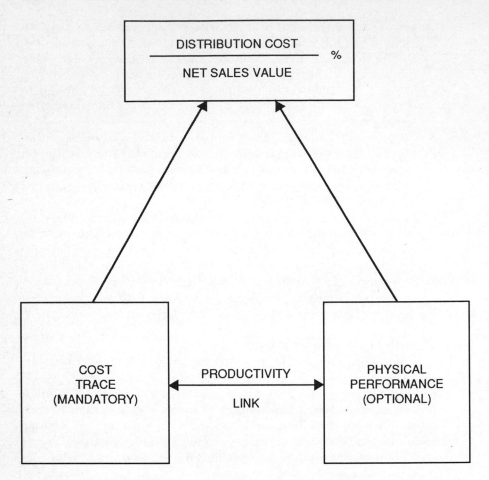

Figure 10.6   Distribution audit: key performance ratio

appropriate. It does not matter which key ratio is selected, so long as it is consistently monitored and does not give a distorted view of the system's true performance.

If the key ratio to monitor is total distribution cost as a percentage of net sales, then it may be broken down into a number of 'intermediate' ratios and finally 'grass-roots' ratios. The intermediate ratios will relate to the five elements which constitute the distribution function: facilities, inventory, transportation, communications, and unitization. Together, these give an internal albeit indirect measure of customer service performance. The hierarchical nature of the control

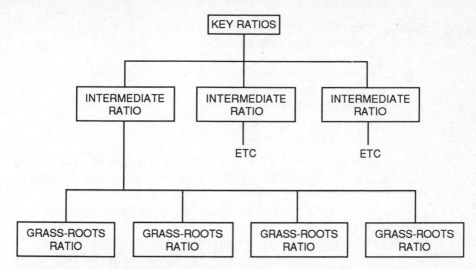

Figure 10.7   Distribution audit: hierarchy of control ratios

ratios depicted in Figure 10.7 facilitates giving responsibility for specific ratios to personnel at different levels within the distribution function of the organization. Each of the intermediate ratios can be built up from a number of constituent grass-root ratios. Below is a list of the intermediate ratios and corresponding grass-root ratios for a typical organization. Note that each contains at least one cost ratio, but the activity ratios may vary in number.

1   Facilities Utilization
   1.1   warehouse activity factors
   1.2   operating costs
   1.3   cube utilization of the facility
2   Inventory management
   2.1   inventory carrying costs
   2.2   stock-turn velocity
   2.3   stock shrinkage
   2.4   intra-company transfers
   2.5   stock rotation
   2.6   stock-out performance
3   Transportation
   3.1   operating costs
   3.2   transport task performance
   3.3   vehicle utilization
4   Communications systems

4.1   operating costs
4.2   documentation activity
4.3   customer contact
4.4   performance measures
5   Unitization degree
5.1   cost – benefit of mechanization
5.2   modular units
5.3   productivity measures

The distribution audit outlined in the previous paragraphs addresses but one of the elements comprising the organization's logistics function. Even the fairly general list of ratios outlined above may not contain some of the ratios which are found necessary effectively to monitor certain distribution functions. Essentially, the process is one of building up individual information modules from the basic operating level of each of the organization's logistics elements. From these will ultimately be selected the few key operational parameters in each area to monitor each period in detail. These parameters will differ between industries and organizations.

Distribution audit output
The audit methodology is capable of uncovering some unexpected results, often in areas of the organization outside distribution – in particular, marketing and production. The types of findings detailed below reveal areas requiring attention; they do not provide solutions. It is only by approaching the audit with an open mind that these areas are revealed.

1   Equal volume-based discounts given for both delivery to central warehouse and numerous retail outlets. Why?
2   Levels of delivery service are very high: 3–5 days countrywide. Reliability of delivery service is high and there exist well developed relationships between driver and customer. Are levels of customer service therefore too high?
3   Twenty per cent of customer accounts produce 89 per cent of sales. Twenty per cent of delivery points produce 81 per cent of sales. Is this pattern of business healthy? What are the implications for distribution?
4   At present no minimum drop size/value policy exists. Analysis reveals 14 per cent of drops for a month were below average distribution cost per drop, and only 15 per cent were above the organization's break-even cost. Should a drop size/value policy be

introduced? Should it be based on average cost per drop or break-even cost?

5 The subject organization handles spares and repairs as well as finished goods. Should the organization mix the distribution or are different levels of service required?

Communicating the findings of an audit

The findings should first be discussed with the responsible managers to obtain their agreement to the underlying facts. Their commitment to corrective action within a specified time period should then be obtained and included in the draft audit report. The report should note corrective action that has already been taken. The findings in draft form should be submitted to the responsible managers for a full two-way discussion.

The final report should be structured as an 'action' document with emphasis on recommendations for improvement. Weaknesses should only be used as evidence to support recommendations.

11 Management Support Systems for Logistics Including EDI

Kees de Leeuw

Introduction

Systems requirements

Due to the complexity of logistics, it is nowadays almost inconceivable to manage the logistics operation without the support of computers and management information systems. Two main categories of management support systems in logistics exist:

- systems supporting the operation;
- systems supporting the decision process.

The main reasons for the implementation of these systems are:

- cost reduction through increases in productivity;
- improved customer service through reductions in time lags;
- improved decisions through more accurate input data.

Management support systems in logistics should also aim at integrating the various logistics functions. This means that a common data-base should be used, input data should be keyed in only once and the systems should provide information about the trade-offs between the various functions so that the overall logistics function can be optimized.

However, few companies have succeeded in implementing systems which really integrate all functions and assist management in optimizing the logistics operation. This will cause a growing demand for new and improved systems in the near future, a growth which will be amplified by constantly increasing pressures further to reduce the logistics cost and to improve customer service.

There are some additional reasons for requiring new systems, one being that the scope of logistics is broadening and will increasingly include global issues. Another reason for the growing demand for management support systems is the introduction of new technologies which will not only concern computer hardware and software, such as electronic data interchange (EDI), and improved communication, networking and distributed processing, but will also include factors such as further mechanization and automation in materials handling and the introduction of new techniques in, for example, forecasting and scheduling processes.

Computer hardware and software

Due to the rapid rate of development over the last 40 years, computer hardware and software provide a solid basis for computer systems to be used in logistics. Developments in computer hardware specifically have a significant influence on the performance, capacity and reliability of computers: for example, between 1958 and 1980, the time required for one electronic operation fell by a factor of 80 million. Computer hardware developments are expected to continue at a similar rate for at least one or two decades and will have a significant effect on the way we are doing business.

Future developments in computer hardware will be focused particularly on:

- performance and capacity;
- communications and networks;
- interconnectivity between computers;
- distributed processing, where processing and databases are distributed over the various processors in a network;
- data capture and user interface.

Spectacular developments are likewise taking place in the software industry. The more recent developments especially concern the areas of operating systems, software tools and languages, data-base management systems and application software. One important recent example is the development of Computer Aided Software Engineering or CASE, which is evolving analogously to CAD/CAM in engineering. CASE uses computers to interactively specify software requirements and to translate those specifications automatically into computer programs. The CASE technology will eliminate large parts of the actual programming tasks and will soon be used to build large applications. CASE is expected to change the software industry

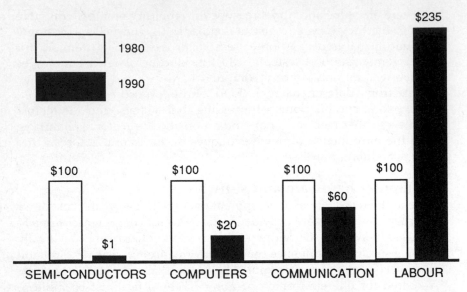

Source: Stone B. and Wyman J., *Successful Telemarketing*, NTC Business Books, 1986.

Figure 11.1   Cost comparisons 1980 vs. 1990

significantly before the year 2000 and will have important influence on future logistics systems.

Parallel to the developments in hardware and software, the cost–performance ratio of computing has significantly improved and, over the next decade, is expected to improve further at an annual rate of approximately 30 per cent. This implies that equal power and capacity will be available at a price that is falling at a rate of 30 per cent per year or that 30 per cent more power and capacity can be provided at constant price.

Figure 11.1 shows a comparison between 1980 and 1990 costs for computer-related products and operations on the one hand and for labour on the other. Other major cost components in logistics, such as rent, energy, transport and mail, will, like labour costs, also increase over time.

From this very brief overview we can conclude that, from a technological point of view, the recent and future developments in computer hardware and software will provide a very solid platform for using computer systems in logistics. Our present computers are fast, have very large data storage capabilities, are reliable and can be interconnected in a network using fast communications methods. As the cost – performance ratio improves, it can be concluded that there will be a growing need for the use of computer systems in logistics to increase productivity.

Types of systems

The first practical computer applications for logistics were developed in the early 1960s and can be categorized as stage one applications. These applications typically concern the recording of what has happened, which means that the system is only updated after the event and is only used for 'book-keeping' and reporting purposes. Examples are stock-keeping systems, accounts receivable and general ledger accounting. Typical outputs of these systems are a stock status report, a customer ageing report and a cost variance report. Stage one applications are hardly integrated.

Stage two applications started to emerge in the early 1970s and concern on-line transaction processing systems. The system is updated at the time a transaction occurs and will then also process the consequences of such a transaction. A typical example of a stage two application is an on-line customer order processing system which, in one form or another, has been implemented by almost every company. Common features of such systems are that, at the time an order is entered, the system usually will perform an on-line customer credit check, a stock availability check, will allocate stock and produce a picking list so that the order can be picked in the warehouse.

Stage two applications are more integrated than stage one applications. For example, a customer order processing system is usually integrated with inventory management and accounts receivable, which means that data about stocks and invoices are interfaced and that the 'book-keeping' functions are automatically performed. They also usually provide decision-oriented information for lower and middle management such as, for example, a report with recommended re-order quantities for replenishing the stock levels.

Stage three applications aim at full integration and at providing information for middle and top management decision-making. They will cover all the various logistics functions such that information about these functions, their interfaces and trade-offs are accessible to all users. Moreover, these systems provide for integrated modules for long-and medium-term planning, budgeting and cost control.

Although some stage three-type applications started to be developed in the early 1980s, few companies have been able to implement such systems. Most companies are still in stage two, but are expected to move to stage three within the next few years.

Another way to classify logistics information systems is to base the classification on primary functionality, as has been done at the start of this chapter. In this way, logistics systems can be classified into operational support and decision support systems.

Although the operational support and the decision support systems are usually integrated into one logical information system, the classification is very suitable to discuss the elements and functionality. The next section discusses the functionality of operational support systems and will include support for day-to-day decisions such as credit decisions and information which can be used for stock replenishments. The third section will cover the support systems for medium-and long term decisions and the final section will deal with the major aspects of EDI, as this will have a significant impact on logistics in the near future.

Operational support systems

General requirements
The objectives of operational support systems are to assist in managing and controlling the day-to-day logistics operation, which consists of the following three sub-operations:

1   the physical operation, such as transport, receiving stock and picking and despatching customer orders;
2   the paperwork operation required to trigger and control the physical operation, such as purchase order processing, inventory control and customer order processing;
3   the accounting operation for processing the financial transactions resulting from the physical operation, such as accounts payable and accounts receivable.

These three sub-operations, together with the most important of their functions, are outlined in Figure 11.2.

Each company has its own individuality and is doing business in its own special way. Detailed requirements for operational support systems will therefore differ from company to company, especially as far as the physical operation is concerned. In general, requirements differ less for the paperwork operation, while the least differences in requirements occur for the accounting operation. This is the main

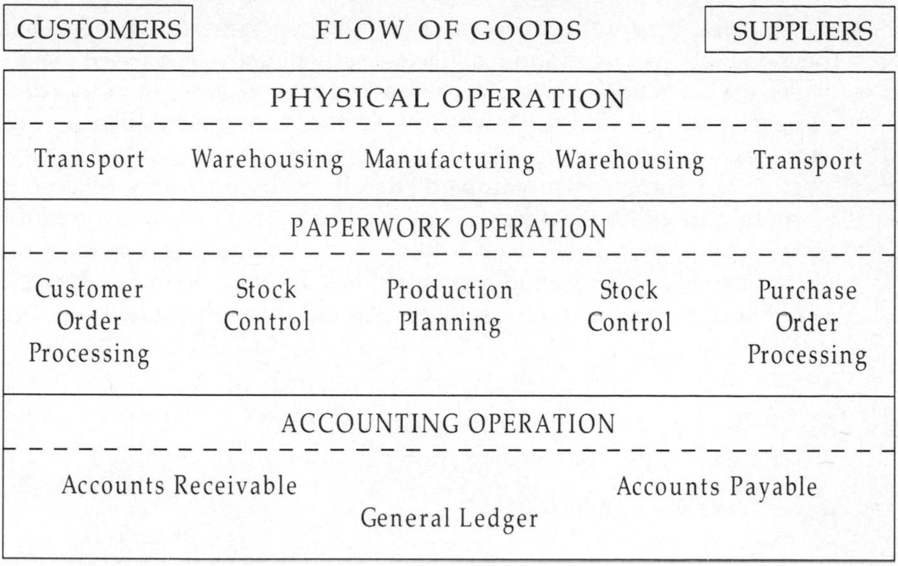

CUSTOMERS	FLOW OF GOODS			SUPPLIERS
PHYSICAL OPERATION				
Transport	Warehousing	Manufacturing	Warehousing	Transport
PAPERWORK OPERATION				
Customer Order Processing	Stock Control	Production Planning	Stock Control	Purchase Order Processing
ACCOUNTING OPERATION				
Accounts Receivable		General Ledger		Accounts Payable

Figure 11.2 The logistics sub-operations

reason why there are many more software packages available for the accounting operation (stage one applications) and the paperwork operation (stage one and two applications) than for the physical operation (mainly stage two applications). Recent developments in software technology have made available an increasing number of packages which include support for the physical operations. These packages also aim at the integration of all the functions involved and can therefore be considered as stage three applications.

The current situation

A sophisticated and fully integrated operational support system assists in managing and controlling all the functions of the three sub-operations. Such systems usually consist of interfacing modules. Each module can clearly be identified with one of the functions of the three sub-operations (physical, paperwork and accounting), examples being an order processing module, which assists the paperwork operation as far as customer order processing is concerned, and a warehouse module, which assists in the physical operation of receiving, order picking and despatch.

Few companies have as yet succeeded in implementing a fully integrated system, although most companies have in place a support system which addresses a limited number of these functions. The functions of the accounting operation are usually addressed best, while the functions of the physical operation are often hardly addressed at all. The main features of the various modules of an operation support system will briefly be discussed below.

As stated earlier, each company has its individual way of doing business and will have different detailed requirements for an operational support system. Since it is beyond the scope of this chapter to discuss all requirements and features in detail, only the main features of the various modules of a fully integrated support system will be outlined.

Modules for the accounting operation

The main modules for the accounting operation are:

- accounts receivable
- accounts payable
- general ledger

These modules process the financial consequences of distribution transactions and will provide a significant amount of management information. They will largely be updated through interfaces with the modules for the paperwork operation.

Modules for the paperwork operation

The main modules for the paperwork operation are:

- stock control
- order processing
- purchasing
- interface with manufacturing

Stock control module

The primary objective of a stock control module is to keep track of the total stock per product for each individual warehouse. It also monitors the status of the stock such as 'free for sale', 'allocated', 'reserved' and 'damaged'. Changes in the total stock are caused by inventory transactions, such as receivals, withdrawals and adjustments.

The stock control module is generally automatically updated

through interfaces with the warehousing module, order processing module and the purchasing module.

A stock control module also assists in the replenishment of stock levels by providing data about recommended quantities to be ordered from third-party suppliers or to be produced in their own plant (see Chapter 1). The recommended quantities are based on forecasts of demand and on the re-ordered algorithms. Sophisticated systems also make use of the technique of distribution resource planning or DRP (see Chapter 21).

Order processing module
The main objective of an order processing module is to provide for the features of entering, processing and keeping track of customer orders. Some of its major features are:

- customer credit check
- stock availability check
- automatic pricing and discount calculations
- back order management

The order processing module will provide comprehensive management information including sales analysis (for example, sales by geographic area, by types of customers, by salesmen and so on) and will provide this information both in the form of on-line screen enquiries and reports.

Purchasing module
The main objectives of a purchasing module are to provide for the features of entering, processing and keeping track of purchase orders.

Purchase orders will usually be based on the output of the re-order algorithms of the stock control module, in which case the data will be automatically loaded into the purchase order.

The purchasing module will also keep track of the status of purchase orders, such as 'placed', 'acknowledged', 'shipped', and 'in custom clearance'. It also interfaces with accounts receivable. The interface mainly concerns quantities and prices on the purchase order which are used for the reconciliation with suppliers' invoices.

The purchase order module will provide comprehensive management information including suppliers' performance analysis and will provide this information both in the form of on-line screen enquiries and reports.

Interfaces with manufacturing systems

If a company has its own production facilities, interfaces are required between the distribution system and the manufacturing system. These concern both finished products and raw materials and components, as well as such data as recommended production quantities, planned production completion dates, requirements for raw materials and components and stock availability information (see chapter 24).

Modules for the physical operation
Warehousing

Two main levels of computer systems exist for warehouse applications. The first level, which we will call the warehouse module, assists in the day-to-day planning, managing and control of all warehouse operations, the most important of which are:

- receiving;
- order picking and despatch;
- control of stock by warehouse location;
- physical stock-takes;
- replenishment of pick locations.

One of the main features of the warehouse module is that information will be transformed into a form which is useful for warehouse management – for example, quantities to be received from suppliers and quantities to be shipped to customers will be expressed in the number of pallets and the number of cartons, as well as in the number of cubic metres. This type of information can significantly assist in the planning and scheduling of the various operations.

The warehouse module will keep track of stock by warehouse location (for example, pallet location, bin location) and will store data such as the product identifier, the quantity, the arrival date, the use-by date and lot number.

The module will also ensure that stock is rotated according to preset rules such as 'first in – first out' (FIFO) and will also assist in physical stock-takes. By keeping track of stock by warehouse location, cyclic stock takes can be performed where, frequently (that is daily), only a small part of the store is counted. This will cause far less interruption than a total stock count which, because of the time involved, is usually only done once or twice a year. Cyclic stock-takes will ensure far more accurate stock levels.

The second level of systems concerns the control of mechanized and automated materials handling systems, such as paperless picking systems, carousels, automatic stacker cranes and automatic conveyor sorting systems. There are a number of interfaces between first-and second-level systems. For instance, a paperless picking system or a carousel receives data from the warehouse module about products and quantities to be picked (see chapter 12–16).

Transport

Several systems exist which support the physical operation of transport. Two of the most important ones will be briefly discussed.

The first system is used for load scheduling and can be seen as an extension of the order scheduling part of the warehousing module. In order to schedule transport loads, the module will provide information about the cube of orders to be transported and the weight of the orders, as well as the dimension of boxes involved. The information thus provided can be used for decisions such as how many and what size trucks to use for a specific geographic area, or whether geographic areas should be combined into one truck or whether the delivery of part of the orders should be postponed to the next day. The second system to support the physical operation of transport is usually called a vehicle scheduling system.

In addition to scheduling transport loads, this type of system will also schedule the geographic routes of the trucks. Given the workload of orders to be delivered (as supplied by the warehouse module), the optimal use of a transport fleet and the optimal route per truck is calculated. This means that a comprehensive data base is required containing data concerning geographic maps and traffic conditions.

Decision support systems

General

The decision support systems which will be discussed in this section will support medium-and long-term decisions. Day-to-day decisions, such as decisions about re-ordering stock, scheduling of orders and scheduling of transport are supported by the operational support systems and were briefly discussed in the previous section.

A variety of decision support systems exist with various levels of sophistication. These sophistication levels can be classified into three main categories: level one, level two and level three.

Level one systems

Level one systems provide management with information which can be used as input for decision processes, but these play no further role in these processes. The main function of level one systems is to convert historical data into useful information.

Examples of level one systems' output are information about the flow of goods measured in cubic metres and data about costs.

Level two systems

Level two systems assist the decision process by evaluating the consequences of various alternatives ('what if?' questions). The decision-maker determines the alternatives to be evaluated, and the system will then calculate the consequences for specific criteria, but will not make a selection between the various criteria.

Level two systems often do not calculate all the consequences of alternatives. So long as the decision-maker is aware of these limitations, the results of level two systems can often effectively be used in decision processes and can lead to significantly better decisions.

Relatively simple level two applications can be carried out by making use of spreadsheets.

Level three systems

Level three systems will assist the decision process by calculating the optimal decision based on mathematical models and optimization techniques. This implies that a level three system actually selects the optimal alternative.

The structure of level two, and especially level three, systems is considerably more complex than that of level one systems. Although they are designed for more than day-to-day decisions, it is difficult and sometimes impossible to capture within a system all the aspects and constraints of real life required for medium-and long-term decisions. Level two and three systems should therefore only be used if there is a basic understanding about their functioning and limitations.

In the past, a number of level three systems were developed which, because of computational and mathematical constraints, had so many limitations that the results were often unrealistic. However, due to the tremendous developments in the computer technology, some level three systems have recently been developed which have over-come these problems and, if used correctly, can lead to significantly better decisions. These systems are dealt with in detail in Chapter 9.

Input for decision support systems

Decision support and operational support systems are often inte-grated into one logical information system. The main reason for this is that the operational support systems can provide a significant amount of input data which can be used for medium-and long-term decisions.

When the initial transaction data is stored in the data-base of a decision support system, a wealth of data is available from which all sorts of information for medium-and long-term decisions can be constructed. The detailed transaction data still has to be processed in order to provide information. This processing mainly concerns select-ing, sorting and summarizing the data. Without this processing, a system can be categorized as 'data rich' but 'information poor'.

Sophisticated operational support systems are normally developed such that they provide a significant amount of standard information. In addition, information is often required on a dynamic and *ad hoc* basis. In order to generate this type of information, use can be made of report generators – software tools which make it possible for non-EDP-oriented users to generate their own reports and enquiries based on a data-base containing detailed data.

By making use of report generators, users are more independent from EDP departments with the consequence that lead times are often significantly reduced. The use of report generators will also make users more aware of the potential information which can be generated.

Report generators can therefore be seen as extremely powerful tools, which can transform operational support systems into effective level one decision support systems.

Applications of decision support systems

It is beyond the scope of this chapter to discuss the technical aspects of the various decision support systems, but some examples of important applications will be briefly outlined below.

It will depend on the detailed requirements as well as on the skill and experience within the company whether a level one, two or three system should be used.

Applications for long term planning

Long-term decisions in logistics concern the logistics structure. They include decisions about the number, size and geographic location of facilities such as warehouses, the type of materials handling systems and whether to use own or third-party transport.

The decision process consists of the evaluation of (usually) a large number of alternatives, and the process is complex because of the numerous interactions between the various aspects involved and the very large number of input data required in order to arrive at the best possible decision.

The input data include data about physical flows (for example, the number of pallets, number of cartons, volumes and weights), data about costs (for example, labour, transport and rent), data about storage requirements, data about transport times, data about supplier lead times and data about the effect of different levels of customer service.

Applications for medium-term planning and control

Medium-term planning and control mainly concerns decisions about how optimally to use an existing logistics structure. The time-frame of medium-term planning varies between one month and four years.

Several application areas for support systems in medium term planning and control exist, two of which are described below.

Ad Hoc applications

The first application area concerns the evaluation of alternatives which is usually done more on an *ad hoc*, rather than a regular, basis.

An example of an *ad hoc* medium-term decision is whether to store all products in the regional warehouses or whether to store only fast movers and supply slow movers directly to all customers from the central warehouse.

These types of medium-term decisions are very similar to long-term decisions as they involve the evaluation of alternatives, interactions between the various aspects and usually a large amount of input data. They are, however, usually less complex in structure.

Standard Applications

Standard applications for medium-term support systems are applications which can be used periodically and for which a standard approach and a standard system can be developed. Typical examples are a logistics budget system and a logistics performance and control system.

A logistics budget system is a system which transforms a sales budget into logistics quantities. Examples of such quantities are the number of pallets and cartons to be handled, the number of pallets to be stored and the volume and weight of goods flows to be transported. A far more accurate logistics budget can be derived based on these quantities than by using conventional methods.

Such a logistics budget can be controlled by making use of a logistics performance and control system which will calculate periodically (say monthly) the actual values of quantities as determined by the budget. By combining these values with actual costs incurred, a number of comparisons can be made with budgeted quantities and rates. These comparisons will not only provide early warnings when the actual situation deviates from a planned or budget situation, but will also provide indications of where problems are occurring.

The implementation of a logistics budget system, together with a logisitics performance and control system, is an important step towards really controlling the logistics operation and its costs.

Electronic data interchange

Electronic data interchange or EDI is currently one of the most important subjects in the area of computer applications in logistics.

A commonly accepted definition of EDI is: the computer-to-computer exchange of inter- and intracompany business and technical data, based on the use of agreed standards.

The use of EDI in logistics applications mainly concerns the electronic interchange of trading documents such as purchase orders, acknowledgements and invoices. For several reasons, including legal and government conditions, different requirements per industry often exist concerning the format and content of these documents. Different standards are therefore being developed for different industries such as the automotive industry, the chemical industry and the retail and distribution industry.

Besides trading data, other data such as technical data (for example CAD, quality and performance data), electronic funds transfers (EFT), interactive queries (for example order status) and general business information (for example, price lists, promotions) can be interchanged as well.

Although EDI is already implemented in several industries, it is still in its infancy. A fully grown EDI application in logistics might be described by the following scenario.

The operational support system of company A generates suggested re-order quantities for a number of products which are supplied by company B. After the recommendations are approved by the Purchase Manager, the system generates a purchase order which is sent electronically to company B. Based on this purchase order, the operational support system of company B will automatically generate a sales order and perform a credit and a stock availability check. If these checks are passed, company B system will electronically send an acknowledgement and will further process the order for order picking and despatch. An electronic advice will be sent to the transport company so that transport will be available on time. At the time of despatch, an invoice will be sent electronically to company A and, after the goods have been received, the accounts receivable module will check the invoice against the prices and quantities on the purchase order and against the prices and the quantities actually received. If these tests are passed, an electronic message will be sent to the bank in order to trigger an electronic funds transfer or EFT, after which the amounts payable module of company B will be updated.

In this scenario, human intervention is only required when actions have to be authorized (for example, purchasing by the computer – suggested re-order quantities) or when certain tests are not met (for example, when quantity invoiced does not match the quantity received). Documents generated by the computer might only consist of exception reports and summarized overviews of transactions carried out.

In addition to banks and transport companies, customs and customs agents are other users of EDI for international trading.

EDI was first introduced in the grocery industry in the USA, and is now in full swing in the US automotive industry which has implemented EDI with many suppliers.

The primary savings consist of reduction in clerical activities, reduction in processing errors, tighter inventory control and time savings. EDI is an ideal tool to be combined with JIT techniques.

In addition to cost-saving reasons, its implementation may also be triggered by pressures from trading partners. In some industries it will soon be difficult to do business without EDI.

There are two ways for companies to communicate when using EDI. The first is to use direct connections (such as leased lines); the

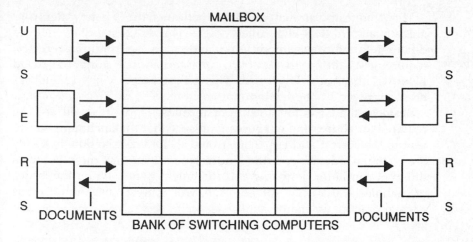

Figure 11.3   A value-added network

second is to make use of a third party which provides store and forward capabilities. The role of the third party is similar to that of a post office. The service provided is called a value-added network (VAN).

The principle of a value-added network is outlined in Figure 11.3. Using direct connections is only practical when the number of participants is relatively small and is relatively stable.

The VAN solution will therefore become the most common one, and more and more software packages are becoming available which will make the technical implementation and use of EDI relatively simple.

For many companies, how to implement and use EDI in the best possible way will be a more difficult problem to solve, and aspects such as analysing the business requirements, as well as overcoming resistence to change, will have to be tackled.

Another important issue which has to be further solved before EDI will take off in full flight is the issue of standards. When using EDI, the format of the data has to be precisely defined for example, the first three characters define the type of document; the next eight characters contain the document number; the next six characters contain the date and so on. Initially, each group of companies which started to use EDI developed their own set of formats and there are now a number of different approaches in use which are virtually incompatible.

The American National Standard Institute (ANSI) is now developing a standard for EDI called X.12. The X.12 standard defines different EDI formats for different industries, as trading and legal requirements differ. In addition, an international standard, called EDIFACT, has been developed. This is based on ANSI X.12 and has been approved by the United Nations.

Besides standards for document formats, standards will also be required for addressing purposes to ensure that the document will be sent to the correct address. The strongest candidate to date is X.400, the standard developed for addressing electronic mail between different computer networks and mailing systems. When the issues of standards are fully solved, EDI will almost certainly become normal practice for many companies.

Part V

DESIGNING AND MANAGING THE PHYSICAL INFRASTRUCTURE OF LOGISTICS

Overview to Part V

In this part Gerry Hatton provides a series of comprehensive guidelines for designing and developing logistics facilities. In Chapter 12 he draws on many years of industry experience to provide a methodology for approaching the design of a warehouse or distribution centre.

In Chapter 13 Hatton describes the methods of analysis and outlines some of the alternatives that should be considered when choosing materials handling systems so as to optimize available cube in warehouse and distribution facilities. He details the characteristics, advantages and disadvantages of a wide range of materials handling equipment currently available.

Chapter 14 describes the various alternatives available for storing product, whether in unitized loads or loose form. Hatton details the benefits, drawbacks and typical applications for each storage type.

Having stored the product, Hatton devotes Chapter 15 to discussing the alternatives available for picking product from stock. Again, he draws on extensive experience in the design and development of major order picking systems across a wide range of industries. This chapter will prove of great benefit to any logistics manager faced with designing an order picking operation for his organization.

In Chapter 16 Hatton succinctly outlines the key considerations for cost-efficient warehouse design. Of vital importance is Hatton's warning that the total cost, including operating costs must be considered when choosing between available alternatives.

Finally, in Chapter 17, Campbell provides an operational perspective for effectively managing a logistics facility. Like so many successful logistics managers, Campbell emphasizes the role of the people who operate the facility in producing desired outcomes. This reinforces the view that technological sophistication cannot by itself provide competitive advantage.

12 Designing a Warehouse or Distribution Centre

Gerry Hatton

Introduction

The warehouse or distribution centre plays a key role in an organization's logistical strategy. It is usually the point at which the organization succeeds or fails in fulfilling the sales and marketing promise. Whereas sophisticated management and technology have been freely applied in manufacturing, marketing and finance, warehousing and distribution is, for most companies, the last frontier of opportunity for truly significant improvement.

Properly designed, planned, organized and managed, a distribution centre can offer higher levels of service with lower inventory and lower costs. This not only improves profitability and increases the competitive edge, it also allows an organization to win market share by offering an improved level of service.

This critical strategic role of the distribution centre in the organization's overall performance merely underlines the importance of developing the best and most cost-effective system. Unfortunately what is best and most cost-effective varies hugely from place to place. Different land, buildings, labour and transport costs change the equation: and the number of line items, the throughput rates, the methods of infeed and outfeed all significantly alter the design. There are, therefore, no standard answers. The proper design of a system requires very specialized knowledge and input, usually from several different skill areas.

Clearly, in the pages that follow we will not be able to examine all of the options in detail. What we can do, however, is to understand the general design approach so that the reader can obtain the most appropriate design working in conjunction with others on the project team.

175

The role of the warehouse and when does it become a distribution centre?

A warehouse is so named since its original purpose was a building which stored wares or goods. These days management has recognized that the best logistical answer is much more complicated than that: indeed, just-in-time (JIT) techniques are significantly reducing the storage task. We therefore prefer to talk in terms of a distribution centre which is more descriptive of its purpose.

Whilst, to some degree, the difference is semantic, it also represents an attitude of mind. What we need here is to build an image of a facility where goods are constantly moving towards their ultimate destination, thereby minimizing storage and its attendant costs.

The principal functions that take place are:

- *Receiving*: often including functions like quality and quantity checks;
- *Storing*: with the attendant task of moving goods from receiving to the storage location;
- *Order picking*: which often also includes transportation from storage to an order picking location and other tasks like further checking and packing;
- *Despatch*: which often includes staging or interim storage.

As can be seen, most of the functions are indeed concerned with movement. In fact when all costs, other than the cost of inventory, are taken into account the cost of storage alone would ordinarily only fall between 20 per cent and 30 per cent of all costs where orders are picked in cartons and less than carton lots.

Clearly, therefore, it is an important part of our thinking to do away with the concept of static storage in a warehouse and to move towards the concept of a distribution centre.

Optimizing the operational pressures

Our distribution centre is being pressed from all sides and has to resolve these conflicting pressures.

- *The finance director* would like minimum investment in inventory and distribution centre facilities plus minimum operating costs.
- *The buyer or the manufacturing manager* would like to supply the fewest number of line items in the largest possible quantities with minimum frequency.

- *The sales and marketing manager* would like the widest range of inventory, all available ex-stock, with instant delivery, in any quantity that the client might request.

Each of these wishes would satisfy the needs of one department but of course all of them are, within themselves, contrary to the needs of the organization. It is no part of these chapters to talk about the resolution of these pressures, but it is important that the system designer should understand them and ensure that they are resolved before design commences.

The location and the number of distribution centres

Here again, conflicting demands have to be resolved. There are clearly benefits in having the distribution centres adjacent to each of the principal markets: however, the purchasing costs and the cost of shipping goods may well be significantly lower if they are located nearer to the source or sources of supply. In a business which manufactures its own products this is usually directly adjacent to manufacturing.

As the number of distribution centres required to service a given number of markets is increased, so is the cost of inventory – and the overall cost of the distribution centres escalates.

Unfortunately, it is usual for the overall service level, in terms of the number of line items available, to fall as the number of distribution centres rises since it is rarely possible to hold sufficient stock of each line item in each distribution centre. On the other hand, smaller facilities, adjacent to the market, can often offer a faster delivery and a lower overall freight cost.

Measuring and resolving these issues is a science in itself. It is no part of these chapters to describe that process, only to make the designer aware of the issues. In general terms, however, there has been a pronounced move in recent years to fewer, better managed, better organized and more mechanized distribution centres.

Fewer distribution centres permit better-quality management, sophisticated computer and administrative services, higher levels of mechanization and lower overall investment – all of which conspire to result in an overall lower cost and a higher service level. The huge improvement in overnight parcel delivery services, with their own high levels of mechanization, freight consolidation and sophisticated control, has reinforced this trend.

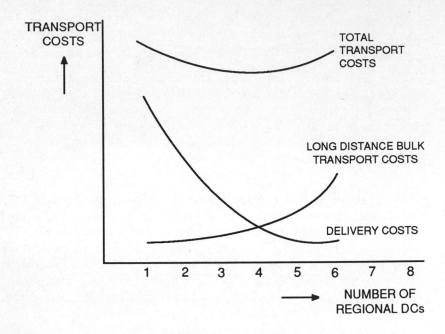

Figure 12.1   How total transport costs vary with the number of regional distribution centres

Designing the distribution centre

Once the ideal number of distribution centres has been resolved, a general location selected, and the market that it has to serve determined, we can commence the task of designing the facility.

The five elements of the system

We should at all times bear in mind that we are designing a sophisticated system, the elements of which are interdependent and comprise:

- land and building,
- management and staff,
- equipment,
- computer and its software,
- operating methods and procedures.

There is little point in considering any one of these elements on its

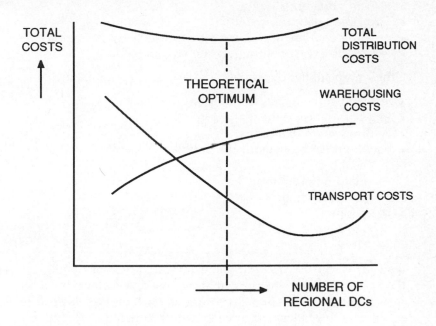

Figure 12.2   How total distribution costs vary with the number of regional distribution centres

own for its cost may directly affect other costs and, therefore prevent an overall optimum solution. For example, an inexpensive piece of land that results in high building costs may be no saving at all: low equipment costs which increase the number of people required may not be cost-effective, and so on.

How, then, do we know where to start? Well, the answers in each area are usually determined by the tasks and the constraints! We will therefore examine each of these separately.

Constraints

Although it is usual to hear designers complaining about constraints that are applied to them, it could be said that constraints make design easier by eliminating some of the options. It is for this reason that they should be identified first. Identifying the constraints is often not easy; some are self-evident, others more nebulous. Typical self-evident constraints include:

- existing land,

- existing buildings,
- available finance,
- existing equipment that must be re-used,
- return-on-investment requirements and so on.

Other more subtle, but equally important, constraints include:

- existing software,
- the preference of the management,
- staff or union objections,
- Government regulations, including
  - health and safety,
  - building ordinances,
  - fire protection,
  - parking,
  - plot ratios, and
  - street access.

Nowadays, the views of our domestic and industrial neighbours as to the hours we work, the noise that we make, the views we block and the sunlight that we cut out are often important. Possible future uses of the building, its smart appearance or imposing presentation are, for some companies, important internal constraints.

Determining the task

Data collection

Data collection and analysis is the most difficult and time-consuming element of the task of designing a distribution centre and its facilities, even for the most experienced designer. It requires considerable skill to know what data to collect and how. Generally speaking, the task of data collection and analysis and establishing the design level takes two-thirds of the total time necessary to design the facility.

The reason for the difficulty is that data exists in different forms in every organization. To make matters more complex the data required varies from operation to operation and then varies again depending upon the design solutions which are likely to be used. The larger the product range and the more complex the order profile, then the larger and more complex is the data collection phase of the project. For example, a manufacturer with 100 or 200 line items which are largely sold in full pallet quantities or in a limited range of standard carton sizes is a relatively simple data collection task. On the other hand, a company selling hardware or motor vehicle spare parts may well have between 20,000 and 120,000 line items which may sell in pallet lots, full carton quantities and individual line items. They may have large stock orders for regional distribution centres and rush orders for spares, and of course they will have a large variety of different-sized items.

An example of the way in which the data required varies with the possible design solution is determining whether or not products are conveyable. Checking out a large product range, determining those that are certainly conveyable, probably conveyable and certainly not conveyable is a time-consuming task. It is only relevant if the final design solution includes the option of conveying the goods without their being placed in a tote bin or other conveyable container.

Data collection by function

In almost all circumstances we need to know:

1   How goods are received and in what volume. How are they to be stored and put away – and at what rates and volumes?
2   How many lines are kept in stock (these are called stock-keeping units or SKUs) and what are the physical characteristics of each SKU to be stored and handled?
3   What volume of goods have to be stored in each of the sub-groups that emerge from (2) above and in any other division or family group?
4   What are typical order profiles (broken down into division and family groups or other sub-groups defined in (2) above)? Must orders be checked and/or repacked? What is the work content and physical volume to be handled in each task area?
5   Must goods be staged if they can be direct-loaded? What type and quantity of vehicles have to be accommodated, loaded and despatched?
6   What effect do days of the week or month or other seasonality factors have on the throughputs and inventory levels?

The designer must think through precisely what data is needed in each area in order that the volume and throughput rates can be defined by each SKU group. Whilst in general terms this means measuring the cube of the inventory for storage, and the unit 'movement rates' for receiving, order picking and despatch, there are

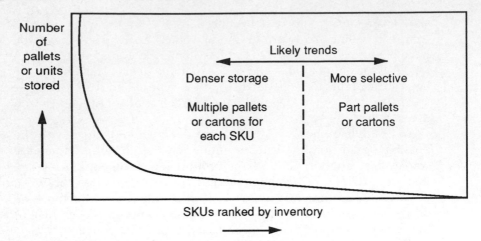

Figure 12.3   Typical product quantity graph

no standard businesses and therefore no standard methods and answers that will apply for all businesses.

However, there are two basic data collection tasks that, in one form or another, almost always apply.

Product quantity analysis

The efficient compromise between storage/access extremes can significantly reduce storage costs and handling expenses. These compromises can only be made after proper analysis of goods to be stored and the rates at which they have to move through the warehouse. In this regard, compilation of ranked product quantity and ranked product movement rate data is invaluable. For clarity we shall discuss this data in graph format.

The product quantity (PQ) graph in Figure 12.3 shows the number of pallets or units to be stored in each line. It shows at a glance how dense or selective the storage system can be. This information, combined with the total quantity of pallets or units to be stored, is a quick and accurate guide in the selection of storage systems.

Product movement analysis

A product movement graph as illustrated by Figure 12.4 shows the rate at which each product line moves through the warehouse with

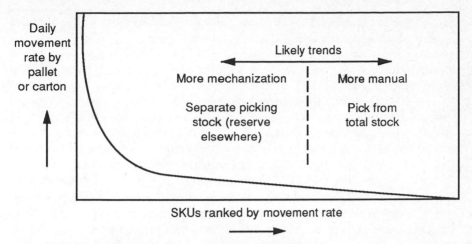

Figure 12.4 Typical product movement graph

indications of whether they move out in carton or pallet lots. This is a further guide to the selection of the storage system and a positive guide to the selection of the most appropriate handling equipment and, in particular, the order picking system.

In a small operation this information can be observed and/or gathered manually. As the size and complexity of the task grows, the only practical way is to collect information from the computer and/or to convert it to machine-readable form. If this is done then here are some notes that will give you some guidance on how to access and reorganize the data.

The use of a computer for data collection and analysis

It is the availability of a database in machine-readable form from which one can obtain the required information that has made much more sophisticated design possible. Computers are an ideal tool for collecting data and then massaging it into a useful format.

Unfortunately, as has been said earlier, not all computer systems store the information requested above and, when they do, it is often in a different format. For example, many companies keep details of product movement by value or some other measurement. One example is the number of litres sold in, say, the paint industry. Whilst this is useful for financial control or for manufacturing planning and scheduling, it is not useful for measuring the storage and inventory movement task. It is therefore frequently necessary to work out some form of conversion.

Few companies have all of the information necessary in the product master file concerning the nature of each product. This data includes carton sizes, cartons per pallet, sales units per carton and other relatively static information. (A sample from a product master file is shown in Figure 12.5). In some industries this changes at a relatively rapid rate and, in these cases, companies are rarely prepared to invest the time and effort in keeping the product master file up-to-date. This is especially so if there is a large and diverse product range.

However, if the designer is contemplating a sophisticated design, and particularly if a high level of mechanization is planned, then this information is essential. Often, therefore, the designer is faced with weeks of work in building a database before design can commence.

Even in the best organized operation, information on most matters like movement rates or inventory level will rarely be in a convenient form. It is therefore necessary to write special programmes to summarize the data in a useful way. Many organizations which are constantly involved in the design of facilities have written software to do this.

It is therefore much easier to use the services of someone skilled in analysing data than to go through the learning curve of developing special software for a one-off application. Moreover, experienced system designers know what to collect and learn short-cut methods of collecting data or converting inappropriate data into a useful form.

Divisions and family groups

The question of determining the division under which each product is handled is only relevant in certain instances. In some cases companies have orders placed quite separately: for example, the wine and spirits division of a supermarket chain quite frequently takes the orders separately and stores and picks them separately from, say, non-food products.

Similarly, the issue of family groups is sometimes very important. Again in supermarkets, it is usual to keep paper products together and pick them separately from, say, food items. This is because, when the goods are delivered, the task of feeding them to the supermarket shelves is hugely simplified if each family group is in some way kept separate. In other cases, family groups require different storage – for example inflammable goods, products requiring special security and goods requiring a temperature-controlled environment.

From this information it will be possible to compile a summary of

Product Code	Description	Family Group	Carton Dimensions (mm) L	W	H	Wt	Ctns /Plt	Inventory Pallets	Full/ Split Case	Units /Ctn	Hits /Day	Ctns /Day
63792	Baked Beans 250g	A	614	205	205	11.2	48	40	F	24	211.4	327.2
71874	Spaghetti 250g	A	585	220	190	9.8	54	34	F	12	197.2	244.5
61636	Plum Jam 125g	A	570	210	185	9.9	40	38	F	12	201.2	231.6
52811	Paper Towels 4pk	C	685	685	420	2.1	64	52	S	6	84.2	191.1
49962	Baby Powder 125g	D	572	196	175	6.2	64	21	F/S	24	278.4	184.2
65482	Custard Van 1lt	C	310	232	285	15.0	52	82	F	32	164.8	228.3
52463	Drink Orange 2lt	B	450	251	300	12.3	80	32	S	12	150.4	312.5
48592	Butter Home 250g	B	328	200	160	8.9	100	25	F/S	24	80.9	120.5

Figure 12.5 Sample from a product master file

most of the data that is required for design purposes. What will be required and the way in which this can be done will vary so much from business to business that these pages can provide only the most general guidance.

Split-case and full-case items

In many companies, products exist in several pack types. For example, they frequently have a large shipper which contains a number of cartons, each of which might contain 100 units. Within this carton there are inner cartons in packs of, say, 10 and of course within each carton there are 10 individual units.

In these circumstances it is important to identify the pack sizes and types in which goods are sold. Frequently, computer information presents only the number of units sold, whereas in the distribution centre we are concerned with the number of shippers, outers, inners or units handled. We must therefore, in each case, determine a methodology of recognizing each order and separating it into the pack types in which they are likely to be picked.

Simplified analysis for complex product ranges

In some instances the product range is so large and complex, with different pack types and different order types, that the analysis described above is simply not cost-effective. We must remember that any analysis that is done is only a 'snapshot' of the way things were at the time that the data was analysed. Since pack types, order quantities, movement rates and order profiles vary over time, care should be taken not to spend an inordinate time analysing a very complex product range only to find that by the time analysis is finished it has changed sufficiently to make the work done not totally relevant.

When the task of using a computer to determine the quantity of inventory and its cube is too complicated it is better to use an approximate method. Bear in mind that the larger the product range usually the more uneven is the distribution of movement.

Whilst Pareto's analysis shows that, on average, 80 per cent of the movement comes from 20 per cent of the line items, in spare parts for example this frequently becomes 90 per cent of the movement coming from 10 per cent of the line items. When this technique is combined with detailed analysis of faster-moving line items, then a moderately accurate database can be compiled in a fraction of the time. (Figure 12.6)

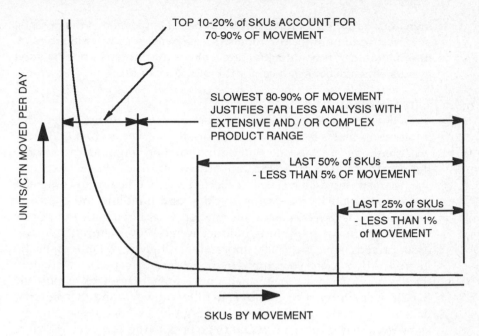

Figure 12.6 Typical Pareto analysis

Summarizing the data

Obviously with anything but the simplest product range, the results of the above analysis in their fullest form are totally incomprehensible. It is therefore very important that the data be broken down into useful sub-groups and massaged in a way that it becomes understandable. For example, breaking down a product range by family groups and then by pack types within each family group leaves a manageable list of information.

Within each of these sub-groups it is then important that we should massage the data into an even more understandable format. Here one of the most useful techniques is using the computer to rank the product range. In many instances it is necessary to rank the information regarding each product in different ways for different elements of the design task.

For example, when designing an order picking system we may rank the goods by movement rate, taking the number of picks or the number of hits (accesses to a given line item) per day. On the other hand, for the storage task we may rank it by the number of cartons stored or, if we have sufficient information, we might cube the inventory and then rank it by the number of cubic metres of goods to be stored or the number of pallets. In this way, a very wide range of information can be gradually consolidated into understandable sub-groups which become critical for the purposes of designing a system.

Extra information

It is almost impossible to know before one starts the analysis all of the information that will be required before the design is completed. As was mentioned earlier, the type of information required varies with the design solution proposed.

Once all of the data has been collected and one begins to contemplate the alternatives for storing, picking and handling the goods, it frequently emerges that extra information is required concerning one product group or the entire product range. For example, average order profiles may give a false impression. Often a few large clients or internal orders to the company's own distribution centres may distort the average of many other small local orders. One may choose to handle such different-sized orders in different ways, and this requires data on the order profile of each sub-group. Under these circumstances there is no alternative but to go back to the raw data and start again or, if the data does not exist, to go out and create a database.

Establishing the design level

All of the data and all of the information analysed and massaged so far is historic. Of course the distribution centre has to deal not with the past but with the future. Accordingly it is necessary to determine what is to be the design level.

Here one should consult with the Sales and Marketing Departments, and perhaps Manufacturing or Purchasing. We should determine the likely growth in the number of line items and the expected growth in sales. Of course a growth in sales is unlikely to occur evenly over the entire product range so that different growth factors may have to be collected for each sub-group.

We should concurrently determine for what year we are designing the facility. It would be rare to design a facility for less than five years after start-up and, in some instances, we may want to design it for 10 years hence. It is worth remembering that if a new facility is involved or a high level of mechanization is planned, then start-up may well be one or two years away so that a design level of five years after start-up has to take into account seven years of growth from the current figures.

The development of alternative concepts

Now the task has been clearly determined and the constraints established it is possible to begin the, perhaps more exciting, task of designing the facility. Here it is important that experienced system designers should be involved. Today there is a huge range of equipment on the market and a very wide range of options for the handling of each task. More importantly, the integration of the various elements requires considerable skill.

As a rule-of-thumb, one should establish at least two, and preferably three, alternative designs. It is suggested that these should include:

1   a simple conventional system;
2   a system with a medium level of mechanization;
3   a system with a high level of mechanization and technology.

It should always be borne in mind that any one design approach is rarely applicable for the entire product range. More mechanization can often only be justified for the faster-moving line items. Dense, non-selective storage systems almost always need supplementing with selective systems for items with a low inventory.

Of course, with a wide product range, this may mean that there are many designs for the total system: for example, we may want to develop three designs for each division or major family group. Since these can be put together in a total facility in a variety of different ways, a wide range of options results.

An experienced designer can eliminate some options without analysis, because he will know from experience that, for a given throughput or a given type of product, certain methods of storage and handling are inappropriate or cannot be cost-justified. Using this experience to reduce the number of options obviously greatly simplifies the task.

At this stage we should bear in mind that we are not in this phase trying to comprehensively design a system – we are only trying to eliminate options. There is therefore little point in designing each sub-element in any great detail. On the other hand, the design needs to be sufficiently accurate to ensure that it can accommodate the range of inventory and the required throughput without making it larger or smaller and more or less expensive than it needs to be.

Once the task has been defined, site visits to comparable facilities are valuable. Only now will the designer be able to ask appropriate questions as to capacity, throughput and so on and be able to understand the answers in relation to his own tasks.

Nor should we forget the effects of compound growth. A 5 per cent annual growth rate for five years is not 25 per cent more since the growth in each succeeding year is based on a higher level than the previous year. In this way, over several years, quite significant growth levels can occur.

On the other hand, we may need to stage the growth of the facility in terms of storage and throughput capacity. Often it may be more practical to work overtime or extra shifts to cope with seasonal peaks than to provide sufficient throughput capacity on a single shift.

As can be seen, the setting of an agreed design level is an important task that requires senior management input.

The final database report

When all of the above data has been collected, massaged, analysed and summarized, it should be put into a database report which clearly depicts the existing task and projects the future task. Special emphasis should be given on the level of the design that has been selected with some notes as to why this level was chosen. This report should be widely circulated to all of those involved in establishing the design level. Clearly, setting a design level for 10 years hence, with a 10 per cent annual growth rate based on the highest sales that occur in the peak period of a seasonal business can result in a facility which is many times larger than that initially necessary. Under such circumstances, phased construction should be planned.

It is very important that we have a clear database summary which accurately reflects a wide consensus, since the implications for the organization are significant.

Budget costing

Once these preliminary designs have been completed, each sub-element should be budget-costed. One should budget all of the elements of the system, including the land, the building, the equipment (including fire protection costs) and the computer and software. In this way the total capital cost of each alternative can be determined.

Next, it is important to establish the annual operating cost. Here various manning levels and total costs need to be established which is best done in conjunction with experienced designers. Depreciation and other costs like heating or cooling (especially in a temperature-controlled facility), local government charges, insurance and so on also have to be calculated.

Once the capital and operating costs have been budget-estimated, it is worth making a summary of the qualitative issues, subdividing them into perceived advantages and disadvantages. Here such issues as durability, expandability, adaptability, simplicity and so on need to be considered. Once this has been done a report can be presented which contains the range of options.

Selecting the preferred option

Here once more we want to involve all of those people involved in the final decision, particularly those who have to operate the system. If they are involved in the decision as to what is appropriate at this stage, they are likely to support that decision and try hard to make it work. Without their support the system will certainly fail to realize its potential.

Return-on-investment calculations can be done in accordance with the company's policy on such matters: however, these calculations themselves cannot make a selection, since they take no account of such matters as risk and the company's strategic plans for example.

Of equal importance is the fact that there is no return on investment on a great many aspects. For example, if the company wishes to store more inventory, then it is simply going to cost more. The return-on-investment calculation, therefore, should be to justify the difference in cost between one storage and handling method and another, and not the total cost.

In some cases no return-on-investment calculations can be done at all. For instance, if it is necessary to weigh goods as part of a new procedure, the cost of appropriate scales will be incurred and no savings are available to justify this cost.

It should be borne in mind that such calculations make assumptions on inflation, manning costs, manning levels, the life of the equipment and so on which may prove not to be totally accurate: thus, the budget may not be accurate.

More importantly, the decision as to what solution best suits the company should be determined by reasons other than cost alone. For example, the company may wish to embrace a high level of technology to give them a marketing edge or to maintain a particular image in the marketplace. These are matters of company management style and part of the company's overall strategy, which cannot be determined by simple financial analysis alone.

Working as a group, the design team and the management should select that option or those combinations of options which best suit their needs. Incidentally, it is at this stage that most benefit is gained by visiting other sites – if necessary – for a second time. When the designers have carefully considered the options that may be applied to their task, it is valuable to see how they work elsewhere before making a decision.

Developing the selected design option

Finally, it is then possible to expand upon the basic designs, fully develop them and finally specify them in order to begin the exciting task of implementing the project.

It should be remembered that the more complex the system, the more detailed should be the design and specification. Calling tenders or a loosely specified complex system will result in offers that cannot reasonably be compared and may or may not meet performance requirements.

The management system

Operating methods, procedures and software

At the beginning of this chapter emphasis was placed on the interdependence of the following five elements:

- land and building,
- management and staff,
- storage and handling equipment,
- computer and its software,
- operating methods and procedures.

So far we have only discussed the physical elements, but this in no way should undermine the critical importance of redesigning the last two elements which constitute the management system. In existing operations, such systems have often been developed piecemeal over the years and most people give them little thought. However, no sophisticated distribution centre can operate effectively without a good management system any more than a road system can operate without signals, signs and a highway code.

Ideally, the management system needs to be developed by the people who are going to operate the system. If these people do not understand the system, if they do not believe in it and if they do not support it then it simply will not work.

The more mechanized the new system, the more different and more important will be a new management system (just as properly controlling a busy airport is more critical than controlling the transportation system of a century ago).

When the design of the physical system is almost complete, work should start on the design of the management system. This typically takes as long to do and implement as does building the physical facility – often longer if significant new software is required. There are no more standard answers here than in the physical system and its proper design is an equally important and parallel task.

13 Materials Handling

Gerry Hatton

Materials handling options: techniques and alternatives

In the last several years materials handling has become a new, complex, rapidly evolving science. A huge range of new techniques, devices and machines has been introduced, and different methods have been developed for handling different products. In these pages it will not be possible to dwell on all of the special materials handling devices available: instead we shall concentrate on discussing the more common items which handle tote bins, cartons or palletized goods. Space permits only a brief reference to the handling of long items, sheets and other difficult material.

Any type of goods movement that is performed more than a few times per hour is worth mechanizing. The higher the volume, the greater the advantage that can be gained by mechanization. However, determining which system is appropriate is not easy. When only the cost of transportation is taken into account, the number of loads and the distance over which they have to be carried determines the correct economic solution. Because there are so many materials handling solutions it is easy to get lost in the variables and lose sight of the principles but, in fact, for the common carton there are only four basic handling methods. Each has its particular role and the designer should be careful to correctly apply each method to an appropriate application.

Each method will be discussed in turn before examining them in detail.

Manual
From the beginning of time man has moved materials by hand. In many cases it is still relevant. Man can lift, lower, turn, stack and unstack cartons or components as well as move them. He can also

process the goods at the same time. If the volume to be handled is low and the travel distance is small we have still not developed a machine to replace the versatility of man.

But he is not a machine and these days he is too valuable to perform simple transportation of anything but the smallest quantity over the smallest distance.

Trolleys

The simple wheel was the next step in improving handling and it still has wide application today. Hand trolleys are relatively small and slow so they are really only efficient with small volumes over short distances. Motorized trolleys like tow trains, conveyor towed trolleys and automated guided vehicles (AGVs) can carry multiple unit loads over long distances with relatively low labour costs.

With moderate volumes of unit loads over a long distance these savings can sometimes offset the higher capital cost and the cost of loading and unloading and make motorized trolleys more economic than forklift trucks.

Forklift trucks

The forklift truck – and with it the introduction of pallet or unit loads – was a major materials movement breakthrough. Now there are many types and they have rightly been accepted as an excellent universal handling machine. Their main advantage is that, as well as transporting material, they can load and unload other vehicles and lift pallet loads up high for storage.

Nevertheless, as a transportation device, the forklift has a few disadvantages: for example, even if each product is of sufficient volume to justify a pallet load, the cost of building and dismantling the pallet will still be incurred, unless it is received and shipped in pallet load quantities. Forklifts also require large aisles, and handling costs will increase as throughput volumes rise.

Conveyors

Conveyors excel at straightforward transportation because they eliminate rehandling before and after each function. These days they can also be loaded and unloaded automatically. They have the advantage of being able to deliver or take away a carton, a work tote or a unit load as it becomes available. No extra labour is needed but the cost increases with the distance to be travelled. Generally speaking, this

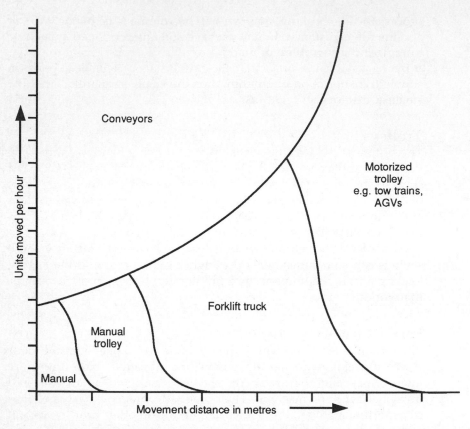

Figure 13.1   Comparison of handling technologies

makes them more appropriate for high-volume throughputs over shorter distances.

Another major reason why conveyors are replacing traditional handling methods is that they can do far more than simply transport goods so that their application is even wider than the graph in Figure 13.1 would suggest.

Criteria for the selection of a handling system

When only the cost of transportation is taken into account, the number of loads and the distance they have to be transported determines the correct economic solution. The graph in Figure 13.1 illustrates approximately where each of the basic handling techniques is appropriate. For instance, if there is a moderately high volume of goods moved regularly over a short or medium distance, then a conveyor is the most economic method. Forklift trucks are generally more cost-effective with a moderate volume over a moderate distance.

However, to consider transportation only is to include only part of the cost. The cost of building and dismantling a load should also be taken into account, as should the space required and such issues as damage, reliability and flexibility. Perhaps the most important issue is that it is very rare that the goods are transported only once. One should therefore bear in mind costs of staging, moving forward, load-building and unbuilding which take place before and after each process.

A more detailed look at the major handling devices for cartons and unit loads

Trolleys
Trolleys were the earliest materials handling device using the wheel to make man's efforts more effective.

Manual trolleys
Even today, manual trolleys still have their place. If a relatively low number of heavy items need to be conveyed over a moderate distance, they are still cost-effective. For example, if, say, 20 cartons had to be shipped 15 metres every hour, some being picked up and dropped off at different places in a small operation or in a small part of a large operation, then a manual trolley would still be appropriate.

They come in a variety of forms to suit different goods. Special frameworks and additional shelves are easy to add: larger wheels and better bearings make trolleys easier to push and handle.

Roll pallets
One form of trolley that has found wide application in the last several years is a roll pallet. This is in fact a combination of trolley and pallet. Its major benefit over a pallet is that it can be handled to and from vehicles without the use of a forklift truck.

Its widest application is in delivering goods to retail outlets where mechanized handling equipment is rarely available. However, the concept has many other applications: for example, security versions with lockable gates can be used for the delivery of valuable goods, drugs and other such items.

Motorized trolleys

As the volume of goods and/or the distance to be travelled increases so does the argument for mechanizing the trolley. There is a very wide range of mechanized trolleys available: some carry the operator, some require the operator to walk in front or behind. Clearly, the greater the distance that has to be travelled, the greater the argument for the machine to carry the operator to reduce fatigue and to increase efficiency.

The serious disadvantages of trolleys are that they have to be loaded at the pick-up point and unloaded at the drop-off point. This problem is usually overcome by using a pallet mover which is the most common mechanized device for moving goods to or from transport or storage where there is no lifting involved.

Tow trains

As the number of unit loads to be handled increases and the distance over which they must be transported increases, then the number of powered units and the number of operators required can be reduced by using a tow train. Under this arrangement one powered vehicle is able to tow, say, four or six tracking trailers, each carrying one or more pallets or unit loads.

Clearly, these vehicles also have to be loaded and unloaded, a cost which must be offset by the saving in transportation.

If there are a limited number of pick up and drop off points, loading and unloading can be done automatically: however, this means further costs of power-fed rollers on the trolley and at pick-up and deposit stations. This can be done automatically if there are high volumes involved: more often it is done using a forklift truck. Here care should be taken to ensure that the task of loading and unloading and the intermittent nature of those tasks does not involve an overall higher cost than having fast forklift trucks do the lifting and the transportation.

Forklift trucks have the advantage that they can retrieve the load initially and put it away at the delivery point. Clearly, therefore, quite considerable distances have to be involved before tow trains are appropriate.

Driverless trolleys

To further minimize labour, a number of driverless trolleys have been developed over the years. In the early days the most common type was that towed by an overhead or in-ground conveyor. This had the advantage that trolleys could be fed on to or off the line at numerous points, making it more flexible than a tow train. Later versions were developed which permitted loads to be discharged or diverted at the required points by simple preprogramming methods.

In-floor tow lines of this nature were popular in the 1960s and 1970s for taking goods from receipt to various parts of a large distribution centre where they could be fed into storage. Indeed, such transportation methods are still frequently cost-effective where the high cost of the conveyor is offset by the relatively low cost of the trolley.

Automatic guided vehicle systems (AGVs)

The disadvantage of conveyor tow trolleys is that they are relatively inflexible in layout and have a high start-up cost for the conveyor. In recent years great advances have been made in AGVs. These are battery electric vehicles which follow a predetermined track.

The tracks are determined electronically, either by setting coordinates and writing software to determine the track between certain feedback points, or more usually by following a wire laid in a small slot cut in the concrete slab. With this method, whilst there is a relatively high cost per AGV, the track cost is quite low. As for in-floor conveyors, it is possible to join the line at various points and to have the AGVs drop off and stop at required points. On-board logic permits the vehicle to carry out a number of functions which extend its use and value.

One important consideration here is that it can become a driverless tow train pulling several unpowered trolleys each containing its own load. These can offset the cost of the AGVs and make the overall system more economic if the transportation task lends itself to this approach.

If automatic loading and unloading points are constructed, then it is possible to programme the AGV to index itself forward to receive and discharge loads to and from each trolley.

All of the motorized trolleys are most effective when there are relatively large distances to be travelled (say 50–500 metres) and where there are several pick-up and drop-off points. Naturally, at the same time there has to be sufficient volume to justify the capital cost.

The distances need to be large to ensure that it is not more economic to use a forklift truck and yet not so large as to ensure that road transport vehicles are appropriate.

Generally speaking AGVs are not appropriate for outdoor use so that, for medium distance, outdoor hauling tow trains are more common and as the distance increases it usually becomes more appropriate to use a road vehicle.

Forklift trucks

The forklift truck represented perhaps the greatest single innovation in materials handling in the post-war era and was largely responsible for the widespread introduction of pallets or unit loads. Many different types have been developed, and each has its specific role.

The main advantage of a forklift truck is that, as well as transporting material, it can pick up and put down, load and unload other vehicles and lift pallet loads up high to take advantage of the available headroom in a storage location. Since goods are frequently being moved from and/or to a storage location, it is often cost-effective to use a forklift truck for the transportation task where it would otherwise not be cost-effective.

Major types of forklift trucks
Straddle truck
These machines have two straddle legs which protrude in front of the body of the machine to give it stability when lifting. The straddle legs must either pass around the outside of the pallet or, if the pallet has an open base, they can pass underneath.

Straddle trucks are available with manual, battery electric and mains power movement and lift. Many are pedestrian-controlled but ride-on versions are to be preferred, especially when travelling any distance.

The straddle legs preclude the use of these machines on a loading dock. In fact they are generally difficult to use for loading or unloading in almost any circumstance since the straddle leg cannot avoid the vehicle wheels.

Whilst lift capacities of up to two tonnes are available, they are most often used for lighter loads and storage heights up to only five metres in distribution centres with a relatively low throughput rate. Operating aisles of a little over two metres are possible but allowance

Figure 13.2   Reach truck

should be made for the extra left-to-right clearance necessary because of the straddle legs. This often precludes their use in drive-in racks unless the straddle legs can be placed beneath the pallet.

Reach truck

Reach trucks are commonly available with lifts of up to two tonnes to a height of up to nine metres. Operating aisles with a 1200mm by 1200mm pallet need to be 2.4 metres to 2.9 metres depending on the machine type, the load size and the lift height.

A reach truck overcomes the disadvantages of a straddle truck by having a mechanism that reaches the load out beyond the end of the straddle legs. This is usually achieved by the entire mast sliding down the straddle legs or by a pantograph device fitted to the mast. These machines are almost always battery electric and are ideal for general-purpose work within the distribution centre. They are suitable for loading and unloading trucks and for moving to and from storage.

Because of the extra mechanism involved they are more expensive than straddle trucks and counter balanced forklift trucks and are usually used where their versatility and space conservation are important. In a racking system, straddle legs cause the loss of some vertical height which should be taken into account as the system is designed.

On some high-lift machines the wide straddles preclude the use of such machines for drive-in racking, especially if pallets narrower than the truck width are to be used.

Because of the extra operations involved, reach trucks are slower than other types of trucks and should not be used for transportation over long distances.

Counterbalanced forklift truck
This machine is available in a very wide range of capacities. Typically, in a distribution centre, it would have a capacity of around two tonnes and the ability to lift loads to around five metres. Several greater and lesser lift heights and capacities are available.

The machine maintains stability by a heavy counterweight set over the rear wheels. They are available in battery electric and internal combustion engine versions. They have a moderate cost and are the general all-purpose workhorse of many manufacturing and physical distribution facilities. They are good for loading and unloading vehicles and transporting over a distance.

Operating aisles are typically three metres through to four metres which is not consistent with good space utilization. However, if the order picking system requires that forklift trucks or operators should pass in the operating aisle, then an aisle of three metres will be required in any event. Under these circumstances some distribution centres, where fast movement is more important than space utilization, use counterbalanced forklift trucks for almost all of their pallet movement activities.

The great majority of counterbalanced forklift trucks have the man on board. A few pedestrian-operated versions are available for the slower-movement, shorter-travel applications.

Free-path narrow-aisle machines
The relatively wide aisles required by all previously described trucks are brought about by the need for the mast to be able to turn and stack at right angles. In recent years a number of machines have been developed where a separate device is fitted so that the load can be

rotated and stacked without the truck changing direction. These machines are often called turret trucks but many of them do not use a turret to rotate the pallet.

Narrow aisle trucks typically lift loads of up to two tonnes to heights up to 12 metres in aisles of around 1.6 metres to 1.9 metres. Their optimum operating range is with loads of around one tonne and heights of around nine metres. They are relatively fast within guided aisles. The larger machines are too large and too expensive to be used extensively outside the operating aisle. Such machines normally collect pallets from a specially designed pick-up and delivery (P&D) station at the end of each aisle.

In recent years new generations of narrow aisle trucks have lowered their cost and increased their flexibility. Some machines are able to load to the front and to the left and right. They are therefore able to load and unload trucks as well as place goods into storage in a narrow aisle.

Free-path, ultra-narrow aisle machines

The machines described above use forks to enter a pallet, even if it has boards across its base. The forks are fixed to a support framework which must be capable of rotating to face either way. This support mechanism necessitates an aisle some 500mm to 600mm wider than the pallet. The width of the aisle can be further reduced to only 200mm or 300mm more than the pallet by the use of traversing plattens instead of forks. Traversing plattens can be fitted to most types of narrow aisle machines with similar lift capacities and heights to those described above.

However, as the height increases the very narrow machines become unstable. This problem can be overcome by using a fixed-mast machine which, whilst free to transfer between the aisles, engages a top-steady rail when in the aisle.

These machines are amongst the fastest and most stable of the free-path narrow-aisle machines and are commonly used for lift heights of eight metres to 12 metres and more.

Rising cabs

As the lift height increases in the narrow aisles, pallet recognition becomes a problem so that many of the higher lifting machines have a rising cab. Some rise with the load and permit occasional order picking. Others rise independently only when required.

Many machines are fitted with automatic height selection devices

Figure 13.3   Narrow aisle truck

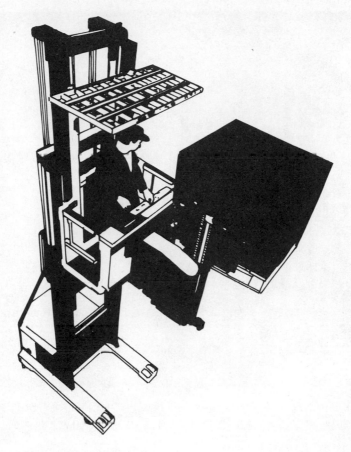

Figure 13.4   Rising cab forklift truck

and/or with closed circuit televisions which give the driver a close-up view of the forks and the pallet storage position.

Two-deep reach
Reach trucks, narrow-aisle trucks and stacker cranes can be fitted with a range of devices that allow them to reach beyond the first storage position to a second storage position. In this way pallets can be stored two-deep on either side of each aisle. Naturally the speed of operation and selectivity are reduced: load capacity and visibility are restricted and, often, the operating aisle is increased.

However there are applications where two-deep reach machines

Figure 13.5   Double reach mechanism allows pallets to be stored two deep – thus increasing capacity by 40%

offer a useful compromise between totally selective and non-selective storage.

Stacker cranes

Stacker cranes are driven by mains power. They operate on a fixed rail at the base and top of each aisle. They typically lift loads of around two tonnes to storage heights of around 20 metres. They are rarely economic below 15 metres. Some machines have been constructed with lift heights of around 30 metres. The operating aisle can be as little as 200mm or 300mm wider than the pallet.

Stacker cranes are very fast in their travel and lift, and it is now relatively economic to operate them automatically. On man-aboard machines the operator normally travels adjacent to the load.

The cranes collect the pallets from pick-up and delivery stations which are used to accurately position and square the pallet. Most installations have one machine per aisle but it is possible to transfer machines between aisles on a specially designed transfer car which is usually constructed in a seven metre-wide aisle at the rear of the pallet storage installation.

Since stacker crane installations typically store more than 1,000 pallets in each aisle, they are generally only used for large installations.

Conveyors

Conveyors excel at straightforward transportation because they eliminate rehandling before and after each function. Nowadays, they can even be loaded and unloaded automatically. It is meeting this need of causing the materials to flow, as opposed to being independently transported from time to time, that separates conveyors from the other handling techniques.

The use of conveyors to achieve lower handling costs and constant flow rather than intermittent movement has grown exponentially in the developed industrial countries in the last few years. It therefore represents perhaps the greatest single opportunity for improvement in materials handling in most distribution centres and factories.

Another major reason why conveyors are replacing traditional handling methods is that they can do far more than simply transport goods: thus their application is even wider than Figure 13.1 (p. 196) would suggest. The other ways in which conveyors can lower the total materials movement cost is therefore examined below.

Capability of conveyors

Conveyors join processes together; they deliver and take away goods automatically, and on cue. They can store goods until the next person or machine wants them; they can sort out goods, or merge them intelligently.

Conveyors of various types – belts, rollers, wheels and chains – have been around for a long time. They can work horizontally,

Figure 13.6   Typical stacker crane

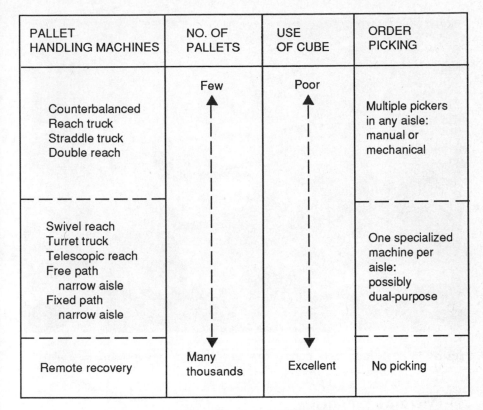

PALLET HANDLING MACHINES	NO. OF PALLETS	USE OF CUBE	ORDER PICKING
	Few ↑	Poor ↑	
Counterbalanced Reach truck Straddle truck Double reach	⋮	⋮	Multiple pickers in any aisle: manual or mechanical
Swivel reach Turret truck Telescopic reach Free path narrow aisle Fixed path narrow aisle	⋮	⋮	One specialized machine per aisle: possibly dual-purpose
Remote recovery	Many thousands ↓	Excellent ↓	No picking

Figure 13.7   Summary of the use of pallet-handling machines

vertically, around corners, up and down inclines: usually they are electric, but often gravity (a very cheap source of power) plays a part.

The simplest and most widely used power conveyor is a belt sliding on a sheet metal bed, called a 'slider bed'. This is fine for most cartons and many other types of loads. But as loads increase, so does friction and eventually the belt must be supported on rollers – called 'belt on roller'. Even heavier loads, like pallets, can be carried on chains sliding in channelled tracks. If goods have to be merged, diverted, or accumulated, a powered roller or wheel conveyor is usually best. If cartons or totes have to be pushed on to or off the conveyor they slide sideways better on rollers than belts or wheels. Powered roller conveyors are usually driven from below by belts, padded chains or bands driven by a rotating shaft, called a 'line shaft'.

Figure 13.8   Slider bed conveyors are the most economical form of powered conveyor

Merging products

Different processes take different times to perform, so that it is often desirable to take the output from several sources and merge them before going on to the next step. For example, a single weighing and strapping station may accept the output from 10 packing benches. In some systems, goods can be sent into the main stream in a random mix, but in others the sequence and quantity must be predetermined.

For low-volume, random merging, an operator or a mechanical arm controlling the traffic from each conveyor is sufficient. If more precise control is needed, and as volumes rise, everything has to work very much faster, and so electronic 'policemen' are built into the lines to control the traffic. The potential of well designed systems is up to around 150 cartons per minute, or 2.5 per second.

Sorting goods

Merging lines to be more efficient often means that the goods have to be re-sorted. However, the number of outputs does not have to equal

Figure 13.9   Gravity roller conveyors on each side of a power roller conveyor are the key elements in this order pick system

the number of inputs. For example, four palletizers may be able to cope with 10 production lines, so 10 lines could merge into one and then be sorted four ways to give a flexible, economic system.

In a distribution centre or freight depot both in- and outbound goods can be sorted by type or destination. In packing areas, goods can be sorted to balance the workload between zones. In order picking, huge increases in human productivity can be achieved by 'batching' or picking many orders at the same time and sorting them later, mechanically.

Manual sortation

There are numerous levels of sortation mechanization available. Selection depends on volume and the number of sort destinations. In manual systems an operator has to recognize and remove products from a recirculating conveyor loop, or divert the product down a chute or another conveyor.

With anything up to a few thousand cartons and a few sorts per

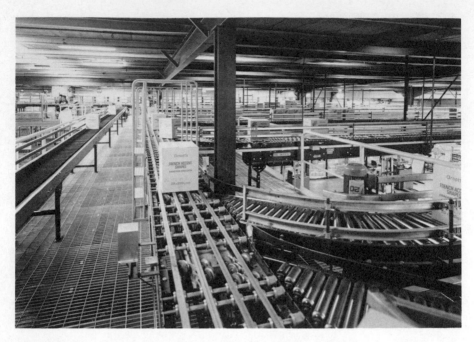

Figure 13.10   This high speed automatic sorter will divert up to 120 cases per minute

day, people can do a pretty good job, but as the volumes and the variables go up, the task gets tougher.

Automatic sortation

As volumes rise and the number of destinations grow, people can no longer cope and some level of mechanical sorting must be included. With medium volume and a few destinations, a simple tag or reflector can be used to direct the goods. As the volume and number of destinations rises, it becomes economic to use coding devices or to have an operator who recognizes the products and keys in their destination.

When this capacity has been exceeded, laser scanners can read barcoded information and pass it to the brains of the sorter – a programmable sort controller (PSC). The PSC can sort the goods according to preprogrammed instructions and pass on information to the distribution centre computer, providing precise control for shipping documentation, work balancing and inventory. Sorting systems

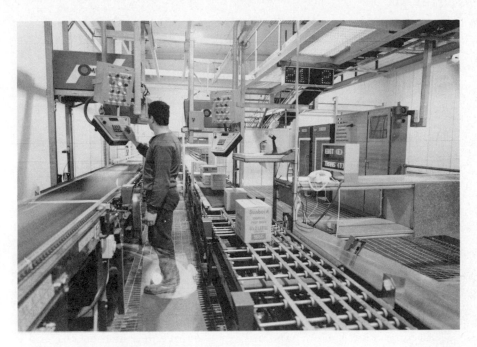

Figure 13.11   **Sophisticated computer controls track cartons accurately for high speed automatic sortation**

already in wide use can sort 20 ways or more and can cope with up to 150 cartons per minute.

Accumulation is the key to productivity

It is not often that goods can be fed from one process to another at a consistent rate to suit both processes, so good conveyor systems must be able to absorb surges in supply and demand by queuing or 'accumulating' goods to form a buffer between functions.

Imagine a barrier across the conveyor. This certainly accumulates the traffic, but pressure on the first carton increases as other cartons build up behind it. This 'line pressure' means that accumulation has to be well designed otherwise fragile cartons would crush and irregular items would jam or jack-knife right off the conveyor.

The first step is the minimum line pressure conveyor

There are many different types of conveyor that minimize this problem by reducing the drive. Each type has its applications

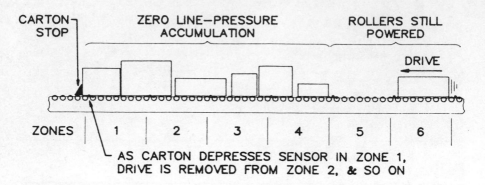

Figure 13.12　A zero-pressure accumulation conveyor

according to the speed and load. But these systems should not be used with irregular, fragile cartons or large volumes of standard cartons at high speed.

The zero-pressure accumulation conveyor

Modern high-speed conveyors demand a sophisticated built-in accumulation system. The answer was invented in the USA and it revolutionized materials handling by making conveyors infinitely more useful. Figure 13.12 shows how it works.

Sensor devices mounted in the conveyor at regular stages monitor the goods as they pass. If the first carton is stopped, the sensor disengages the drive from the section behind it, and so on. Thus the whole line behind is safely halted by stopping any particular carton. As the first carton moves off again, so too will the second, and the third, and so on. As one function becomes overburdened, goods simply wait until they are required. Surges in productivity are ironed out so that all processes can perform at their maximum capacity.

14 Storing the Inventory

Gerry Hatton

Pallet storage

The warehousing compromise
All warehousing systems are a compromise between the efficient use of warehouse space and ready access to the goods.

Maximizing use of the cube
Maximum utilization of the available storage cube offers extremely poor access. For instance, it would theoretically be possible to start in one corner of an empty warehouse and block-stack goods one on top of another until every available cubic metre of space was occupied. However, even though this would utilize 100 per cent of the storage capacity, this situation would present an enormous access problem. The incidence of damage, caused either by crushing as goods are piled one on top of another or by handling in congested conditions, would be high. Also, stock control would be difficult, and there would be no opportunity to rotate goods on a first-in/first-out basis. Finally, a large staff would be needed to remove pallets from the warehouse in order to provide access to a required pallet buried at the centre.

Whilst this system offers the lowest possible capital cost so far as warehouse and storage equipment is concerned, it would have the highest operating cost from damage and labour costs.

Maximizing ease of access
At the other extreme, goods could simply be placed one-high on the warehouse floor in an orderly manner that allows for wide aisles. Access to each product would be direct, with no need to move one product to get at another, and damage from crushing and congested handling would be eliminated. In addition, a system of coding would simplify stock rotation.

215

This system would reduce labour operating costs enormously but would use such a small percentage of the available space that an unreasonably high capital cost for the warehouse would result.

Apart from the small proportion of goods which, for various reasons, can fall into one of these two extremes, the overwhelming majority of warehouses need to make an adequate compromise between maximum storage and maximum access if they are to operate efficiently.

A mixture of the two systems described above can sometimes prove advantageous, but the advances in the last 20 years have enabled much better compromises to be made.

Generally speaking, the lower the capital cost of the system, the lower the benefits in effective space utilization and reduced handling costs. As the capital cost of the storage and handling system increases, it is usual for building and operating costs to be reduced. As systems grow more complex and more sophisticated, however, they become less flexible, so that their applications are limited to a specific set of circumstances.

Hopefully, readers of these pages will recognize the circumstances that apply in their business and after consulting with storage and materials handling experts, will be able to make the compromise that results in the lowest overall cost.

Pallet storage systems

Selective pallet storage

In cases where immediate access must be available to all or most of the pallets within a storage system a range of storage and handling options must be considered.

Figure 14.1 represents a product quantity graph which is typical of a warehouse where there are a relatively large number of lines with only a few pallets of each product. Such product quantity graphs are typical of wholesalers and retailers where the number of product lines frequently extend into the thousands.   Whilst in this case the graph indicates that the 80/20 rule will still apply, this is not always the case for a wholesaler or retailer product quantity graph (although it is usually the case for a product movement graph).

Wholesalers and retailers tend to hold only a few pallets of each

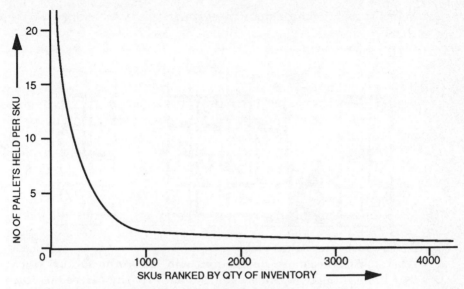

Figure 14.1 Typical product quantity graph

product. If the movement rate of popular lines is high they use the manufacturers' warehouse to limit their own stock holding.

Selective pallet racking

Where the warehouse is storing a large number of lines with a relatively low volume in each line, then direct access must be provided to each pallet within the system if very high handling costs are to be avoided.

The most widely used pallet racking system is, in fact, selective pallet racking. In this system pallets are stored one-deep on either side of a forklift truck operating aisle. For most 1000mm to 1200mm wide pallets it is more economic to store the pallets 2-wide between the upright posts in the racking system. The number of pallets that can be stored in any given stack is limited by the height of the pallets, the lifting height of the fork truck and the available headroom in an existing building.

The system offers:

- immediate access to any given pallet;
- the lowest cost of any racking system;
- versatility and ease of alteration or relocation;
- order picking from almost all pallets within the system (but usually only the lowest one or two);

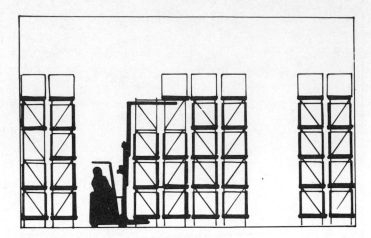

Figure 14.2   Two-deep reach racks
When used in conjunction with telescopic forklift trucks reaching two pallets deep, storage capacity can be increased by 40 whilst offering selectivity to 50 per cent of all pallets.

- relatively low level of stock damage.

Unfortunately, this impressive list of benefits is offset by the fact that this system has the lowest use of the available cube so when the cost of warehouse is taken into account it is perhaps the most expensive system available. Nonetheless, for many applications, it is the most versatile solution.

Two-deep selective racks

Two-deep selective racking is a recently introduced variation of the system. Forklift trucks and other machines are now available that are able to reach into the use of the cube but, of course, at the price of reducing selectivity. It is also somewhat slower in operation and, since visibility can be a problem as the rack height increases, stock damage is somewhat higher. For some applications, however, this is a reasonable compromise between the high-density storage systems discussed earlier and totally selective systems.

Medium-rise narrow aisle selective racks

As we have discussed elsewhere, the cost per cubic metre of a building reduces as the headroom increases. To take advantage of this a number of floor-mounted, high-lifting forklift trucks have been developed.

They lift from between eight and 12 metres and operate in aisles of as little as 200mm more than the pallet width. Whilst the capital cost of these machines is double or more than that of conventional electric forklift trucks, they operate at a higher speed and, of course, they use the cubic capacity of the warehouse much more effectively.

One disadvantage of this system is that, as goods are stored higher, order picking of individual cartons becomes more difficult. Frequently, the best solution is to provide a separate order picking area or to introduce high-level stock picking machines. The other disadvantage of this system is that the high capital cost of the machines limits their selection to the larger warehouses where at least 1,000 to 2,000 pallets and probably more are to be stored.

Automatic storage and retrieval systems (AS/RS)

AS/RS or stacker cranes are a simple extension of the floor-mounted narrow aisle machines. They are faster in operation than any floor-mounted truck and they operate in aisles only 200mm wider than the pallet. They are capable of lifting almost any load up to 20 or 30 metres but the normal range is around 16m to 24m, or eight to 12 pallets high.

The order picking and capital cost disadvantages of narrow aisle stackers are, of course, magnified so that stacker cranes are only applicable for very large warehouses. The system may include transfer cars to move cranes from one aisle to the other or a stacker crane must be included in each aisle. Lane changing cranes are also available.

Stacker cranes are applicable in installations where:

- there are at least 3,000 to 4,000 pallets stored (to amortize the high capital cost per unit);
- the rate of movement is relatively high;
- the site is expensive and/or limited;
- a totally new facility is being constructed;
- the site is long and relatively narrow since the high speed of the crane and its travelling and lifting ratios can only be used effectively without frequent aisle transfers.

The case for constructing the building using the rack framework is even stronger with a stacker crane high-rise warehouse than for a

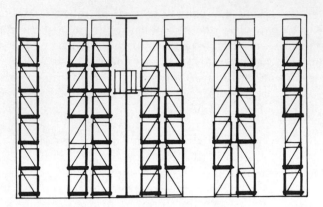

Figure 14.3   High-rise warehousing
This is normally constructed to heights of around 30m.

turret truck. In many cases a warehouse of this type can be classified as plant and equipment, which can attract certain taxation benefits.

The cost of automating the cranes decreases as the number of cranes rises. Such systems normally also justify automatic pallet infeed and outfeed conveyors fed by fork trucks, pallet conveyors or AGVs.

Power-mobile pallet racks

The most serious disadvantage of selective racking systems is that the very low use of the available cube makes them a most expensive system, despite the fact that the rack structure itself is inexpensive.

In some cases, costs can be reduced by installing selective racks on a mobile base so that they can be moved from side to side. The concept is similar to that employed in the manually operated cabinets for office supplies which have been in use for many years. The prime difference is that the movement of the racks is controlled by an electric motor driving steel wheels mounted on guided rails built into the floor. With this scheme a single aisle can give individual access to perhaps 10 separate racks. Utilization of the available cube is by far the highest of all of the available selective systems. In fact, the system competes with most of the high-density storage systems discussed elsewhere.

The power driven racks can be controlled from push button panels located on the end of the racks or from a central console. For safety, trip bars run the full length of either side of each mobile rack unit. When meeting an obstruction the spring-loaded trip bar activates a dual safety electric circuit bringing the rack to a halt.

The system has the following benefits:

- it can be used with almost any type of handling equipment except fixed aisle cranes;
- there is a relatively low rate of damage compared with other high-density storage systems;
- cubic utilization is very high.

There are only two disadvantages of note. The movement of product cannot be too high as only one forklift truck can operate in a given block of racks at a given time and the relatively high capital cost of the system is aggravated by the need to build the rails into the floor. In an existing warehouse this might mean moving much of the stock before the system can be installed.

The principal application for this system is in controlled-temperature warehouses and confined or expensive sites where the higher cost of the space more than justifies the capital cost of the racking system.

High density pallet storage systems

This title is somewhat misleading since there are many selective storage systems that offer very high-density storage. However, generally speaking, if there are only a few product lines and a large number of products in each line access to any given pallet is not important so that the number of aisles can be reduced to achieve high-density storage.

Figure 14.4 illustrates a typical product quantity graph that would be appropriate for one of the systems that we shall consider. Such a product quantity graph is typical of a manufacturer as opposed to a distributor or retailer.

It should be noted that the 80/20 rule works almost always in this particular type of product quantity graph. Some 20 per cent of the products represent 80 per cent of the total volume of stock. This allows for much denser storage systems to be used across this part of the product range.

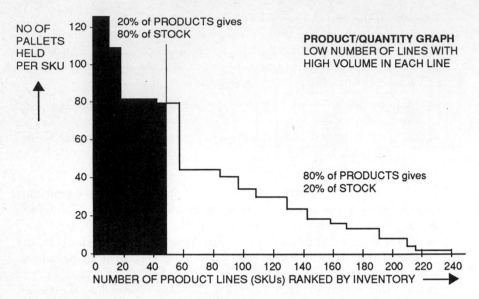

Figure 14.4   Typical product quantity graph

Occupancy

This is the name given to the percentage of storage locations that can effectively be used. It is never more than 90–95 per cent in selective systems and can fall to 70 per cent or less in non-selective systems.

Accordingly, great care must be used in designing these systems. The length of the lanes needs to be closely tailored to the product volumes as indicated in the product quantity analysis referred to earlier. Some provision must always be made to store low quantities of different types of product which may occasionally be left over. If this is not done, occupancy of the system can be dramatically reduced by having lanes that store, say, 12 pallets with only one or two pallets in them.

It should also be borne in mind that the quantity of inventory for each line item varies constantly and, usually, stock has to be rotated. Inexperienced designers often make systems ineffective and difficult to use by trying to improve storage density without considering access and occupancy.

Block stacking

For some products no storage racking system is necessary. The goods can be stacked several pallets high by several pallets deep on either

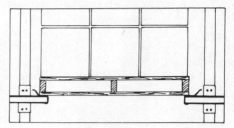

Figure 14.5   Drive-in pallet storage
The rails on which pallets are stored are spaced so that
forklift trucks can pass between them

side of an operating aisle. The system can be used with almost any type of forklift truck. It provides very dense storage and, of course, the cost of the system is limited to the cost of the warehouse and the truck. There the benefits end.

The disadvantages are that stock cannot be rotated, rigidity and stability are low, carton and product damage is likely to be high. Selection of pallets is limited to the top pallet at the front of a row, practical usable occupancy of available storage slots is likely to be low and carton order picking is not possible.

Mezzanine floors
Some of the disadvantages of block stacking mentioned above can be reduced or eliminated by the installation of a mezzanine floor. For the handling of pallet loads such a scheme has nothing to commend it in most circumstances. It precludes the proper use of materials handling equipment, it is expensive and the warehouse designer becomes involved in matters of additional lighting, ventilation, sprinkler systems and the like. Despite this, it is surprising how frequently the system is used.

Drive-in and drive-through pallet racking
This is perhaps the most popular system of storing pallets where there is a limited number of lines and relatively high volume of pallets in each line.

Drive-in racks are simply a framework with rails running from front to back off the forklift truck aisle. This enables the fork to drive down between the rails carrying the pallets between them. In this way pallets can be stored two, three, four, five or more deep by as many high as can be reached with standard forklift trucks. The system is popular because it:

- reduces crushing and stock damage;
- provides selection of any pallet from the front face;
- allows some order picking of cartons from the lower pallets;
- has a moderate capital cost.

Like block stacking and pallet convertors, however, it offers poor selectivity, no rotation of stock, is limited to an overall height of approximately nine metres, and provides relatively slow operating speeds. The trucks, the racks and the products are subject to damage while being moved to and from the system.

For these reasons, drive-in racks should be used only when there is a relatively slow movement rate and a high number of identical pallets. Lane depth should normally be restricted to two to five pallets to minimize these problems.

Pallet live storage

This storage system is also a handling system. The goods are fed into the rear of the rack and they flow through the rack to a selection aisle. This overcomes many of the disadvantages described in the previous high density storage systems.

It provides:

- automatic stock rotation;
- very high utilization of the cube;
- simplified selectivity;
- simplified inventory control;
- individual cartons can be selected from pallets on the front face;
- utilization of high-level narrow aisle trucks and cranes, as well as conventional machines.

Stock damage is low because the goods spend most of their time in the centre of the rack away from the handling equipment. However, because of the conveyors required, the capital cost of this system is very high. This is particularly so because of the slatted base configuration of many pallets which demand an expensive conveyor arrangement.

The slope of each lane must be such that self-feeding of pallets to the front of the rack takes place automatically as each pallet is removed. Unfortunately, the scope required to guarantee self-feeding

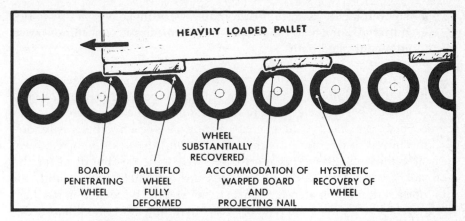

Figure 14.6   The use of polymer-tyred wheels to convey pallets

is such that a speed control mechanism must be incorporated to control the movement of pallets being fed into an empty lane. Most of these are mechanical or hydraulic devices.

Alternatively, to avoid the use of special pallets or slave pallets special high hysteresis, polymer-tyred wheels can be used for conveying pallets and controlling their speed.

Remote recovery module

One of the serious limitations of drive-in racking for a modern warehouse is that narrow aisle trucks and high-rise stacker cranes are not able to enter the drive-in lane. This limitation is overcome by the use of a remote-controlled retrieval machine, resembling a small radio-controlled hydraulic pallet jack, which is carried down the central aisle by a high-lifting, narrow aisle truck or crane. At a given station it leaves the crane and enters the rack running along a specially shaped rail positioned immediately below the pallets. From this position it can be commanded to lift the pallets and bring them back to the handling equipment. The majority of these installations are between 10 and 20 metres in height so that the high capital cost of the equipment is offset by the progressively reducing cost of the cubic space as the building gets higher. This system gives:

- perhaps the highest-density storage;
- reasonable access when compared with, say, drive-in rack;

- stock rotation (with fully automated versions);
- minimal damage to the goods and the racks since machines move in a controlled path.

The disadvantages of this system are that the special racking and handling equipment is quite costly and must be amortized over a very large number of pallets before this system can be considered.

Since the fixed path cranes cannot pass each other, only one machine can operate in each aisle, limiting the system to relatively slow-moving lines. This is probably the least flexible of all of the storage systems: scope for changes are extremely limited and, for normal non-automated versions, stock can only be rotated in batches.

Table 14.1 shows the type of pallet handling equipment and order picking systems that can be used with each of the rack types that we have just discussed.

Fitting together pallet storage and handling systems

Unfortunately it is not possible to choose an ideal pallet storage system and handling system in isolation. First, they naturally have to be mutually compatible within themselves but, secondly, an order picking system has to be accommodated.

Table 14.1 and Figure 14.7 show something of the way in which these various sub-elements can be interfaced: for example, it is not possible to do order picking in an automatic narrow aisle system.

Figure 14.7 is illustrative only. It indicates the likely mechanized storage and handling system that would be appropriate with a given number of line items and a given number of pallets stored.

Naturally this does not take into account the order picking task, nor the constraints of the shape of the building or the headroom available. It is, however, perhaps a useful indication of at which level the various types of more mechanized storage and handling might be considered. It also graphically demonstrates the likely storage system if only the number of SKUs and the number of pallets stored are considered.

Using an appropriate range of storage systems with appropriate handling equipment dominates the design of most distribution

Table 14.1
Order picking from pallet racking

	Selective Pallet Storage	
Rack Types	Appropriate Machines	Picking Options
Standard selective	Counterbalanced or reach	Multiple-operator manual or machine
Modified selective	Straddle or double reach	in-aisle picking
Power-mobile	Counter balanced or reach	Limited picking
Medium-rise narrow aisle	Turret or swivel reach	Limited
Medium/highrise	Telescopic plattens, free path or over head steady	picking
		with specialized
Highrise	Fixed or transferable stacker (AS/RS)	machine

	Non-selective Pallet Storage	
Double reach	Only telescopic reach	Order picking very limited
Drive-in	Counterbalanced or reach	↑
Palletflo	All machines (except REM)	↓
Remote recovery	Only REM crane	No order picking possible

centres. It is therefore a critical task deserving much analysis and consideration.

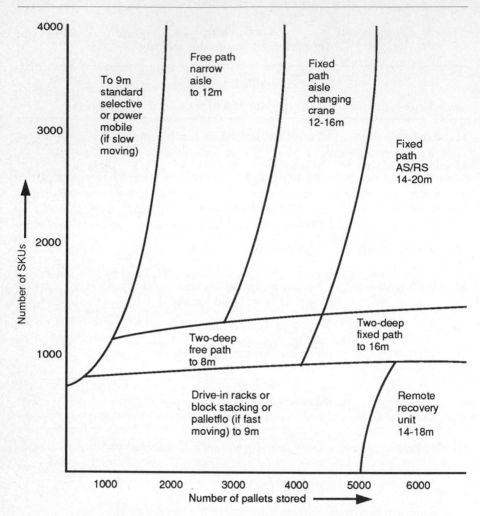

**Figure 14.7   Criteria for the selection of pallet storage systems
Copyright Colby Handling Systems.**

Small parts storage and Uglies*

When small parts are stored in sufficient quantities it is possible to justify their being stored in cartons which can be made into a unit load. However, where small parts are held in relatively small

*Uglies are the awkward to store parts, due to their difficult shapes and sizes eg exhaust systems.

quantities, then there are quite different methods of storing and handling them.

At first there seems to be a baffling range of options but in fact there are only four basic methodologies. They are:-

1   A multiple location tray or draw
2   A tote or container
3   Steel binning with solid backs and side
4   Open shelving

These basic methods of storing are shown in ascending order of the size or volume of the components to be stored. A few tiny components are best stored in a larger tray or draw that is subdivided. As the quantity of component grow it becomes easier to have each line item stored in a tote or container large enough to carry the total inventory.

The above two options are portable and, as we shall see later, can themselves be stored and handled in a variety of ways. The next two options are essentially static. Binning, usually of steel, has solid backs and sides and often has a retainer to hold components within the pigeon holes that can be created. As the size of the components to be stored increases then the goods can eventually be placed on a shelf that needs no side retention.

Once it is recognized that there are only four ways of actually storing the goods we have to decide how to store the containers that are storing the goods or how to present most effectively the storage medium for ready access.

Plastic or metal totes are sometimes suspended off a rear panel. This method is most often used in display areas or to present components in a work area.

Steel binning
More often the basic storage units are grouped together into a steel binning system that can contain any proportion of each storage medium. These come in a variety of widths, depths and heights, with and without drawers, with and without doors, to suit the size and the nature of the goods to be stored.

The size of bins, trays, drawers or shelves should be varied to suit the merchandise to be stored and handled, which involves considerable analysis. Faster-moving inventory should be positioned in more accessible levels and the overall height and spacing of shelves should be carefully designed.

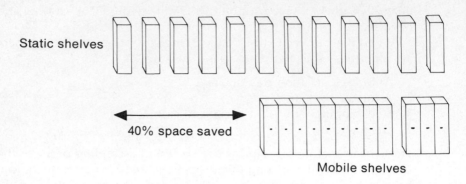

Figure 14.8   Representation of space-saving potential of mobile binning

The main disadvantages of this now quite old system are that binning fails to use the headroom and it is labour-intensive, both in putting away and in retrieving the goods.

Mobile binning

Where the space is limited and the headroom and the movement rates are low, then the single-tier steel bins can be mounted on a mobile base so that a single aisle can be moved around to service several bins. Generally speaking, this reduces the area required for storage by, typically, 40 per cent, as illustrated in Figure 14.8.

Naturally such systems cost more than static binning but, when the cost of the space is taken into account, the overall cost per cubic metre of goods stored is much lower. The disadvantage is that the goods must be relatively slow-moving for it is clearly not possible to have operators simultaneously picking and replenishing goods in various aisles in a mobile system.

Use of the headroom with binning

There are two ways in which the headroom can be effectively used. Firstly, bins can be placed one upon the other forming a two or three tier system as illustrated in Figure 14.9.

The disadvantage of this approach is that, whilst it uses the headroom, it intensifies the problem of access – the labour involved in raising the goods to and from the second level being higher than that involved if the bins were only one tier-high. It is therefore more appropriate for slow-moving goods, particularly at the upper level.

To some extent, these costs can be reduced by using conveyors to

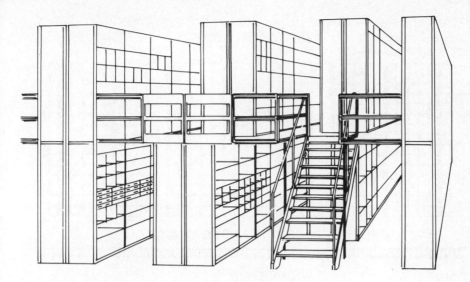

Figure 14.9 Two-tier binning system

feed goods to the various points of the system and to take them away again to despatch.

Another alternative is to consider the use of high-rise, narrow aisle order pickers. The savings in the cost of the walkway and staircases in a multi-tier system can pay for the order picking machines in some cases.

High-rise, fixed-path, narrow aisle or free-path order pickers like this are more appropriate for high-volume throughput systems. Their role will further be discussed in chapter 15.

Mini-stacker retrieval system

If small parts are stored in bins that form part of a large tray or unit load they can be automatically stored and retrieved from high-rise narrow aisle racking. Whilst this saves labour and is often a good order picking system a mini-stacker is often cost-effective as a storage system in its own right.

This system will be further discussed in chapter 15.

Carton live storage

Small parts stored in cartons or containers can frequently economically be stored in carton live storage since this is not only a valuable aid to order picking but also a dense storage system.

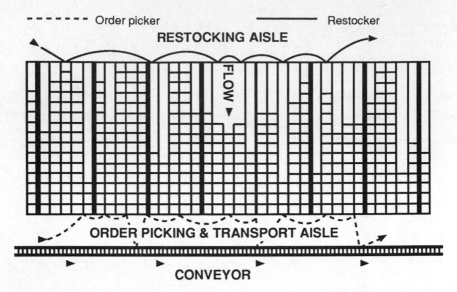

Figure 14.10   Carton live storage

As Figure 14.10 shows, carton live storage, as well as reducing travel distance by between 50–80 per cent, also eliminates the aisles required for standard binning and increases storage capacity by 50–60 per cent.

Vertical and horizontal carousels

Whilst small parts are often stored in vertical and/or horizontal carousels it should be recognized that they are primarily retrieval order picking systems.

Vertical carousels use headroom effectively and are well suited to store trays and totes for very small as well as medium-sized components. Horizontal carousels are more often like rotating bins and therefore are more suitable for medium-sized components and items.

The high cost of storage must be offset by savings in labour. Accordingly, these systems will be further discussed in chapter 15.

Long lengths

Many companies have to store and handle goods like aluminium extrusion, tube, bar, timber slats and so on which range in lengths from one or two metres through to many metres. The best method of storing and handling them varies with the length and weight of the goods and the volumes to be handled.

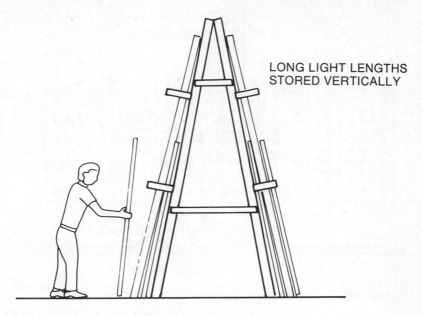

LONG LIGHT LENGTHS
STORED VERTICALLY

Figure 14.11 End view of 'A'-frame rack

Vertical A-frame racks

For lightweight sections stored and picked in relatively small quantities, the cheapest and easiest method is to store the goods on A-frame racks. This system effectively uses the headroom and has moderately good use of the cube whilst allowing direct access to each item. The goods must be light enough for an operator to be able to handle them to and from the vertical position.

Pigeon-hole bar racks

Where there is insufficient headroom to store the goods vertically it is sometimes more convenient to store them in a simple pigeon-hole rack. Here the goods are slid endways in to a small compartment, usually one for each different product to be stored. As the goods become heavier, a number of devices have been developed to enable such racks to be loaded with the use of an overhead crane. However, this is a relatively rare system.

Broadloom carpet racks

One variation for using pigeon-hole racks of this type is for the storage of broadloom carpets and other long rolls. These are most

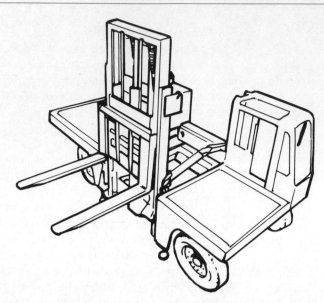

Figure 14.12   Sideloading narrow aisle machine

often stored in decked racks, sometimes with a number of vertical dividers. They are usually handled by a forklift truck with a special pole fixed in place of the normal fork tynes. This pole is inserted down the core of the broadloom carpet so that it can be inserted endways into its storage location. Such a handling method requires aisles wide enough to accept the length of the goods and the associated handling equipment. Other narrower aisle methods have been developed for very high-volume throughput systems, although these are relatively rare in their application.

Cantilever racks

As the volume and/or weight of goods to be handled increases, it becomes necessary to use some type of handling equipment. For relatively small volumes, special reach trucks can be adapted so that they are able to move sideways down an aisle carrying a long length. These are called four-way reach trucks. They are then able to feed goods into cantilever racks which effectively use the headroom.

As the volume of goods to be handled increases then so does the justification for using a specialized side-loading narrow aisle machine. This machine operates in aisles of only one to two metres, depending on the size of the unit load to be handled, and can lift loads up to several tonnes up to several metres.

As the height and volumes increase further still a variety of overhead stacker cranes is available to service goods in this way.

Also available is a number of specialized machines that lift the operator up with the goods in order that individual bar order picking can take place with a machine that is also capable of handling unit loads of, say, two to five tonnes.

Block stacking: tube or bar stock

Very high volumes of almost identical inventory are frequently cost-effectively stored on the floor. Dunnage is put in between stacks to assist the bundles to be put into position and moved with slings using an overhead crane. Whilst this is a cheap storage system, it is, of course, labour-intensive and it does not use very much headroom unless there are very considerable quantities of identical inventory.

To some degree, these disadvantages have been overcome with the use of stacking bar racks. In this way, bundles of long lengths of inventory are formed up into a unit load which can be handled with an overhead 'grab'. Additional headroom can be used and labour costs are somewhat lower. However, this system has not found wide popularity because of the additional cost over block-stacking systems and the very limited access compared to cantilever racking.

Sheet and plate storage

Wooden and metal sheets and other similar materials are rarely as long as pipes and bars. For these reasons, it is occasionally more economic to use a more standard forklift truck and store the goods in racking with left-to-right beams. This is only so if there are only a few limited sizes of sheet and the maximum length is around three metres.

As the range of sizes to be handled and the length of sheet increases it becomes very much more practical to use cantilever racking. In the same way it becomes more appropriate to use either a four-directional reach truck or eventually one of the specialized side loading trucks mentioned earlier.

Furniture storage

Whilst many businesses have shapeless articles that fall into none of the previous categories which cannot be described in the limited space available, it is perhaps worth dwelling briefly on the storage of furniture and similar goods. Despite extensive research, where it is not possible to make these goods into a unit load, it is still usually

Figure 14.13   Stackable bar racks are an alternative to cantilever racks for the storage of long lengths

found to be most effective to store the goods into a wide-shelved and decked cantilever storage rack.

These require that the goods be manhandled to and from the storage location by operators on a special type of high level order picker. A number of types have been developed with safety cages that totally enclose the operators whilst they are accomplishing this task.

In many businesses there are items which fit neither into small parts

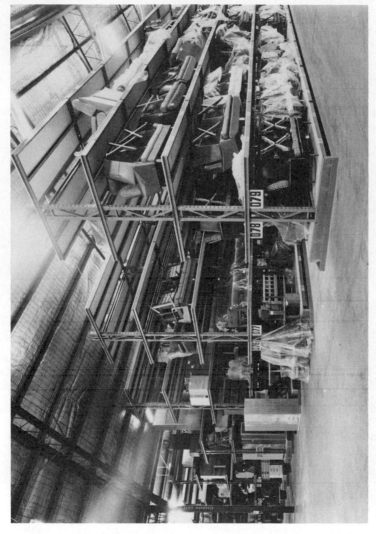

Figure 14.14   Decked cantilever racks cope with most shapes and sizes

storage systems nor into pallets or unit loads: companies selling machines, large sheets, coils, bars and tubes are examples. Storing and handling of these types of goods is a special science within itself beyond the scope of this chapter. It is sufficient, therefore, to say that if a company has some of these goods to be stored, as well as a range of conventional goods, then they are better stored separately in appropriately designed, customized equipment.

Unit loads

History
Less than 100 years ago, the great majority of goods were handled individually by hand. For long-distance shipping some type of case was common, but certainly no attempt was made to standardize. Gradually, the concept of the unit load evolved. As mass production of consumer goods became more common, items were placed in cartons of a standard shape and size. It was found that such cases could be more easily stacked and handled. Moreover they protected the goods while simplifying stocktaking and other aspects of inventory control. The size of these early unit loads was, however, limited to a weight that could be easily lifted by one man.

The invention of the forklift truck in the United States in the 1920s was the beginning of a worldwide revolution in materials handling. As has been discussed elsewhere, great steps have been made in the development of different types of forklift trucks, each designed for a specific purpose. Here, it is worth dwelling upon some of the issues concerned with unit loads that they can handle.

Definition
Fundamentally, unit loads are constructed by in some way bringing together a number of sub-elements to make one large load that can be handled mechanically.

Pallet construction
By far the commonest unit load is constructed on a pallet. This is a rigid platform that supports the goods and usually allows entry below for the tines of a forklift truck or other lifting device. They are generally made of wood, although metal and plastic pallets have been developed. Generally speaking, non-wooden pallets are more costly and therefore limited to applications where their additional cost can

be justified. For example, regulations frequently prohibit the use of timber pallets for handling produce in a food manufacturing area.

Obviously, plastic pallets have the advantage that they can be washed down and are resistant to a wide range of chemicals. Metal pallets in some instances have strength advantages, and both plastic and metal pallets are, in some cases, lighter than wooden pallets. For example, aluminium pallets are often used in the air freight industry. However, the great majority of all pallets are constructed of wood.

Constraints on pallet sizes

Over the years, most developed nations have made an attempt to develop a standard pallet or a series of standard pallets. Different regulations in different countries act as constraints. One major constraint is the maximum vehicle width available. This tends to be in the area of 2.5 metres. Since the pallets would ordinarily preferably be stored two-wide and sometimes be inside the walls of the vehicle, it leads to the requirement of pallets not exceeding, say, 1200mm in that dimension.

The widespread introduction of International Standards Organization (ISO) shipping containers in the post-war era is yet another constraint. Unfortunately, of necessity these containers had to be no wider than the maximum that could be permitted in the countries in which they were to be used on both rail and road. As a result, their external dimension has now been set at 2.4 metres. Because of the wall thickness this means that pallets of 1200mm cannot be fitted two wide inside it. Accordingly, 1100mm square pallets have been developed for this application.

Square or rectangular pallets

Generally speaking, there is a wider range of stacking patterns available on a rectangular pallet than on a square pallet. Thus, better use of the cube is obtained.

Of equal importance is the question of the space required to present an order picking face within the distribution centre. Pallets only 800mm or 1000mm say, can substantially reduce the length of the picking aisle. If there are, say, 4,000 or 5,000 pallets so presented this can be a significant issue. On the other hand, the picking depth should not be too great. In this regard there are few pallets which exceed 1200mm. This is partly because of the maximum vehicle road width mentioned earlier and partly because this is the greatest distance that an operator can be expected to reach to retrieve a carton. In fact, of course, if the average carton is 300mm deep the operator only has to reach 900mm into the pallet to grasp the front of the carton.

Two-way entry pallets

Earlier pallets were only two-way entry, having solid side members. This had the disadvantage that they must be picked up in the same or opposite direction in which they were loaded.

Two-way pallets of this type have become standard in Australia, the United States and certain other countries. In Australia the pallets are 1170 × 1170 × 150mm deep. Since they are constructed from hardwood they have the disadvantage of weighing around 60kgs. In the United States the standard GMA (Grocery Manufacturers' Association) pallet is made from softwood and is 48 in. deep by 40 in. wide.

The two-way access is an important constraint in handling to and from conveyor and narrow aisle storage systems, where the ability to pick up on all faces is frequently important. The closed base of these pallets also precludes them being used in racking systems with the telescopic plattens of narrow aisle machines without the additional cost and space required for fork spacer bars. The slatted base of the pallet also makes it unsatisfactory for handling on wheel or roller conveyor systems since it must travel in the direction in which it is loaded. This tends to substantially decrease the cost-effectiveness of pallet live storage systems.

Four-way entry pallets

These pallets were initially developed in Europe and have now become the international standard.

Standard sizes are 1200 × 1200 and 1000 × 800. Apart from the four-way access which overcomes the disadvantages of the two-way entry pallet, they are usually made from soft, and therefore much lighter, timber, reducing pay-load and improving manual handling where necessary. Their biggest disadvantage is that they are some-what less robust.

New Zealand has compromised by cutting small openings in the sides of two-way entry pallets 1200mm wide by 1000mm deep, making them into partial four-way entry pallets.

Four-way pallets are more versatile in their application. One example is that, in narrow aisle storage systems, pallets can be dropped on one face by the infeed machine and picked up on the other face by the narrow aisle machine only if a four-way entry pallet

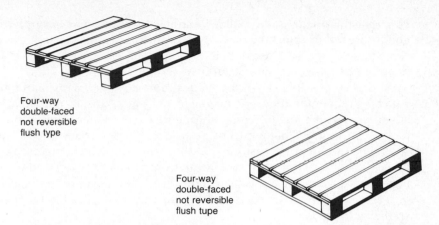

Four-way
double-faced
not reversible
flush type

Four-way
double-faced
not reversible
flush tupe

Figure 14.15   Four way entry pallets

is used. In some four-way pallets two faces have an open base which
facilitates access.

The base of the pallet
If pallets have to be stored one on top of the other it is desirable that
the base of the pallet is as extensive as possible so that the load can be
evenly distributed. This strengthens the pallet but, of course,
increases its weight and cost.

Where it is necessary to pick up the pallet using hand or powered
pallet jacks, then there must be room for the front pick-up wheels to
pass through the base in order that the load can be elevated. The
quickest and easiest way to do this is to have base boards only in the
direction of pick-up underneath two or three main bearers, but of
course this reduces the base-bearing area.

A wide number of compromises has been developed. Figure 14.15
shows two of the pallets in use that have become standards in certain
parts of the world.

The selection of an appropriate pallet
A pallet should be as large as is practical, consistent with the number of
goods that has to be carried and stored and the mode of transport,
because larger pallets reduce the number of unit loads to be handled.
However, as can be seen above, vehicle and container sizes and manual
pallet building and unloading limit the size; hence the majority of pallets
are in the range of 800mm to 1200mm in width or depth.

Another consideration is that the pallet should in many instances be at least as wide as the pallet handling machine. For example, if goods are to be block-stacked or fed into drive-in racking, then considerable space is wasted if a 1200mm wide forklift truck is handling pallets only, say, 800mm wide.

Wherever possible it is clearly desirable to stick with standard pallets. Frequently they are available on hire. This is particularly advantageous if they are being shipped to users where they can be de-hired instead of having to be returned. On the other hand, one should be careful not to assume that the standard pallet being used by others is best for your purposes. Many companies have derived great benefit by developing a special in-house pallet that is perhaps smaller or larger, lighter or stronger, or in some way more flexible for their specialized needs.

Pallet stacking height

If goods are stacked high on each pallet, then the total number of pallets to be stored and handled is reduced: however, the pallet weight is often increased, which might lead to the need for a bigger machine to handle it. Load stability is also often impaired; sometimes crushing of the lower cartons results.

Most importantly, if individual cartons are to be picked from pallets by staff not standing on elevating order picking equipment, then the height from which they can pick is limited. In many cases, it is necessary to pick from two levels high, in which case either the operator must be raised or the overall height of pallet and load should be restricted to a maximum of, say, 1200mm.

In a sophisticated distribution centre one should design the pallet stacking pattern for each carton and establish how many cartons are to be stored on each pallet in order that replenishment requests for order picking stock can be automatically generated by the computer.

If using power mobile rack or pallet live storage, one should be doubly concerned about load stability: if using narrow aisle equipment, then the squareness of the pallet and the amount of stock overhang are important factors in determining the minimum width of the aisle. It should be borne in mind that some cartons compress sideways when frozen or when other cases are stacked upon them, making the final load size longer than the one originally calculated.

Pallet cages

Many items cannot be built into a unit load and are unstable when stacked up on a standard pallet. In some cases the easiest way to

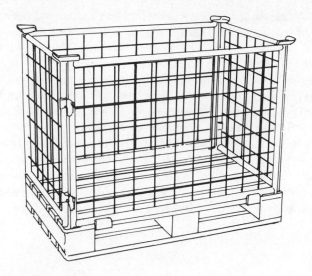

Figure 14.16 Pallet cage

solve this problem is to mount a rigid or demountable cage around the pallet. In this way, fragile or unstable goods can be safely contained.

It is of course possible to make the framework sufficiently strong to support the weight of other such units so that they can be stacked up to use the available headroom. If goods have to be order picked, then the lower units cannot be removed when empty: also selectivity of pallets is significantly reduced when racking is not used.

Since pallet frames and pallet cages are more expensive than most racking systems their applications are restricted to where the goods to be stored need lateral restraints.

Post pallets and stacking containers

For many items, wooden pallets with pallet cages are simply not appropriate. For this reason, a very wide range of unit loads have been developed over the years. They are known variously as stillages or post-pallets. They can have fixed or collapsible sides, full-drop or half-drop gates, they can be lined with sheet metal, plywood, wire mesh or a variety of items specifically designed to meet unusual requirements.

Such units have wider application in manufacturing than in distrbution but they do have their place, even if only to service part of the total product range. Even long items can sometimes best be handled in such a unit load.

Other types of unit loads

Unit loads of bricks and concrete blocks are built by strapping them together, leaving out certain layers so that fork tines can be inserted.

Another example is the use of slip sheets. These are flat sheets of cardboard onto which a unit load of cartons is constructed. A special forklift truck is able to grab the protruding piece of cardboard and to push and pull the unit load to and from a special flat carrying platform. Since slip sheets cannot be used in storage racking systems unless they are first placed on a pallet, they tend to be used when the goods can be directly loaded into a shipping container or vehicle.

15   Order Picking

Gerry Hatton

It is from the point at which a client places an order with a supplier that the supplier is obliged to fulfil the sales and marketing promise. If the company is to maintain or increase market share, it must supply a maximum number of order lines from a minimum inventory, quickly and accurately. The goods and paperwork should be well presented in good order and in a reliable time-frame; and all of this labour-intensive work must be accomplished at a minimum cost. Thus, of all of the tasks that take place in the distribution centre, few are more important than order picking.

What is order picking?

Order picking is the task of selecting from bulk the items the customer wants, in the quantities he wants, when he wants them. It is the breaking down of neatly packed and often palletized bulk into handfuls. It generally involves taking cartons from a pallet or items from a carton. Often these have to be marked, checked and then repacked.

Clearly, order picking involves a number of labour-intensive functions, including deciding what has to be picked, where it is and how to get there – and where to take it next. It is, indeed, by far the most costly labour function in operating a distribution centre. Whilst the figures obviously vary from business to business depending on the nature of the orders and the goods to be picked, on average, order picking accounts for some two-thirds of the labour costs.

Can order picking be carried out automatically?

Whilst automatic order picking systems have been developed they have not been widely adopted due to their very high capital cost and hitherto insufficient payback in most circumstances.

One system has been developed in the United States, and now has variants elsewhere, that dispenses items in full-case or less than full-case quantities. As yet, the items must be picked from the case into a live storage lane. From this lane they can be released onto a conveyor. Such systems have proved to be viable only in certain very limited circumstances.

Accordingly, the only significant opportunities to mechanize order picking of full cartons are likely to occur when there are very high volumes of less-than-full pallet quantities of a very limited product range. Under these circumstances, goods can be automatically depalletized and each line item fed into a separate accumulation conveyor.

The accumulation conveyor can then be used to discharge the required quantity of goods. In the event that the size of the cartons is common for all of the line items, then the order so discharged onto a take-away conveyor can be automatically palletized. If cartons vary in size, then it is possible to build tier quantities automatically; otherwise the final palletizing task must be done manually.

Finally, packing and palletizing a wide range of items must still be carried out manually, no matter how orders are picked. For the great majority of order picking tasks, and almost all other associated tasks, it is still necessary to use people. The task is therefore to make sure that the people are used as effectively as possible – in fact, the potential for improvement is enormous.

What is the potential for improvement?

If an operator were to pick cartons from waist height onto a conveyor also at waist height, then he could comfortably pick between 700 and 1,200 cartons per man-hour, depending on the size and weight of the cartons. Compare this with the typical productivity for full-case order picking in a distribution centre which is likely to be in the range of 60 to 150 cartons per man-hour.

Precisely the same lost time occurs for split-case order picking but the erosion in productivity tends to be even higher, especially for spare parts and similar businesses where there is a very large number of line items and a number of small orders.

The pie chart in Figure 15.1 shows a typical profile of the time spent on various tasks by people picking orders. It is the 70–90 per cent of the time spent in tasks other than actually picking the orders that constitutes the huge opportunity for improvement. In order to increase productivity we should therefore turn our attention much

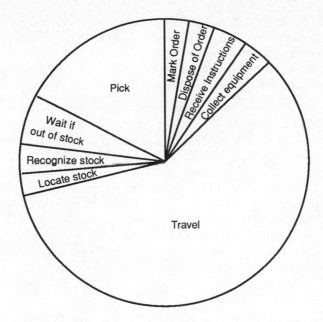

Figure 15.1 Proportions of time spent on various tasks in the order picking process

less to the picking task and far more to minimizing the non-productive areas.

It is rare to examine any conventional system and not find that productivity can be improved by 50–150 per cent by applying the following techniques to eliminate non-productive functions.

The five basic techniques to increase order picking productivity

As the range of options increases, the task of determining what should apply to a given application becomes increasingly difficult. One can well imagine that, for the average distribution centre manager, determining what might best apply in his business has become an onerous task.

Whilst there is a huge variety of different machines and devices on the market to assist in the order picking task, there are fundamentally only five techniques that can be used to improve productivity. They are:

1   travelling faster;
2   travelling less;
3   cutting out the paperwork;
4   picking several orders at once;
5   bringing the goods to the man.

Each of these techniques helps reduce the non-productive element in the order picking task. The designer should bear in mind that the correct solution for any given operation is often a combination of systems. First, the fast-moving line items may be handled in a different way from the slow-moving line items: full-case differently from split-case, and so on. Second, one should bear in mind that two or more techniques can usually be used concurrently within a single system, no matter which of the other techniques is used.

Overlapping these five techniques is the opportunity to use the computer in a way that better organizes the documentation, layout, stock control, manpower planning and so on.

The following subsections examine which of the techniques applies in a particular instance.

Travelling faster

Travel distance grows as the volume of picking stock is increased. To pass, say, 10,000 line items stacked on pallets can mean a run of 15 kilometres. So the first objective with a long picking run is to get the operators to where they have to pick and then back to the shipping dock as fast as possible.

Low-level order pickers

The low-level order picker is an inexpensive machine for picking from the lower pallets or shelves of a racking system. It is one of the most widely used devices to aid order picking productivity. They usually carry the operator as well as his picking pallet (or trolley or container). For larger orders, some machines can carry two or three unit loads so they do not have to travel back to Shipping so often.

Variations of the low-level order picker allow the operator to step up to the second or third pallet level. This can halve the picking run and increase productivity further.

Low-level order pickers are ideal for handling full-case orders or large, bulky items. They are normally used in wide aisle pallet racking systems where several order pickers and replenishment forklifts can work together – which is important for fast moving items. The headroom above the order picking stock stores reserve stock and services orders for full pallet loads.

High-level order pickers

Taller buildings cost less per cubic metre, so we have to go up to store goods economically. But as the number of lines increases, it is unlikely that all of the high-level storage solely for reserve stock can be used. High-level order pickers allow us to put picking stock up there too.

High-level order pickers can raise the operator up to six or even 10 metres in a relatively stable and comfortable cabin, ergonomically designed so that reaching, bending and lifting are minimized. Picking productivity is high: by going up and down as they travel along – and being able to pick from both sides of narrow aisles – they combine the desirability of high-density storage with the practicality of efficient order picking. However, they cannot pass in an aisle so that, as movement volumes rise, it is usually more convenient to pick from lower levels in a wider aisle or use a totally different technique.

Another limitation of not being able to pass in the aisle is that each operator on each machine must pick only that part of the product range allocated to the aisle or aisles served by that machine. The sub-component of an order picked in this way must either be passed on to the next operator or consolidated in some other way.

Fixed-path high-level order pickers are more efficient if the activity in one aisle is sufficient to justify their cost. In fixed-path high-level order picking systems goods are often fed in by conveyor for put-away. Conveyors are also often used to progressively feed split-case orders from one machine to another until the total order is picked or a shipping container is filled.

Reducing the travel distance

There are three major means of reducing the travel distance in any order picking system. The use of one or more of these systems should be considered in conjunction with almost any of the other design approaches. The three techniques are:

1 To slot the stock according to its movement rate.
2 To design the racks so that there is a condensed picking face.
3 To use conveyors to feed goods to and from the operator.

Each of these techniques is examined below.

**Figure 15.2   High-level order picker ensures stock is always at right
height to place or pick up cartons**

Locating stock according to movement rate
In all systems we should seek to reduce the travel distance by
logically grouping inventory. Since 50 per cent of the line items

ordinarily account for 96 per cent of the movement, then clearly we should position them where they are more readily accessible: conversely, since the last 50 per cent of lines average only 4.6 per cent of stock movement, these can be stored in a more out-of-the-way location.

In a walk-pick-to-pallet or trolley operation, a layout which puts the faster-moving goods near Shipping can dramatically reduce the average travel distance. In many pick-to-conveyor operations better results can be obtained by having operators work in zones. Under these circumstances, fast-moving items should be between knee level and eye level where picking is faster and more accurate.

Unfortunately many more factors other than movement rate have to be taken into account when slotting inventory. Frequently it is necessary to store them in 'family' groups, to separate out full-case and split-case items, to have special areas for handling different products or goods which are heavy or fragile. All of these factors make the proper slotting of inventory to obtain the best results an important science on its own.

Live storage racks to reduce the picking face
In most static racking systems some reserve inventory has to be stored as well as the inventory that has to be picked next. Ordinarily, this reserve inventory is stored longitudinally alongside the picking stock.

By using live storage racks the reserve inventory can be stored on roll-tracks behind the picking inventory in a way that dramatically reduces the picking face. Naturally the extent of the reduction is determined by the nature of the goods and the amount of inventory stored on-line but, in most instances, a reduction of in the order of 80 per cent could be expected.

There are a number of other advantages for using live storage which are as follows:

a) Inventory is automatically rotated.
b) Picking and replenishment functions are separated.
c) In split-case picking the last carton can be tilted towards the operator, giving better access.
d) The front frame can be laid back, further improving access.
e) Because the number of aisles is reduced, storage density is typically increased by up to 60 per cent.
f) Picking and replenishment activities are confined to a clearly

defined area which makes illumination, heating and cooling, supervision and other activities more practical and economic.

g) A shorter, in-line picking face makes it cheaper and enables the use of conveyors as described in a later section.

Carton live storage is particularly appropriate for split-case order picking in a range of movement rates and for full-case order picking only with slow-moving line items. Fast-moving full-case items are more generally best picked from a pallet.

Use of the headroom
Like static shelving systems, carton live storage racks can be constructed two or three tiers high to cost-effectively use the headroom.

The inventory in the second or third levels of the mezzanine structure can be replenished either from a high-level order picker or by having replenishment aisles adjacent to a selective rack into which replenishment inventory can be placed by the forklift truck. From here the operators can move the inventory to replenish the carton live storage racks.

Pallet live storage is almost always used in walk-pick-to-belt full case picking systems which generally incorporate batch picking techniques which will be discussed later. Since it is most important that picking inventory is not exhausted during the picking of a batch, on-line reserve inventory is essential.

The length of the picking conveyor can be reduced if this reserve inventory is stored in pallet live storage behind the picking pallet. Moreover, such an arrangement increases the effective use of the cube. It is much less common to find justifications for the use of pallet live storage in discrete order picking operations where goods are being picked to a trolley or some type of order picking machine.

Using conveyors to move goods to and from the picking operation
As a quite separate exercise from condensing the picking face we can reduce the travel distance in a picking operation by mechanically conveying materials that would otherwise have to be handled by the operator. The use of conveyors falls into three quite separate categories:

1   *To feed picking totes or cartons into a split-case picking operation:* Shipping totes or cartons can be fed into a picking area either on a gravity carton conveyor or an overhead conveyor. With carton

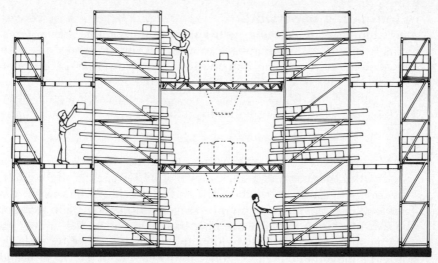

Figure 15.3   Use of three techniques in split-case picking operations

conveyors it is possible to queue them in sequence in various areas until they are required.

2   *Taking out the finished order:* Once an order has been completed, or a tote or shipping carton filled, then the picking operator can place it onto a central take-away conveyor. In this way it is moved to the next operation, be it Checking or Packing, without the operator having to travel.

3   *The disposal of trash:* In split-case picking operations it is usually practical and cost-effective to have an overhead conveyor with tall sides into which empty cartons and other packing material can be placed. This conveyor can be switched on from time to time, conveying the surplus packing materials to a central area for further processing.

Conveyors are frequently also used to accumulate picked orders during the Checking and Packing operations and to take away packed orders to Shipping. The principal application of conveyors in a full-case picking operation is when batch picking is also used; this will be discussed in a later section.

As is illustrated in Figure 15.3, in split-case picking operations all three techniques for reducing the travel distance are generally used to good effect.

Eliminating paperwork

Distributing order picking instructions, locating the relevant pick slots, marking off, feeding back information on shortages or out-of-stock items all cost time and money. More importantly, in many industries it leads to a high number of errors.

Computer-aided picking systems (CAPS) streamline the entire picking process by using lights to guide the operator rather than a written list.

For faster-moving line items   A bay light indicates that a pick is required in that bay and a 'pick module' under each product guides the operator straight to the bin and shows how many of that particular item to pick. Simply pressing a button allows him to report back to the computer that the pick has been concluded or that the item is out of stock. The bay light cannot be extinguished, nor can the order be moved into the next zone, until every item has been picked.

Paperless order picking is most often used for split-case picking, usually in conjunction with carton live storage where there is a condensed picking activity.

For slower-moving line items   In addition to the system described above, a number of portable paperless picking systems has recently been developed. Here, a picking cart either carries picking instructions with it or receives them by radio link. The operator is advised as to which pick slot he should visit next. Once there he can use a portable scanning wand on the pick cart to scan a bar code on the front of the picking bin. This verifies that he is in the correct location, at which time the paperless picking system on the pick cart can give the operator picking instructions.

Under this arrangement it is quite usual, when there is a number of small orders involved, to pick several orders concurrently. This paperless order picking system therefore has a wide approach where there is a large number of line items and a relatively slow movement rate per line item.

Often computer-aided picking systems (CAPS) can double output, but the biggest boost can be the reduction of errors by up to 90 per cent, saving money and keeping customers happy. This factor alone often justifies the cost of paperless order picking.

Finally, management and control is simpler and infinitely better than with a paper-driven system because the computer can generate a wide range of reports on exactly what is happening. Bottlenecks can

Figure 15.4 Display panels (on shelf face) allow operator to communicate directly with computer

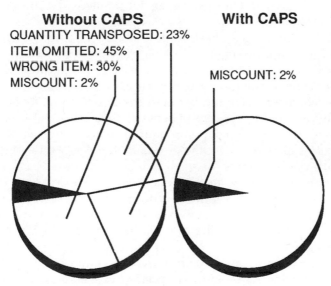

Figure 15.5 Advantages of using CAPS

be identified and eliminated by reslotting; zones can be balanced to share the workload; projections for next day's manning are available instantly; shortages can be reported as they happen and more stock can be called for automatically – even the quantity and location of the reserve stock can be monitored.

Batch picking

By having the computer add together, say, five or ten orders, all of the non-productive functions are divided by as many orders as are batched. Picking productivity is therefore typically tripled or quadrupled.

Because orders then need to be re-sorted, most batch picking systems require orders to be picked to a conveyor, which permits them to be quickly sorted on the dock either manually for low volumes or automatically for high volumes.

The great majority of instances where batch picking can be used is in filling full-case orders. This is because it is normal to apply a label in order that goods can be scanned or manually recognized in the sorting operation.

The smaller the average order, the higher the downtime in the picking cycle and the stronger the argument for batch picking. As the number of line items increases and the percentage that are picked in the average order decreases, again so increases the argument for batch picking.

With a very high number of line items, the walk-pick-to-belt batch picking system is often supplemented with the use of a pick car, which acts like a high level order picker but, because it has a take-away conveyor, allows batch picking.

Mechanized batch picking systems might normally be considered with full-case throughputs of between 5,000 and 10,000 cases per day. Above 10,000 cases a day automatic sortation can usually be justified. The best method to sort the orders depends upon the order size and the throughput rates.

Often, with many small orders, it is possible and economic to carry out a secondary sort at the Shipping dock. These days, in automatic sorting systems laser scanners read the barcodes on the labels or the cartons prior to diverting directly into the despatch vehicle or to a palletizing station.

The barcodes can contain a wealth of information like the customer's name and address, prices, order numbers, picking slot locations and so on – all of which can be scanned, analysed and sent

Figure 15.6 Rapistan pick car

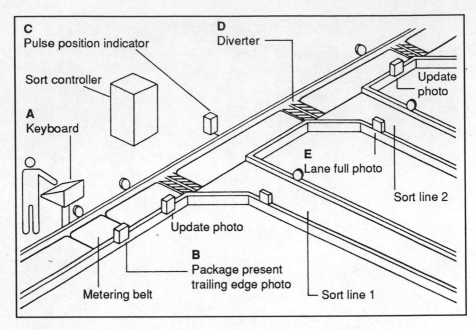

Figure 15.7 Automatic sorting system operated by laser scanner

back to the mainframe. By checking off the cartons scanned against the order in the computer an automatic check of exactly what was shipped is possible.

Bringing the goods to the man

This significantly reduces the travel distance and therefore makes the operator much more productive. There are two quite different types of systems that achieve this function and two sub-groups within each type. Each should be used for a different product range and a different movement profile.

Carousels

Carousels are a relatively expensive form of storage and are generally only used where their higher cost can be justified by the labour savings in order picking. On the other hand, care should be taken not to use them for very fast-moving goods because, like all goods-to-the-man systems, their throughput capacity is limited to machine capacity. The designer should also bear in mind that some machine time is taken up to replenish picking stock as well as to pick it.

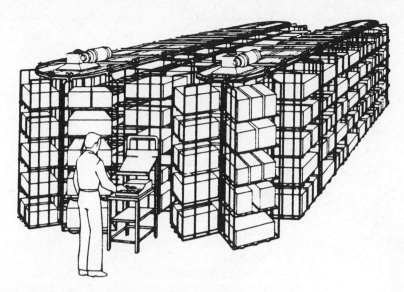

Figure 15.8   Horizontal carousel storage

Nowadays, carousels are almost always computer-controlled and can often be combined with paperless order picking to good effect. They fall into two main sub-categories, each of which in turn has a different range of appropriate applications.

Horizontal carousels   Whilst horizontal carousels are expensive per cubic metre of storage when compared with static or live storage racking systems, they are much cheaper per cubic metre than vertical carousels. Since they are also often constructed with a wire mesh framework they tend to be used to store medium-sized items. They have particularly wide application in the garment and footwear industries, for example.

Apart from being suitable for a wide range of standard order picking tasks, another common application for horizontal carousels is the picking of 'kits' or the total allocation of a range of merchandise – for example, flatwear fashion delivered to a central distribution centre frequently has to be allocated in random quantities to a number of retail stores, which function is sometimes well suited to horizontal carousels.

Vertical carousels   The cost per cubic metre of vertical carousels is around three times higher than horizontal carousels. On the other

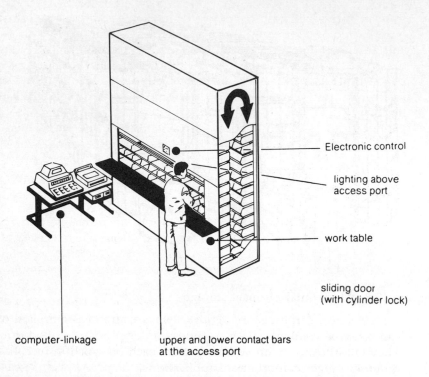

Electronic control

lighting above
access port

work table

sliding door
(with cylinder lock)

computer-linkage

upper and lower contact bars
at the access port

Figure 15.9   Vertical carousel storage

hand, they make far better use of the available headroom and also
have the advantage that goods are kept in a cleaner and more secure
environment. These reasons alone often determine their selection
over horizontal carousels.

Perhaps more importantly, the storage medium is usually a series
of steel shelves which can be subdivided and fitted in a number of
ways which make them very appropriate for storing large quantities
of loose, small parts.

Vertical carousels also have the advantage that the goods can be
presented at waist height for picking, which increases picking speed
and accuracy.

Retrieval systems

Pallet and mini-stacker retrieval systems can be used for goods-to-
the-man order picking: however, their prime purpose is to provide a
cost-effective storage system for a large amount of inventory. Once

this can be justified it is then possible to provide additional savings in order picking by bringing the goods to the operator.

It should, however, be remembered that such retrieval systems must have a limited number of picks in each aisle during a given period otherwise the captive machines will not be able to cope with the throughput. Obviously an operator on a high-level order picking machine could access many more line items per hour than an automatic machine. This is because it can only pick up one line item at a time, feed to an operator and then replace it in its storage slot.

Automatic retrieval systems　These systems can be broadly divided into two types:

1　*Pallet AS/RS:* where the goods are stored on pallets so that full-case and split-case picking can take place from relevant pallets.

Such pallet retrieval systems usually need a fairly extensive conveyor system to bring out and accumulate pallets to feed them past a picking and processing area and then back into the highrise narrow aisle system: however, such conveyors in the main would form part of the infeed/outfeed systems for an AS/RS system anyway.

Finally, of course, in any storage system it is possible to retrieve goods with whatever pallet handling machine has been used to store them: however, since this involves the use of an operator it is very rare that such systems are cost-effective.

An isometric AS/RS plan is shown in Figure 15.10.

2　*Mini-stacker system:*　The goods are stored in boxes or drawer-like totes so that split-case orders and small part components can be picked. It is not unusual for a large box to be sub-divided and several SKUs stored in it in order that a standard-sized container can be used for a very wide range of SKU volumes.

These containers are normally retrieved to a workbench area where picking and, if appropriate, packing take place. One operator can normally service other machines so that he can be picking whilst the machine is putting away and retrieving.

Automatic retrieval systems are used under the following circumstances:

a)　Pallet retrieval systems are used for high cube inventory, and mini-stackers for low cube inventory.

b)　They are used where there is a considerable quantity of inventory

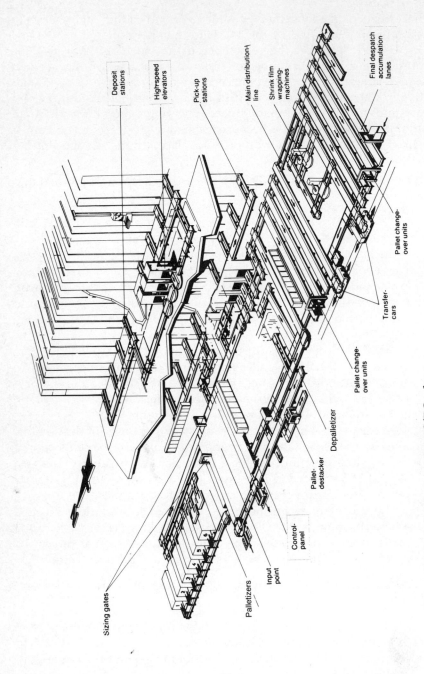

Deposit stations

Highspeed elevators

Pick-up stations

Main distribution line

Shrink film wrapping-machines

Final despatch accumulation lanes

Pallet change-over units

Transfer-cars

Pallet change-over units

Depalletizer

Pallet-destacker

Sizing gates

Palletizers

Input point

Control-panel

Figure 15.10   An isometric AS/RS plan

262

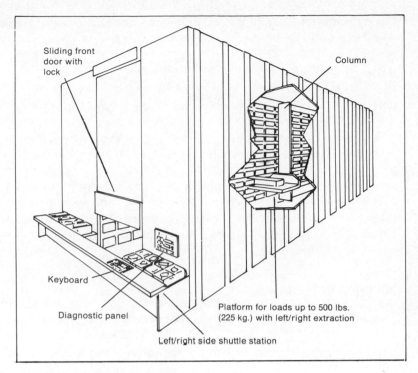

Figure 15.11   A mini-stacker system

that is relatively slow-moving so that the prime concern in the
operation is the effective use of the cube.

c) They are also used where there are very low pick rates, typically
no more than, say, 20 to 30 hits per aisle per hour.

As can be seen these are not great pick rates, but because retrieval
systems are good storage media they still have their place. It should
also be borne in mind that, with a high volume of inventory and a
low-hit density even these pick rates would be difficult to achieve
manually. If the cranes were not automated then four crane operators
may be required to undertake the same work as one picker/operator
of four automatic cranes.

When should high technology methods be used?

Perhaps it would be clearer if we were to ask: 'What level of
mechanization will be applicable?' Clearly there is no easy answer to

this complex question: however, there are some fairly clear guidelines which are outlined below.

Rule of thumb
Full-case picking
One might start to consider using some level of mechanization between 5,000 and 10,000 full case picks per day.

One could consider using a smart storage system where there were several thousand SKUs and between, say, 4,000 and 6,000 pallet loads of inventory. A decision to use a smart storage system might imply a relatively high level of mechanization for order picking: for example, a narrow aisle automatic retrieval system might be appropriate if the throughput was low. If the throughput exceeded 5,000 to 10,000 picks per single shift, then a separate mechanized order picking system might be justifiable.

Split-case picking
With a relatively low number of line items, then one would expect between 10,000 and 15,000 hits per day which would typically represent 20,000 to 40,000 items picked. This would be the level at which one might consider using a higher level of mechanization for order picking.

As the number of SKUs exceeds 10,000 but, more relatively, as the cube of inventory exceeds, say, 5,000 cubic metres, then the argument for having a smarter, more dense storage system increases, which would in turn point to the need for a higher level of mechanization in order picking.

Different techniques for different sections of product range
As was outlined earlier, any given technique is rarely the answer for the whole product range. It is frequently appropriate to pick fast movers in a different way to medium movers, which is different again for slow-moving line items.

Typically, for example, slow-moving line items might well be picked from the bulk or total stock, whereas a more conveniently located and arranged separate picking stock is usually more cost-effective for faster moving line items. Under these circumstances, the reserve inventory is stored elsewhere and picking stock is replenished from time to time.

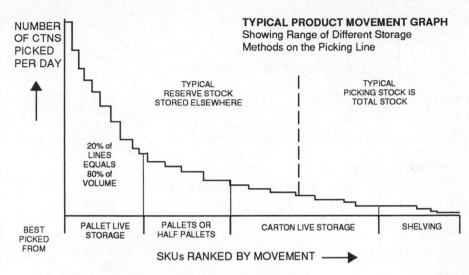

Figure 15.12   Typical product movement graph

The picking task vs the storage task

As the number of line items or stock keeping units (SKUs) increases, so does the argument increase for using a dense storage system to store the goods cost-effectively. Once this decision has been taken, then one has also taken the decision that the method of order picking must, by definition, also be more mechanized unless it is to be done outside the storage system.

For example, if one wishes to store several thousand line items with several thousand cubic metres of inventory, one might determine that the most cost-effective storage system is a high-rise narrow aisle design. Having stored the goods in this way, we now either have to have man-aboard high-level order pickers, fixed- or free-path, or an automatic retrieval system.

In this instance, therefore, a DC with a relatively low throughput rate employing, say, only 10 to 20 people, might finish up with a relatively high level of mechanization.

Obviously, if we have a high number of line items and a significant storage task *plus* a high throughput, then the argument for the smartest level of mechanization of both the storage and the order picking tasks becomes even stronger.

The term 'hit' is used to describe the action of accessing a particular line item or SKU. Hits have a greater influence on the work content of picking than do the number of picks if the items are small and less

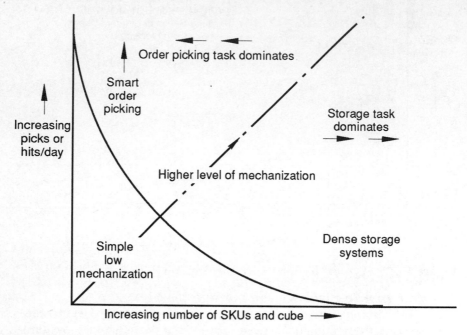

Figure 15.13   Relationship between 'hits' and number of SKUs

than full-case quantities. Where the goods to be picked are in cartons, then the number of picks predominates in determining the work content.

In a distribution centre where there is only a relatively low number of line items but a high number of picks or hits, the storage task becomes far less relevant and the picking method dominates the design of the DC. Under these circumstances, as the number of picks or hits per day increases, so does the work content, and so does the argument for an increased level of mechanization. Figure 15.13 graphically demonstrates this argument.

What might seem a high number of SKUs to a biscuit manufacturer would be a blessing to an automobile spare parts company. The former might have 100 to 300 SKUs and the latter 50,000 to 200,000!

Twenty thousand full-case picks per day represent a huge volume of merchandise, whereas the same number of picks in a split case or small components parts would be a minimal cubic movement rate.

16 Building Design and Layout

Gerry Hatton

Optimizing the building design

Often, the designer of a distribution operation will be faced with an existing building design, in which case a great number of compromises have to be made. However, the principles which apply to the design of a new building can sometimes be retrospectively added to an existing building.

Ideally we should first develop our ideal storage and handling system and then build a building around it. When this is not possible, or when there are few site constraints, there are some guidelines on building shape.

The ideal building shape

The building shape is most often determined by the shape of the available site. Another major controlling factor is the optimum position and the size of the docks. Given required dock space on, say, one face of the building naturally determines at least a minimum for that dimension.

Generally speaking there are considerable disadvantages in allowing the ratio of a building shape to exceed 2:1. The main exceptions to this general rule are with high-rise warehouses where the ratios of 6:1 and 8:1 are common.

The reason for limiting ratios is related to the travelling distances required. Obviously, by this criterion alone, the ideal building should be round with Receipt and Despatch in the centre. Since this is impossible the buildings more usually approximate a rectangle with

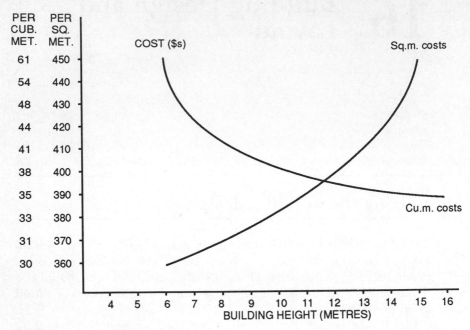

Figure 16.1 Relationship between cubic cost of warehouse and clear headroom

either equal dimensions or a 2:1 ratio with Receiving and Despatch most generally on the same shorter face.

Building heights

Higher warehouses cost less

Figure 16.1 demonstrates clearly the way in which the cubic cost of the warehouse reduces dramatically as the clear headroom inside the warehouse is increased. It should be noted, however, that the costs mentioned are illustrative only.

Since most storage systems are concerned with using the available cube and not the available square, this phenomenon has strongly influenced modern warehouses to use storage and handling equipment that can reach higher.

The ideal general-purpose building height

Of course the ideal building height is determined by what functions have to take place within the building. For instance, sorting goods for allocation only requires three or four metres of headroom: on the other hand, if palletized storage and handling is to be involved, then there are some useful general rules.

These days, most forklift trucks can simply and economically lift to in the order of six to eight metres. If the pallet height is, say, 1.5 metres and some room is left for ventilation and sprinklers, then a minimum building height of eight metres, and more likely 10 metres, is generally appropriate. This headroom will not only accommodate most standard pallet handling and order picking machines but is also appropriate for three-high split- or full-case order picking modules.

Using taller buildings

The headroom in buildings of over 10 metres clear can only be used if analysis shows that some form of higher lifting storage and/or order picking machines is appropriate for any given task.

Making existing buildings taller

If there is insufficient space in an existing building, it is occasionally practical to raise the roof level. The cost of doing this is usually in the order of one-third of the cost of building a new building.

With a low-roofed building of, say, four metres being raised to, say, eight metres, the cubic capacity of the building is doubled. This is frequently an appropriate answer if there is little or no further space on site to develop a new building. One of the main disadvantages of this approach is the difficulty of implementation. It is very difficult to raise the roof whilst continuing to operate within the facility, although it can sometimes be raised in segments depending on building size and design.

Issues concerning the determination of the building shape and the ideal layout are best considered under the subsections to be covered later on selecting storage and order picking methodology.

Docks and offices

Docks

Docks are usually grossly underdesigned. The area required for bringing in vehicles, turning them and positioning them, unloading, staging and loading approximates the area required for all other functions. The dock areas inside the building are themselves usually in the order of 25 per cent of the distribution centre area. They should

Figure 16.2   Example of a covered weatherproof dock

therefore be carefully designed with adequate space for all necessary operations.

The aspect of the docks is also important. Generally, it is preferable that they face the sun and away from prevailing, inclement weather. Stopping the movement of large volumes of air through the building is usually easier if all of the docks are on the same face of the building. Temperature and dust control is then much improved. However, weatherproof docks can be constructed if climate or location dictate. (Figure 16.2)

Offices

One control office is best positioned somewhere between Receiving and Despatch. There are benefits in having these functions separate but adjacent in order that people and machines can be moved from one area to the other as the workload varies: however, any other offices are best built above ground level to conserve valuable floor working area.

Since the Receiving, Staging and Despatch operations can only use two or three metres of headroom effectively, one economic and practical solution is to build the balance of the offices and any other facilities overhead in this area.

Right-hand-down turning

Too many designers overlook the fact that it is much easier to reverse a right-hand drive vehicle into a loading dock in a right-hand-down position. If this is not done, then either the docks have to be more widely spaced, or the reversing area has to be increased by another fifteen metres.

A model arrangement

(Figure 16.3) shows the way in which the most common functions can frequently be neatly and economically positioned on the site: this is only possible, however, in an ideal world and these notes are therefore only for general guidance of building designers.

As will be seen from the Figure, the fast movers should ideally be positioned adjacent to Receiving and Despatch with medium and slower movers further away. Arranging functions in this way can often significantly reduce the total travelling time and minimize handling costs.

Floor design

Because the warehouse or distribution centre floor has to meet a number of special requirements that do not occur in most other types of buildings, it is therefore worth separate discussion. In particular, the floors should be designed to withstand the unusually high loads that are likely to occur. These fall into two principal categories:

1   *Static loading.* The construction of two- or three-tier mezzanine floors for small-part order picking, packing and other low headroom functions, or the building of storage racks for pallets or other heavy items is likely to induce a number of high point loads on the floor.

    The designer should ensure that the base below the slab and the slab itself have been adequately constructed to cater for the worst circumstances that are likely to occur. In particular, he should allow the overall floor loading to be such that, in most circumstances, racks and other storage equipment can be relocated as

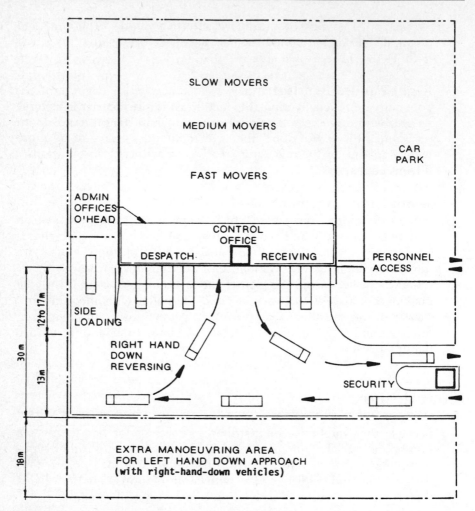

Figure 16.3   Ideal layout for docks and offices

required to suit changing needs without consideration of limited
floor loading.

2   *Dynamic loading.* In addition to the load applied by storage and
other equipment, quite high dynamic loads are applied by the
wheels of pallet handling or order picking equipment. This is
especially so with free-path high-rise narrow aisle machines.
These machines may well each weigh five tonnes or more, to
which must be added the load that they carry. When this load is

being picked up or deposited most of the applied load tends to fall on to one wheel, with substantial dynamic point loads.

It is particularly important that the joints between slabs be 'keyed' in a way that takes into account such loads. If individual slabs are free to deflect under the load applied by pallet handling equipment wheels, then they will flex independently, leading to an uneven floor surface for the machine and the breaking of the edge of the slabs.

Floor surfaces

The floor surface itself is also worth separate consideration for two reasons. First, there is an unusual amount of wear, particularly in operating aisles: second, many products must be protected from the 'dusting' which occurs from ordinary concrete floors.

In most circumstances, therefore, the use of floor hardeners, special extra-hard concrete and surface sealers are often desirable to prolong the life of the floor and minimize the generation of dust. The hardener is usually cast into the floor and reduces the effect of wear whereas sealers are usually applied afterwards.

Level floors

Warehouses and distribution centres have particular requirements concerning levels. It is often unacceptable to have the whole slab slope to one side in a way that might be quite acceptable in a factory. This is because tall storage racks and the machines that service them would also be required to lean over with most undesirable results.

Free-path, narrow aisle machines in particular require extremely flat floors if dynamic sway is not to be introduced as they lift to heights of ten or twelve metres. A level difference of 4mm across a 1500mm wide aisle can represent a 32mm deflection with a machine lifting to 12 metres. When the deflection in the mast and compression of the tyres is added, then unacceptable overall deflection can result.

Apart from being flat in this way, such aisles should be even with minimal sharp changes in level. For example, whilst a 4mm change in level over a length of five metres down an aisle would be quite acceptable, a 4mm change in level over a distance of 200 metres would be quite unacceptable because of the way in which it would induce dynamic sway into high-lift narrow aisle machines.

The design of warehouse floors is a very specialized subject and one on which specific advice should be taken – which includes accounting for the issues discussed above.

Building column spacing

These days it is economic to design buildings with clear spans of around 30 metres or more by the use of modern portal frame design. The number of columns in a building should be kept to a minimum in order to maximize the flexibility of future operations and to minimize the lost space in the initial design.

Ideally, the storage, handling and order picking system should be first designed to define the building 'envelope'. In this way columns can then be positioned in the centre-line of racks and in other areas where they do not interfere significantly with the operation.

Rack-supported buildings

Rack-supported buildings are occasionally viable, especially with automatic stacker and retrieval systems (AS/RS) and occasionally in other high-rise, high-density storage systems. They are rarely economic for other types of operations.

Even where they are economic it is usually only the major storage area to which this design applies. The balance of the area – for example receiving and despatch docks, staging and so on – are usually constructed by conventional means. (Figure 16.4)

The use of rack-clad structures sometimes changes the way in which the whole facility might be treated for taxation purposes (the rules vary from place to place). Another benefit is that it is sometimes faster to construct a building in this way. On the other hand, such a design approach is inflexible and one must be very certain that there would be no need to make any changes in the design of the internal structure at a later date before proceeding on such a path.

Unless the overall cost is significantly less, users will seldom accept the inflexibility that comes with such a design approach. The only way to know what is appropriate in a given application is to calculate the relevant construction costs and taxation rules to determine the most appropriate design approach.

Roof and wall design and cladding

Clearly, the most appropriate solution for cladding the walls and roof of the distribution centre changes from location to location. In many

Figure 16.4   Construction of a rack clad building

instances, local government regulations or fire safety regulations will determine that fire-rated masonry walls be constructed.

Failing these constraints, in most circumstances nowadays light-weight steel cladding materials, or a combination of these with masonry, are usually found to be the most cost-effective.

For the comfort of operators and the care of merchandise the designer should provide adequate ventilation and protection from both extremes of temperature. Obviously, in many buildings where goods are being controlled at different temperatures or inflammable goods are being stored for example, then special construction techniques of the floor, the walls and the roof are required.

Fire protection and security

Security requirements will vary from company to company due to varying company policies and, of course, the relative value and portability of the merchandise to be stored and handled. In the notional ideal layout provided in Figure 16.3 some thought has been given to separating staff access from delivery and despatch vehicle access and the provision of security gates for both groups. The inclusion of other security techniques is a matter that should be separately considered by the designer of the facility.

The level of fire protection is usually determined by a combination of the company's insurance underwriters and government regulations. Whilst, again, these rules vary from location to location they are normally directly related to the flammability of the goods. Clearly, highly flammable goods need to be more carefully protected than would otherwise be the case.

Another matter which affects fire protection is the building height. As goods are stored to increasing heights, then they are more likely to become affected by a fire which starts at the lower levels of the storage system. As the heat rises there is an exponential increase in the amount of damage induced. Accordingly, if the height is sufficient and the goods to be stored are rated at an appropriate level, it is usually prescribed that fire protection devices should be fitted within the storage racking system as well as into the roof of the building.

17 Managing Logistics Facilities

Keith Campbell

The management of logistics facilities is concerned with the management of the total distribution channels utilized in the movement of merchandise from the source of supply to the customer. Depending on the industry, the source will be either at the raw materials procurement or manufactured product level. Every company therefore must identify the distribution channels affecting its business and accept responsibility for involvement in channel management with the other trading partners involved.

It is imperative to recognize that the flow and exchange of information within the channels and the effectiveness and speed with which this is achieved is the most direct impact on the efficiency of the physical function of goods movement. The information flow facilitates planning, scheduling, costing, assessment of alternatives and quick response feedback for all members of the channel.

The physical distribution facilities in terms of distribution centres, warehouses, depots and transport fleet are a part of the channel to be managed in the context of the total channel as another distribution alternative, in achieving the company marketing objectives. Management of the physical distribution facilities in isolation from the rest of the distribution channel cannot be effective: concern with managing only the activities within the distribution centre, will not best utilize the total company resources and will probably add a greater cost burden elsewhere in the channel – usually in another part of the organization.

The logistics facilities must be managed as an integral part of the marketing thrust of the company, giving the company a competitive advantage, and providing value-added services, more efficiently and economically than they can be done by other members of the channels.

Operating service levels, costs, performance and productivity levels for activities must be determined, measured and controlled. Trends must be established at a macro level to enable monitoring of performance at a high level, and assessment of alternatives within the total channel performance.

Ongoing communication with all groups involved is a vital ingredient for success. Communication must be relevant and productive whether it be with a vendor, transport company, distribution centre staff, company purchasing personnel or customer. It must also be timely, accurate and regular. Communication must be such that people need it to play their part in the process effectively, can act upon it and use it to assist in their interactions with other parties. Lack of credibility or usefulness of information not only lessens effectiveness at the time, it affects the value of future communications.

Management organization

The organization structure of the logistics management group must consider the following factors:

- Closeness to the customer and supply function. Must be outward looking.
- Impact of technology and expertise to manage internally and externally to the company.
- Alignment to critical success areas.
- Achievement of long-term objectives.
- Effective management of the physical distribution functions. Emphasis on effective work teams, leadership, communication channels.

A mission statement, brief, concise, expressing the groups mission in terms of its contribution to the overall company objectives is important.

The vision must be stated. What is the view of the future? Given the strategic direction of the company, what should the distribution channels and logistics functions be like in three to five years, and then in the longer term. It is imperative to visualize the next three to five years in detail as a basis for planning, setting objectives and milestones to achieve the desired future. The longer term is a less specific, more speculative view given that many things, not the least technology will change significantly five years or more into the future.

In considering the *vision*, we must consider *differences* to the current situation:

- What do we *know* we will be doing differently?
- What do we *think* we will be doing differently?
- What are we going to *make* happen differently?

The establishment of *goals* and *objectives* are the next step. The goals are general statements of the aspects of focus to manage the business consistently with the *mission* and *vision*.

The objectives, then, are a specific target in terms of timing, costing, result. They must be:

- quantifiable,
- measurable, and
- achievable/realistic.

For example, a goal may be: 'To improve productivity performance through the quality of work and new technology.' The corresponding objectives may be:

- Improve productivity by 3 per cent by . . . (date).
- Improve productivity by 5 per cent by . . . (date).
- Implement quality improvement programme in distribution centre by . . . (date).
- Install barcode label printers in distribution centre and specified vendor premises by . . . (date).
- Implement Electronic Data Interchange programme with priority suppliers and customer by . . . (date).

Implementation dates will, of course, be reviewed as the projects progress; the important consideration is that the broad and specific directions and measurements are established.

The *key issues* for each must then be identified, documented and addressed. Each group in the company will have different issues to consider, and there will be some common issues such as customer service, systems and channel relationships. Key issues relate to the objectives set in terms of the facilities, resources, environment required to achieve them.

Examples of key issues that may relate to the objectives above are as follows:

- development resources

- systems availability
- capital available
- employee relations/morale
- change in work practices
- customer service
- channel relationships

Documenting the mission, vision, goals, objectives and key issues provides a blueprint for the management of the logistics facilities.

It is absolutely vital that this blueprint is developed through discussion, involvement, and agreement with the people responsible to make it happen. Everybody involved must have input to, and ownership of, the plan to ensure commitment and success.

Distribution channels

Identification of the distribution channels in which a company is involved, the various members of those channels and the part they play is a first step in addressing the management of the channels.

It is a useful exercise to document the channels and the relationships. Figure 17.1 is an example of a channel diagram showing typical direct merchandise flow channels for the retail industry. Figure 17.2 shows more complex relationships with the flow of information to and from channel members.

It is not only the physical flow of goods which determines the channel members, the information flow embraces a wider integrated group. The old phrase that 'merchandise moves on information' has never been more valid, with the rapid developments in information technology.

The efficiency and productivity of the physical distribution facilities depend on how well a company manages the information, merchandise and communication flows between all members of the distribution channels. The productivity and efficiency of a distribution centre are affected as much by the processes that take place prior to merchandise being received and following despatch as they are by the management of the processes within the distribution centre.

Having identified and documented the channels, it is possible to analyse the relationships and seek opportunities to manage them more effectively for all concerned.

Partnership marketing with all members of a channel working together leads to mutual gains. This process provides opportunities for:

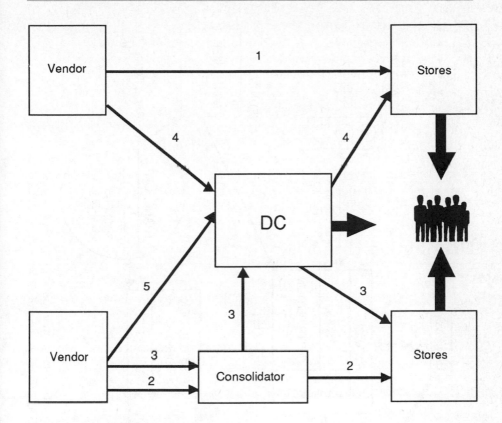

1. Vendor-Store-Customer
2. Vendor-Consolidator-Store-Customer
3. Vendor-Consolidator-DC-Store-Customer
4. Vendor-DC-Store-Customer
5. Vendor-DC-Customer

Figure 17.1   Distribution channels

- cost efficiencies
- trade-off negotiation
- competitive advantage
- reduced inventories
- improved customer service
- value-added services

Channel members need to be concerned with an understanding of

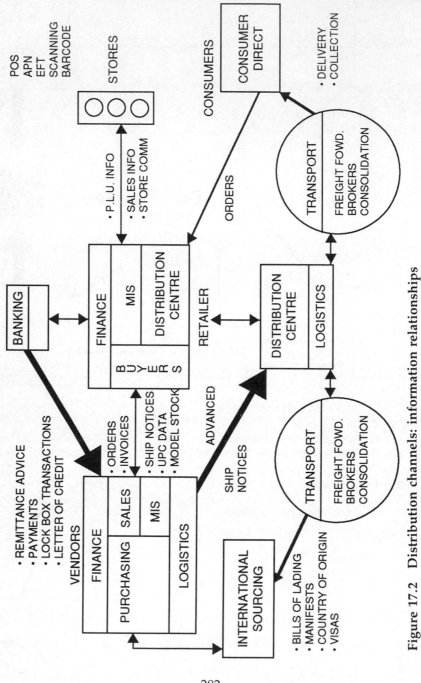

Figure 17.2 Distribution channels: information relationships
Figure reproduced courtesy of G.E. Information Services

each others' business, and contribute to the improvement of each. Trading partners usually have experience and perspective of others' systems (receiving, ordering, delivery and so on) which is both different and valuable. An atmosphere must therefore be created which encourages open, frank discussion and cooperation, seeking mutual gains from the experience.

Assessment of alternatives is possible with the application of costing and service requirements to different channels. Changes can be maintained: 'what if?' simulations are a simple matter once the parameters of performance are established.

Performance/productivity measurement

In terms of managing the logistics facility, measurement, control, reporting systems are necessary for:

- key performance factors
- service levels
- operating costs
- productivity performance

Key performance factors

The critical success factors for each operation must be identified, together with the relevant unit of measurement. The facility management must identify the factors on which reporting is needed to assess the performance of the facility and indicate areas where corrective action is necessary. It is a common error for management to believe that reporting is required for every function performed in a distribution centre – for example, on a daily or weekly basis. The result is usually unnecessary cost incurred recording and reporting information which is of little (if any) consequence, and not used. The danger is, once started, it is difficult to stop.

Wherever possible, computer systems should be networked to provide the reporting required without labour-intensive input from staff. The development of computer systems, whether they be inventory, financial, materials handling, merchandise or management information systems must consider the *key performance factors* and be specified in the systems design.

Barcoding provides the facility to design into systems the automatic collection of a wide range of data, which can then be related in many different forms of reporting.

Service levels

Operational and inventory service levels must be set for each operating area. Inventory service levels are largely a function of inventory systems which forecast requirements and automatically generate re-orders.

Operational service levels must be set in conjunction with customer service requirements. They are usually expressed in terms of hours or days, but may be expressed in other terms which relate to the customer service policy. Service levels within the same facility may vary also according to company marketing requirements.

An example of a range of service levels for order servicing within a facility could well be:

- Standard stock replenishment – Class I stores   = 2 days
- Standard stock replenishment – Class II stores   = 4 days
- Customer special orders   = 1 day
- Advertised merchandise   = 2 days
- General order processing   = 5 days

Service levels for order processing in a distribution centre must be measured from the time the merchandise is received, or the time a replenishment requisition is received to the despatch time. Barcoding provides the necessary tracking and removes any subjectivity from the measurement. Other processes, such as stock location, re-order work and materials supply will have different time measurements; they must be related to the commencement and completion of a process.

Operational service levels are vital ingredients in order/personnel scheduling and workload forecasting. The establishment of operational service levels facilitates the work hours required to maintain them with differing throughput volumes and configuration of order sizes.

Operating costs

The basis of operational costing is the expense budget for operating a facility. Control is enhanced when the expense budget is broken down into cost centres which reflect the responsibility and accountability of each manager. The principle of a manager being accountable for the total costs incurred in the operating area ensures closer control and acceptance of that responsibility. The number of cost centres depends on the size of the facility, the span of control and the autonomy of operating sections. All costs should be included – labour, statutory provisions, supplies, maintenance and overheads – to give relevant unit costs and comparisons.

With cost centres allocated to operating section level, the manager (who may manage several cost centres) is entitled to operate within the agreed budget without interference. Control reporting indicates to senior management if expenses are not controlled consistent with merchandise throughput variations.

Unit costing is important for control, comparison and alternative methods assessment. The relevant unit of measurement for each area must be identified, agreed and understood by everybody. Depending on the operations, it may be:

- pallets stored
- truck loads received/despatched
- customer telephone contacts made
- orders processed
- invoices processed
- units picked/packed

Whatever the unit of measurement,

- it must be the measure which relates most closely to the work performed;
- the terminology must be that which is used by the people doing the work; and
- reporting must reflect the input.

Credibility is paramount; people must be able to read unit costing reports and be confident that they reflect the work they performed.

Unit costing provides a basis for mission costing by alternative distribution channels and assessing trade-offs possible by relocating processes either up or down the channel. It also provides the basis for assessing internal impacts of methods application, equipment changes, personnel and system changes.

Every relevant function must be costed to facilitate informed analysis and decision making.

Productivity measurement

Productivity performance measurement and reporting have identical characteristics to unit costing in that every relevant function is involved, and must reflect the work performed.

The unit of measurement is the same for productivity measurement as it is for unit costing. The expression of costing is the difference between the two measures.

Productivity performance is considered at both macro and micro levels. Macro level measurement relates to trend indicators of performance for the total facility or group of operations. Macro measures for a distribution centre could be:

- Total operating expenses $ as % of total $ value of goods processed.
- Total operating expenses $ as % of total $ value of goods received.
- Total operating expenses $ as % of total $ value of goods despatched.

If the facility processes 100 per cent of the company stock, total $ operating costs as percentage of sales could be a macro measure.

The important issue is that the measure be consistent and that the resultant percentage can be used as a trend indicator of productivity, taking into consideration fluctuating volumes and conditions.

Micro level measurement relates to operating section level, building through a heirarchy to the key performance report for the facility. Typical micro level measurement could be:

- Number pallets located per hour
- Number units picked/packed per hour
- Number invoices processed per hour
- Number trucks loaded per hour
- Cost per delivery
- Cost per hour for each operating section

Each facility tailors the reporting to the level and measurement required to suit the particular business.

The actual results achieved are compared to a standard, and a performance percentage calculated. Standards may be engineered standards, based either on history or on peer performance. The method of standards determination needs to be considered by each enterprise in terms of what is to be achieved. The concern is not with precision, rather it is with providing a management tool for assessment of trends, exceptions and motivation. The level to which measurement is related is also an enterprise decision, whether it be to work group, operating section, individual operator or management area of responsibility.

Leading the team

Every manager must accept the responsibility for developing and leading strong teams, and creating the environment for team achievement. Every manager is a member of at least two work teams: first, his leaders team; and, second, the team he personally leads.

The manager must have the attitude, and develop the relationship, of 'doing with' the people, rather than 'doing for or to'. Only when the team is comfortable and contributes to this environment will the relationship be effective.

The power of small, strong groups has been long established, enabling an individual to be more than he would otherwise be. Small group interaction and motivation results in positive contribution to increased productivity and efficiency.

The manager or supervisor is the leader of his team; it is his role to ensure continuity and provide the team with the information, facilities, access to other resources and feedback needed for it to function effectively. He must listen, encourage participation of all members, be objective, and be able to accept suggestions and comments in such a way that they become constructive attempts to improve the operation rather than criticism of his leadership. When the team accepts that its input is appreciated and being acted upon, members will contribute more freely and constructively. The important issue is for the relationship to change, for the manager to be recognized as the team leader and the person to work *with* to improve work methods and solve problems. Each group must be encouraged to have input to their objectives. At first they may be reluctant and the input very minor: the way in which progress is managed will determine how more active this participation becomes. If it is used in a negative way continually to criticize or be held as a yardstick for non-achievement, people will react negatively, distrustfully, and industrial problems will most probably result.

As important, then, as encouraging the staff to be involved is working with the managers to ensure that they approach team-building in the proper way and come to see the benefits which they can realize in their area of operation.

The responsibility of the team leader involves:

- working with the team to set and maintain the team objectives and targets;
- ensuring that the total team is involved, as one, in achievements;

- maintenance of unity within the team and the elimination of both internally and externally derived threats;
- effective, and regular, communication with the team as a whole, discussing the operation of its work area;
- maintenance of the group's trust, by discussion of decisions which affect it;
- ensuring that high standards are met and maintained for the team (the ethic must not condone the lowering of standards);
- provision of feedback to the team on its performance and contribution;
- development of a 'CAN DO' attitude and a culture within the group 'to find a way';
- provision of the opportunity for team members to grow in themselves.

All too often, supervisors and managers are appointed on their technical competence rather than their leadership ability or potential. Whilst management must have the technical knowledge to do the job, it is more important that they have the skills to manage the work of a group of people.

Communication

Communication is the vital ingredient for success. For any of the foregoing considerations to be successful they must be discussed with, clearly understood and agreed as realistic by everybody involved. There must be no secrets: if people are expected to operate at a certain level and toward certain goals they must know what the expectations are and the progress being made toward achievement. The *vision* must be shared.

To this end, regular review meetings with everybody involved are invaluable. Within the company, not only the managers and supervisors but also every staff member appreciate attending review meetings to hear progress, what has been achieved, whether objectives have been met, what has changed and what are the next goals. Review meetings held three to four times per year are well worth the time spent.

With other channel members – such as vendors, buyers and customers – the same review process is necessary: the timing may vary, the 'where are we at, where are we going?' process is the same.

Developments in information technology facilitate economies and speed in the technical areas of communication. This gives everybody in the channel the opportunity to have access to the same information at the same time, bringing its own pressures and eliminating many traditional excuses for non-performance. The responsibility of the logistics manager is to ensure that expertise is available to keep abreast of the developments and recognize the opportunities, and to apply them to the best advantage of the company and its trading partners.

Competitive advantage

Logistics facilities are, and must be, managed as an integral part of the company marketing thrust. They must not be managed purely as a cost.

The objective and direction are to provide the company with an advantage over its competition. Working with trading partners to reduce lead times from order decision point to customer delivery, reducing inventory, increasing stock turn through application of JIT principles, providing first-class customer service, managing physical distribution facilities and alternatives at the required service quality levels, and competitive cost, are the challenges in managing logistics facilities. How well it is achieved determines the contribution to the competitive advantage realized by the company.

Part VI
MATERIALS MANAGEMENT

Overview to Part VI

The logistics mix depicted in Figure 10.1 (p. 142) clearly shows logistics comprising two major areas of activity: materials management on the input side of production; and distribution management on the finished goods side. It is only in recent years that the importance of these input side activities have been acknowledged at senior management level.

As Aschner points out in Chapter 18, inventory impacts the effectiveness of virtually every aspect of an organization's activities. He outlines the scope of inventory management, presenting the basic issues involved and reasons for holding inventory. In so doing, he challenges the validity of many of the mathematical formulae still blindly used by so many organizations. After outlining most of the commonly used inventory management systems, Aschner briefly discusses some of the new approaches being successfully adopted, including improved product design and process layout as well as just-in-time techniques.

Whilst more commonly considered as part of the distribution side of logistics, transport does play a significant role in the delivery of raw materials and sub-assemblies. In Chapter 19 Slater provides a comprehensive practitioner's guide to choosing the most appropriate mode of transport. Solutions offered range from the simple to the sophisticated; however, ultimate choice is dependent upon the logistics practitioner's skill in identifying and quantifying the significant options.

Farmer has long been concerned with the input side of the logistics equation and in Chapter 20 provides a convincing argument for the coordination of both the materials management and distribution subsystems if the organization is to operate effectively. The benefits to be gained from giving equal emphasis to incoming materials management is again highlighted in Chapter 27 which discusses the use of electronic data interchange (EDI) to control the inward flow of material.

In Chapter 21 Heenan traces the difficult, but rewarding, path to successful implementation of distribution resources planning (DRP) in manufacturing and distribution organizations. He stresses that successful implementation can only be achieved if there is a total visible commitment to the process from senior management. Organizations may undergo a culture change in the process of implementing DRP and the overall result can be a distinct competitive edge.

Finally in Chapter 22 Mitchelson defines then outlines some of the key materials management issues and success factors facing the capital-intensive sector of the economy. Mitchelson highlights the different materials management emphases and benefits in capital-intensive industries. Mitchelson goes on to provide a methodology for developing an effective materials management strategy in this important area.

18 Managing and Controlling Logistics Inventories

Andrew Aschner

Introduction

Inventory management is central to every enterprise engaged in the manufacture, warehousing, shipping and selling of products and commodities. The effective execution of this function has a major influence on overall performance and impacts the effectiveness of virtually every aspect of an organization's daily business activities.

The scope of inventory management extends well beyond the traditional practices of record-keeping, valuations and stock counts. Modern concepts challenge many of the traditional views and control practices. In particular, leading Japanese concerns have clearly demonstrated to the rest of the world how to run very efficiently with minimum inventory levels by adopting different philosophies and techniques. As a result, practitioners are having to re-evaluate and rethink conventional approaches. The art of effective management involves, first, the understanding of the techniques available, followed by the planned use of those systems and procedures most appropriate of each enterprise.

The basic issues

Each business has its own strategic and business objectives. While these may be many and varied, there are certain issues or objectives which tend to be common, namely:

- profitability;
- current assets;

- sales and customer service levels.

In a manufacturing environment, related investment goals may include effective resource utilization – that is, labour, energy, equipment and facilities.

Investments in inventories impact business objectives in all three areas and much has been written regarding the interrelationships between the three. Conventional wisdom maintains the three are in perpetual conflict. For example, higher customer service is typically associated with higher inventories, as the old saying 'stocks make sales' implies. Management science also holds this belief; there are well documented mathematical relationships between safety stock policies and target customer service percentages. Similarly, lower inventories require smaller order quantities and batch sizes which are believed to lead to higher operating costs, hence lower profits. Camp's formula for calculating economic order quantities (EOQ) shows this relationship:

$$EOQ = \sqrt{\frac{2RS}{cI}}$$

where   R = the annual usage in currency
         S = set up or ordering costs
         c = cost per stock keeping unit
         I = interest costs of holding inventory as a percentage

This formula and its variations, and these tenets, have now been clearly proved dated and incorrect. The role of managers and practitioners is to maintain pressure on all three of the business objectives mentioned, through better use of inventory management techniques – not by making compromising trade-offs.

This is not intended to imply that complex and sophisticated mathematical optimization models are required. Where complexity is inevitable, computer software is readily available to accommodate.

The right tools help, but success factors more importantly require the right direction and include:

- inventory objectives set by top management;
- consistency in maintaining objectives and performance;
- equal emphasis on objectives in all three issue areas as opposed to shifts in emphasis;
- continuous pressure to drive out unnecessary inventories.

Table 18.1
Traditional cost trade-offs

Holding Costs   – Opportunity (Interest)
                   – Storage and Warehousing
                   – Insurance
                   – Obsolescence, shrinkage, deterioration,
                     depreciation
                   – Rates

                        versus

Ordering Costs   – Set up and skills
                   – Waste
                   – Quality Control
                   – Administration

Stock-out Costs

Production and Transportation Costs

Reasons for holding inventory

Notwithstanding existing accounting conventions, not all inventories are assets. If inventory holdings are to be considered of true value they must serve specific primary functions, including protection against the uncertainties of customer demand versus the ability of the logistics operation to supply against the demand, and also against the uncertainty of supply, either in between various manufacturing steps or from external sources of supply. Inventories permit the decoupling of demand from immediate dependence on supply sources.

The recognized functional stock classifications reflect the different conditions under which inventories provide safety:

1 *Demand/supply fluctuations.* Safety stocks, buffer stocks or reserves are the terms commonly used to describe inventories held to absorb:
   • variations in sales demand during the replenishment period not able to be addressed by rescheduling action so that customer service levels may be maintained;

- uncertainty of vendor performance resulting in greater than average lead times to avoid material and product shortages.

2 *Anticipation.* Typically, anticipation inventory comprises finished goods inventory to meet seasonal demand, sales promotions and holidays. This approach is used to avoid forcing major changes in capacity and the operational disruptions such changes bring.

3 *Transportation.* Products and materials may travel considerable distances between suppliers, warehouses, distributors and customers. The amounts of this pipeline stock depend on the rates at which stocks can be moved, which implies a trade-off with transportation costs, and the level of business activity.

The extent to which a pipeline can be kept full also depends on procedures ancillary to shipping including timing for order processing and transmission, receiving, stocking and review periods. These stocks may be quantified using the equation:

$$I = R \times T$$

where I = transportation inventories
     R = average sales for the period used (e.g.: weeks)
     T = number of periods

4 *Hedge.* Inventory accumulations in advance may be profitable if opportunistic purchases can be made to avoid price fluctuations or to take advantage of 'specials'. Varying prices and volumes from purchase to purchase is speculative; hence much analysis and caution is required before commitments are finalized.

5 *Lot size.* Inventories often exist in an attempt to improve operational efficiency by separating purchasing and manufacturing rates from consumption rates. Such trade-offs include purchases in excess of immediate requirements to improve shipping costs, quantity discounts and set-up costs. It is interesting to note that there is one class of inventory which is unaffected by changes in order or batch quantities. Work-in-process inventory holdings are lead-time dependent; whether work is carried out in small lots or not, inventory levels are not decremented until the work is completed.

Controls

Inventories are goods which await conversion into sales dollars. They appear on financial statements and thus are of vital concern to management and shareholders. Since inventories impact on earnings, accounting conventions reflect the concern of government authorities and are strict regarding the use of inventory pricing methods. This is the main reason for the active participation of accounting personnel familiar with costing methods, taxation regulations and financial accounting procedures in controlling inventories. The resultant financial controls reflect these legal and financial concerns and often require extensive detailed control procedures.

Classes of inventory

Direct responsibility for inventory levels may rest with any of the functional heads in an organization. Of the three main classes of inventory,

- raw materials, components, operating supplies, sub-assemblies (items which await further processing and possibly storage before conversion into intermediate or finished products);
- intermediate stage or work-in-process items, which are materials with labour and overhead added and await conversion into finished goods (this conversion may be in-house or subcontracted); and
- finished goods, manufactured or purchased for resale, locally or imported.

The first two are typically controlled by manufacturing personnel, while finished goods may be the responsibility of marketing, logistics, manufacturing, or even the administrative functions. Operational controls over stocks on hand aim at having accurate and up-to-date records, adequate physical storage, efficient handling and maintaining reliable replenishment systems for all inventory classes. In contrast with financial controls, the unit of control is stock-keeping units (SKUs) rather than currency.

Both financial and operational controls for all classes of inventory require a structural approach based on sound plans, timely feedback and appropriate corrective action. Specifically this means that the following steps are in place:

1 the inventory plan;

2   budgets;
3   accurate records;
4   timely feedback of significant variances;
5   corrective action.

Each of these steps is discussed below.

Inventory planning

Controlling inventories requires much more than controlling individual supply transactions which, while an essential feature of any inventory control system, will not in itself ensure the availability of the right amounts of stock in the right place and at the right time. Effective control begins with the development of plans against which actual performance can be compared. The starting-point for an inventory plan is the sales and marketing plan, which is the main input to business plans. Since business planning is an iterative process, it is reasonable to expect several inventory plans may be prepared before a firm plan is accepted as the starting point for a given period.

Once an organization commits itself to sales levels and product mix, the plan will form the basis for budgets and for operational controls. The planning process itself has the key objective of providing a predictive model for aggregate controls – the ability to predict serious imbalances before they occur. It helps to conceptualize inventories as a flow process with inputs and outputs – that is, goods received and consumed.

When the two are not synchronized, surpluses and shortages occur, each creating a sequence of events resulting in unscheduled activities and costs. The model will vary considerably from one business to the next but in its simplest form may be viewed as follows, time-phased in monthly periods for not less than 12 months.

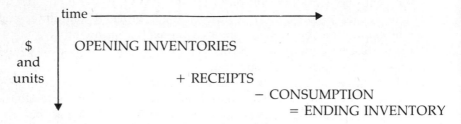

By definition, the plan is recalculated each period and is rolled over to the next. The levels of aggregation are typically by product families, geographical locations, by major stocking locations and, in general, wherever accountability for profits and assets exist. Figures are expressed in currency, and units where it makes sense – that is, if SKUs are homogeneous.

The simplicity of the concept belies the difficulties in obtaining the data necessary for reporting. Opening inventories are easily obtained, but to capture all receipts, both committed and planned, requires replenishment systems capable of predicting demands and planned usages over the planning horizon. In the case of a distribution operation, this implies the ability to aggregate all demand estimates and sales orders (plus any other independent demand) and then offset these demands for procurement lead times to calculate when replenishments are due. In the manufacturing environment this process is much more complex for, in addition to finished goods planned replenishments, purchase of lower-level goods used in production and replenishments arising from manufacture also need to be predicted.

Similarly, all estimates of consumption whether issues, sales or other usage must be offset against the anticipated receipts to arrive at predicted closing balances.

On reports it is useful to show the aggregates of receipts and consumption which give rise to the closing inventories for, if the predicted inventory levels are unacceptable, future activity levels may be altered; for example, a reduction in receipts to a level which will yield target inventory totals may be indicated.

Planning tools provide management and professionals with the foundation for control. The type of reporting described here has to be underpinned by accounting and record-keeping systems which provide trails and information for measuring, analysing and impacting every category of inventory by location and by item.

Budgeting

Inventory plans, like sales and shipping plans, provide a basis for budgets and operational controls, following negotiations and agreements to specific objectives with top management. For the resultant controls to work effectively through progress reports, senior management involvement in objectives-setting, negotiations and progress reviews is essential.

Budget formats may vary between organizations, but every organization produces a monthly comparison of actual results with budgets. This analysis is mandatory if inventory objectives, and hence profitability and other business objectives, are to be achieved. Yet the main benefit of this type of comparison lies in the analysis of the reported variances, not in the results.

Over- or underachievement may be due to a number of factors and is typically in step with the performance of some other budgeted activities. Sales, production, supply and labour deviations from budgets will be reflected in inventories. If sales are significantly different from budgeted activity, this will create difficulties in achieving targeted inventory levels. Flexible budgets varying with sales is one way to help maintain the relationship between inventory levels and rising or falling sales. It can be shown that even this measure is insufficient for precise performance assessment, especially as inventories tend to rise with increases, as well as decreases, in sales.

It is for this reason that assessments should rely on explanations of variances, as well as the quantitative measures. Inventory managers are accountable for interpretations and for demonstrating the ability to follow market trends in a non-static commercial world.

The increased availability of packaged computer software such as materials requirements planning (MRP), using bills of material or recipes, can readily provide projections of requirements consistent with planned levels of activity. By multiplying quantities with standard costs over the budget period, for every type of inventory, a basis for a budget is obtained.

The final budget may contain additional figures such as allowances for revaluation, new product introductions, special build-ups and known obsolescence, to mention some.

Accurate records

The costs of inaccurate records are becoming increasingly clearer. Shortages and excesses resulting from faulty computer records and the resulting wasteful activities of expediting, irregular counting, obsolescence, extra handling and overheads are a high priority on inventory managers' and financial controllers' lists of improvements.

Inventory accounting and physical controls are the two main mechanisms for monitoring the accuracy of inventory information. These are specifically systems and records, inventory audits and warehouse procedures.

Systems and records   Traditional methods of periodic recording have given way to perpetual recording using computer-based systems. Static data is typically resident in a database while dynamic data is updated either instantaneously, on-line, or in a batch mode – that is, at regular intervals but not exceeding one day. As lead times for manufacture and delivery become shorter, it is becoming increasingly important to have access to the latest inventory status as soon as inventory movements occur.

Since inventory information is provided and used by several functions in a company, the maintenance of records is a major issue. Several approaches are popular, ranging from decentralized maintenance by users, to a central database administration type of control. The degree of difficulty must not be underestimated. Accurate records require:

- considerable education and training in concepts and in the use of computer systems;
- management attention and support;
- systems and practices designed for, and supportive of, the particular business;
- support systems for recording transactions in each functional area affected; and
- regular use of the information to spot discrepancies as they occur.

As in the case of any other business activity, regular measures and performance assessment are needed for continuous improvements.

Inventory audits Physically counting quantities of each SKU in each location is the traditional accounting and auditing approach for validating inventory values for financial reporting. It is a misconception that periodic counts verify or improve the accuracy of records. Such counts are often inaccurate and give little information regarding the day-to-day activities which affect recording.

Periodic counts also tend to be expensive and disruptive to on-going activities. The use of untrained personnel in these counts reduces the reliability of results.

Increasingly, cycle counting is replacing periodic counts. The idea behind cycle counts is to rely on well-trained operating personnel to count a selected number of items every day as part of normal daily activities. Any discrepancies with records are immediately analysed to determine the cause and action is taken to correct problems and to improve accuracy. Measures are kept to assess quality improvements in warehousing and recording over time. A good example is a cumulative variance report displaying variances by classification, in money and percentages, by month and year to date.

Although the usual ABC classification system is used to determine how frequently an item will be counted, every item must be counted at least once per annum. In large areas, it is practical to identify separate logical areas or zones and assign them to different operators. By involving accounting and auditing personnel – both internal and external – in the design of the procedures, it is feasible for cycle counts to be also acceptable for financial valuation purposes.

Warehousing procedures   Where storage areas exist, physical controls, systems and administrative controls are interdependent. Correct warehousing procedures require locked storerooms and tight controls over all receipts and issues. If locked storage areas are not practical, suitable control points by location, whether fixed, random or logical warehousing storage schemes are used, are required to record movements and changes in status. Computer systems are useful in this task: through radio contact with operators, modern systems can capture data as early as during the materials handling phase.

More conventional aids include storage according to frequency of use, fixed locations in item number sequence as much as possible, and the use of clearly visible and significant numbering systems.

Modern methods, particularly in manufacturing, are increasing the emphasis on waste reduction, which implies minimum inventories and the avoidance of storage areas. Typically, one day's inventory is in the operation next to production areas or in shipping docks awaiting despatch. This approach greatly reduces complexities in storage and handling, and obviates the need for the classical issues and receipts recording procedures.

Usages can be automatically deducted from balances at standard, extra usage and scrap are identified during cycle counts and are recorded as adjustments. Either approach requires the prompt and accurate recording of changes in status and a rigorous adherence to record keeping procedures.

Timely feedback

Central to any control mechanism is the timely feedback of relevant information which describes the process, measures and flags out of tolerance conditions. There are two classes of information necessary for control:

1   variances from budgets, targets and standards;
2   historical data for analysis as the basis for improvements.

Accounting systems typically provide information on a historical basis and thus fall in the second category. Business pressures require more timely, and more frequent, feedback for control than accounting reports provide. Since inventory management issues affect a number of functions in an enterprise; information needs to be available in different formats as applicable to each function. Provided accurate and timely data has been collected and stored, modern computer systems have the capability – through the use of report writers and high-level languages – to aggregate and report information at the appropriate level of detail, distributed across functions and across geographical locations.

Daily exception reports and on-demand enquiries through computer terminals can provide all the information management and operating personnel require for executing short-term plans and schedules. Technology allows problems to be communicated instantaneously throughout an enterprise over a computer network.

In this manner, any quality issues, shortages and operational breakdowns are immediately known and alternative plans can be put into effect. By collecting these problems and applying statistical analysis, such as frequency distributions and Pareto charts, recurring problems may be addressed in order of magnitude. While different reports will be required in each situation, the overriding consideration is to obtain quantitative rather than subjective information, in a form that permits immediate corrective action when feasible or otherwise following a thorough and well considered evaluation.

Corrective action

The loop of a planning and control system may be closed following execution and feedback, but a modern process is not complete unless continuous improvements are part of this loop. Feedback concerning operational problems, accounting reports of financial variances, and performance measurement reports to management, all highlight status.

More importantly, they will highlight symptoms of problem areas. Since inventories reflect so much of business activity, such problems may be a multitude of issues in purchasing, sales, shipping, distribution, accounting and others. Modern systems provide excellent information to highlight problems as they occur in each of these areas.

Problem recognition is the first, and easiest, step in correcting the underlying causes of operational problems and inhibitors of progress.

In line with total quality control concepts, there are three other stages:

1 identification of the cause;
2 development of a solution;
3 monitoring to prevent recurrence.

These three are significantly more difficult than the first. Only the simplest of problems are easily analysed as to cause. Significant gains can only be realized by collecting sufficient data and carrying out the required analysis to determine precisely the nature of an operational problem. After this, solutions are relatively easy to arrive at, based on experience. Monitoring only requires persistence. Many organizations which are achieving dramatic improvements in inventory performance have embraced this approach of systematic problem-solving.

Whether the corrective action is simple or requires extensive effort, management has the task of insisting performance be measured, variances are acted upon and permanent solutions to problems, and not to symptoms, are introduced.

Replenishment systems

Ultimately, the success of any inventory management function depends on how well inventories are planned. Inventory plans can only be executed if an appropriate system for replenishing inventories is implemented. Over time, these systems have evolved from relatively simple clerical procedures to complex computer-controlled systems. The primary questions are:

1 How much to order?
2 When to re-order?

Another issue arising is the limitation on resources; thus not every item receives the same amount of attention. Based on Pareto's law, inventory items are classified in decreasing order of annual dollar value or other criteria of importance. This method of inventory classification is referred to as ABC classification, since the analysis results in the grouping of items into A, B or C categories.

Since class A items represent the highest dollar value, or some other equally high priority, they receive the most attention. Class B items receive less attention, and class C items fall under simple routine control procedures. The philosophy is that effort saved on controlling low-value items is applied to the improved control of more important items. For these reasons, it is not uncommon to find several methods of replenishment for different classes and types of inventories in the one organization. The more popular replenishment methods are briefly described below.

Manual records

Manual stock control practices are quickly disappearing, although stock card systems are still used where valuable commodities warrant individual attention by item. Operating supplies, spare parts and maintenance supplies are often controlled in this manner.

Fixed order quantity

As stock levels – that is, amounts on hand plus on order – drop to an order point, a predetermined fixed quantity, or multiples thereof, are re-ordered. This method requires that inventory levels are constantly monitored.

Two-bin system

This term is generally used to describe fixed-order quantity systems, and it is the simplest of these types of systems. Inventory is carried in two bins or other containers and a replenishment quantity equal to one bin is ordered when the first bin becomes empty. On receipt, the material is used to refill the second bin and the excess is to put into the first bin.

Other characteristics of this system are low and regular usage; and the items controlled are comparatively inexpensive.

Order point systems

In general, these systems are referred to as statistical order point systems and are defined as methods which trigger replenishment orders when the order point is reached. Order points are calculated as estimated demand during lead time plus safety stock. Statistical methods are applied in two ways:

1 to demand, if statistical sales forecasting techniques are used;
2 to safety stock calculations, if safety stock calculations are linked to target customer service levels and forecast errors, adjusted for the ratio of lead time to the length of the forecast period.

Historically, EOQ and fixed-order quantity lot-sizing approaches are associated with this method.

Topping-up system

This is the simplest of the periodic review systems, and applies to short lead-time items. At each review period, stock is ordered to bring levels up to a predetermined maximum level. This method should not be used for long lead-time items as overstocking will result.

Min-Max system

When on-hand and on-order stocks are at, or below, the minimum level, a variable quantity of stock is ordered to bring levels up to the maximum inventory level. Typical review periods are weeks or months.

Visual review systems

Perpetual recording – that is, recording each transaction as it occurs – is the most common form of recording here, although periodic recording may be more practical in some situations, such as retail for example. Physical reviews of stocks on hand may be more appropriate in special situations than order point and periodic review systems.

Time-phased order point

This approach is used for planning independent demand items, items whose requirements are forecast or estimated rather than exploded from a higher level demand. The logic is similar to material requirements planning (MRP), and enables the planning of replenishments by time periods. Distribution centre and spare parts inventories are well handled by this technique.

Material requirements planning (MRP)

Demand passed down from master schedules (production forecasts) is exploded using bills of material for dependent demand items and is then applied to inventory data to calculate requirements for materials. MRP is both an inventory management and a prioritizing tool and requires computer technology to cope with the inherent large volume of calculations. The time-phasing capability is used for rescheduling deliveries when need dates and due dates are not in phase.

MRP is part of the manufacturing resource planning (MRPII) technology which evolved from MRP and is a planning and control system used for managing the resources of a manufacturing company.

Distribution requirements planning

A time-phased order point approach is used to determine inventory replenishment at branch warehouses by exploding planned orders at the warehouse level, using MRP logic, to become the demand on the supplying source. This process is applied to every level in a multi-level distribution operation and the demand on each supplying source is considered as dependent. Distribution resource planning (DRP) is the extension of distribution requirements planning technology, which is used in the planning of key resources in a distribution system.

Performance measurements

Depending on the inventory goals and operational plans of each organization, reports will contain information for some or all of the categories listed:

1 Financial
   - Inventory impact on profit and loss, including purchase price variance analysis
   - Investments in inventories, performance against budgets
   - Operating and inventory holding costs
   - Results of stock-counts
2 Operational
   - Customer service levels, statistics
   - Inventory accuracy
   - Performance against targets or plans, units and financial, stock turnover ratios
   - Quality of purchased items
3 Marketing
   - Availability, shortages, lost sales and back-orders
   - Service and warranty costs
   - Obsolescence due to sales shortfalls
   - Sales forecasts – accuracy

Top management generally receives summaries of these reports; increasingly, exception reports are available to highlight significant deviations from plans obviating the need for extensive reporting and

Table 18.2
Examples of customer service levels measures

1   Market share
2   Number of customer complaints
3   Number/value of lost sales
4   Number/value of units on back-order
5   Number of customers not supplied from stock (No. of orders with shortage)
6   Number of days out of stock
7   Number of months in which stockout occurred
8   Number of stockouts per year
9   Number of lines out of stock at month-end
10 Probability of stock-out
11 Percentage of demand supplied from stock (units/line/items/dollars)

analysis. Effective inventory management demands performance be tracked and measured so that management understand how well plans are executed and pinpoint operational problems.

New approaches

In recent years, Japanese techniques for achieving excellence in manufacturing and logistics have been replacing traditional planning and control approaches. There are powerful philosophies behind these techniques aiming at continuous improvements, the elimination of waste and the achievement of the highest quality. These new philosophies are pervasive and affect every function. It is therefore not surprising to find inventories playing a key role in the success of these new approaches once again.

Characteristics of successful implementations are many and include dramatic reductions in inventory holdings, particularly work-in-process. Just-in-time (JIT) and total quality control (TQC) are the two most recognized terms for these techniques. While inventory reductions result, these schemes must not be undertaken as inventory reduction programmes. Inventories play a central role, however, as inventories are considered wasteful and hide operational inefficiencies.

To achieve continuous improvements, problems need to be

Table 18.3
Factors influencing buffer stock

Just-in-Case
Interruptions = Inventories

- Demand Protection
  - Demand variability
  - Confidence in forecasts
  - Exposure to stock-out
  - Remember when??

- Supply Protection
  - Lead time variability
  - Confidence in lead time estimates
  - Security of supply

- Existing Philosophies
  - Consequences of stock-out
  - Item cost
  - Obsolescence
  - Scrap rate
  - Space requirements
  - Comfort

- Existing Conditions
  - Materials handling
  - Set-up of machines
  - Imbalance of machines
  - Quality checking
  - Machine breakdown
  - Waiting for parts, tools, inspection, forklifts
  - Plant and warehouse layout

exposed, solved and prevented from recurring. The procedure involved is a planned reduction in inventory levels to expose inefficiencies. As improvements are made, inventories are lowered again to expose further opportunities for operational improvements, repeating the procedure over and over. Quality improvements also serve to reduce inventories through reductions of rework, safety stocks, inspection stocks, scrap and returns.

New approaches to product design and process layouts serve to reduce queues of stock awaiting work, reduce transportation stocks, eliminate storerooms and facilitate the flow of material and product, thereby reducing the overall time goods are on the premises. Such initiatives seek out and eliminate all unwanted inventory, the dogma being that inventories are liabilities and not assets, and that they cover up wasteful activities, resulting in a remorseless pursuit of waste reductions.

Waste reduction and value adding have the inevitable result of simplification. The removal of unnecessary activities presents an ideal basis for the application of other technologies – principally automation. The resultant use of modern techniques, such as computer-integrated manufacturing (CIM), which in itself comprises a wide range of technologies, serves to further improve planning and control techniques, and to reduce processing and information lead times. Decisions may be made in split seconds, optimum batch sizes are reduced to one since one of an item can be manufactured as efficiently as any other quantity, quality is further improved through the use of fail-safe techniques and reduced complexity, and supply lead times and quantities are collapsed to the bare minimum.

Robotics, automated materials handling, computer-aided design, group technology and computer-aided manufacturing, plus a range of new computing technologies, are all reshaping traditional approaches; and their contributions are starting to be well understood. Even newer technologies, such as electronic data interchange, will serve to reduce supply and distribution lines and further reduce in-transit and distribution stocks. It is only a matter of time before artificial intelligence routines may begin to impact on inventory management in a major way.

Conclusions

Inventory management is both art and science, and is ultimately concerned with three main questions:

1   How much inventory is enough?
2   Are inventories assets or liabilities?
3   Who should carry the responsibility for inventory management and performance?

The quantitative answer as to how much inventory is enough is provided by replenishment systems and statistical computations of safety stocks based on target customer service levels, order quantities and lead times. Since it is now clear that inventories are only assets in an accounting sense and, more importantly, if they are useful stocks awaiting short-term conversion into sales, a better answer to the first question is: the absolute minimum quantity required to achieve plans, expressed in number of days work or sales, not weeks or months. Pressure to drive out unwanted stocks must be relentless.

It follows that all unnecessary inventories are liabilities and wasteful in that they tie up money and space. Even more undesirable side-effects are the impact of excess inventories in covering up problems and impeding the adoption of modern management methods.

Accounting conventions showing inventories as current assets may actually work against inventory reductions by avoiding decisions to revalue or write off unwanted stock for fear of unfavourable reporting of financial performance.

Responsibility for inventories ultimately rests with management. Clearly, inventories are impacted on by all functions, and inventory performance affects bottom-line performance. The expertise essential for effective planning and control must be provided by educated and experienced professionals and managers in logistics, manufacturing, accounting and marketing. Nevertheless, senior management must retain accountability for:

- setting goals and objectives;
- maintaining pressures on performance;
- insisting that problems, and not symptoms, are solved;
- Coordinating the plans and activities of the different functions to ensure that they all work towards common ends.

It is this combination of applied expertise and management direction, underpinned by information systems, which provides the foundation for effectively managing and controlling logistics inventories.

19 Choice of the Transport Mode

Alan Slater

The choice of the transport mode is a fundamental part of distribution management which should be analysed carefully because of the impact upon a company's operational efficiency. Failure to identify the most appropriate transport mode may incur higher costs than are necessary and may provide a lower customer service level than is potentially possible.

The decision upon the choice of the transport mode is extremely complex because of the vast volume of choice available together with the numerous methods of examination and evaluation of each choice.

Every organization involved with physical goods will require transport services. The nature of the transport services operated by each organization will vary considerably, depending upon such factors as the nature of the product, the size of the order, the service level required by the customer and the alternative transport methods available. Once a transport method is selected, other choices may include the equipment required, the method of finance, and the operating techniques to be adopted.

The transport selection process is extremely complex because of the vast volume of choice available. Failure to identify the most appropriate transport method will lead to either incurring higher costs than are necessary and/or to providing a lower customer service than potentially possible.

However, the application of a technique based upon matrix analysis will assist in the examination and evaluation of transport requirements for individual organizations. Adopting the matrix technique will invariably result in the selection of a transport profile which includes a number of different types of transport for one or more tasks.

In order to be able to identify the 'optimum' transport mode, it will be necessary to:

1   identify the significance of the choice by determining the impact of transport on the supply chain system;
2   identify the factors which determine the choice of the transport mode;
3   identify a method of choice;
4   receive subsequent feedback that the choice is correct.

Further complications occur if the impact of potential changes is calculated, since the operating environment is dynamic and even the fundamental requirements of the transport mode may change over time, rendering it impossible to obtain the optimum transport mode for more than a short period.

The significance of the choice

Transport costs include all the costs directly associated with the movement of product from one location to another.

In order to identify the significance of the choice of the transport mode, it is necessary to be able to determine the impact of transport upon the overall supply chain. This could be achieved by an analysis of existing transport cost, realization of the profit leverage effect and analysis of the impact of transport upon the other elements of the distribution system.

Transport costs

Transport costs vary from less than 1 per cent (for machinery) to in excess of 30 per cent (for food) of the recommended selling price of products, depending upon the nature of the product range and its market. However, the average transport cost is between 5 per cent and 6 per cent of the recommended retail price of a product.

Generally, transport costs rise in line with inflation because the major components are labour (drivers and maintenance mechanics), fuel, components for maintenance, depreciation and interest charges. Occasionally, however, fiscal measures such as increases or decreases in fuel charges do draw transport cost increases above the rate of inflation.

Productivity also impacts upon costs, and the recent trends to increase unit weight movements, particularly in road movements, significantly increase overall productivity.

Profit Leverage

Transport represents a direct cost added to the price of the product and any reduction in transport costs would lead to an increase in profit, (assuming that the price remains constant). The impact of reducing transport costs is shown by the profit leverage effect in two ways. Assuming that a company has a 10 per cent profit margin on sales turnover and prices do not change, then:

1   A cost reduction in transport expense of £100,000 is equivalent to an increase in sales turnover of £1,000,000;
2   If transport costs are estimated at 20 per cent of total costs, a 1 per cent reduction in total transport costs would give a 2 per cent increase in profits.

Supply chain systems

Transport cannot be considered alone because it offers a service which moves product from one location to another and at each terminal, capital and labour facilities exist. Throughout the movement process, the product will need to be monitored with documentation in order that its approximate location is known.

Transport, therefore, is a process or system which transfers the product between two or more locations; and the form of transport used must be compatible, not only with the terminal systems at both ends, but also the operating environment through which the movement takes place. Sufficient information should be generated to enable this movement to take place and enable the producer, customer, haulier, government agencies, financial institutions and other relevant groups to monitor the progress at all times.

Transport profile

The transport requirements of the organization will be governed by its operating characteristics. If, for example, the organization's major operating features included:

- two domestic and two overseas factories,
- six domestic warehouses,
- large numbers of domestic and overseas customers,
- a large range of products and,
- variable customer service levels to each major category of customers,

then it would be feasible to expect the transport requirements to include:

- contract hire with driver for day and night movements between factories and warehouses;
- own fleet for some domestic customer deliveries;
- contract agreements for some domestic customer deliveries and all overseas deliveries either to the port or direct in the case of Europe;
- parcel carrier for small orders;
- high-capacity vans for emergency deliveries.

The significant feature of this profile is that there is a number of different types of transport requirements according to the task to be performed. Thus, to generalize, an organization which tackles a number of different tasks in a similar manner with the same vehicles will almost certainly be operating below the optimum. efficiency levels.

Operational factors

The operational factors which determine the transport mode include environmental factors and the characteristics of alternative transport modes, and the combination of these factors gives rise to potential customer service levels and costs incurred (see Figure 19.1).

The operational factors to be considered may include such issues as:

- International:
  - national economic conditions (inflation, value of currency)
  - taxation and export incentives (tax advantages and grants)
  - barriers to trade (import quotas, and customs duty)
  - export controls and licensing
  - conditions of trade (penalty clauses)
  - cultural system and national practices
  - development of communications system
  - availability of international banking services
- National:
  - bureaucratic system
  - operating infrastructure
  - legal system (control on movement and marketing)
  - level of technology
  - local labour costs, availability, skills and productivity

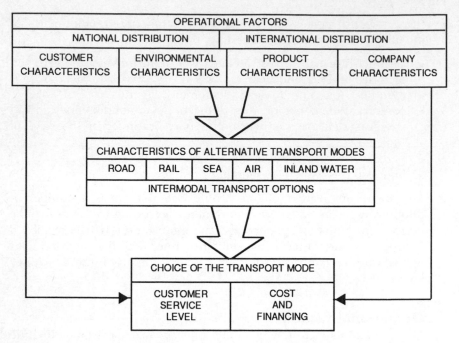

Figure 19.1   Operational factors which determine the transport mode

 - relative costs, availability and quality of service support requirements (particularly at the terminal facilities)
 - availability of local capital, the credit situation and interest rates
 - characteristics of alternative transport modes.

Characteristics of alternative transport modes

It is important to determine accurately the operating characteristics of each available transport mode, to establish whether it would suitably match the important operating factors. The important features are:

 - Useful load – physical capability and maximum load as a percentage of gross weight
 - Density – cargo density (weight per cubic unit)
 - Overheads – fixed costs as a percentage of total cost (as an indicator of risk for price increases and support requirements)
 - Productivity – calculated in ton miles per direct man hour.

It is significant to note that each type of transport offers different characteristics as shown in Table 19.1 where

Table 19.1
Characteristics of various transport modes

	Useful Load	Density	Overheads	Productivity
	Maximum Load as % of Gross Weight	Cargo Density lbs/cu. ft.	Fixed Costs as % of Total Costs	Ton Miles per Direct.Man-Hour
(1) Cargo Aircraft (32 tons)	48	11	24	8,250
(2) Cargo Vessel (1,500 ton displacement)	69	42	35	6,000
(3) Freight Train (wagon 12 tons)	64	30	34	5,200
(4) Lorry (12 tons 3 Axle)	73	23	6	420

- the 12 ton lorry offers the highest useful load;
- the cargo vessel offers the highest density;
- the freight train has the highest overheads;
- the cargo aircraft has the highest productivity.

Each mode of transport also has its own individual characteristics which affect the preparation of product before movement (for example, packaging for sea freight must be more substantial than for air freight). These characteristics are particularly important when considering intercontinental traffic utilizing more than one mode of transport.

Channel strategy

The choice of the transport mode is not merely a choice between one form or type of transport, but between a system or process of transportation between the manufacturer or seller and the customer or buyer. This process involves separate sectors (for example, production line to warehouse), material handling interfaces at each terminal facility and documentation which is processed to support the product.

The complete marketing channel must be defined and each sector

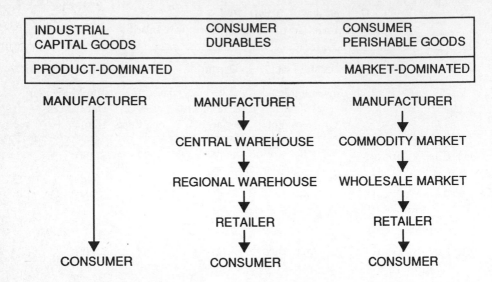

Figure 19.2   Type of channel

where movement takes place clearly established (see Figure 19.2). Each sector should be analysed separately for transport requirements in accordance with the terminal customer characteristics, the volume of product moved and the operating environment between the stages of the channel. Each sector of movement throughout the channel may require separate transport methods and it is important that all the operating characteristics for each sector are clearly identified (see Table 19.2). The important factors to consider when analysing the transport requirements of each sector are:

1 Control
   – ownership
   – security (documentation and product)
   – financial standing
   – information processing systems
2 Product Movement
   – mechanical handling interfaces
   – stock levels required at each terminal
   – packaging
   – safety (for product, capital and manpower)
3 Marketing Factors
   – variations in service level requirements

Table 19.2

Characteristics of the marketing channel

Channel	Factors	Important Operating Characteristics			
Manufacturer	(1) Control	Ownership	Documentation (Information Processing)	Security (Documentation Product)	Credit-Worthiness
Central Warehouse	(2) Product Movement	Mechanical Handling Interfaces	Variations in Stock Holding	Product Marketing and Packaging	Safety (Product Labour)
Regional Warehouse	(3) Marketing	Variations in Service Level	Advertising and Promotion Policy		
Retailer	(4) Labour Related	Labour Training	Labour Turnover		
Customer	(5) Risk	Potential Changes	Inter-type Competition	Profit Potential	Government influence

4   Labour Factors
- training requirements turnover
5   Risk Factors
- potential changes
- inter-type competition
- government influence
- profit potential

The major influence upon the choice of the transport mode may be the ability of the transport concern to match or adapt the requirements of two parts of the marketing channel to maximize the use of the transport offered.

Specialization of transport modes is created by the impact of channel costs which are incurred either before or after transportation - where the introduction of specialization reduces the mechanical handling costs, packaging costs and so on during the terminal function. Only rarely will specialization of the transport mode be introduced purely to maximize the movement of transit costs.

Objective assessment

The objective by which the transport mode should be chosen depends upon whether the company is using revenue or capital to buy the transport. In the case of *revenue*, minimum cost throughout the transport process should be the objective, and in the case of *capital*, maximum after tax return upon capital should be the target since both of these objectives give the shareholders maximum return.

In certain cases both capital and revenue expenditure will be included in the operation; under these circumstances, the combination of the minimum revenue expenditure and maximum after-tax capital return could be calculated by determining the net cash flow after tax for the life of the capital asset. The criteria for choice will then become the maximum discounted return or mimimum discount cost in terms of net cash flow, calculated with a discount rate equivalent to the cost of capital.

Although these criteria for assessment are relatively simple, complications could be added by identifying the need to calculate:
- all revenue expenditure incurred by the utilization of a particular transport mode (for example, packaging);
- all capital expenditure incurred by the utilization of a particular

transport mode (for example, mechanical equipment at the terminals);

- the risk associated with any capital asset with a life of over two years, where the asset may need to be modified to meet changing operating or environmental characteristics.

Even when a method of assessment has been determined, the degree to which calculations are taken becomes an important factor to ensure that a correct decision is made.

One basic rule is that any capital or revenue cost incurred in the operation of a particular transport mode, should be taken into account in the calculation. Similarly, any significant risk incurred by capital assets which may be reasonably calculated should be accounted for in the financial calculations based upon the probability of occurrence.

A further rule is that, where possible, trade-off analysis should be used to assess the impact of each transport mode upon other functions in the business system, and to indicate the impact of changes upon the distribution system as a whole.

Method of selection

The selection procedure for the choice of the transport mode could vary from the simple decision either to identify one feasible method of distribution or to follow the competitors' procedures, to the complex decision which calculates every cost incurred and produces an optimum solution. There are four potential selection methods:

1 *Judgement*. Where the transport manager identifies the important factors affecting the transport problem, and identifies a transport mode from a short list of alternatives, which are considered to be available, in order that the most important features of the transport requirements are satisfied. The shortcomings of this particular selection method are numerous: factors other than transport matters are ignored, and transport is considered as a service rather than part of the distribution system; a complete list of alternative transport methods may not be considered; and costs are not important because the decision is made upon operational ability.

2 *Cost trade-off*. Where the impact of transport is calculated in relation to its immediate terminal activities and the total cost of the distribution system optimized. This approach acknowledges the

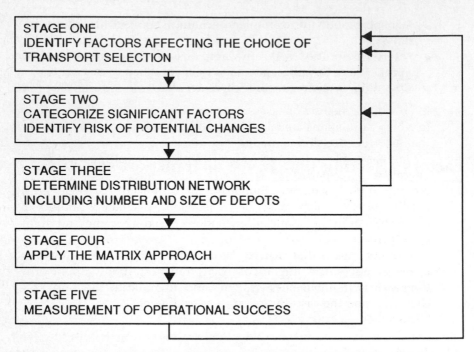

Figure 19.3 Framework for alternative transport selection

existence of trade-offs within the numerous alternative approaches in an attempt to assess the situation to minimize total costs.

3 *Distribution models*. Which identify and explain the interrelationships between the components of the distribution system at various levels of daily/weekly/monthly demand. These models could be built to examine the impact of alternative transport modes and methods, as either the demand changes or the components in the system change.

Systematic selection

In order to resolve the issue of transport selection, a framework consisting of five stages is recommended. These stages are described in Figure 19.3 and include:

- Stage One: Identify those factors affecting the choice of transport selection.

- Stage Two: Categorize the significant factors, and identify potential risks.
- Stage Three: Determine the distribution network in terms of numbers and size of depots.
- Stage Four: Apply matrix analysis to select the most appropriate transport method.
- Stage Five: Measure operational success.

Factors affecting the choice of transport selection

Those factors which may fundamentally affect the choice of transport selection, may be classified into four groups:

- customer characteristics;
- product characteristics;
- environmental characteristics;
- company characteristics.

Customer characteristics

The key factor in terms of customer characteristics is that, in the final analysis, the delivery must be profitable – that is, the sum of the delivery cost per order must be less than the gross margin earned on the order before distribution costs are incurred. Thus, a small order travelling a long distance to a timed delivery may be unprofitable because the effective cost of delivery is greater than the sum of the gross margin earned on the sale of all the items included in that order. The main customer characteristics to consider include:

- geographical location (distance from supplying depot);
- delivery point features (access);
- time restrictions (day of week, time of day);
- size of order (and annual turnover);
- product knowledge (to avoid damage upon and after delivery);
- mechanical handling equipment used;
- service level requirement (receipt of order to delivery);
- type of sale (COD or FOB);
- after-sales service requirements.

Product characteristics

Essentially, all product characteristics must be considered, but transport resources should not be overspecified to deal with the isolated and unusual product delivery particularly where alternatives may be found or where transport may be hired for that purpose. This would apply where, for example a crane was added for each vehicle in the fleet, when the product which requires heavy-lift equipment is only carried on those vehicles once every two weeks. Here, the additional cost of that crane may not be recovered by the gross margin before distribution costs of the product which requires heavy-lift equipment. The main product characteristics to consider include:

- weight;
- size and shape;
- fragile nature;
- obsolescence and deterioration;
- danger (for example, toxic);
- value.

Environmental characteristics

Transport operations may be affected by environmental factors in three different ways. First, other road users may have a significant impact upon operational efficiency particularly where heavy demand creates congestion and leads to missing timed deliveries. Similar factors may affect the operational efficiency of alternative transport methods (for example, the Christmas peak may extend the lead time for postal deliveries). Second, there are operational constraints imposed by terrain, weather and legal restrictions, which restrict the type of vehicle used for particular routes (for example, town centres may have axle weight restrictions which limit the type of vehicle). Third, there are technological changes in equipment and the infrastructure which may improve productivity (for example, the development of close coupling drawbar rigs, or the opening of a new section of motorway).

Up-to-date knowledge of the environment is essential to operate efficiently. The important features to monitor and assess the effect of include:

- other road users (effects);
- infrastructure;
- technology (vehicle and equipment);
- climate;
- legal considerations;
- road patterns.

It is now possible to monitor the majority of these factors through:

- radio/television (climate, road usage);
- telephone enquiries (road patterns); and
- published literature (technology, legal infrastructure).

Company characteristics

It is essential that distribution management fully understands all significant company policies to avoid over-reacting to pressure from customers or management colleagues. Cases are all too common where the distribution manager is thrown into 'blind panic' to deliver an order 'today' because a management colleague believes this is necessary, when the customer will neither need nor use the product for three to four days after delivery. A defined delivery policy which is only over-ridden by a named manager is the acceptable and practical solution. Tight management control will ensure that the question of urgent deliveries should arise infrequently rather than weekly or daily. The important company characteristics to consider include:

- service level policy;
- sales territories;
- warehouse locations;
- manufacturing locations;
- financial policies;
- performance of competition.

Impact of these factors

A large number of factors have been identified so it is important that, during an analysis, the factors are categorized in order of significance, and the risk of change for each factor is determined over the potential maximum time span or any capital commitments.

It is the significant factors which are selected for use in the matrix analysis which help determine what options should be considered. How important each option will become may depend upon the potential risk of change in the key determining factors.

Decision framework

In order to determine an organization's transport requirements there are five basic decisions to consider:

1 the number and size of depots – including the movement require-

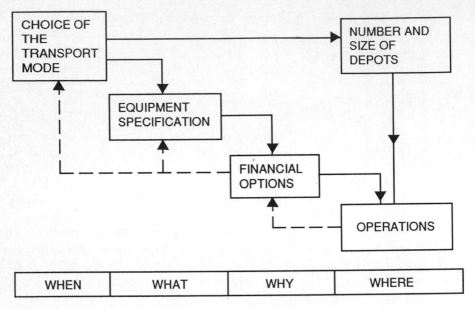

Figure 19.4   Framework for transport decisions

ments of raw materials to factories and finished product from
factories to customers;

2   the choice of the transport mode required – in terms of *when* each
type of transport will be appropriate for each potential movement
defined by distance travelled;

3   the choice of equipment specification – in terms of *what* type of
transport will be appropriate for each requirement defined by the
product characteristics;

4   the choice of which financial option – in terms of *why* commit
financial resources to individual types of equipment; and

5   the choice of operational needs – in terms of *where* to use the
equipment to maximize the utilization and minimize the operational cost.

All of these decisions are interrelated (see Figure 19.4) but the first
question is to determine the distribution network by determining the
number and size of depots to be used.

Number and size of depots

The outline of the distribution network is defined by the number and
size of depots required to link the sources of production to the market

place. The network of depots will be defined by determining the number, size and location of depots which, when combined, minimize the cost between ex-factory delivery and local distribution depot delivery for each order. Essentially, the distribution depots provide the resource to balance the cost to achieve optimum ex-factory loads and optimum local delivery loads.

Once the distribution network is defined, it is possible to classify the transport operational requirements into tasks, for example:

- management of raw materials to factories;
- inter-factory movements;
- deliveries to warehouses;
- deliveries to third-party transport facilities;
- deliveries to satellite depots;
- deliveries to customers (normal, priority and emergency).

These tasks represent the operational requirement for which transport resources must be selected.

The matrix approach

In order to determine the most appropriate transport option from the substantial range available, a matrix approach may be adopted. This approach uses six basic steps:

1 Selection of initial decisions required based upon known alternatives, for example:
    - choice of the transport mode
    - choice of equipment specifications
    - choice of financial options
    - choice of operational needs.
2 Selection of two important factors affecting each decision required, so that a matrix may be produced using one factor on the vertical axis and one factor on the horizontal axis. For example, to determine the choice of equipment specification, the vertical axis may be volume (cubic metres) and the horizontal axis may be weight (tonnes).
3 Selection of the basic alternatives which adequately cover the conditions imposed by the vertical and horizontal axis. For example, when considering the choice of the transport mode where size of the order represents the vertical axis and distance the horizontal axis, then a very small order travelling over five miles may use the postal system as the most appropriate means of delivery.

4   Determination of the organization's needs by analysis of the important factors generated to produce the matrix and use of the matrix to select the options required.
5   Selection of the resources required by considering the results of the matrix analysis plus other factors of importance. For example, if an organization has a high-volume, low-weight product, the most economic vehicle selection may be a drawbar trailer combination, but access constraints at customers may restrict the organization to operating rigid vehicles.
6   The combination of the matrix solutions to provide an efficient transport profile, which identifies transport tasks and appropriate resources for the task.

This approach requires imagination to develop the selection of the initial decisions, to determine the important factors to use for the vertical axis and horizontal axis on the matrix, and to construct the matrix. However, the majority of these questions may be answered by a combination of brainstorming, plus analysis and categorization of the important factors which affect the choice of transport selection.

The choice of the transport mode

One way to identify the appropriate choice of the transport mode is to select the two most significant factors affecting this decision. These could be the size of the order (cubic metres or weight) and the distance to travel in miles from the supplying depot.

The creation of a matrix using order size as the vertical axis and distance as the horizontal axis, as in Figure 19.5, indicates the most appropriate transport mode to select at any level of order size and distance. Thus, the small order delivered in close proximity to the source may use a local courier and small orders for overseas may be despatched by airmail. This form of analysis will help identify when each transport mode is appropriate.

There is a number of alternative transport methods for both national and international movements (see Figures 19.6 and 19.7).

The choice of equipment specification

One way to identify the appropriate choice of outline equipment specification is to consider the two most significant factors affecting this decision. These may be, for example, volume carried and weight carried.

The creation of a matrix using volume as the vertical axis and

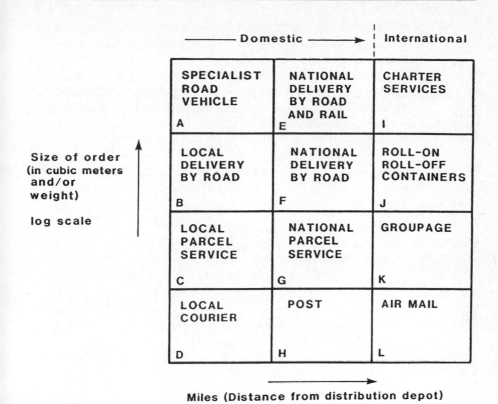

Figure 19.5 Choice of the transport mode: options

weight as the horizontal axis, as in Figure 19.8, indicates the most appropriate vehicle type to select for products with a defined volume to weight relationship. Thus, very heavy product, with a low volume, will be best suited to a four axle rigid vehicle; whereas light product with a high volume, may be best suited to a drawbar combination. Since vehicle weights and cube (assuming a reasonable height) are limited by the Construction and Use Regulations, this comparison may be achieved as an absolute calculation and compared to actual product characteristics.

The choice of financial option

Again, it is possible to consider the level of financial spend in terms of two factors: commitment to vehicle ownership; and commitment to the employment of a driver.

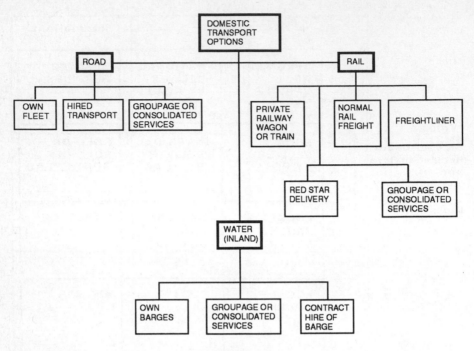

Figure 19.6   Domestic transport options

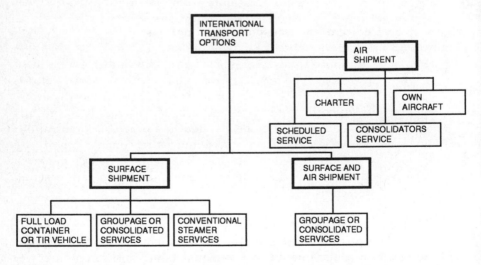

Figure 19.7   International transport options

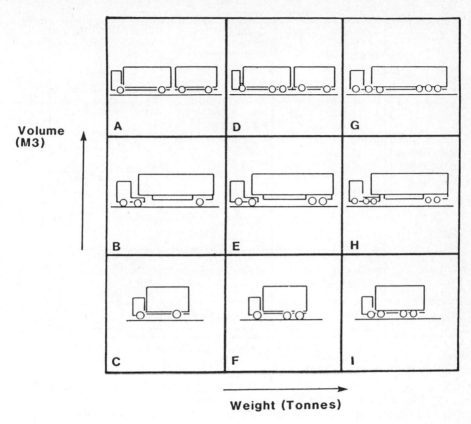

Volume (M3)

Weight (Tonnes)

Figure 19.8   Vehicle selection by type: options

The creation of a matrix using commitment to vehicle ownership on the vertical axis and commitment to the employment of a driver on the horizontal axis, as in Figure 19.9, suggests that a number of alternative options is available. For example, where a company has a low commitment to employment of a driver but a relatively high commitment to vehicle ownership, the company may choose to own the special body of a vehicle and contract hire the chassis cab and driver (case B in Figure 19.9).

This analysis could also be undertaken using two other significant factors:

- potential vehicle utilization; and
- probability of vehicle availability.

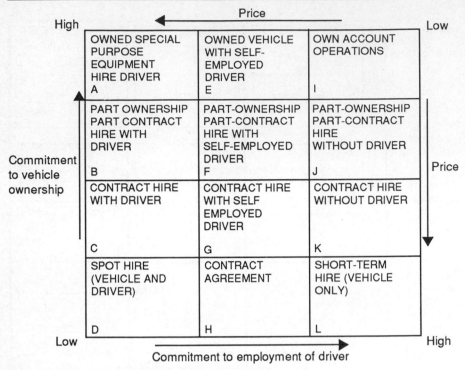

Figure 19.9   Vehicle ownership/operations: options

The choice of operational needs

Similar analytical methods may be used to determine the choice of operational needs. The two important factors may include:

- customer service level; and
- vehicle utilization.

If operational needs are expressed in terms of order pattern options with vehicle utilization on the vertical axis and customer service level on the horizontal axis, as in Figure 19.10, the required order pattern may be defined.

Alternative transport selection

Since there are so many combinations, to choose the selection of the alternative transport options may be narrowed down by the use of a matrix analysis. Both the horizontal axis and vertical factors affect the

ADDITIONAL TELEPHONE SALES AND FIXED ROUTES	ADDITIONAL TELEPHONE SALES AND VARIABLE ROUTES	CONTROLLED ORDERS AND DELIVERIES
A	D	G
RANDOM ORDERS WITH VARIABLE ROUTE DELIVERY PATTERNS	SALESMAN'S ROUTE PRECEEDS FIXED ROUTE DELIVERY PATTERN	VAN SALES
B	E	H
RANDOM ORDERS FIXED ROUTE DELIVERY PATTERN	RANDOM SALESMAN'S ROUTE VARIABLE ROUTE PATTERN	RANDOM ORDERS AND DAILY DELIVERIES
C	F	I

Vehicle utilization →

Customer service level →

Figure 19.10 Selection of order pattern: options

parameter selected, and a matrix of alternative options can be constructed to suit the conditions described by the axes.

A large number of parameters may be selected and a matrix constructed for each one. In the final analysis, the important ones are combined to identify the overall transport requirement, which will probably result in a combination of alternative transport options for different transport tasks.

For example, the domestic distribution of consumer electronics equipment may generate a specific transport profile, as in Figure 19.11 where:

- the choice of the transport mode will include a combination of:
  - local delivery by road (B),
  - national delivery by road and rail (F), and
  - national parcel service (for spare parts orders) (G).
- the equipment specification for road will include a combination of:
  - local delivery rigid box vans (16 tonnes) (C),

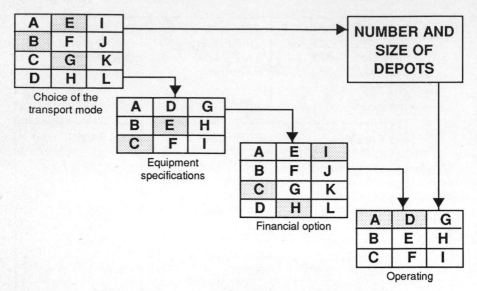

Figure 19.11   The solution is a combination of alternatives
- articulated box vans (32 tonnes) (E), and
- high-capacity transit vans (for emergency deliveries).
- The ownership choice will include a combination of:
  - contract hire with driver (for inter factory/ depot movements), (C)
  - contract agreements (for some local deliveries) (H), and
  - own-account operations for the high-capacity transit vans.
- The operating methods and order patterns will include:
  - additional telephone sales and fixed routes (A), and
  - additional telephone sales and variable routes (D).

The profile generated includes a number of different transport methods depending upon the task to be performed.

Measurement of success

In order to test whether the correct transport methods are selected it will be necessary to generate certain methods of measurement. At the macro level the most important measures are express as ratios including:

- cost per tonne, or cost per cubic metre;
- cost per drop, or cost per delivery.

These ratios relate cost to a physical characteristic of the product or the delivery other than the value of the product. In some cases it may be possible to evaluate each transport alternative in terms of cost, distance, and service level, by defining:

- cost per tonne/mile; and
- order to delivery time in days.

If targets are established for each transport activity it will be possible to determine where and what differences occur. It will also be important to monitor those factors identified as significant in the decision-making process.

Improving the choice over time

Throughout the life of any capital asset, there will be a number of changes and it is important to monitor these changes in order to adapt the choice of the transport mode to the new circumstances, or change the transport mode if necessary. The main areas which should be monitored include:

- technology – particularly of transport and mechanical handling systems, in order to change or adapt quickly if cheaper or better alternatives appear;
- environment – the operating environment should be continually monitored to ensure that the system does not infringe laws and maximises all available opportunities;
- volumes carried – particularly if they are moving up or down dramatically, to ensure that the correct volume of capital is being utilized;
- competitors – to ensure that the correct customer service level is being maintained.

It should be remembered that once the choice of the transport mode is made, it is not a simple procedure to change, particularly if a large quantity of capital is employed in vehicles and mechanical handling equipment.

Conclusion

The choice of the transport mode is a complex decision involving many factors and one which offers many opportunities. The final selection will depend upon management's skill to determine and quantify the significant options available; and this will be achieved only by a thorough and systematic approach to the problem.

As prices rise and transport becomes identified as a significant cost, then there will be pressure upon management to improve both the method of selection of the transport mode and justify that selection in a rational and defined manner.

Table 19.3
Monthly operating costs analysis

| Distribution Costs | Business: |
| Transport | Period: |

Trends   £000's

Actual this Period	Operating Costs		Moving Annual Totals To		
		Previous Year	P(−8)	P(−4)	This Period
	Wages and Expenses	(1)			
	Fuel and Oil Costs	(2)			
	Depreciation	(3)			
	Maintenance Costs	(4)			
	Insurance Costs	(5)			
	Warehousing Costs	(6)			
	Administrative Overhead	(7)			
	Total Cost	(8)			

Comparative Data		This Period	Previous Year	Year to Date	Same Period Last Year
(9) Number of Vehicles	Number				
(10) Total Vehicle Capacity	Tons				
(11) Total Working Days Available	Days				
(12) Total Working Days Lost	Days				
(13) Total Delivery Cap Available	Tons				
(14) Total Tonnage Delivered	Tons				
(15) Total Number of Journeys	Number				
(16) Total Miles Clocked	Miles				
(17) Total Number of Drops	Number				
(18) Total Hours Worked (Clocked)	Hours				
(19) Overtime Hours Worked	Hours				
(20) Number of Employees	Number				
(21) Value of Goods Delivered	£000's				

£

Costs	This Period	Year To Date	Ratios	This Period	Year To Date
Total Costs:			(31) Miles per Drop		
(22) −to Deliveries			(32) Weight per Drop (Tons)		
(23) −per Employee			(33) Miles per Journey		
Transport Costs:			(34) Miles per Day		
(24) −per Drop			(35) Weight per Journey (Tons)		
(25) −per Journey					
(26) −per Mile			(36) Deliveries per Day (£)		
(27) −per Ton			(37) Deliveries per Journey (£)		
Administrative Cost:					
(28) −per Journey					
(29) −per Ton			(38) % Load Capacity		
Warehouse Cost:			(39) % Vehicle Days Lost		
(30) −per Ton			(40) % Overtime worked		

20 Incoming Materials Management: a Case of Reverse Distribution

David Farmer

Introduction

Any comprehensive view of a business system must include consideration of input as well as output. For example, in a manufacturing system there is a need for input of parts and materials to allow manufacture and subsequent distribution of those manufactures. Further, in any physical distribution or logistics system, by definition, purchasers of the goods which are being distributed must exist. This chapter is concerned with the purchasing and materials management element of the system.

The approach taken should serve several purposes in respect of the readership of this chapter. First it should help to apprise those concerned with physical distribution management (PDM) of the many implications of materials management which affect their own performance. Second, it should help them to relate more effectively to the various aspects of the input system of their own customers. Third, it should provide those who are contemplating the development of a systems approach within their own organization with an alternative starting-point for the introduction of such a philosophy. Then it should provide the reader who is, as yet, uncommitted to the systems philosophy with a view of its potential in an alternative environment. Finally, it may also serve as a reminder of the importance of both long- and short-term input management, in strategic as well as operational terms, to the efficiency and effectiveness of, for example, the majority of firms engaged in manufacturing.

Conceptually, the relationship between materials management and the remainder of the system may be illustrated as in Figure 20.1. The

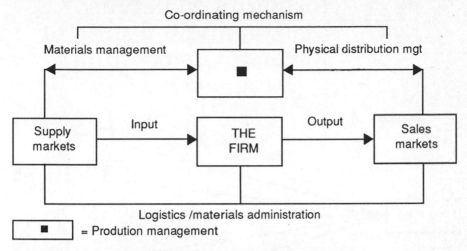

Figure 20.1   A conceptual view of a manufacturing firm

scope of materials management in this view can be seen to be the obverse of PDM, since it embraces the management of the flow of materials from the supply market into the firm. It may be defined as:

> The concept concerned with the management of the flow of materials into an organization to the point where those materials are converted into the firm's end product(s). Responsibilities include collaboration with designers on material component specifications, purchasing – which includes the search for, and location of, suitable economic sources of supply, incoming traffic, goods receiving and inspection, supplier quality control, inventory control (raw materials and components and, possibly, work-in-progress) and material control. In some cases internal materials handling would also be included.

Clearly, if a systems approach has not been adopted, then the various functions which are embraced by the definition would generally be seen as separate departments, or as elements within more traditional departments – for example, Production Control.

However, as experience in many industries during the last decade has shown, the liaison role with the remainder of the system is vital if materials management is to be effective. For example, the trend towards so-called 'pull' systems presupposes a resource system which can react quickly to changing patterns of need from the end market.

As with all systems approaches, the main thrust of the materials management concept is to avoid sub-optimization; to look for

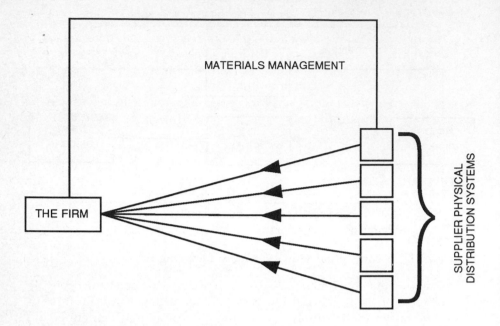

Figure 20.2   The link with supplier systems

systems efficiency and effectiveness; and to help ensure the achievement of common objectives rather than those that apply to elements within the system, which may be competing one with another. In addition, it should be concerned with 'supply marketing' which implies an orientation towards the environment within which the firm operates as a buyer.

This latter part of the task may be seen as the linking mechanism with the many PD systems with which it is in contact. This is suggested by Figure 20.2, which illustrates the mutuality of these relationships as regards efficiency and effectiveness.

The scope of activity is, thus, considerable and, as has been argued elsewhere, it has important potential in terms of the efficiency and effectiveness of the total system. While many firms in the recent past tended to treat the supply segment of their business as mundane and strategically unimportant, things are changing fast.

For instance, many major manufacturing concerns have recognized the importance of effective supplier liaison in (for example) setting up 'co-makership' projects. They have become aware, in the process, of major factors which impact upon their businesses, such as using their purchase power most effectively. Moreover, and in some respects more importantly, they have recognized that the time taken to establish and manage supplier relationships properly can be considerable. From this it followed that it was beneficial, in certain circumstances, to reduce the number of suppliers with whom they dealt, and consequently several European manufacturers reduced the number of their production material suppliers by as much as 70 per cent.

The potential

Several studies over the last two decades sought to explore the potential of the materials management approach. In general, the arguments put forward, valid as they were, were largely ignored until the early 1980s when competitive pressures were such that they were recognized by some organizations – in particular, it is worth noting, by those organizations which were facing intense competition from Japanese businesses. The lessons which were learnt, albeit late in the day, were those which the Japanese themselves had learnt as a result of considering the fundamentals of any system, one of the key factors in this regard being that input and output should be in balance. This was a fundamental tenet which, as long ago as 1915, Shaw, when writing in the USA, had expressed as: 'the twin requirements of success are interdependence and balance'.[1]

Notwithstanding the foregoing, it is worth considering, for present purposes, some of the work of the last 20 years which has sought to identify fundamental aspects of business systems which either impact upon materials management or are affected by input systems.

Zenz, in an extensive research published in 1969 stated:

> Materials Management provides concise delegation of responsibility and authority, eliminating the possibility that departments may have overlapping responsibilities. In so doing it recognizes the importance of the manager principle of accountability by providing a materials management which is responsible for all aspects of materials decisions – a condition lacking conventional organization.[2]

Ammer,[3] writing 10 years earlier, had listed the possible conflicts which exist between objectives relating to materials in a conventional departmental organization (20.1). His thesis was that effective coordination through the adoption of the materials management approach

Table 20.1
Possible conflicts between departmental materials objectives

Primary Objective	Interrelated Objectives that are Adversely Affected
1 Minimum prices for materials	High inventory turnover, continuity of supply consistency of quality, low payroll costs, favourable relations with supply sources.
2 High inventory turnover	Minimum prices, low cost of acquisition and possession, continuity of supply, low payroll costs.
3 Low cost of acquisition and possession	High inventory turnover (sometimes), good records, continuity of supply, consistency of quality.
4 Continuity of supply	Minimum prices for materials, high inventory turnover, favourable relations with suppliers, consistency of quality.
5 Consistency of quality	Minimum prices for materials, high inventory turnover, continuity of supply, favourable relations with suppliers, low payroll costs, low costs of acquisition and possession
6 Low payroll costs	Maximum achievement of this objective is possible only by sacrificing all other objectives.
7 Good supplier relations	Low payroll costs, minimum prices, high inventory turnover.
8 Development of personnel	Low payroll costs (other objectives might also be affected).
9 Good records	Low payroll costs (other objectives might also be affected).

would eliminate many of the problems associated with these conflicts. Since the conflicts are recognizable to all who work in the materials area, the promise is considerable.

Fearon, too, saw the potential of the concept. In reviewing the progress of materials management up to 1973, he argued that 'The Materials Manager, placed in a position to exercise direct control over all materials functions, can maintain the necessary overview and can assure that needed balance of functions is, in fact, achieved'.[4] He went on to argue that this balancing of functions results from two subsidiary objectives of materials management, the first of these being 'to co-ordinate the performance of the materials function into a total materials system, in which the whole is greater than the sum of the parts'. The second objective was then 'to provide a communications network among the several materials functions that provide a quick, accurate, and comprehensive transfer of data, regarding demands occurring anywhere along the system'.

Fearon's list of benefits which firms believed they had realized from adopting the materials management approach included the following: elimination of buck-passing; better interdepartmental cooperation; lower prices of materials and equipment; faster inventory turnover; continuity of supply; reduced material lead times; reduced transportation costs; less duplication of effort; better morale; development of personnel; reduced materials obsolescence; improved supplier relationships; and better records and information. This tends to confirm the view put forward by Ammer but, if Ammer's conclusions held considerable promise, then this list of Fearon's suggests an even greater potential. And since Fearon had the benefit of reviewing the literature on the subject up to 1973 (including Zenz's comprehensive study), that potential appears to be achievable under competent and committed management. Events since that time have confirmed that potential.

Since Fearon's article appeared, the pressures on material supply, including cost and availability, have grown probably at a faster rate than ever before. The 1973 oil crisis, with its aftermath of material shortages and frightening levels of inflation, forced managements to pay greater attention to supply factors. The area in many organizations which has been thought of in operational terms was now emphasized as of strategic concern. Inventory costs in the light of extremely expensive money became a focal point of activity in every organization of any size. In the UK, for example, purchase prices seemingly continued changing in an upward spiral as internal inflation was fuelled by the decline of the pound against other currencies. The importance of materials to the economy of manufacturing concerns was then not in question. Yet, as was argued earlier, the stimulus for action was not as effective as it should have been.

As I have shown, most of this action, unfortunately, was reactive rather than proactive, so that the measures taken to alleviate the problems which occurred most significantly in 1973–74 were of a defensive nature. Since that time the downturn in world trade has eased the pressure on supply availability, if not on the financial implications. Consequently, many organizations had the opportunity to reorganize themselves to take advantage of the lessons learned from 1973. However, further changes in world economics were to have greater impact. As the 1980s began, the levels of unemployment, in the UK for example and in parts of Europe, were more significant than at any time since the 1930s. The companies which survived found themselves with slimmer workforces, and, whilst costs rose, the end market remained persistently unwilling to accept price increases. With lower levels of labour plus a trend towards greater automation, material costs emerged as an even more significant element of total costs.

Before continuing with the present discussion it would be helpful to consider the results of another study[5] which was carried out in the UK in the mid-1970s, which was concerned with the benefits of improved buyer–supplier relationships.

The advantages of the improved liaison cited by respondents in this study were, not surprisingly, closely related to those suggested by Fearon. They included 'better liaison Purchasing/Production', 'better utilization of own production facilities' 'better utilization of stores, warehouses, and stockyards' and 'better relationships with sources of supply'. It would appear that improved liaison between parties in the total system is crucial to such benefits. However, there is little doubt that the advantages will accrue most readily and most quickly where the internal organization is in a position to control its activities as it mates with those of its suppliers. The materials management approach would appear to offer a sound base from which to relate to supplier organizations.

However, as has been suggested, materials management requires the commitment of top management to the concept and professional, capable management of the area if the objectives discussed earlier are to be achieved. The materials manager should be of a calibre commensurate with the importance of the task he has to undertake. He should be able to relate to colleagues within his own organization, and in those of suppliers, at the highest level. The objectives, goals and policies towards and within which he needs to work should be clearly defined. Like his marketing colleagues he needs to be consumer-oriented but with the added responsibility of extending that orientation into his supplier's systems.

Ericsson,[6] writing about materials administration, suggests that several other requirements need to be present in the company system if the approach is to be effective. He argues that management expertise should exist within the company to enable the approach to be adopted, and that management should have available to it the appropriate information-processing equipment and techniques. Further, costs – especially those connected with the materials system – should be capable of being analysed and accounted for with a reasonable degree of accuracy; and top management, as well as those concerned with the materials system, should be wedded to the concept.

These requirements for system effectiveness are just as applicable to either PDM or materials management; and while it is true that many current accounting arrangements, for example, are unsuitable for systems approaches there would appear to be a better chance for successful adaptation on a subsystem basis as a first step. It is probably true to say, however, that the relevant deficiencies at the input end of many company systems are greater than in the majority of others. Nonetheless, the potential rewards – once recognized – are so great that the motivation to implement the materials management approach should ensure that these deficiencies are made good relatively quickly.

Certainly, at the end of the 1980s the concept of systems approaches are more widely accepted whilst the power and 'transparency' of information systems are greater than ever before.

Many systems problems stem from product decisions. Indeed, virtually all the main business decisions in manufacturing organizations are influenced by the basic product question, 'what products should we have in our range?' The complexity, quality level and number of products which result from such questions impinge upon materials management to a considerable degree; and it is extremely important that relevant attention is paid to this aspect of system management.

There is a positive materials management role in which the key objectives include working with other managers in the system to reduce the time taken to get the product into the rapid growth stage of the product life cycle; and as life cycles shorten this aspect of the task becomes increasingly important. Indeed, in some circumstances, this is crucial. For example, in 1988 a consumer electronics business in Europe was working with a life cycle of eight months for a piece of audio equipment. At the same time its new product development sequence was estimated at 18 months. Closer marketing – design – materials management liaison on an *on-going basis* was highlighted as a result of this dilemma.

One approach to solving this problem which has been used successfully in several businesses has been the re-orientation of (new) product development teams. In these cases materials management plays a far more significant part than hitherto, and often involves key suppliers in the process. Clearly, the shorter the life cycle of a product, the greater the need to get the product to the market on time and in the right condition. Where that does not happen the product will fail. Consequently, it is of extreme importance that the right materials are available at the right time so that production may manufacture the item to meet the schedule which the market demands. Another aspect of this which has exercised the minds of managers is the ability of the manufacturing system to respond quickly to market needs.

One example which illustrates the impact on, and of, materials management on the manufacturing system as a whole relates to a cycle company. The company had problems meeting demand for its products which, in the market concerned, tended to peak in July–August and November–December. Some 80 per cent of the company's sales were made in those periods. The planning process in the business required the sales people to forecast sales of some 163 lines (including colour variations) six months ahead. In turn, Production forecast its demand based upon the sales figures, whilst materials management placed purchase orders for the relevant components based upon the production schedules.

In the event the forecast error by line was ± 50 per cent with the result that many wrong cycles were in stock when compared with market demand, whilst materials management, also, had the wrong components. Among the 'results' of this state of affairs was that the inventory turn in the business was just twice per annum, whilst the business was losing money.

A simple analysis of the situation might have suggested that the key difficulty was the inability of the sales department to forecast effectively. However the core problems stemmed around the ability of the business system to respond quickly enough to market demands. Careful analysis revealed a series of interacting decisions, several of which hinged upon materials management issues.

The outcome of the analysis was a new approach to managing the system as a whole which recognized the impossibility of accurately forecasting 163 lines six months in advance. The key was to find what has been called the 'decoupling point' between the 'pull' of the market and the 'push' of production/materials. This was achieved by identifying 15 'families' of cycles and forecasting at that level. This facilitated manufacturing forecasting to an accuracy level of ± 6 per cent, with a subsequent marked improvement in all aspects of the business.

From the materials management viewpoint, it also identified the length of the supply pipeline as being crucial. From that analysis resulted strategies which promoted either the development of local sources or arrangements with distant suppliers to hold stock in the UK.

This case is a classical example of the potential impact of effective materials management on a business system. Clearly, all logistics systems have input and output and the previous discussion on balancing the two is deceptively obvious; nevertheless, in many business situations, it has patently not been given adequate attention.

The role of materials management in the organization

No attempt will be made here to discuss the general aspects of organization for materials management, since this topic is well covered in the books listed under Further Reading at the end of this chapter. Instead, discussion will be related to the total system and the function of materials management within it. The emphasis will be on the need to recognize the importance of liaison between functions in the system and of having the right people to perform those functions; for, whatever form of organization is adopted, the quality and attitude of the people engaged in it are extremely important.

Materials management and the environment

It is important for the organization to be aware of the potential impact of changes in its environments, and supply markets can be as crucial as sales markets in this regard. So far as supply markets are concerned, the events of the mid- and late 1970s and the early 1980s all illustrated the impact of the supply environment on the system as a whole. Perhaps the Oil Crisis of 1973–74 and the severe recession of 1979–80 were the most significant in this regard. The changes which occurred in these periods emphasized the importance of effective market study in procurement as much as in respect of sales.

For example, such study should include a general scenario relating to aspects such as mergers, key suppliers' activities and plans, alternative suppliers' activities and plans, other buyers' activities and plans and related legislation. It will be necessary to have: (i) staff in the procurement area who have the necessary attributes to undertake this work; and (ii) a suitable mechanism to ensure that the resulting pertinent data is fed into the corporate decision-making and planning system, both long- and short-term.

At the strategic level this might include consideration of such factors as the need to integrate vertically or abandon certain products. In other cases it might call for participation in plant location, production methodology and 'make-or-buy' decision-making. The essence of strategy is in the ability to concentrate strength against competitive weakness. The considerations listed above are among those which may have a considerable effect on the recognition, as well as use, of such strengths.

It should be the task of procurement (in the present sense, part of materials management) to keep product designers in touch with developments in the supply market. Not only should this include data on new materials, but also projected comparative economics of available alternatives. Among other things, consideration of potential changes in currency parities and transportation methods might be included. In the multinational company environment it could also involve consideration of the availability of material at the various company manufacturing locations. Other factors might include an analysis of material/product availability with respect to potential demand, not only as regards the company itself, but also as regards other users and potential users. Changes in the supply–demand balance can also have a considerable effect on production economics and on end-product selling prices. Given the proportion of material cost to total cost in many products, sound supply market information may be critical to the selection of the right formula for a new product.

The roles suggested by the foregoing discussion are not the kind which, traditionally, have been applied to procurement. However, in many cases, if the company system is to be effective, they need to be undertaken efficiently and effectively. Such roles necessitate staff who have a corporate perspective, who understand the objectives of the business as a whole, and are aware of how they might contribute to the achievement of those objectives. They need to monitor potential changes in their external environment and plan and act with a view to minimizing the adverse effects of those changes while seizing every advantage. And, in the context of the present text, they need to be aware of systems concepts and of the roles which they have to play in that regard.

Internal liaison and suppliers

The foregoing may be considered as examples of aspects of the strategic role of the materials functions. There are other important liaison roles in respect of what may be termed operational activity. A manufacturing organization receives materials and/or components which it converts into finished products. As has been suggested, one task of Procurement is to ensure that those materials and components are there when they are required at the most economic cost to the buying company. This means close liaison – for example, with Production, Production Control and Cost Analysis departments.

Production is perhaps the function with the most obvious liaison requirements. A failure in supply which results in idle men or machines is always expensive. Not only is there the direct cost of idle men and machines, but when equipment stops, overheads are not being recovered, and the finished product may be delivered late to the customer with consequent damage to relationships. In addition, if goods are delivered late, payment will be made at a later date, which may in turn affect cash flow and, in extreme cases, solvency. These dangers are among those which result in many organizations when they attempt to ensure against supply failure through, for example, increasing inventory. The case example of the cycle company which was referred to earlier illustrates the futility of such measures, as will many of the contributions to this text.

In servicing Production, one element of the materials management role involves calling forward 'sets' of components and/or materials from suppliers in accordance with the company's own production schedule. There is no doubt that much can be done in terms of making such call-off automatic. For example, period contracts may be placed with suppliers in which the estimated daily/weekly/monthly call-off is stated. The supplier then sets up to meet that demand but delivers against an 'actual' schedule provided, say, one week in advance. This approach works well where there are limited variations in supply and demand. It can also work well where there are changes, but communications within the production–procurement––suppliers system need to be effective. Such circumstances require fast response to changes, intelligent anticipation and prompt action. The growing interest in the MRP and JIT concepts reflects these ideas.

It is impossible in the space available to do anything other than touch on some of the key materials management issues which relate to manufacturing systems, for instance. Nonetheless, before concluding this chapter it may be helpful to describe, briefly, two widely used approaches in input control.

The first of these is MRP which, at the outset was referred to as materials requirements planning. A typical MRP system utilizes a computer connected to a series of work stations. It starts with a master production schedule (or list of products which are to be completed within the period in question) and 'explodes' this into time-phased schedules of items which make up the products. These schedules may relate to sub-assemblies, parts and other material requirements and allow for stock-in-hand and purchases which are due for delivery. From all this data the system produces a schedule of net requirements per period. This can be printed on hard copy, for example as a purchase order or, in some cases, can be connected to supplier systems. This net requirement can be shown on VDUs as necessary and gradually converted into finished products.

As the MRP concept developed, so did its scope, for the reality of effective manufacturing systems, as has been argued, necessitates effective integration and balance. Both these requirements imply *interactive* communication. Out of this came MRPII now renamed manufacturing resource planning. A definition used by one company of MRPII is: 'it is an integral approach in which all essential resources are consistently planned in their mutual relationships in order to achieve a total "closed loop" control'.[7] This rather complex definition covers an approach which has three levels. Figure 20.3 illustrates the interrelationships.

What may be seen from this figure is the recognition of the importance of continually refining the information being used for management through the feedback loops. The system sets out to harmonize the various elements of the system. Clearly the 'input' aspects of this system are vital ingredients in the whole process.

The JIT approach

The second, and increasingly popular, approach to the management of materials flow is the so-called 'Just-in-Time' (JIT) approach. It is

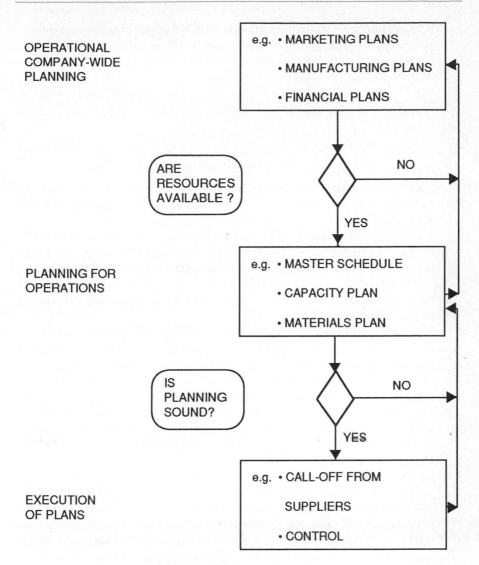

Figure 20.3 A 'closed loop' MRPII system

based upon the simple idea that components (for example) should be delivered to the production line 'just-in-time' for them to be assembled into the product or sub-assembly being made. Again, the original concept was focused upon incoming components in order to obviate inventory at that stage whilst facilitating production. Now, however, there is the recognition that, in order to ensure system-wide effectiveness JIT should be applied throughout the business.

Consequently in more sophisticated situations, at least, the concept is applied to:

- finished goods which are manufactured *just-in-time* to be sold;
- sub-assemblies which are delivered or produced *just-in-time* to be assembled into finished products;
- components which are delivered or produced *just-in-time* to go into sub-assemblies or finished products.

Clearly, the concept necessitates absolute precision and control at all points in the system and it is for that reason that few organizations (if any) can claim total success.

From the incoming materials point of view, a key for success is the quality of relationship between the company and its suppliers. Apart from anything else this necessitates a relationship which is *collaborative* rather than *adversarial*. The need to benefit from the system for both parties and cooperation should begin at the earliest stage of product development.

In short, the approach necessitates a change in attitude to what has been termed a 'co-makership' approach. That will not happen overnight, since there needs to be a great deal of management attention paid to developing such a way of working. It is for that reason that the European companies which have sought to employ the approach have all reduced their supplier base. Finally, it should be stressed that JIT is not universally applicable. A sensible approach is to use one or two suppliers to pilot the scheme. If those suppliers have experience of JIT systems with other customers then much time can be gained in 'going up the Learning Curve'.

Some useful questions which may be asked in deciding on suppliers in these circumstances are: Do they have experience with JIT systems? What can we learn from them? Should we select a supplier which is located near to us? Can we focus more business upon the supplier? Can he work with us at the development stage, and is his quality control system good enough?

Conclusion

As is implied, if not made explicit, in the foregoing discussion, the materials management role within the business system is a key factor in its success. Whilst the majority of the discussion here has been concerned with manufacturing operations, the implications are as important, if not more so for retailing. The drive towards replacing inventory with information will necessitate even greater care and attention being paid to the function in the future.

It is the view of author that input management will become even more important during the next decade as the proportion of 'output' income disposed of on 'inputs' increases whilst other costs fall.

References

1 Shaw, A. W.; *Some problems in Market Distribution*; Boston, H.V.P., 1915.
2 Zenz, G. J., 'Materials Management: Threat to Purchasing', *Journal of Purchasing*, vol. 4, May 1969.
3 Ammer, D., 'There are no "Right" Answers to Materials Management', *Purchasing*, vol. 46, 16 February 1959.
4 Fearon, H. E., 'Materials Management, a Synthesis and Current Review', *Journal of Purchasing*, vol. 9, no.1, February 1973.
5 Farmer, D. H. and MacMillan, K., 'Voluntary Collaboration -v- "Disloyalty" ', *Journal of Purchasing and Materials Management*, vol. 12, no.4, Winter 1976.
6. Ericsson, D. 'Materials Administration', *The Scandinavian Journal of Materials Administration*, Trial Issue, November 1975.
7 Response given during an unpublished research study, Farmer, D. H., 1988.

Further Reading

Baily, P. J. H. and Farmer, D., *Purchasing Principles and Management*, (5th ed.), London: Pitman, 1986.
Farmer, D. (ed.), *Purchasing Management Handbook*, Aldershot: Gower, 1985.

21 The Path of Successful Implementation of DRP

Phil Heenan

Introduction

Buzzwords, buzzwords, buzzwords . . . . During the past 10 years we have been inundated with terminology. Acronyms such as MRP, MRP II, DRP, DRP II, JIT, TQC, TQM, SPC, CAD, CAM – the list is endless. Managers find it difficult enough to work out what the letters stand for, let alone whether or not they can help their company. This is unfortunate, since many of the letters can be summed up as OCS – Organized Common Sense!

This chapter sets out to achieve two objectives:

1 to clarify some of the terminology that has been thrown around;
2 to facilitate the succesful implementation of DRP in your company.

Distribution resource planning

The philosophy of distribution resource planning (DRP II) has been popular in the USA and Canada since the early 1970s. DRP II evolved over the years from distribution requirements planning which was based on Joe Orlickey's technique called material requirements planning (or MRP). It was the late Oliver Wight who became famous for taking MRP and other management processes and turning them into the business philosophy 'manufacturing resource planning'. Then André Martin adopted the MRP principles and first developed distribution requirements planning or, as we know it today, distribution resource planning.

Today, then, when we talk about distribution resource planning (hereafter referred to as DRP) we are talking about a philosophy not

356

just a technique. It is a tool-box containing a proven set of reliable tools ready for the successful manager to put to good use.

My past involvements in successful implementations of DRP and MRPII highlighted two things to me:

1 The path to successful implementation is straightforward provided you follow the 'proven path'.
2 If you do not follow the 'proven path' it is an agonizing and frustrating, expensive experience for all concerned.

The company I worked with operated with nine manufacturing plants and distribution centres throughout the country with a growing import and export business. MRP II and DRP were both implemented throughout the company, and one division became the second company in Australia to be awarded the prestigious 'Class A' award in July 1988.

The DRP 'Proven Path'

André Martin, author of the book *Distribution Resource Planning*, President of Oliver Wight Education Associates, developed the proven path when he first implemented MRPII and DRP to 'Class A' at Abbott Laboratories in Canada. Since then, working with companies throughout the world, he has developed this proven path to a point where, if followed religiously, outstanding benefits and 'Class A' recognition is guaranteed.

The rest of this chapter will be devoted to the 'proven path'. I will outline my experience in each area, where we made mistakes along the way and how you can avoid them in your implementation.

Initial education

Although the philosophy of DRP is not difficult to grasp, prior to embarking on this path, initial education for both senior and middle management is absolutely vital. Time and time again I have seen senior managers attempt to 'delegate' to the project leader or middle managers the task of 'installing' DRP, rather than accepting the responsibility themselves for 'implementing' this philosophy. I have chosen the words 'installing' and 'implementing' with deliberation and care.

Before implementing DRP, the managing director (or CEO of that division), along with his direct reports, should accompany the project leader (if one exists) to an external course on DRP to achieve the following objectives:

1   To find out what DRP is.
2   To estimate the benefits.
3   To understand their responsibilities in implementation.
4   To determine if DRP is for their company.

Upon their return, the management of this company may now progress to the next stage of implementation, which is the justification stage.

George Plossl, a well known consultant in the USA, once said: 'if you think education is expensive then try ignorance'. This hits the nail right on the head.

Justification

The justification, or cost – benefit analysis, is the next phase in implementation, and it is important to understand that this process is not just to satisfy the financial department or head office. It must be carried out to outline clearly to everyone precisely why the company is implementing DRP.

In one company the pay-back for implementing MRPII and DRP amounted to an additional US $750,000 profit per month. This figure, which became 'the cost of a one month delay' was neatly placed on paper and framed for all senior managers and directors to put up on their walls as a reminder of the importance of the project to the company. How much would your sales need to increase to obtain such a profit?

An additional benefit of publicizing the amount to be saved is that it enables personnel to get things into perspective when problems arise – particularly resource issues.

For example, a manufacturing director, when confronted with the need to recruit a full-time cycle counter, stated that the person was not included in the budget and could not be recruited. The managing director, however, pointed out that by not hiring the cycle counter the project would be delayed some months. And, with a pay-back sum of over US $500,000 per month, a sum of US $30,000 per year did not seem to be a significant amount. The cycle counter was recruited immediately.

I like to suggest to my clients that their justification should be prepared with a view to overstating the costs whilst understating the benefits. Then, if the return on investment is acceptable, everyone is aware that the figures are realistic and achievable.

Another important aspect of the justification is 'ownership of the benefits'. That is, each functional head should sign off on the benefits associated with his or her area. Of course, the project leader may prepare a rough justification initially, but the final justification must be 'owned' by the functional head of each department.

One question often asked is 'how do I know what benefits we will get and how big will they be?'. Ten years ago this may have been a valid question. However, today there are so many companies successfully implementing DRP that contact with a number of them will give you a very good answer.

The steering committee

The DRP steering committee should comprise the chief executive officer, his or her direct reports plus the DRP project leader. Whilst the project leader is responsible for the day-to-day activities and detailed planning of the project, the steering committee must take overall responsibility for ensuring that DRP is successful.

Many times throughout our implementation, we encountered issues which we could not resolve. These obstacles must be discussed with the steering committee and the problems resolved.

Resource constraints or money problems will be the most common issues raised and, if the steering committee does not resolve them for the project team, then it is highly likely that they will never be resolved.

The project team

I held the position of logistics manager in my company when I volunteered to become project leader. As the logistics manager, I had the following persons reporting to me; planning manager, purchasing manager, stores manager, despatch manager and customs manager. As such, my day was fairly hectic without any additional tasks to complete.

After four months I realized that something had to go. When the managing director gave me the choice, I decided on becoming the full-time DRP project leader. My view is that the project leader must be full-time and, depending upon the size of the company, some members of the project team may also need to be full-time.

The project leader should be the person in the company who you can least afford to lose. This could be the planning manager, accounting manager, purchasing manager, human resources manager – but not the EDP/MIS manager. Unfortunately, when the person in charge of the computer becomes the DRP project leader, then everyone in the company thinks that DRP is just another computer system. It is not. DRP is a 'people' system made possible by the computer's massive data manipulative capabilities.

The balance of the DRP project team should be made up of key senior managers representing each major department.

A statement I hear continually is that 'we are not like some companies who have spare people hanging around – in fact we are all absolutely flat out'. Smaller companies say that larger companies are lucky because they obviously have people to spare; larger companies say the same about the smaller ones and so on.

Only once have I ever heard a company say that it had spare people to put on the project, due to a rationalization involving a plant closedown. Yet, amazingly, the DRP project leader said to me 'Oh yes, we have spare people but I really don't want them because they are not the "type" I need'. Sometimes you just can't win!

Maybe you believe that you cannot afford to put people on a project like this – which brings us back to the justification or cost – benefit analysis mentioned earlier. All the required personnel should be included in the cost justification. If your return on investment is acceptable, with full-time DRP project team members included, then the whole process becomes a business proposition. Make the decision, appoint the personnel, redesign the organization chart and make a start. For every month you delay you lose profit.

The project plan

Many companies spend months carefully preparing objectives, tasks and detailed activities neatly printed on beautifully bound packages that have been painstakingly prepared on the latest project management packages. This is fine if you have a secretary to do this for you. However, if you are like most project leaders, you rarely have the support you need and therefore much of the work that needs to be done is done by yourself.

Therefore, your motto should be: 'Ready, Fire, Aim'. I admit that I have been guilty of spending too much time on the MacIntosh and not enough time on getting results.

What changed my approach was a visit to a company in Ireland which had its project plan hand written on pieces of paper. There were no fancy binders, no MacIntosh printouts, just objectives to be achieved, people to achieve them and dates for the action items to be completed by.

Prepare an overall plan based on the 'proven path'. Break that plan down into each area, then detail the tasks required to be completed. Monitor progress weekly and take corrective action as soon as required. Set up task groups consisting of users within the various areas. Appoint one member of the project team to assist the task force, but not as task force leader. Appoint a sponsor from the senior management team to each task force to assist them with difficult problems and to show top management commitment.

Finally, make sure that the project plan is broken down into achievable tasks. Achieving small successes builds confidence and makes for easier monitoring of progress.

Professional guidance

If you are going to learn to fly an aeroplane, would you take advice from someone who has 'watched' someone fly an aeroplane, or would you seek advice from someone who has actually 'flown' one? Implementing DRP is really not much different to flying an aeroplane.

The first step must be to get a consultant who has a proven track record in implementing DRP – not someone who has merely read about it. He or she should be able to provide you with references. You owe it to your company, and yourself, to check those references, visit the companies, and see the results they obtained.

A consultant should 'guide' you along the 'proven path', not do the work for you. If this happens then the ownership does not rest with you, but with the consultant, so that when he or she leaves, so too does all the activity. 'Thank goodness the consultant has gone, now we can get on with our own jobs!'

The consultant should also be an outside objective voice and be able to advise the CEO when progress is off course.

Project team education

All the project team members should attend external public classes on DRP. These classes will provide them with the knowledge required to implement DRP and educate their own company personnel.

Where there is a manufacturing interface, then key members of the team should also attend public classes on MRPII.

Once the project team members have attended outside classes they may then begin teaching other personnel. Education is vital to the project team not only because they need to be the 'in-house experts', but also so they can marry the 'philosophy' of DRP with the software purchased and the company culture.

Internal education

The best way to educate your company personnel is to obtain DRP videos then, using the project team members and key personnel who have attended public classes, run in-house classes. There are some excellent videos available which have been produced by the leading practitioners in the field.

Using your own managers to educate your personnel is much more effective than having an 'outsider' come in and do it for you. A person is much more likely to want to change his behaviour if his or her supervisor or manager is up front outlining how, in the future, the department will be operated.

However, be careful not to fall into the trap my project team did when 'watching' the videos. There is a temptation to watch the video and, when it is finished, walk out of the training room without changing the company in any way. This is called 'fact transfer' and, unfortunately, does little to change the company culture.

What we are really looking for is 'behaviour change' and the way to achieve this is as follows. First, at the start of the 'business session' (a better description of these video-assisted education sessions) review action items from the previous meeting. Do not start the new session until all action has been completed, otherwise nothing has been achieved. Second, start the new session by reading the introduction materials and watching the video. Third, discuss the principles and techniques raised in the video then carefully review the action listed in the video workbooks. This is how you achieve 'behavioural change'.

Using the analogy of reading a book on dieting serves to illustrate the difference between 'fact transfer' and 'behavioural change'. We all read books on dieting at some stage of our life. Once we have finished reading the book we have completed the 'fact transfer stage'. However, this does not mean we will change our behaviour and immediately start our diet. First we have to review the material, relate the theories to our own life, discuss the situation with members of the family, and so on. Finally we will make a decision and 'change our behaviour'.

Fact transfer is important, but useless unless we change our behaviour. Education is the key to DRP success. It is only a minor cost but contributes the most to success of the project.

Data integrity

One of the benefits of implementing DRP is it provides a process which forces us to achieve and maintain accurate data, since without accurate data the whole system will collapse.

If your inventory records do not reflect reality, then the company cannot possibly operate efficiently. Indeed, inventory record accuracy is one of the key areas in data integrity.

Cycle counting, carried out on a daily basis, is the best way to get inventory 100 per cent accurate. However, cycle counting does not involve merely counting the stock in order to make the computer stocks reflect what is actually in the store (although this is a great side benefit). What we are attempting to do is fix (permanently) any errors that may be occurring in the process. Once each error in the process is permanently eliminated, your stock records must be accurate.

Education is the key to achieving data integrity in inventory, forecasting or the item analysis area.

Item analysis

Loading item data into the system is an obvious requirement for successful DRP. Clear responsibilities are required to ensure that each person in the company knows who is responsible for what segment of the system. Further, and this is something most companies fail to do, an audit process should be initiated to ensure that all data remains accurate.

Many companies take six to 12 months to load the data then proceed to forget about it. Eventually, of course, errors creep in, people change jobs, the process is not followed correctly and data integrity declines.

Set up a good, formal process and monitor results regularly; this is the key to having good data.

Purchasing planning and MPS policies

Master scheduling is the filter between supply and demand and unfortunately is non-existent in most companies. A good DRP software package should have a master scheduling process that enables the scheduler to critique the effect sales and receipts have on current on-hand inventories.

Managing this demand, using firm planned orders, ensures that the company operates in a pro-active environment rather than in a reactive one.

A great benefit derived from MRPII was the process called vendor scheduling. There is no reason why vendor scheduling cannot also be introduced into a distribution environment and achieve the same dramatic improvements.

A vendor schedule lists requirements by supplier and shows due dates so that the supplier is informed weekly of the latest requirements.

Pilot vendor scheduling with one of your better suppliers. Spend a day with him outlining what you are trying to achieve (using videos and reports) then, once it is working successfully with that vendor, repeat the process with your other suppliers. You may educate the balance of your suppliers in groups of 15–20.

Remember, what we are trying to achieve is a minimum of 100 per cent quality, at least 98 per cent of the time, 98 per cent on-time performance and a way of ensuring the price we are paying is a 'fair' market price.

Software evaluation and selection

A major headache for many companies is evaluating and selecting software. Whilst I agree that this usually presents a problem, much of the difficulty is due to lack of education. If your management team has been to external, then internal, education sessions, the task of software evaluation and selection becomes much easier.

Try not to change the software but select a good, standard package that best fits your business. Be careful of personnel wishing to 'computerize' the way they currently do their job. I have seen this happen in many companies, and it is such a shame. Here is an ideal opportunity to introduce state-of-the-art technology and all some companies end up with is ten-year-old systems transferred to the latest and greatest computer.

My view is that any modifications should be done 'outside' the package so that updates can be installed without fuss – that is, if there needs to be any modifications! If your company is not particularly well managed at the moment, what gives your management the qualifications to alter a package that maybe hundreds of other users worldwide are using successfully? Many companies believe that they are 'unique', and this belief causes many problems that could be avoided.

Go/no go checklist

Prior to putting DRP finally into operation, you must first ensure that all previous activities have been completed. I would suggest that you have your consultant critique your achievements to date to make certain that you are ready. It is quite common to believe you are 'there' when in fact you have overlooked some vital areas.

Ensure that standard DRP is operating effectively; make certain that your data integrity is being maintained at the required levels; and make sure that top management has been to education sessions. Monitor accountability in each department to ensure that people understand their responsibilities and are following the procedures and policies laid down. Pilot a product, a small group of products or a 'stand alone' section of the business prior to 'going live' in all areas. If the process works in that area, it will work elsewhere. However avoid frustrating your personnel by running the system in parallel.

Cut-over

Once an effective pilot has been completed, the cut-over phase of DRP should not take long at all. Certainly your policies, procedures, education, training and testing should all have taken place preparing you for this activity, and if the product(s) that you chose to pilot were fairly representative of your product range then your cut-over should present minimal problems.

There will naturally be some start-up problems. These should be attended to immediately and resolved to the satisfaction of the users. Allowing problems to drag on will cause the users to lose face and doubt the system and the project team.

Transportation planning

Once basic DRP is operating you may then introduce transportation planning. The major involvement here comes not only from the master scheduler but also from the Traffic department. Initially, manually prepared documents will suffice but at a later stage, on-screen smoothing of future requirements, to tie in with shipping capacities, should be introduced.

Some difficulties will be encountered with problem of 'stock in transit'. One company left this responsibility with the despatch manager. Prior to the weekly 'requirements' run, he would call each distribution centre to ascertain what they had received, then take those figures from the scheduled receipts column. The new numbers would then be input to the computer for computation. Eventually, this process should be totally mechanized.

It is important to note that the weekly 'execution' phase of DRP should be in synchronization with (and be driven by) the sales and operations plan. Failure to do this means that you are still merely reacting to your customers' demands.

Simulation and financial planning

Once the figures contained within the schedule are correct, the financial plans can be simulated. This may well reveal that, although we may have the capacity to sell or ship the product, it makes no financial sense to do so.

On the other hand, we may find that by bringing shipments forward, and building stocks in advance of peak seasons, overtime and/or shifts could be significantly reduced or eliminated, thereby reducing operating costs and increasing customer service and profits.

On-going education plan

Unfortunately, many companies believe that DRP is a destination, whereas in fact the journey to manufacturing or distribution excellence is a continuous journey. Once you achieve one level of excellence, you must progress to the next, otherwise your competitors will catch up whilst you are congratulating yourselves.

Thus, on-going education is vital to the company's continued success. When new personnel join the company, they should go through an induction programme which includes external classes and internal video-assisted business sessions. All too common a company gets to Class A then lets its education programmes slip, resulting eventually in an overall slight drop in efficiency and effectiveness. On-going education and a continuing effort to maintain excellence helps to eliminate this problem.

Further reading

1   Ling, R. and Goddard, W., *Orchestrating Success*, Vermont, USA, Oliver Wight Publications, 1988.
2   Martin, A. J., *Distribution Resource Planning Course*, Oliver Wight Companies,
3   Martin, A. J., *Distribution Resource Planning*, Vermont, USA, Oliver Wight Publications, 1983.
4   Martin, A. J., *The Origins of Distribution Resource Planning*, Atlanta, Management Science Amercia, 1986.
5   Martin, A. J., *Controlling the Marketing Channel*, Atlanta, Management Science America, 1987.

6   Martin, A. J., *'Can you Afford DRP?'*,New York, Thomas Publications Co., 1988.

7   Martin, A. J., *'Is EDI a Dream or a Reality?'*, New York, Thomas Publications Co., 1988.

8   Martin, A. J., *'The functional tunnel vision syndrome'*, New York, Thomas Publications Co., 1988.

9   The Oliver Wight Companies,*The ABCD Checklist*, Vermont, USA, Oliver Wight Publications', 1988.

10 Wight, O. W., *Production and Inventory Management in the Computer Age*, New York, Van Nostrand Reinhold Company Inc, 1984.

11 Palmatier, G. and Shull, J., *The Marketing Edge*, Vermont, USA, Oliver Wight Publications, 1989.

12 Wallace, T, F., *MRP II: Making It Happen*, Vermont, USA, Oliver Wight Publications, 1989.

22 Materials Management in Capital-Intensive Industries

Martin Mitchelson

Definitions

Before examining some of the key materials management issues and success factors in the capital-intensive sector, let us be quite clear about definitions.

By 'capital intensive' we mean those industries in which substantial investment has been made in plant, and in which the availability and performance of that plant are of overriding importance to the success of the business. Examples of such industries include:

- heavy process industries such as steel, bulk chemicals, paper and petrochemical refining;
- public utilities such as railways, electricity generation, and water supply;
- certain parts of the defence sector such as dockyards;
- major manufacturing plants where considerable new investment has gone into automation – the automotive sector itself being a prime example.

By 'materials management' we are referring to all those functions involved in the supply and logistics process from initial identification to final receipt by end-user or customer. Typically, some of these functions will not report through to a materials manager but rather to Finance, Engineering or Production, but for the purposes of this chapter are deemed to include:

- specification;
- sourcing, purchasing and expediting;
- cataloguing and inventory control;

- warehousing and materials handling;
- quality assurance, testing and tracking;
- internal and external distribution.

While all of these functions are just as likely to exist in a pure manufacturing environment, their relative importance and the optimum approach to carrying out each function is generally very different in the capital-intensive sector.

Objectives

In both manufacturing and capital-intensive industries, the materials function is essentially a service operation, the prime aim of which is to support other direct revenue-earning functions such as 'production' or operations. As such, the objectives of 'materials' must be closely aligned to the goals of these other functions and to the overall objectives of the organization.

Unlike in the manufacturing sector, however, where these corporate objectives may be readily defined in financial terms – and the materials objectives therefore also tend to be financially driven, such as unit purchase price and work in progress minimization – the corporate objectives of some of the capital-intensive sectors may be very different.

Thus, for example, we are commonly faced with such stated objectives as:

- security of supply, as in electricity generation;
- vehicle availability, as with transport authorities;
- strategic readiness, as in the defence sector;
- public health, as in water supply.

In such circumstances not only must the objectives of the materials function reflect these very different corporate goals, but the traditional measures such as inventory levels and unit prices frequently become minor issues.

The need for a different emphasis and different key performance indicators is further compounded by two factors:

1 the different *types of operation* which exist within a capital-intensive organization;
2 the diverse *range of materials categories* involved.

In the majority of sectors, there will be a combination of three distinct *types of operation*:

a) production or manufacturing (where, even in a service operation such as the public utilities, there are generally service shops to support maintenance and repair operations);
b) plant support or maintenance (which frequently accounts for a much higher proportion of operating costs in terms of labour and materials than the direct production operations);
c) construction or project work, related to the installation of new plant and facilities or major refurbishment of existing assets.

In each case the key interfunctional relationships and driving forces, and hence the approach to each of the materials activities, is very different. Thus, for example, the approach to stock control:

- is driven by the production schedule in a manufacturing environment and emphasizes work-in-progress minimization, just in time deliveries and so on;
- is driven by the maintenance programme in a plant support environment, and requires close interface with engineering to determine optimum spares stockholdings;
- bears a direct correlation to the construction programme in a project situation, and is likely to concentrate on the ready availability of consumable items, and the accurate definition of commissioning and operating spares requirements.

Within these different types of operation it is also clear that there are a number of different *materials categories*, for which the optimum approach to purchasing, inventory control, warehousing and distribution will again be very different. Typical materials categories may include:

- raw materials for both the main production processes and for supporting manufacturing operations;
- insurance and programme spares which may be identified for a specific shutdown operation or which may simply remain in a warehouse as cover against major breakdown of critical plant and lengthy lead times for replacements;
- repairable or rotatable spares – generally complete units such as motors, pumps, large valves and so on – which are subject to replacement by exchange in a maintenance programme, and are later refurbished and returned to stock;

- consumables and common spares – generally low-value items ranging from fasteners, to clothing, to seals and gaskets and so on;
- bulk supplies such as basic metal plate, cabling, lubricants and so on;
- contract services such as transport, cleaning, certification, mobile equipment-hire and so on.

Again, each of these categories needs to be handled very differently, and the approach, style and documentation involved, for example, in the purchasing of one category of material is unlikely to be appropriate for another.

Given the above diversity of objectives, sub-functions and activities, types of operation, and material categories, it is clear that the materials management operation in a capital-intensive environment is not only critical but also extremely complex. As a starting-point to addressing these complex issues and optimizing performance levels, it is therefore crucial to define very clearly both the overall objectives of the organization and the materials functional objectives in support of the overall goal, and the related key performance indicators. In defining these objectives it may therefore prove useful to consider the key issues facing organizations in the capital-intensive sector.

Key issues and performance optimization

In the manufacturing sector, developments both in the marketplace and in process technology, in recent years, have led to fairly fundamental changes both in the key issues facing manufacturing companies and in the response required from an effective materials management operation. Among these changes are:

- the increasing proportion of direct costs associated with materials, and correspondingly lower emphasis on labour costs and productivity;
- the current emphasis on factors such as flexibility, responsiveness and innovation as sources of competitive advantage rather than simply lowest-cost production.

The materials function has had to react accordingly – and in many cases has failed to react quickly enough, at considerable cost to the company – to change emphasis:

- first, away from material availability in support of labour efficiencies, to material cost minimization;

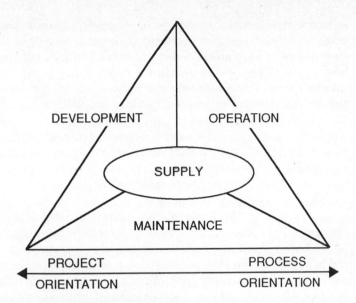

Figure 22.1   Asset management

- later, away from cost minimization alone, to such factors as rapid supply response times, streamlined supply chains, and total quality/zero defects.

In the capital-intensive sectors there has equally been a number of market and technological developments but, unlike in manufacturing, the critical success factor has remained constant: that is, key asset management in terms of availability and performance. Within the asset management cycle of development, operation and maintenance, supply plays a crucial central role as depicted in Figure 22.1 below.

This seeks to demonstrate that the generally substantial materials-related lifetime support costs and the critical role of materials in ensuring availability are of such paramount importance to business results that optimization of materials performance is essential.

The key materials category or sub-function in each situation, is, however, likely to vary but in most cases is likely to be related to spares holdings. Thus:

- In the oil and gas sector, spares availability in line with a preventive or predictive maintenance schedule is crucial. (I recall an early lesson in consulting where I was confident of achieving a substantial reduction in inventories based on historical usage. The production manager soon reminded me that one hour's production stoppage per annum due to non-availability of spares would lose 10,000 barrels of production at US $30 per barrel – and that finances a lot of spares!).

- In steel production or mining, success depends on keeping the blast furnaces or continuous miners operating flat out and where the initial spares identification process becomes critical.
- In rail operations, the availability of revenue-earning rolling stock is crucial and therefore the establishment of local stockholdings or very streamlined supply lines is essential.
- In dockyard operations, where the duration of refit cycles has a major impact on the level of investment on new ships to meet strategic requirements, the ability to source unique spares world-wide at very short notice provides a major financial and operational benefit. (Again, I can remember a couple of recent examples of major dockyards putting substantial effort into reducing stocks at a time when the labour cost associated with materials-related waiting time exceeded stockholding costs by several hundred per cent!).

Thus, while in manufacturing a strong emphasis remains on direct materials costs, in the capital-intensive sector the benefits from an efficient and effective materials operation are more likely to come from other indirect areas, such as:

- improved plant availability and performance;
- increased labour productivity;
- reduced spares obsolescence or redundancy;
- increased maintenance effectiveness;
- reduced expenditure on additional, stand-by facilities.

What then needs to be done to develop and implement an effective *materials management strategy* in the capital-intensive sector?

An approach which I have found useful is based on a number of factors, and can be summarized as follows.

1   An all important first step involves the definition of corporate and functional objectives.
2   There will be a small number of key functions, materials categories and sensitivities which have a major impact on the total operation and which therefore must be addressed. These need to be identified at an early stage.

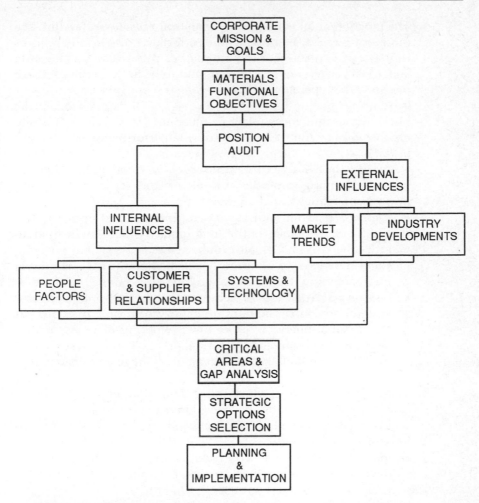

Figure 22.2 Materials management review and development methodology

3   There will be a number of internal and external influences which may constrain or facilitate effectiveness and the relative importance of each needs to be clearly evaluated.

In summary, therefore, the review and development process may involve the stages depicted in Figure 22.2.

Enough has already been said about functional objectives in support of overall corporate goals, but the other steps merit further explanation.

1   The position audit is merely an analytical phase which addresses the question 'how is the function performing at present?' This of course may be measured in a number of ways to reflect the costs and service levels being achieved, and to begin to highlight those parts of the operation where greatest scope for improvement exists.

2   The internal influences relate to those factors largely within the organization's control, which affect performance levels and include:

  • *people factors*, such as organization, style, capabilities, qualifications, training, attitudes, incentives and remuneration, and accountabilities;

  • *relationships*, both with customers (internal and external) and suppliers. This follows the total quality concept which advocates the use of a small number of suppliers with whom a sound relationship has been established on the basis of mutual understanding, trust and commitment;

  • *systems and technology*, which may include not only computer systems for purchasing and inventory control and so on, but also manual operating procedures, working methods, materials handling technology, information and control systems and the technology relating to material tracking such as barcoding, light pens and so on.

3   The external influences which the organization may not be able to control, but which must be considered in the light of changes which need to be made or alternative strategies developed. Such influences may include:

  • market trends such as world commodity prices, new materials developments, changing customer requirements, exchange rate fluctuations and so on;

  • industry developments such as increasing insistence on adherence to quality assurance standards, increasing tendency towards equipment lifetime support contracts, changes in maintenance management practices and so on.

All of the above will affect to some extent the degree to which the functional objectives are achieved, and in conjunction with the position statement from the audit, will enable critical areas to be identified and key 'gaps' assessed.

4   Having identified the major areas for attention – 'the what' – it is also likely that there will be a number of options available for addressing them – 'the how'. For example, if the shortage of

materials management skills is a major limiting factor, options available may include:

- recruitment;
- training and development;
- subcontracting of sub-functions;
- automation of non-critical processes;
- restructuring of the materials function.

These options and associated costs, benefits and risks, need to be carefully evaluated before firm decisions are made;

5 Planning and implementation, perhaps surprisingly, are two of the most crucial areas where organizations frequently fall down, having expended considerable time and energy in carrying out the earlier analytical stages. Any major improvement programme is likely to involve a complex change process, and, given the inherent complexity of the materials function anyway, merits careful planning. An anomaly to which I frequently refer in stressing the need for project planning, draws a comparison with major construction programmes. These are generally well planned, with detailed tasks, timescales, dependencies, resources, milestones and so on. When it comes to materials improvement projects, however – although they may have a far greater impact on corporate results – this level of planning is rarely undertaken.

Only by undertaking the above comprehensive approach can an organization in the capital-intensive sector be confident that all major opportunities for improvement are realized, or that all key issues which might affect future strategy are addressed.

Conclusion

In a brief review such as this it is simply not possible to cover all aspects of materials management in capital-intensive industries, and there are numerous factors which have not been considered here, such as:

- demand pattern variability;
- warranties and lifetime support;
- contractual terms;
- forecast modelling;
- risk analysis;

- service characteristics and measures;
- supply chain complexities.

I trust, however, that sufficient has been said about some of the major issues involved, to demonstrate that:

1   the materials function is not only critical but is highly complex;
2   materials management in capital-intensive industries is very different from in the manufacturing sector;
3   there are several critical success factors involved in optimizing performance, including:
    - relationships to overall business goals;
    - identification of key issues, interfaces and sensitivities;
    - recognition of the diversity of internal and external influences (systems alone will not solve the problems!);
    - the need for detailed project planning of both short- and longer-term tasks.

Few large organizations have successfully addressed all of these factors and, as a result, substantial potential tends still to be available to make dramatic improvements in corporate performance through optimization of the materials management function.

Part VII

CRITICAL INTERFACES
IN LOGISTICS

Overview to Part VII

The two most critical interfaces for logistics – that is, with marketing and manufacturing – are discussed in this part. In Chapter 23 Gattorna and Kerr emphasize the critical role played by logistics in the organization's overall marketing effort. They stress the differing levels of logistics support required as products move through various stages of their lifecycle. The chapter concludes with a discussion on the role of information and information systems in enabling marketing and logistics to coordinate their respective functions more effectively, both internally and across the whole organization as required.

The need for logistics to develop a strategic perspective of the organization is again highlighted by Greenhalgh in Chapter 24 where he argues that the organization's competitive strength is determined by the effectiveness of the manufacturing/logistics network as a whole. Greenhalgh emphasizes the interdependence of these two areas, and identifies a range of issues affecting both which have long-term implications for the organization. In providing a series of guidelines for working through these issues, he highlights the risks and possible pitfalls that can be encountered as well as the benefits that accrue from a well thought-out strategy.

23 The Logistics Interface with Marketing

John Gattorna and Andrew Kerr

There was a time earlier this century when the functions now broadly grouped under the term logistics were part of marketing. During the 1950s and 1960s however, marketers tended to focus on product promotion and development, neglecting the more mundane areas of warehousing, transport and inventory control.

The realization that storage and distribution costs were absorbing an increasing percentage of sales revenue sparked a renewed interest in this area in the late 1960s and early 1970s. However, a different group emerged to manage these areas, as marketers of the day considered warehousing and distribution not to be marketing concerns.

Over time, logistics assumed primary responsibility for warehousing, inventory and transport within many organizations with marketing responsible for negotiation, promotion and selling. As neither group had responsibility for overall channel management, conflicts arose, exacerbated by organizational structures that fostered achievement of functional goals, often at the expense of overall organizational goals.

Gradually the more enlightened organizations heard their customers' demands for solutions and realized that functional interdependence, not internecine conflict, was the key to satisfying customer needs. Whilst surveys show that many marketing and logistics managers cannot fully agree on certain areas of responsibility, there appears to be a general acceptance amongst progressive managers that the interface between logistics and marketing must be effectively managed if organizations are to compete successfully in the difficult markets of the 1990s.

Recognition that effective management of the marketing/logistics interface is necessary for success does not imply an end to conflicting

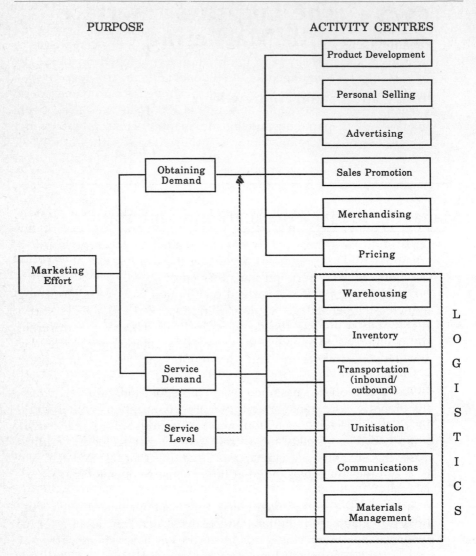

PURPOSE   ACTIVITY CENTRES

Figure 23.1   The division of marketing effort within the firm

interfunctional objectives; these are a fact of life. Rather, it provides a strategic opportunity for organizations which realize that their marketing and logistics functions are strategic resources, best employed as part of an overall strategic plan. Logistics has the task of ensuring that demand generated by marketing is actually serviced or fulfilled, as depicted in Figure 23.1.

Effective utilization of these strategic resources does not necessarily require changes to organizational structure or any realignment of responsibilities. Advances in information technology provide ample opportunity for interdependent functional areas to share information as part of an integrated system. What is required is a fundamental re-evaluation of how organizations think about the resources being managed. Both marketing and logistics managers must adopt a wider perspective of the organization and begin to think strategically.

Managing the logistics/marketing interface

Despite the realization by progressive logistics and marketing managers that cooperation is essential, marketers often criticize logistics departments for being cost-minimizers, having no understanding of customers' needs, whilst logistics departments accuse marketers of chasing sales at any cost. This inability to understand the other group's position is a major factor inhibiting many organizations' marketing efforts.

Conflict between logistics and marketing seldom arises over functions clearly agreed by both groups as being the primary responsibility of one group. For example, most marketers agree that freight rate negotiation, selection of transport mode and investigation of transit loss or damage are logistics responsibilities. Conflict tends to arise when one department has been assigned primary responsibility for a function that the other department feels should be their responsibility. More frequently however, conflict arises when responsibility for a particular function is not clearly defined and agreed. It is these interface areas of potential conflict that need to be effectively managed.

It is essential that organizations identify areas of agreement and potential conflict. Where conflict cannot be easily resolved, senior management must ensure that clear guidelines for cooperation are established and that cooperation is forthcoming. Senior management must be seen to actively support cooperation between the two groups. This can be assisted by performance measurements that reward cooperation and a spirit of interdependence and actively discourage parochial behaviour.

Logistics and the product life cycle

A key marketing concept that affects the relationship between logistics and marketing is the product life cycle (PLC). This concept suggests that products move through definite stages throughout their life which tend to follow the pattern depicted in Figure 23.2.

The PLC model postulates that, if a product is successful with early purchasers (and many products fail at this stage), repeat purchases occur, the more cautious are persuaded to try the product as word-of-mouth spreads, and the rate of sales growth increase. Later, as the market becomes saturated and newer products offering additional benefits are introduced, sales decline and eventually the product is abandoned.

The levels of logistics support required by marketing varies as a product moves through the different stages of the PLC. In the early stages timely cost-effective fulfilment of orders is a major requirement in ensuring initial acceptance of the product. Later, as sales slow and the product moves into the maturity and saturation stages, the emphasis changes to trimming costs as the product faces stiff price competition and consequent pressures on margins. Unless logistics managers understand what marketing is trying to achieve with each product, they cannot hope to provide appropriate levels of logistics support for the marketing effort.

A changing environment

A distinguishing characteristic of the 1980s has been the increase in the pace of change. The pace at which new concepts, products and technological innovations are introduced, gain popularity and are themselves superseded, has increased to the point where it can now take longer to source the components for an item of consumer electronics than the life cycle of the product itself. In this environment it is essential that marketing and logistics work together to gain a competitive advantage.

In many organizations, logistics not only has responsibility for warehousing and distribution of finished goods, but also for sourcing and management of raw materials. By developing an effective logistics/marketing interface and utilizing established technology strategically (see Chapter 27), organizations can implement JIT policies that: ·

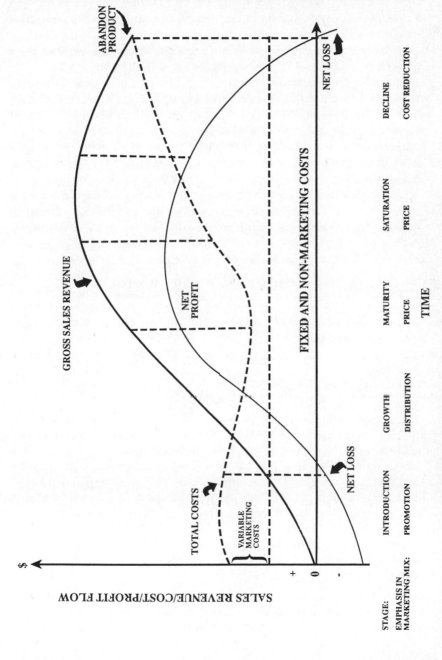

Figure 23.2   The product life cycle and the marketing mix

387

- see manufacturing costs incurred closer to the point of sale;
- substantially reduce raw materials inventories;
- result in finished goods inventory profiles more closely aligned to customer demands; and
- help reduce buffers of prohibitively costly finished goods inventory.

Shortened product life cycles, the pace of technological innovation, regulations such as those in the EEC relating to open-date coding of consumer non-durables and the high cost of capital are forcing organizations to find ways of meeting customer demand other than with large finished goods inventories. Organizations are forced to react to increasingly sophisticated buying groups who order smaller quantities more frequently and demand greater reliability of delivery. Unless internal organizational structures are capable of effectively meeting these demands, profitability and market share will suffer.

Areas of logistics and marketing interaction

Some progressive organizations are utilizing the benefits of their established logistics/marketing interface to negotiate not only product and price, but also logistics services tailored to meet individual customer needs. These organizations are able to differentiate themselves from their competitors by offering a total service, with logistics forming an essential part of the profit equation.

A critical challenge facing both marketing and logistics managers as we move into the 1990s is not how to eliminate conflict, but instead how to effectively manage and reduce the level of conflict more successfully. One of the keys to achieving this lies in information systems design. In his book *Logistics Decisions*, published in 1984, Schary suggested that:

> Logistics as a system transcends organizational boundaries, and therefore does not lend itself to conventional organizational design. Lines of authority and responsibility cannot be extended to every function that must be included in the system. The solution appears to be not along organizational lines, but in the information systems. If decisions are made where sufficient information is available, then developing and controlling the flow of information becomes not only a substitute for organization but

possibly a more effective means of managing a complex set of activities and decision makers.[1]

For some organizations, advances in information technology have turned Schary's prediction into a reality. Progressive logistics and marketing managers use sophisticated computer and communications technology jointly to manage activities that were previously the source of constant conflict.

The major areas of interaction between logistics and marketing include:

- *Product design.* This can have a major effect on warehouse and transportation utilization (and therefore costs).
- *Pricing.* This is the means by which logistics services customer demand affects the overall cost of the product and in turn the organization's pricing policies.
- *Market and sales forecasts.* Marketing forecasts will largely dictate the level of logistics resources needed to move products to customers.
- *Customer service policies.* If marketing opts to offer a very responsive level of service to customers, logistics resources, in the form of facilities and inventory, will need to be very considerable.
- *Number and location of warehouses.* This is one of the greatest areas of contention and can only be satisfactorily resolved if marketing and logistics develop the policy jointly.
- *Inventory policies.* This is another area of contention, as decisions have a significant bearing on operational costs and the extent to which desired levels of customer service are achieved. It is another key area where policy should be developed jointly.
- *Order processing.* Responsibility for who receives customer's orders and the speed and efficiency with which they are processed has a major impact on operational costs and customer's perceptions of service levels. This is another area where joint policy-making is preferable.
- *Channels of distribution.* Decisions to deliver direct to the customer or through intermediaries will greatly influence the level of logistics resources required. As channels change, so too will the resources required. Marketing should definitely consult with logistics when making channel decisions.

These examples are but a few of the areas where logistics and marketing interact; many others exist.

Conclusion

Customers are interested in how consistently their suppliers fulfil orders within agreed service levels. Organizations capable of differentiating themselves from their competitors by meeting these service levels will be perceived by their customers as reliable and even preferred suppliers, becoming longer-term partners in a mutually profitable relationship.

From the supplier's point of view, it is essential that this level of service be provided at a profit. Organizations able to meet the challenges of the 1990s in a cost-effective manner will prosper whilst less effective organizations will decline and even fail. Logistics and marketing together have vital roles in achieving cost-effective performance. Success will come to those who work together in a cooperative spirit.

Note

1   Schary P. B., 'Logistics Decisions', New York: The Dryden Press, 1984, p.344.

24 The Logistics Interface with Manufacturing

Garry Greenhalgh

Introduction

Why is the interface between manufacturing and logistics important? Is it possible for each of the two functions to operate in a related, but independent, manner? If the interface is important, what are the key issues which must be resolved? The answers to these questions are found in the manner in which the organization positions itself in its chosen markets relative to its competitors and the demands then made on manufacturing and logistics by the very nature of that positioning.

Two primary questions for manufacturing organizations are:

1 how to maintain or enhance its responsiveness to the changing needs of the marketplace;
2 how to maintain or enhance profitability.

Then, in developing its position, the organization must consider the following strategic issues:

- the key success factors for the industry;
- its basis for competing in its chosen markets;
- the relevant elements of customer service.

For a manufacturing organization to even maintain its competitive position in a dynamic industry, the manufacturing and logistics functions must respond positively to the strategic issues above by:

- treating the manufacturing/logistics network as whole;
- sustained improvement programmes coordinated across the various activities (for example, delivery service, production priority control, purchasing and so on) to exploit the synergy available.

The remainder of the chapter is concerned with three topics: first, the

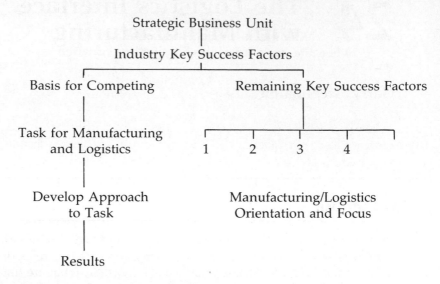

Figure 24.1   The competitive framework

competitive stance of the business and how it may impact on the manufacturing and logistics functions; second, a discussion on the manufacturing logistics network; and third, customer service issues at the manufacturing/logistics interface.

The competitive stance of the business

The orientation of an organization's manufacturing and logistics functions, and consequently the nature of the interface, must be determined against a predetermined competitive framework. The two aspects to this framework are shown in Figure 24.1.

The primary aspect concerns the basis on which the organization has decided to compete and from which many manufacturing and logistics tasks are derived. The second aspect concerns the relevant industry key success factors which provide the manufacturing and logistics functions with further dimensions for focus and orientation.

The relationship between manufacturing and logistics and the organization's predetermined basis for competing in its chosen markets is shown in Tables 24.1 and 24.2. Having decided the market segments in which it will compete, an organization must choose one of two fundamental strategic competitive options:

Table 24.1
Manufacturing/logistics approach
when the basis for competing is differentiation

Basis for Competing:
Product Availability and delivery time

Old Approach	New Approach
Increase investory to act as a buffer	Shorten internal lead times to improve responsiveness to market
Increase number of branch warehouses	
Increases capacity to provide flexibility	Emphasize schedule performance to ensure reliable supply
Release orders early to production	Emphasize product and process quality so as to reduce delays caused by rework, breakdowns etc.
Emphasize production output	
	Utilize express transport and centralized distribution to prevent misallocation of stock
	Initiate superior customer service and order entry systems to enhance customer communication
Which also Results in:	Which also Results in:
Higher costs	Lower costs
Negatives cause by the complexity of the system and poor product quality caused by emphasis on 'getting the product out'	Improved product performance
	Reduced product variability
Long internal lead times caused by early release of works orders to give the plant 'plenty of time'	An image of reliability
	Improved flexibility in volume and product mix
Stock-outs due to work order overload, confused priorities and difficulty in allocating stock to many warehouses	
WHICH INHIBIT THE ABILITY OF MANUFACTURING TO COMPETE DIFFERENTLY 'TOMORROW' OR IF COMPETITIVE CONDITIONS CHANGE RAPIDLY	WHICH ARE POTENTIAL PLATFORMS FOR COMPETING 'TOMORROW' OR IF COMPETITIVE CONDITIONS CHANGE RAPIDLY

Table 24.2
Manufacturing/logistics approach
when the basis for competing is cost leadership

Basis for Competing:
Lowest-cost Competitor

Old Approach	New Approach
Cost-reduction programmes	Eliminate all non-value adding activities/procedures/tasks etc
Reduce inventory	
Trim 10% off all budget allocations	Reduce the need to buy capacity by shortening internal lead times
Defer capital expenditure	Reduce the material conversion cost by simplifying processes through integration and technology
Emphasize control on expenses particularly direct labour	
Reduce support areas/overhead	Emphasize product and process quality so as to reduce costs associated with rework, breakdowns etc
	Reduce need for inventory through superior planning systems, shortened internal lead times; linking processes etc
Which also Results in:	Which also Results in:
Inadequate support	Improved product performance
Poor product quality	Reduced product variability
Ageing equipment/processes	Improved flexibility
Poor customer service	Improved reponsiveness to market
An image of being unreliable	
Poor product availability	
Poor delivery service	
WHICH INHIBIT THE ABILITY OF MANUFACTURING TO COMPETE DIFFERENTLY 'TOMORROW' OR IF COMPETITIVE CONDITIONS CHANGE RAPIDLY	WHICH ARE POTENTIAL PLATFORMS FOR COMPETING 'TOMORROW' OR IF COMPETITIVE CONDITIONS CHANGE RAPIDLY

1 cost leadership – that is, be the lowest-cost participant in the industry

or

2 meaningful differentiation – that is, be visibly superior or significantly different to competitors in some aspect of the business that has value for the customer. Examples of differentiation include delivery time, delivery reliability, superior product, technical service and so on.

In Table 24.1 alternative approaches to the basis for competing (product availability and delivery time) are shown. Two approaches designated 'old' and 'new' are offered, both of which, at least in the short term, would complete the task of ensuring the necessary levels of product availability and delivery service. Each approach, however, has other outcomes which, when understood, would influence the choice of approach. Generally the 'old' approach has a number of negative outcomes while the 'new' approach has essentially positive outcomes.

There are two points to note here. First, as Michael Porter points out in his book *Competitive Advantage*,[1] a competitive strategy based on differentiation still requires the organization to maintain costs within reach of the leaders. Clearly the 'old' approach does not help in this area while the 'new' approach does. The second point to note is that the 'new' approach provides alternative potential platforms to compete if the business so desires or if the competitive environment demands it. Hence the 'new' approach contributes to the reality of a lean and fit business with the capability to ward off, or be resilient to, threats and to take advantage of opportunities. In other words the 'new' approach enhances the capacity for self-renewal and adaptation to a changing environment. The 'old' approach, on the other hand, actually inhibits this.

In Table 24.2 where the basis for competing lies in being the lowest-cost participant a similar argument to the above applies.

In some cases, the issues for manufacturing and logistics are subtle. If the basis for competing is new product introduction there is a requirement for management and the workforce to be adept at coping effectively with continual change and to ensure that the planning and control system is able to deal with an increasing number of products and associated activities.

In developing an approach to achieve the relevant task it is necessary to select goals which also provide strategic flexibility.

Strategies in manufacturing and logistics must not inhibit the business in pursuing other competitive paths in the future.

The manufacturing–logistics network

The effectiveness of the manufacturing/logistics network *as a whole* is what determines competitive strength. Manufacturing and logistics are interrelated and interdependent. Manufacturing cannot be considered in isolation from logistics and vice versa.

Decisions made in these two areas usually commit the organization to relatively long-lasting cost structures and also determine, to a large extent, the manner in which the business competes in its chosen markets. But how is an organization's manufacturing and logistics interrelated and interdependent?

The two prime determinants of location are the location and characteristics of inputs (suppliers of raw materials) and the location and characteristics of the market (customers). For a given manufacturing organization there is a production/branch warehouse configuration which satisfies most constraints or pressures imposed by the inputs or the markets.

Capacity is related to location and logistics in the following way. First, production capacity must be related in some sensible way to the market demand. An obvious extension to this is that the capacity of the logistics network – that is, procurement, receiving, order entry and processing, outbound transport, branch warehouses and final customer delivery – must also be sensibly related to market demand.

The second point is that the capacity issue consists of a number of options:

1 capacity enhancers such as overtime, second and third shifts, third-party contracting, range rationalization and lead-time reduction;
2 an enlarged facility;
3 an additional facility in a new location;
4 a move to new location with expanded capacity.

Options (1) and (2) possess the least risk, and impact on the logistics network only in terms of the additional capacity requirement. Options (3) and (4), however, demand a re-evaluation of the manufacturing/logistics network not only in terms of the capacity of each component but also the strategic necessity and location of each facility (factory, warehouse) in terms of its contribution to the effectiveness of the total network. In other words, a change in location and capacity of any one facility requires a review of the location and capacities of all other facilities. Clearly, the issues involved in location, capacity and logistics are inextricably linked.

To understand the complexity of the interrelationships amongst the elements involved consider Figure 24.2.

The starting-point in determining plant/capacity/branch configuration options is the organization's basis for competing in its chosen markets – that is, lowest-cost competitor or some form of differentiation meaningful to customers, as discussed earlier in this chapter. The organization's basis for competing strongly influences the nature of the configuration particularly with regard to the number of facilities (factories, warehouses). Industry key success factors are also important since they provide a vehicle for further orientation and focus once the requirements of the basis for competing are met. Attention to them helps prevent 'wandering' into activities which do not add value to the primary purpose of the manufacturing/logistics network.

The next step is to consider the various and interrelated issues concerning the characteristics and locations of current and future markets, current and potential suppliers, product characteristics and transport options. Of particular interest is the service level required by the market (customers) both current and future and how the plant/capacity/branch configuration should respond given the organization's basis for competing. If the basis for competing is some aspect of customer service then the decisions regarding the configuration have relatively few risks. The major trap is that overservicing will occur with subsequent unnecessary costs being incurred. However, if the basis for competing is that of being the lowest-cost competitor in the industry, then very real risks surface.

These risks arise in the operational treatment of customer service, particularly at the branch warehouse level where pressure to provide a high level of service to local customers can be considerable. The pressure may come from the customers themselves or the local field sales force. This difficulty in aligning the strategic (lowest-cost competitor) with the operational (service customers) is understandable and raises the issue of how to maintain strategic control. It is made especially difficult in this case by the fact that, even when the lowest-cost competitor strategy is chosen, the overall service level provided by the organization to its customers must be within reach of

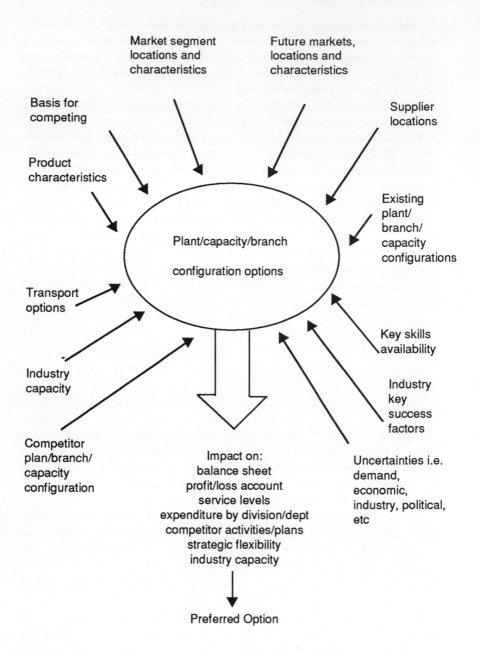

Market segment
locations and
characteristics

Future markets,
locations and
characteristics

Basis for
competing

Supplier
locations

Product
characteristics

Plant/capacity/branch

configuration options

Existing
plant/
branch/
capacity
configurations

Transport
options

Key skills
availability

Industry
capacity

Industry
key
success
factors

Competitor
plan/branch/
capacity
configuration

Impact on:
balance sheet
profit/loss account
service levels
expenditure by division/dept
competitor activities/plans
strategic flexibility
industry capacity

Uncertainties i.e.
demand,
economic,
industry, political,
etc

Preferred Option

Figure 24.2   Relationships within the manufacturing/logistics network

its major competitors. More specifically, the important components of service must not become so poor as to become a liability.

Given supplier locations (and the generally accepted methods of procurement) and the characteristics of the product (for example, perishable, bulky, high or low margin and so on) there are usually alternative transport methods available to service market needs. Transport alternatives need to be considered in conjunction with the number and location of facilities (factories, warehouses). For some industries, express transport may negate the need for a large number of branch warehouses and their corresponding inventory and expenditure.

Any analysis and discussion up to this point would yield a few alternative configurations. These alternatives must then be further considered in relation to:

- key skills availability;
- industry capacity;
- competitor configurations;
- specific uncertainties.

The availability of key skills may not always be relevant but should at least be considered. Crucial managerial and technical skills are not something to be assumed to be available when required.

In the situation where very large increases in manufacturing capacity are contemplated it is necessary to review precisely how the additional capacity will be used as well as the impact on total industry capacity. Significant overcapacity in an industry leads to reduced return on assets and pressure to increase sales volume through price-cutting often resulting in reduced profit for all concerned. The problem is exacerbated when exit costs are high – for example, specialized high-value equipment cannot be sold.

Competitor configurations are worthy of analysis and discussion if only to determine any advantages they might have. This applies particularly to the locations of plants and warehouses. The main questions should centre around why competitors chose the particular locations for plants and warehouses, whether they were correct or incorrect in their decisions and whether or not any major weaknesses which might be exploited are apparent.

Specific uncertainties are those areas of doubt which put at risk what would otherwise be sensible decisions relating to plant/capacity-/branch configurations – such as future demand, economic outlook for example. Where uncertainty is high, strategic flexibility is important and, in the context of this discussion, usually means taking action to ensure a low fixed to variable cost ratio and that all major decisions are reversible. This is more difficult than it might appear, particularly if new plant and equipment or relatively long-term leases on land and buildings for branch warehouses is being considered.

Before the final few options are selected, comparison with the existing plant/capacity/branch configuration should be carried out in order to identify the major discrepancies and to ensure good reasons for them – that change has not occurred simply for the sake of change.

The relevant financial parameters are then fed into the projected balance sheets and profit and loss accounts to estimate the on-going effect on the major financial performance indicators. For each option a final review of service levels offered, strategic flexibility, industry capacity and the impact on known competitor plans is made and the single preferred option is then chosen.

Customer service issues at the manufacturing/logistics interface

Customer service strategy may be thought of as an on-going process of increasing both the quality and number of links between the manufacturing organization and the customer. The ideal would be a series of both human and information based technological relationships that would bind the customer and the organization to the extent that a mutually beneficial alliance is created.

This gradual increase in binding force may come about through the following strategic process:

1 Develop customer service policy, practices and standards relevant to the key elements of service – for example, product availability, delivery service.
2 Redesign of the entire logistics system (including distribution channels) to ensure that service is a competitive strength at the operating level.
3 Formalize human relationships and information links with customers at the functional and general management level. Utilize electronic data interchange technology to transmit information related to changed requirements to reduce uncertainty and potential for conflict.

Table 24.3
Interface issues and emphasis

Interface Issue	Short/Mid term	Longer term
Forecasting	Stock availability	Capacity and flexibility decisions, production planning and control systems
Customer-orientated Systems	Effective production planning and sales order processing	Formalised information links
Supplier-orientated Systems	Effective materials planning and control	Strategic alliance with suppliers. Allow integration into overall customer supply chain
Plant/Branch Warehouse Configuration	Overall cost and service impact	Major structural input to reducing overall supply chain costs
Master Production Schedule	Stock availability	Integrate marketing logistics, manufacturing decision making and suppliers

Given this form of strategic development there are a number of issues at the manufacturing/logistics interface which need to be addressed:

- forecasting;
- customer-orientated systems;
- supplier-orientated systems;
- plant/branch warehouse configuration;
- master scheduling.

Table 24.3 depicts the short-, medium- and long-term significance of these issues for the manufacturing/logistics interface.

The general function of product forecasting in the short to mid term is to contribute to the process of ensuring the availability of stock for customers. This includes the use of distribution requirements planning (DRP) where appropriate. For the longer term, forecasting at product group level and new product forecasting is crucial for manufacturing capacity and flexibility decisions. In industries where the lead time to purchase capital equipment is considerable forecasting is obviously important.

The major weakness of forecasting for the longer term is the inability to forecast new products and the failure to translate forecasts into meaningful statements as to the impact on planning and control systems. The interesting thing about new product forecasts is how little information is actually required by manufacturing. Marketing people tend to be reluctant to commit themselves in this area, but much of the disruption to established products by the launch phase of a new product may be removed by a little preplanning. Primarily, manufacturing management needs to know the following:

- approximate volume increases on current production lines and the number of products this *might* represent;
- approximate volume and number of products which would require production processes different to current processes.

Note that actual product identification is not required. In addition, the information does not necessarily trigger immediate action for capital spend, but rather helps to delineate areas that require further discussion and coordination so that product availability over the long term is carried out smoothly. The same information may be used to evaluate the future usefulness of current production planning and control systems. Systems designed initially for a relatively small range of products become unwieldy as the *number* of products (not volume) increases.

The systems within an organization should, in both theory and practice, be geared towards the achievement of organizational goals. Within the manufacturing and logistics functions the systems tend to be oriented around their day-to-day purpose. Order entry and sales order processing systems are usually designed with the customer in mind. Materials management (production planning and control, purchasing) systems tend to reflect the customer only indirectly. The focus is usually internal rather than external.

Increasingly, however, organizational systems will need to be directly related to the issues of:

- how to bind the customer more tightly to the organization;
- how effectively to integrate suppliers into the overall supply chain with the objective of enhancing significantly customer service.

The systems installed by organizations will need the capability to formally link with the customer in a form that benefits both parties.

The systems will also be required to link up with suppliers in a manner that gives meaning to and supports the concept of strategic alliances. In a strategic alliance the supplier and the manufacturer agree to a relationship that goes beyond the normal commercial relationship such that each obtain synergistic benefits similar to that obtained by forward/backward integration but without the associated risks and negative attributes.

The location, nature and operating performance of manufacturing facilities, central warehouses and branch warehouses impact heavily on both cost structure and service levels. In the longer term, and in conjunction with other factors (systems, suppliers), the plant/branch configuration is a major structural input into reducing overall supply chain costs. When the links between manufacturer and customer and manufacturer and supplier are complete, a rethink of the logistics (supply chain) network from supplier through to customer will be required, for two reasons.

- Available technology, particularly information technology, will allow certain plant/branch configurations, previously ruled out, to be feasible.
- There will be an on-going need to reduce (in real terms) the cost of the network.

A key feature of this process will be the requirement of involving in an appropriate manner both customers and suppliers. This will be new ground for many organizations and will force a re-evaluation of values and mission in some circumstances.

The master production schedule (MPS) is an area where a number of parties (manufacturing, logistics, marketing, finance) have a vested interest in it being done well. Often as not, though, it is done by one group in isolation from the others. In the operational sense the MPS is primarily concerned with stock availability within a set of constraints such as capacity. As such, it is the single instrument which demonstrates the plan for:

- finished goods inventory levels;
- customer service in terms of stock availability;
- machine utilization;
- capacity utilization
- labour productivity;
- output;
- need for overtime/casual employees and so on.

The real power of the MPS, however, is its potential to involve all interested parties. In practice, when people from marketing, logistics and manufacturing get together and agree a schedule the result is a superior schedule. When operational difficulties combine to force a potential stock-out scenario, sensible decisions understood by all may be made. The mere fact that there are 'no surprises' is a significant benefit and reduces the all-to-common negative behaviour and the search for a scapegoat. When suppliers are shown the relevant sections of the MPS the usual result is improved supply performance because suppliers can then schedule according to your planned needs as opposed to reacting to a purchase requisition. Attitudes towards resolving mutual operating problems also improve. When customers, such as large buying groups, are able to supply estimated forward buying requirements, a major chunk of the forecast becomes firm. Clearly the MPS may be used as a vehicle to integrate a number of parties into the planning and decision-making process with the result being a superior plan which, when executed, results in superior customer service.

Conclusion

This chapter has attempted to address the logistics interface with manufacturing at the strategic level. The issues at the interface are different for different organizations. This chapter should help managers define their organizations interface issues through the discussions on the competitive stance of the business and the manufacturing/logistics network. The issue of customer service at the interface is specifically covered.

Reference

1   Porter, M., *Competitive Advantage*, New York: Free Press, 1985.

Part VIII

INTERNATIONAL LOGISTICS

Overview to Part VIII

In Chapter 25 Davies suggests that the increased cost, change of culture and increased complexity of international logistics require a different management emphasis from that currently displayed by many exporters. In suggesting that international logistics practice lags behind domestic practice, Davies argues that international logistics is often well managed at the operational level whilst ignored at the strategic level. He examines the various additional issues involved in international logistics and suggests that detailed management of the outstanding order pipeline is a key to effective control of international logistics. This, he argues, will change the emphasis from cost to service, thereby providing additional value added for the buyer.

25 The Role Logistics can Play in International Competitiveness

Gary Davies

International logistics has to be seen as somewhat different from domestic logistics for three main reasons: increased cost; change of culture and increased complexity. Until comparatively recently, the issue of cost has dominated management thinking in serving international markets. The problems of varying commercial and legal cultures and greater complexity have been afforded secondary consideration, or have been largely ignored, by delegating responsibility to a combination of the external transport specialist and local management in the foreign market. The consequences of concentrating on cost have been both beneficial to exporters of volume or basic products where price competitiveness is paramount, and damaging to companies who need to avoid having the customer compare their offer solely, or mainly, on the basis of relative price.

It would not be totally unfair to draw parallels with the present stage of evolution of practice in international logistics with the situation with domestic logistics management 10 or 20 years ago, when stockholding and transport costs were emphasized, under the banner of physical distribution management (PDM). The second phase of development, based on the potential offered by defining PDM as part of a logistics concept that encompassed a wider totality, has not yet reached the international sphere. Instead, most companies appear to manage a series of subsystems in handling both export and import matters, with the inevitable result that coordination and reliability suffers or costs rise as goods are stockpiled to counterbalance the expected problems caused by not seeing international distribution as a single system worthy of managing in its totality. In a nutshell, international logistics is often well managed at an operational level with an emphasis on reducing costs, but largely ignored at a strategic level where a more open attitude would encompass the potential to operate international logistics systems concentrating more on service.

Who controls delivery?

Defining the limits of responsibility for an international movement between two parties is an issue significant enough for an international body, the International Chamber of Commerce to sponsor a list of standards, INCOTERMS, defining the responsibilities of exporter and importer. The minimum responsibility for the exporter is ex-works (EXW) where the exporter has few duties other than to make the goods available at the factory gate. Selling on free-on board (FOB) terms means that responsibility is extended to the ship's rail. The exporter wishing to manage the entire movement sells on delivered duty-paid (DDP) terms – the equivalent of what was once called Franco Domicile.

In some countries INCOTERMS have to be used by law; in others they are recommended and could be judged to be legally binding in any dispute. Even so, their use is not yet universal and subtle differences in the interpretation of even the more commonly used terms in daily usage can cause problems. For example, many developing countries insist that their importers be responsible for insurance on goods sold on delivered terms. The normal delivery terms of CIP (cost, insurance and freight) might be modified to DCP (as CIP but without insurance) in such circumstances. If the goods disappear or are damaged on route and the importer refuses to pay, the exporter may experience practical difficulties in collecting its remuneration, especially if the importer has overlooked the need to insure!

In practice, most firms seem to distinguish between only a limited number of delivery terms that in turn divide into two broad categories: those where the exporter undertakes most of the responsibility for delivery (CIP, DCP) and those where the importer takes on that role (ex-works, FOB).

A number of surveys of practice in various countries have demonstrated that the majority of firms tend not to sell on delivered terms. This fact has to be interpreted carefully in that smaller firms (who predominate numerically) selling to larger multinational firms will often be instructed to sell ex-works or delivered to a domestic collection point where the larger firm consolidates purchases from a number of exporters. This is the case for example with the Swedish car company Volvo which sources many components in Britain.

Another practical point that helps confuse an overall picture of exporters being reluctant to accept responsibility for delivery is the tendency to quote for delivery separately. For example, many British exporters use the term FOB plus services in quotations, not an INCOTERM, but an attempt to offer the customer choice and simplify the export quotation. One more practical point is the tendency by multinationals to agree on FOB as a standard method of transfer pricing irrespective of who arranges delivery.

Overall, it is believed that British exports are sold about half on delivered terms and half on non-delivered terms. This represents a slightly higher percentage than that for, French and West German industry which tend to be less likely to sell delivered. Again generalizations such as these mask a great deal of variation in practice. French companies seem to view European markets much more as part of an enlarged domestic market and, because of the size of France itself, to see delivery as a more significant issue than some of their European counterparts. West German companies, which tend to be involved in exporting industrial machinery, tend to see freight as a separate part of the contract and rely more on the international freight forwarder to manage that aspect of their international business.

Exporters are advised by almost all sources to sell on delivered terms as a matter of marketing or strategic policy. The importer is, after all, being given a better service and can compare the exporter's offer more readily with those available domestically. Governments and transport lobbies are equally concerned, albeit for somewhat different reasons, to maximize the proportion of exports sold delivered as this helps both the balance of payments and the country's transport industry.

It should follow from the assertion that selling delivered is good marketing, that customers would generally prefer a delivered price. The example of Volvo cited earlier implies that this may be another overgeneralization and the idea was tested with some rigour in a survey of British, French and West German companies in the early 1980s. Companies were asked to define their actual and preferred terms of delivery on both exports and imports. The first observation was that half of firms surveyed preferred to *buy* on ex-works, FOB or similar terms. Even more interesting was the tendency for a nearly

Table 25.1
Strategy on delivery in British, French and West German companies on international trade

Strategy	% of Firms
Freight Controllers	27
Freight Avoiders	36
Neutrals	37

two-thirds of 139 companies who were both exporters and importers to prefer either to sell delivered and buy non-delivered or alternatively to sell non-delivered and buy delivered. What might have been expected is that the majority would prefer to sell delivered and buy non-delivered. In practice, companies tend to look to control freight on both exports and imports or to avoid doing either.

Table 25.1 presents the percentages of those firms surveyed who appeared to have adopted such freight controlling and freight avoiding strategies. Some 37 per cent could not be classified in this way either because they had no dominant preferred terms of delivery or, in a minority of cases, because they fell into the expected category of seeking to please the customer by managing delivery on exports and please themselves by seeking to have their imports delivered to their door.

The benefits of selling delivered

The company which defines an international strategy based on selling delivered, in the belief that this means better customer service, may find problems selling to a customer who is a freight controller. That said, the majority of customers will be expecting at least the option of buying delivered. In a second survey the advantages of moving to more delivered terms were assessed by asking 100 British exporters to identify what were the consequences of any changes they had made to selling on more delivered terms.

Only 28 companies had made such a change, itself a significant figure implying some rigidity in the pricing policies of exporters. Of these 28, 19 reported an increase in orders and sales, only five an increase in profitability, and six companies reported a decrease in profitability.

Some firms reported both an increase in volume and a decrease in profitability, implying perhaps that they had failed to achieve any significant mark-up on the freight costs when these were subsumed within their new selling prices.

If this relatively small sample can be relied upon, selling delivered does produce an increase in sales volume, so long as one is not selling to freight controllers.

Other anecdotal evidence is available to support this general philosophy. One company was more than relieved to see the long queues of vehicles arriving at always the wrong time to pick up consignments on behalf of various importers. A move to delivered pricing meant just the one vehicle waiting to be loaded and all under their own control.

Another exporter tells of their erstwhile Scandinavian agent who was constantly pressing for lower prices from their British factory because of what the agent described as high distribution costs to, and severe price competition in, his market. The exporter discovered that the agent had instead been making substantial profit margins. A change to selling delivered to the final customer and paying the agent a commission proved more profitable for the exporter.

Yet another exporter reported substantial savings in both delivery and stockholding costs by selling delivered. Small consignments were sent under consolidation to each market on a daily basis. The carrier deconsolidated the consignment in each market for local delivery. The exporter eliminated stockholdings in many markets, avoided minimum freight costs and improved control over service levels.

But who manages it?

The company which sells delivered must, of course, manage their delivery system to optimize customer service. The problem faced by many companies lies in the quality of management they retain in their international distribution function.

Most companies grow initially by exploiting opportunities in their domestic markets. Export business grows slowly and can be very much a peripheral activity. The tendency for small firms to sell on non-delivered terms is higher than in firms in general. An export clerk might be retained to liaise with a freight forwarder and prepare some documentation as the only change in personnel or organization.

Twenty years later, export might account for the majority of the company's turnover but the same individual is still responsible for export distribution. Many people can grow with the job. Others cannot and, consequently the general quality of international distribution management is an issue in most countries.

In many countries the real expertise lies with the specialist forwarder. Forwarding is regarded as a professional occupation in countries such as Switzerland and West Germany. In France and the USA it is a licensed trade. Even in Britain where anyone can set up in business as a forwarder there is a strong professional body.

The forwarder offers a wide range of related services from documentation and carriage to advice and many companies use their forwarder as their export expert.

Over the last 20 years the traditional forwarding role has declined. Door-to-door freight services have grown as containerization and Ro-Ro have replaced break-bulk services. Even in air freight the integrated carriers have grown fast, particularly at the premium end of the market. The potential to replace the forwarder in his intermediary role has grown as transport systems have simplified, but to seize that opportunity requires that the exporter retain management capable of fulfilling an enhanced function.

At least as important is the issue of where the international distribution role is placed in the organization. One apparently logical place is within an expanded logistics role. In practice, this is rarely the most logical choice as the two roles have significant differences (more on this later). The most frequent organizational link chosen by exporters is that with export sales and marketing. The logic here is to ensure coordination between the two on what tend to be fewer but larger orders of a more complex nature than in the domestic business.

In a minority of companies, organizational links with the financial function may be desirable. For example, in a company exporting large and expensive plant or selling mainly to developing countries, sales are likely to be against a letter of credit. While letters of credit are, on the surface, an excellent method of trading, offering advantages in terms of cash flow compared to open account dealing and the inevitable open credit which that involves, both banks and the less scrupulous importer are prone to examining the fine print in contracts, letters of credit and export documentation to ensure that the fine print in each is compatible. When an error in the spelling of a ship's name can nullify a letter of credit worth millions, having the export shipping office near to the finance director in both senses of the word can be beneficial.

Centralization in larger companies

Many large, multi-site companies have chosen to centralize their international distribution. The function of the central service varies from offering advice and taking an overview, to the operation of full blown in-house forwarding company. The ideal situation, if it exists at all, seems to lie somewhere between these two extremes. The in-house forwarding company solution seems to be only a temporary one. It might start off as a central service, funded as an overhead or as a direct charge on operating units, but the natural tendency is to evolve this into a separate company or a separate profit centre, allowing it to offer services to other exporters and allowing operating units to seek more favourable rates elsewhere (with normally some covenant that the in-house forwarder must be given the option to match the rates or service level in the market place). It seems to be inevitable that the company forwarder goes its own way, perhaps very profitably, but losing the advantage for the parent of coordination of activities such as consolidation of small consignments to similar markets and central negotiation with carriers.

Many head office groups concern themselves with location strategy. For example, a car company who sells in most European countries may choose to manufacture components and assemble in a significant number of markets. The policies of such truly international companies tend to include having at least a duplication of key capacity as well as taking advantage of the various location incentives offered by individual governments nationally or locally. While such policies make sense at a strategic level, they leave a trail of logistics problems at the operational level.

The cost advantages of cheap location can be lost if the savings have to be spent on transport costs. Even so, a steady flow between factories of components can be organized such that the main stock-holding is held in a container or truck on its way between two operating units, rather than in a warehouse.

The potential contribution to location decisions by logistics management cannot be understated. Mistakes can be made at either end of a spectrum of attitudes towards the issue of whether or not to ignore international frontiers when selecting locations for distribution centres or manufacturing units. At one extreme, a large company may decide to structure its business by country, each market having its own manufacturing, distribution and marketing. At the other extreme, the same company may decide to view a market such as Europe as one, largely homogenous, area.

Many companies have gone far too far towards the first mentioned end of the spectrum. Even within the EEC in the run-up to the complete removal of trade barriers in 1992, multinational companies retained separate plant in individual countries, making similar products selling in different sizes and under different names in each market. One detergent company found itself selling the same basic products, but in one market their toilet soap sold under the name used by a detergent in another. One food company had rules that stopped one arm exporting to another market even though the location of factories was such that one factory in one country was far nearer to part of its neighbour market than the operating unit in that country.

By contrast, a Japanese camera company held stock in just one European market under Customs bond (thus avoiding import duties into that market). They served each individual country market by air and express road freight from the one stockpoint. The costs of transport were higher but the overall costs were far lower. Where the logistics systems are good, either because Customs barriers are low or the transport system has managed to minimize delays because of its relationships with Customs, it is vital to examine the benefits from ignoring frontiers.

The international freight market

The choices of transport mode in international freight are similar to those in some domestic markets. The main differences are the greater importance of sea transport and the potential for air freight to be traded off against low stockholding costs.

Unitization of freight became the norm from the 1960s onwards, and conventional sea services were limited to those developing countries who could not afford container handling equipment. Road has replaced rail in many markets, but the use of rail as an alternative to sea via the North American and Russian landbridges has been an important innovation for the rail mode. Barge traffic is still an important mode, even in Western Europe.

Sea freight

The major trends in the 1980s were probably threefold. First, the traditional power of established shipping lines trading within the cartel structure of the shipping conference system came under attack. The initial challenge was from Eastern European and Third World fleets who often sold on price, eager to earn hard currency for their state owners. The UNCTAD 40:40:20 rule was designed to favour developing country fleets by insisting that only 20 per cent of traffic on any trade could be carried by vessels owned by countries not involved in the trade, with the rest divided equally between trading countries. The main mechanism to operate the UNCTAD rule was meant to be the liner Conference system. In the event, the rule presented the second threat to the very system it hoped to rely upon for implementation.

Another factor was the emergence of a new type of non-Conference operator. Traditionally, the outsider to the Conference system sold on price to balance the irregular service it offered in competition with the Conference members who regulated service levels and rates between them. If the outsider proved successful, it was not unknown for it to be invited to join the Conference.

The new outsiders, such as Evergreen, sold themselves on service relying upon a heavy investment in modern equipment, high capacity and often on a round-the-world rather than a trade basis for their operation. These innovations allowed the new outsiders to compete with Conferences, restricted as they are by the operating efficiency of their weakest member.

From the point of view of the exporter, the attraction of using non-Conference shipping has grown while costs have often fallen in real terms due additionally to gross overcapacity in the shipping market from the early 1980s.

Air freight

The second major trend in the freight market has been the fall in relative price of airfreight. The explosion in long-haul passenger traffic was met by airlines using wide-bodied aircraft, each with a substantial bellyhold capacity. These quickly replaced the use of old planes as all-freight freighters. Because many airlines regarded passenger revenues as their major source of income, freight tended to be costed at little above marginal cost at times.

While the fall in rates on all but the most popular of routes was greeted with pleasure by shippers, there were some disadvantages. One stemmed from the reality that long-haul passenger aircraft tended to fly from a limited number of airports, while freighters were more flexible. Regional traffic tended to be trucked to these centres. On short-haul routes, where wide-bodied capacity was limited, air freight tended to move for all of its journey by road.

Air freight had become cheaper but less flexible and, in some instances, much slower. More recently, door-to-door operations, undertaken normally by independent carriers rather than national airlines, have grown rapidly by offering well marketed time guarantees and simplified rate structures. Prices seemed generally higher than regular air freight but services levels appeared to be better.

Many companies concentrated on the sub-25 kilo market: courier companies moved into small declarable items. The shipper is left with a plethora of services in what has become known as the parcels or express freight sector. Within Europe overnight road services can compete in the mainstream of this growth area and even rail is being used as a linehaul between major centres.

Multimodal services

The third significant trend has been the growth of freight services that depend upon a number of transport modes. This seems to be hardly an innovation in that most seaborne traffic has to move by land and the same is true of air. However, the major transport mode has largely determined the way the service was marketed and the way it was controlled. Different modes required different documentation, safety standards and used different tariff structures.

The ISO container was the source of a change in attitude to transport model choice. What mattered was that the goods were containerized rather than whether they moved by road, rail or sea. Combined bills of lading had to be introduced. Transit times were quoted door-to-door rather than dock-to-dock.

The more substantial change can be seen in the express market where operators now market various service and cost level packages. The slower, cheaper services run on slower and cheaper modal combinations. The use of sea/air combinations can take advantage of low air freight volumes on certain routes to halve transit times with little extra cost.

The result has been more choice for the shipper and more pressure on the transport industry to offer freight 'packages' of varying rates and service levels rather than specialist transport.

Freight purchasing behaviour

This chapter began with the proposition that international logistics had tended to be focused on to cost rather than examining other factors that will affect the service the end-customer will receive. Freight costs can account for around 10 per cent of the delivered price of goods. The range is enormous, from 0.2 per cent for a pharmaceutical company to 100 per cent for an exporter of china clay.

Inevitably there will be pressures on management to reduce freight costs, even in the pharmaceutical business. Freight normally represents a lower percentage of costs than tariffs. Add this observation to the reality that price competitiveness in international marketing is also of paramount importance on commodity items, and the traditional emphasis on buying freight on price is easily explained.

There are two problems with this approach. The first is the difficulty in controlling an international freight budget. International markets tend to fluctuate, sometimes wildly, depending upon currency movements, government actions on key projects linked to development grants and the manipulation of tariff and non-tariff barriers to protect domestic industries. The costs of servicing individual markets can differ by as much as a factor of 10. Second, the exporter can reduce freight expenditure by changing terms of delivery to less delivered terms. It is not surprising that only a minority of exporters use budgetary control on freight.

The second factor promoting an emphasis on price in freight buying is an apparent lack of awareness of the other factors, such as speed and reliability of service. Export sales people in particular have been shown in surveys to have totally erroneous perceptions of transit times on international movements, tending to underestimate Customs delays at major freight centres and overestimate transit times on road and rail modes.

Even freight buyers have been shown to have inadequate data on true transit times. In some ways, this is not surprising. The communication between exporter and importer is more cumbersome than between supplier and customer on domestic business. The importer will often use its own forwarder to effect customs clearance, so that the exporter can, at best, only monitor the transit time to the port or terminal rather than the importer's door.

Documentation

An export consignment may require up to 20 separate documents for transport, Customs, insurance, banking and licensing purposes. In one survey, the complexity and quantity of paperwork was the most important factor dissuading smaller American companies from becoming involved in exporting at all. Costs per consignment have been estimated at around £80, largely due to internal clerical costs and external fees paid to forwarders. Error rates in documentation have been shown to be high, with a substantial number contributing to delays in distribution or delays in payment.

A number of proprietary paperwork systems are available internationally. Most are based upon the concept of alignment. In essence, this means that each data item connected with a consignment (the exporter's and importer's names and addresses, a description of the goods, the size and weight of each package and so on) are allocated a unique space on a master document. As most documents use much the same data, even though they may be for totally different purposes, the potential exists to redesign each document so that the required data appears in the same unique space as on the master document.

Once the master document is prepared and carefully checked, other documents can be produced by screening the master document and photocopying the required data onto the document required. This final process can be automated on a number of photocopiers.

This system is gradually being replaced by laser printing, where the document can be printed on plain paper, with different fonts, company logos and all. Another system within Europe, the Single Administrative Document, or SAD, was introduced in 1988 to replace a whole range of official documents concerned with Customs and transit requirements. Put simply, the same document that is acceptable as a Customs entry in one country on export is now acceptable as a Customs entry on import to another country. Perhaps the real innovation due to the SAD is the agreement on a limited number of data items to document a consignment. This facilitates the introduction of 'paperless documentation' and will help remove a major artificial barrier to trade.

The logistics concept and international trade

The management issues in international logistics are often substantially different from those in domestic logistics. A number of these differences have been highlighted thus far:

- the issue of who controls the delivery process;
- the advantages that accrue when selling delivered;
- the difficulty of placing international distribution in the company organization;
- the reducing complexities of the freight market;
- the need to look beyond market boundaries;
- the lack of data on transit times;
- the complexity of documentation.

To these can be added the following:

- the typical export order being an order of magnitude larger in size than a domestic order;
- the potential to sell on service rather than just price in exporting.

The domestic logistics concept can be described as a device for examining the flow of tangible items, raw materials, semi-manufactures, part-manufactures and finished goods, from suppliers to customers. The counterflow of information helps optimize this flow, reducing costs and increasing service levels simultaneously.

The company's international system must incorporate much of the domestic system, in that the domestic system determines the supply of merchandise. What is missing on the purely domestic system are additional devices for ensuring that the idiosyncrasies of international business can be managed effectively.

The author has argued that many, if not all, the major issues stemming essentially from the international dimension can be met by seeing the movement of the export order into the firm, and out again to the customer as merchandise, as the focal point for 'international logistics'. The key control for such a system is the value of the outstanding order pipeline, which comprises those orders which have been accepted but not yet delivered and paid for.

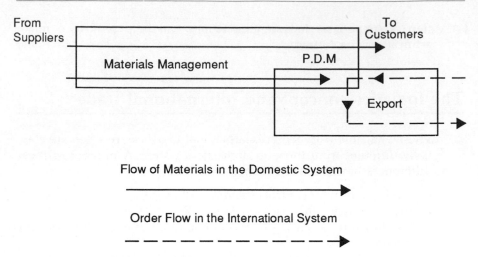

Figure 25.1   **The relationship between domestic and international logistics**

Reducing the size of the pipeline for a given level of trade increases the customer service level because goods are delivered more quickly. Export orders where the customer has not raised an appropriate letter of credit or negotiated an import licence are less likely to be accepted into the system as apparently firm orders needing stock allocation. The progress of the typically large complex export order must be monitored to minimize delays in the preparation of documentation. The delivery system must be appraised even if the customer is buying on less than delivered terms, but the emphasis will be on selling delivered where possible.

Conceptually the international and domestic systems appear as in Figure 25.1. Each system has a counterflow of information to help in the management of the system. The two systems overlap in the allocation of stock.

Unlike the domestic system, international logistics would seem to require much closer cooperation and coordination between sales and distribution. In the domestic process, logistics is more of a reactive function responding to relatively regular order flows. On international business, the processing of the order is more complex and customer service more difficult to monitor. It does seem to follow that an organizational link to marketing has advantages in optimizing international logistics management.

International competitiveness

Theories on international trade emphasize the competitive advantage in one economy, allowing it to sell more cheaply in another. Such theories can promote the idea that price is the dominant factor in trade. While this is true in many market sectors, a company can also succeed by maximizing service especially if the company strategy is to aim for a niche rather than a main market position. Selling on price clearly involves reducing logistics costs along with all others. Selling on service in niche marketing does not mean the opposite, but allows the exporter to concentrate more on managing the distribution pipeline in a more pro-active way. Both approaches require elevating the role of logistics to a more central position in international business.

Part IX
THE NEW WAVE IN LOGISTICS

Overview to Part IX

In this part we look at a number of strategically significant, emerging issues that are likely to affect organizations in the 1990s.

In Chapter 26 Ericsson provides a breakdown of the issues impeding productivity improvement, and suggests that the climate for change is right. Arguing that a wholly analytical approach in complex organizations does not provide the answer, he states that improved understanding of how and why parts of an organization work together is sorely needed. He offers Business Resource Management (BRM), not as a new management technique but rather as a philosophy for working at the interfaces between the four key business resources of materials, capital, information and human resources. This philosophy involves changing management attitudes and building a holistic approach out of the best parts of existing structures.

In Chapter 27 Gattorna and Kerr assess the strategic implications of technology, especially information technology as it relates to logistics practices. Whilst technology offers many opportunities for organizations to gain a competitive advantage, they warn that both the positive and negative impacts of various parts of the organization must be considered to ensure a net positive outcome.

In Chapter 28 Lancioni addresses the dual questions of waste disposal and product recall, suggesting that the majority of organizations are currently poorly placed to cope with these emerging critical issues. Having detailed the issues involved, he then outlines a methodology for developing an effective reverse distribution strategy.

Chorn can draw some comfort from the fact that, despite the placing of his chapter on human resources management at the end of this book, the vital importance of human resources has been a recurrent theme in the preceding chapters. In Chapter 29 Chorn provides a comprehensive human resources view of logistics, covering the interaction of organizational characteristics, group dynamics and the individual's attributes. Apart from providing practising logistics managers with an insightful guide to human resource management, Chorn provides ample evidence that an organization's human resources are indeed a potential source of significant competitive advantage.

Finally in Chapter 30 Chorn provides us with a vision of the logistics organization of the future. Having described an organization radically different from some of those existing today, he goes on to offer a number of guidelines for organizational architects. Implicit in

Chorn's argument is the notion that only those organizations that successfully adopt a new mind-set will survive the sometimes vicious competitive climate of the 1990s and beyond.

26 Business Resource Management: a Framework for Strategic Management of the Materials Flow

Dag Ericsson

Introduction

For quite some time, productivity growth has been slow in Western industrial countries, threatening the real standard of living and the competitiveness and profitability of companies working in international competition. Improved productivity is a must for the profitability which is essential to provide for the future capital requirements. Therefore Swedish industry has worked hard, especially in the 1980s, to improve productivity in order to produce the capital necessary to maintain growth and to make investments in further improvement. The downturn in the growth of the GNP in the mid-1970s, and the simultaneous decrease of profitability, made it necessary for top management to rethink and open up new avenues to profitability. Management tasks can be divided into two groups – administration and innovation. 'Administration' refers to tactical and operational approaches to improve utilization of *given* resources in a *given* surrounding. The term 'innovation' on the other hand, refers to strategic approaches aiming at creation and development of resources. The term 'resource' is used to denote the basic 'ingredients' of business: people, capital, materials and information. In times of rapid growth it is possible to rely on administration for the creation of profitability, but in times of stagnation or slow growth, it is necessary to stress innovation for profitability and survival.

Resources

During the 1960s resources were taken for granted and considered to be almost limitless. Goals were focused on growth, and the availability of material, capital and people were taken for granted. The acceptance of the 'customer orientation' and 'the new marketing concept' stressed and encouraged this frame of reference. The central issue seemed to be to identify needs and to administer resources to satisfy them. In a way, this was a rather natural evolution from the earlier 'production orientation' with the overcapacity it created. The marketing concept offered the frame of reference and also the tools which were needed. And it also provided the change agents – for example, in terms of product managers – necessary for the initiation of the process. In this way, the evolution from the seller's market with its production orientation into the buyer's market with its customer orientation was carried out.

During the 1970s, however, priorities changed again. Politicians and economists were talking about 'zero growth' as a necessary, possible, and even desirable goal. The energy crises and high raw materials costs showed that exponential growth was no longer possible, even if it were desirable, and the number of speeches, books and articles on recycling, preservation and allocation or resources increased dramatically. For many reasons 1974 has been labelled the turning-point. This was the year when post-war economic growth went over to stagnation. It was also the 'year of surplus profit' which was followed by a downturn in profitability that lasted until 1977–78. The confusion and anxiety of the late 1970s was further accentuated by the simultaneous evolution of the traditional 'industrial society' into an 'information society'. In the 1970s companies started to rethink, and the difference between administration and innovation became clear. The time was ripe for a new frame of reference and a new set of tools to face the new challenges. What was needed was rethinking and enantiodramia – that is the ability to develop and accept new approaches which may even conflict with existing 'traditional' ones. To be the best you need rethinking and development of resources. You need courage to break out of the norms and conventional wisdom. Renewal calls for enantiodramia! For top management this implies that it is important to define visions as well as provide tools to make the company successful.

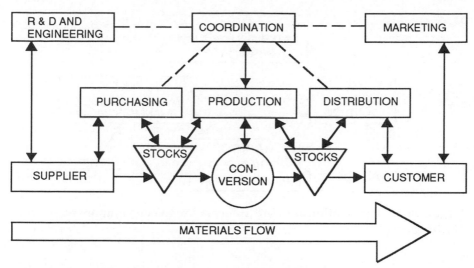

Figure 26.1   The philosophy of materials resource management

Avenues to productivity improvement

For a long time, productivity improvement in manufacturing had the highest priority for management attention. Then there was a shift of focus to marketing and, later, to physical distribution and materials management. However, the time is now ripe for focusing the whole materials flow and treat it as an entity not only in theory, but also in practice. The development of modern manufacturing strategies and principles, such as flexible manufacturing systems, JIT and KANBAN (what we in Sweden call market-oriented production), has once again put focus of attention back on manufacturing.

What top management needs is a frame of reference which really integrates the traditional concepts of materials management, production management and physical distribution management into a coherent whole. In many cases, traditional logistics concepts treat manufacturing as a black box, which is not very fruitful in practice. The Swedish concept of materials resource management (MRM) has, from the start, stressed that it stands for the coordination and coplanning of R&D and engineering, purchasing, manufacturing, physical distribution and marketing (see Figure 26.1). The MRM concept, which is a strategic, innovation concept, is explicitly distinguished from its tactical/operational subconcepts materials control

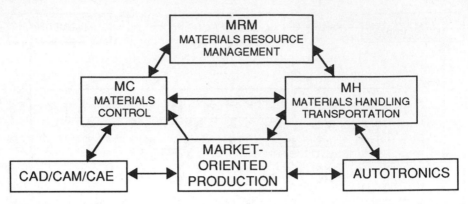

Figure 26.2   The relationship and interplay between components in the MRM concept

and materials handling/transportation. In this way the distinction, but also the interplay, between innovation and administration; between doing the right things and doing things right is highlighted (see Figure 26.2). The MRM concept is defined as 'planning, development, coordination, organization, control and review of the materials flow from raw materials supplier to the ultimate user'.[1] This means that the concept, from the very start, has stressed the whole flow and all types of interorganizational issues raised along the flow.

The design and development of vertical marketing systems (VMS) is a key area within the MRM field.[2] In a VMS, the role of the channel captain and the creation of rules of the game are vital. The development of flexible manufacturing systems has stressed the need for flexible procurement, and flexible distribution systems, and it has also initiated the development of 'dependent sourcing' (as opposed to 'multiple sourcing') and various types of stockless buying systems.

This type of broad, interorganizational approach is now also spreading to the traditional field of logistics under headings, such as 'supply chain management' and so on. The Swedish concept also emphasizes very strongly the interplay between administrative systems for control and review of information flows and systems for physical handling and transportation. The interplay and symbiosis in this area grows increasingly important with the development of autotronics and CAD/CAM/CAE, which breeds the evolution of computer-integrated manufacturing systems (CIM) for market oriented production and CID for computer-integrated distribution.

Climate for change

Some of the methods, techniques and technologies for CIM have been around for quite some time, and some are rather recently developed. What is important to note, however, is that the climate for change is the proper one now. In order for change to be permanent it is necessary for four forces to work together and in the same direction. *Technological, economic, social* and *personnel* preconditions must be fulfilled at the same time and they have to be working in the same phase. This is highlighted by the simple 'Tenth Commandment' of MRM which states that the result (R) of our efforts equals the technical/economic systems efficiency (S) times the social acceptance (A) of the proposed change; $R = S \times A$. Neither S nor A can be zero if we want to achieve something. This means that the change process has to be well managed.

Materials resource management

There are three factors which have dramatically changed the climate for productivity improvement in MRM since the beginning of the 1980s. These factors are:

1 the greater attention focused on MRM by top management;
2 development within transportation and materials handling;
3 the electronic revolution with exploding computer power and the development within the field of information resource management (IRM).

A number of external forces have drawn the attention of top management to MRM in recent years. First, high interest rates have focused attention on inventories of raw materials, work-in-progress, and finished goods. Second, rapidly increasing fuel prices drew attention onto handling and transportation systems in the late 1970s. This was further accentuated when highly competitive markets increased the importance of reliability and speed of customer service. Labour-intensive activities, such as warehousing, aroused top management attention when labour costs increased rapidly.

The result of this senior management attention on the materials flow has been an important consolidation of management responsibility for MRM in recent years. The broadening scope of responsibility has allowed materials resource managers to widen the perspective of

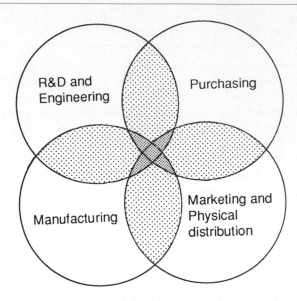

Figure 26.3   A holistic approach to MRM

productivity improvement from a purely functional focus on outbound transportation and finished goods warehousing (PDM) or
inbound transportation and raw materials storage (MM) to a total
view of the entire materials flow. But, even more important, top
management attention has allowed more and more companies to
begin addressing interface issues with engineering, marketing and
manufacturing to improve the effectiveness of the total corporation
according to Figure 26.3. The largest challenge and opportunity
within transportation comes from tailoring transportation services to
improve the underlying productivity of the carrier operations and
sharing those benefits between carrier and shipper. Companies with
well conceived strategies for transportation, supported by effective
information resource management (IRM), will have major opportunities to further reduce transportation costs through productivity
improvement. Computer power has grown enormously in recent
years. The real value of computers and information technology in
MRM lies in innovation not administration – that is, in developing
new approaches for management, capitalizing on vastly increased
information, communication, and storage capabilities, instead of
merely 'computerizing' existing processes for accounting, control and
review.

Inexpensive, small computer terminals allow the capture of order-

Table 26.1
Reliable delivery performance

Country	Speed	Punctuality	Integration with prod.	Delivery info.
Sweden	66	107	58	90
Germany	34	96	40	99
France	−11	87	58	41
Italy	−58	−33	41	19
Britain	−84	−56	16	−23

Source: Turnbull and Cunningham, 1981

ing or inventory data directly from the shelf at a level of detail and accuracy never before available at a reasonable cost. Telecommunication advances have allowed the instantaneous transmission of order, shipment and receipt data, elimination of delay and cutting of cycle times for many materials flow activities. Massive databases allow for more sophisticated analysis and planning of the flow process to eliminate unnecessary transportation, inventory and warehouse space, which means real productivity improvement.

In summary then, the dramatic development within IRM, the increased mutual understanding between carrier and shipper, and the increased willingness of top management to provide support and resources, have served as catalysts to encourage companies to re-evaluate long-standing goals, guidelines and strategies for material flows. The broadening scope of the MRM concept provides a climate for drastically improved productivity in the years ahead, which is vastly superior to the opportunities in the mid-1970s. Most important is that the acceptance of MRM as a top management philosophy has shifted the focus from techniques within materials control and materials handling/transportation to strategic issues in MRM – in other words, from administration to innovation. Management by logistics has evolved and become an integral part of the management by holistics approach.

Some empirical facts

A recent British study of the opinions of European buyers of engineering products asked for a rating of supplier nations on their delivery performance.[3] Of the five countries surveyed the rank order, from best to worst, was Sweden, West Germany, France, Italy and Britain as shown in Table 26.1.

An in-depth study of British companies shows that the root of the difficulties lies in management and is not a problem of basic inability in British industry. British companies tend to work in larger units than is common elsewhere in Europe. This leads to greater specialization, larger compartmentalization and lack of coordination according to the philosophy pictured in Figure 26.1.

According to a study of 70 successful Swedish companies, the situation is different in Sweden.[4] The MRM concept has attracted top management attention and the approach to productivity increase in the materials flow has evolved from scattered, isolated (and often sub-optimizing) rationalization efforts into a fully-fledged, coordinated concept.

The study revealed four dominating approaches put forward by most companies:

1   Push inventories 'upstream' – from finished goods inventory to inventory of components and parts and to raw materials storage; and also from customer to supplier, from retailer to wholesaler and/or manufacturer.
2   Revitalize the assortment – for example, by replacing slow movers and carefully reviewing the turnover rate.
3   Build bridges of mutual understanding among internal departments and divisions and also with external companies.
4   Rely on 'trial and success'. Do not put too much emphasis on analysis but more on action.

A 'typical' result of this approach in mechanical industry is a 30 per cent reduction of the capital tied up in the materials flow, an 80 per cent increase in reliability of delivery, and a 20 per cent reduction of leadtime.

There are 10 common and overriding ideas behind the high-achieving companies' approach:

1   increased market orientation;
2   warehouse delocalization – that is reduction of inventory accompanied by disposal of warehouses;
3   increased coordination in the whole supply chain;
4   simplified systems and increased flexibility;
5   close ties with suppliers, customers and especially one's own

resellers – that is, a focus on interorganizational aspects and vertical marketing systems;

6   MRM as an active means of competition to increase revenue.
7   simple measurements of effectiveness such as
   • delivery performance,
   • punctuality,
   • quality;
8   simple measurements of effectiveness and efficiency in the interfaces between design and engineering, purchasing, manufacturing, marketing and physical distribution. (see Figure 26.3);
9   a focus on the whole flow and avoidance of functional sub-optimization;
10   management by holistics (MbH).

The change process has several important characteristics:

• The total process lasts for several years.
• It is important, with explicit terms and concepts at an early stage.
• No mammoth projects but step-by-step processes where progress breeds action.
• More intuition and 'trial and success' than analysis and calculation.
• Changes of the formal organizational structure are secondary rather than primary activities and they should come as self-evident adaptations when the time is right.
• There are several problems because:
   – it is hard to get acceptance;
   – the process is time-consuming;
   – it is a continuous struggle.
• There are three important steps in the change process:
   – defrosting,
   – change,
   – refreezing.
• Active support and backing from top management is a must.
• Visions and objectives have to be communicated in simple terms and translated into operational activities.
• Results have to be measured in profitability terms, preferably in terms of Du Pont diagrams.
• In too many cases companies are dominated by specialists; their minds have to be broadened by education and training.
• Remember that it is harder to get people to forget old ideas than to accept new ones.

- It is important to take advantage of all new tools created in the development of information technology, and in finance and accounting. And remember that people provide the leverage effect in the application of tools.

According to this in-depth study of excellent companies, successful productivity improvement processes in MRM tend to have the following characteristics.

- The process of change (innovation) is managed with the same attention and care as the management of day-to-day administration.
- Successful companies employ a process orientation for change with explicitly stated visions, clear goals and measurements of the results achieved.
- Focus is on real productivity improvement coming from utilization and development of operational technology rather than simple 'cost reduction techniques'. This requires physical, and not just financial, measurement systems to support it.
- Successful companies start out with rather a modest pilot process to achieve early success, and then they build more ambitious programmes as they gain experience and support. They know that trying to grasp too much in one all-embracing bite leads to failure.
- Successful companies apply management by network (MbN) – that is, people working in informal networks, communicating success and sharing the credit upwards, laterally and downwards.
- In almost every successful process, there is a key executive considered as the catalyst and motivating force by others in the organization. The process is highly dependent on such a strong leader to provide:
  - visions,
  - a holistic approach,
  - intuition,
  - action orientation, and
  - penetration of the whole organization.

The fourth generation of integrated MRM leads to major, structural improvements in flow productivity, which cannot be achieved by more traditional piecemeal approaches based on functional techniques. The piecemeal approach is an example of administration – doing things right. The first approach is an example of innovation. Both approaches have their rationale for existence, and they should not be considered as substitutes. An integral MRM approach is always backed by top management and, hence, allows the systematic definition and balance of interfaces between R&D and engineering, purchasing, manufacturing, marketing and physical distribution, which makes it possible to support the total business idea and strategy in the most effective way.

In the really successful companies, there is a total integration of the MRM improvement process in an even broader innovation process based on a MbH approach sponsored and executed by top management.

The process starts by a definition of what value (value=quality-/cost) is to customers in different segments; the overriding vision and business idea is explicitly stated and realistic customer service objectives are defined to support the overall business strategy. Based on the marketing plans, a materials deployment strategy is developed which trades off the timing of raw materials receipt, master production scheduling needs and finished goods inventory requirements to meet the service objectives. This gives the basis to determine the right number of factories and warehouses and the allocation of products and markets. In this way a long-term materials flow strategy can be developed to support effectively and efficiently the movement of materials from raw material sources to the final user. In the same way strategies for supporting information, capital and human resource management can be developed and synthesized into a whole.

Among the most important reasons for success in MRM discussed above, the following are worth repeating. First, there is a very high degree of internal integration and cooperation between engineering, purchasing, manufacturing, marketing and physical distribution in the excellent companies. Second, there is the high degree of interorganizational cooperation in successful marketing channels. Dependent sourcing and organized vertical marketing systems are two key concepts in this context. Third, the acceptance of materials resource management is accepted as a top management philosophy – as a strategic tool for increasing profitability. This means, among other things, that the interest is focused not so much on techniques within materials control, but more on trade-offs and trade-ups between departments and companies. The last sentence implies that MRM has to be integrated in a still broader top management frame of reference.

The conception of MRM as a top management, strategic concept also leads to an emphasis on the human resources in business. The principal maxim is 'systems make it possible – people make it happen'. This leads to the fourth, and perhaps most vital, aspect of the Swedish approach to physical distribution and materials flow – the integration of the concept of MRM in a top management philosophy and toolbox called Business Resource Management (BRM). BRM is a frame of reference or philosophy for management, but it also contains four sets of 'toolboxes' for the implementation of the concept. Hence, the BRM concept recognizes the fact that companies need visions to 'know why' and tools to 'know how' to do it. Hence, it is important for executives always to remember the simple formula $R = S \times A$ mentioned above.

Business resource management (BRM)

One of the main tasks for top management is to increase and develop the productivity of all resources in the company. Productivity can be increased in the utilization of equipment, machinery, materials, capital and information by improving the technical systems efficiency. However, results can be multiplied if the leverage effect of motivated people is also taken into account. If employees know not only *how* to do things but also *why*, effectiveness, as well as efficiency, can be improved.

Following from this, the leader of the 1990s has two major tasks:

- to achieve high technical systems efficiency; and
- to develop the human resources in the organization.

In production management, the four Ms – men, machines, materials and money – were discussed, and trade-offs between them were emphasized. The achievement of an optimal balance between these four basic resources was the goal. Today, we also have to include information as a basic resource to be taken into consideration in strategic, as well as operational, thinking.

If we allow the term 'capital' to cover all assets in their different shapes – from fixed assets to cash – and the term 'materials' to cover everything in the chain from raw materials to finished products, then we will, as mentioned, have four basic resources in the company:

- materials;
- capital;
- information; and
- personnel,

For each of these four resources there are methods and techniques

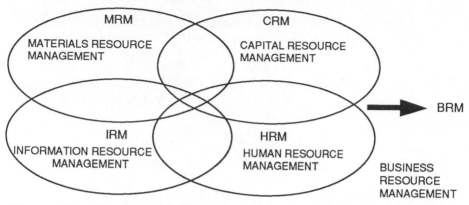

Figure 26.4   The four cornerstones of the BRM philosophy

developed to increase productivity. Focus has for a long time been on increasing efficiency in the utilization of the 'hard' resource materials, capital and information. In the early days, human resources were also approached from this technical point of view. Today, however, the human resource management approach takes the unique abilities of people into consideration. And results are multiplied!

Earlier, it was quite common to take the complex whole of business management and break it into manoeuverable parts. Of course, this analysis is still important in obtaining an understandable picture of the complex reality. However, an analytic approach is not enough. We need to combine it with synthesis – that is, an understanding of how and why the parts work together. We have to improve on work done in the interface between the areas. The whole is greater than the sum of its parts!

A specialist is often accused of only seeing the trees and not the forest, and generalists vice versa. What is needed now is a 'synthesist' who can see both the trees and the forest and who can supplement the analyst by improving not only efficiency but also effectiveness.

The BRM toolbox consists of four subsets as depicted in Figure 26.4. One of the important things with the holistic approach is that it focuses on the interfaces among activities and functions as well as departments, divisions or companies. Uncoordinated work leads to isolation and suboptimal behaviour. It may lead to efficiency, but it will certainly not lead to effectiveness for the total company or for the total marketing channel (the VMS).

MRM is one of the four cornerstones of BRM and, from the

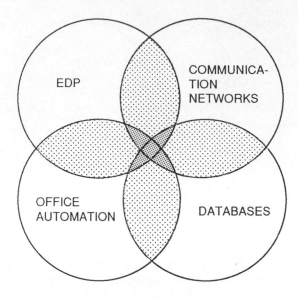

Figure 26.5   A holistic approach to IRM

discussion above, it follows that human resource management (HRM) is another. The increasing importance and cost of capital employed in business gives the third cornerstone – capital resource management (CRM). CRM deals with acquisition and use of capital – for example, capital tied up in the materials flow and also in other physical resources. The fourth cornerstone is based on the increasing importance of information technology and systems for management behaviour – for example, within the area of logistics. Information Resource Management (IRM), as it is called, combines methods and techniques from 'traditional' EDP, office automation, communication systems and information search, storage and retrieval into an integrated whole.

Together, the four concepts of MRM, HRM, CRM and IRM make up a stringent and coherent framework and makes it possible to really implement 'management by holistics'.

Activities within IRM should be approached according to Figure 26.5 and not according to Figure 26.6. In the same way, activities within materials resource management (MRM) should be approached according to Figure 26.3 (p. 434) and not according to Figure 26.7.

In industry, the materials flow was the first area to awake interest from a holistic point of view. Already in the 1960s, efforts to cover

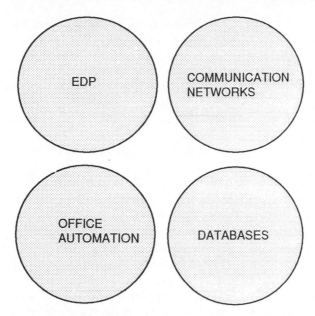

Figure 26.6 Isolated approaches to IRM

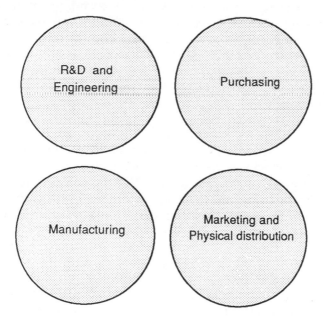

Figure 26.7 Isolated approaches to MRM

larger and larger parts of the total materials flow had started to evolve. The purchasing concept evolved into procurement and materials management, and transportation and handling into physical distribution and logistics. In Sweden, the term 'materials administration' was first used to denote 'planning, coordination, organization, control and review of the total materials flow from raw materials supplier to the ultimate user'. Later this concept evolved into MRM – that is 'planning, *development*, coordination, organization, control and review of the total materials flow from raw materials supplier to the ultimate user'.

Hence, for quite some time, efforts were focused on increasing efficiency within separate areas related to the materials flow as shown in Figure 26.7. This was a 'specialist' approach based on the assumption that, if productivity was increased in the sub-parts, productivity in the whole would be increased. In many cases, however, this was not so, and severe problems with sub-optimization appeared. The first holistic approaches – for example logistics – were also concerned with how to find trade-offs between functions. Optimal solutions were the vogue of the day, and these solutions were often cost-centred. The trade-off between level of service and cost was also one of the most important issues. Much time and effort was spent on finding methods and techniques for optimal solutions of the balance between, for example, level of inventory and service. Later, heuristics and different sorts of computer models were used to find solutions. Today, we know that the problem was stated in the wrong way. It is not a question of trade-off, it is a question of trade up! Decreased levels of inventory lead to increased service and reduced costs – at the same time! Increased flexibility in manufacturing leads to reduced cost and increased service! It has also been proved that, if the capital tied up in the materials flow is decreased by, say, US $1 million, the total improvement in profitability will be worth US $3 to 4 million! The advantages of working according to the holistic MRM concept as shown in Figure 26.3 became more and more obvious. This synthesist view of MRM was also clearly stated in one of the more 'humorous' definitions of the concept 'The unique thing with MRM is the *integration* of several related areas of knowledge into a frame of reference for decision making'. In the early MRM concept, engineering was not included in the frame of reference. However, it soon became evident that design and engineering had to be included (cf. Figure 26.1, p. 431). Today, some of the best results are achieved in the interface between design and engineering and manufacturing.

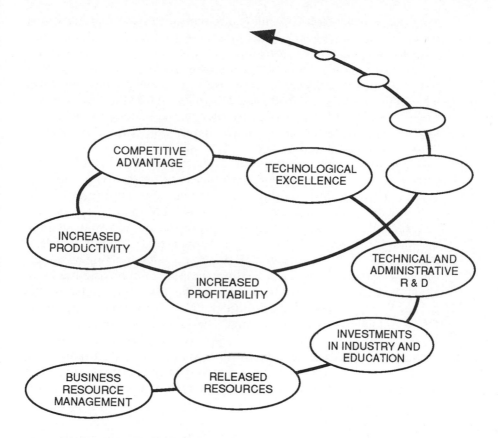

Figure 26.8   The positive spiral of the BRM approach

This cooperation, for example, has helped Saab to reduce the number of components in the doors from 27 in the Saab 900 to seven in the Saab 9000. In the same way, the number of components in the cabins of the Scania has been reduced from 3,300 to 1,050. The effects on cost, capital tied up in the materials flow and lead time are obvious!

BRM can be used to release resources, such as capital tied up in the materials flow. These resources can be invested in research and development and education, which means that the company achieves technological excellence, which in turn means competitive advantage. This competitive advantage leads to higher profitability and more possibilities for the creation of resources, which breeds success and the positive spiral is at work (see Figure 26.8). Saab-Scania, for example, has released 2.8 billion kroners out of the materials flow during the last five years. In addition, 500 million kroners has been released from accounts receivable. These resources are used for investment in education and development, which leads to technological and commercial excellence via R&D. The company has invested 6.9 billion SEK in fixed assets and 8.3 billion in R&D in five years! In 1985 4.4 billion were invested, 2.5 billion in R&D. The goal, of course, is to achieve competitive advantage; that is, being best in the chosen market-niche.

It has to be remembered that even though integral MRM has proven to give approximately three times the productivity improvement achieved by more traditional materials control approaches, it is not something to leap blindly into. Integral MRM requires a corporate culture which can only be created by a daring top management believing in 'enantiodramia'. This means that a genuine MRM approach based on BRM demands top management acting as renaissance sovereigns – people to whom nothing human is unknown. With this knowledge it is possible for the manager to choose the proper timing for launching an integral MRM process for improving total productivity in the company. The launch may or may not be triggered by an external force or crisis, but in most companies it is evident that productivity improvement in the total materials flow is a mission whose time has come. Something has been trying to happen for so long that when somebody finally presses the start button it is like the launching of a satellite – a slow start is followed by rapidly increasing acceleration.

One of the problems in implementing holistic approaches like MRM is the deeply-rooted urge to defend one's own territory and to fight off attacks. Some people prefer to be a big fish in a small pond rather than being a small fish in a big pond! However, the MRM concept has come to stay, and it is now spreading into several new areas of use.

Today, we can also witness the rapid diffusion of another holistic concept – IRM. Even in this area we have tried to increase productivity by working in isolation within areas such as EDP, office automation, communication networks, and information search storage and retrieval. It has also been possible to see headlines like 'Revolution in the offices – electronics takes over' and 'The best thing for everybody is to slow down on the development of office automation' in the same issue of a computer journal! Something was wrong, and in many cases, it was shown that too many people were focusing

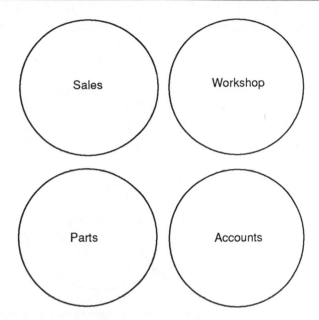

Figure 26.9   An isolated approach to organization of a sales outlet

on efficiency by looking at revenues and costs in traditional systems evaluations while too few were focusing on effectiveness in terms of flexibility and adaptability to the environment and to users. 'The computer people who listen' was a battle cry to induce some courage in the suffering users out in the desert!

The efficiency approach had led to sub-optimization and many isolated islands in the huge information sea. Efforts were made to build bridges and headlines like 'Office automation is dependent on rethinking within the area of administration and it demands a holistic view' became more common. So the IRM concept according to Figure 26.5 had a fertile soil waiting when it started to evolve in the mid-1970s.

Within personal and human resource management, the growing interest in holistics can be illustrated in the following way. Once upon a time there was a car dealer who used to work according to a specialist approach as illustrated in Figure 26.9. He had sales people who were specialists and, within the group, there were new car and used car specialists. He had specialists in the workshop, in the parts and in the accounts divisions. They were all very skilful and hard-working, spending a great deal of time on increasing efficiency.

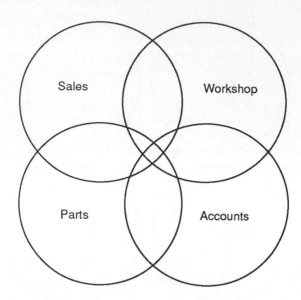

Figure 26.10   A holistic approach to the organization of a sales outlet

However, they did not have much time to talk to other specialists – no time for 'gossip'. Suppose that you sell say 20 cars to a company to be used by salesmen out on the road all day. If these cars are supplied with air conditioning, turbo and intercooler, you know from statistics that a certain number will be back within a certain amount of time for repair and maintenance, and you will need some spare parts and some time in the workshop. It may be worthwhile, then, to talk to the fellow specialists in other departments! Figure 26.10 shows the new guidelines for cooperation in the company.

The BRM approach is, in theory, a straightforward and logical approach. In practice, however, there are some difficulties in the implementation of this frame of reference. One problem is that some people believe that their autonomy may be decreased. Another problem is that the approach demands a different state of mind, one which is based on synthesis rather than analysis, on the perception of the whole as greater than the sum of the parts. In summary, the approach demands synthesists who can see both the trees and the forest at the same time. Leaders need this kind of split vision, which makes the difference between a 'superstar' and the rest in ice hockey, soccer, and tennis!

The implementation of BRM does not mean the application of a whole new set of tools and techniques. It is more of a philosophy for working in the interfaces between functions and some guidelines for choice and use of the appropriate tools. This, however, is both the strength and the weakness of the approach, because it demands changes in attitudes. It is a long and never-ending process to change the attitudes, values and norms in an organization. It takes time and training and education, and time and training and education again. The old corporate culture should not be thrown away and replaced by a brand new one – the roots are too important. The famous Swedish writer August Strindberg once wrote, 'Here houses are torn down to create open space and light – isn't that enough?' It is not enough in business anyway!

In business we have to build on the existing, and to improve and take the best parts with us into the new building. We need a structure for innovation and renewal to work hand-in-hand with a structure for administration and continuous work. The reason for this is that an organization is like an iceberg – 90 per cent is below the surface. Above the surface are visible factors like policies and objectives, technology, the formal organizational structure, the financial situation, skills and knowledge. Under the surface is the corporate culture in terms of attitudes, values, norms, feelings, personal relations, power structures and so on. Therefore it is not enough to try to work only with systems efficiency (above the surface), we also have to work with acceptance in the culture (below the surface). Remember $R = S \times A$!

References

1   Ericsson, D., and Persson, G., *Materials resource management – A Top Management Responsibility*, Malmo, LIBER, 1981.
2   Ericsson, D., *Vertical Marketing Systems*, Goteborg, SIMS, 1976.
3   Turnbull, P. W. and Cunningham, M. T., *International Marketing and Purchasing*, London: Macmillan, 1981.
4   Ericsson D., Sary, H. and Backman, G., *Materials Administration Today*, Malmo, LIBER, 1985.

27 The Impact of Technology on Delivered Costs

John Gattorna and Andrew Kerr

Introduction

Technology, especially information technology, is creating strategic opportunities for progressive organizations to build competitive advantage. There is, however, an increasing gap between the opportunities created by technology and the effective utilization of technology by organizations. In part, this gap can be explained by the fact that few managers have experience or backgrounds in managing technology and therefore have difficulty relating new forms of strategic opportunities to their organization's business.

The massive increase in functionality and cost performance of computers and telecommunications equipment has created a whole new range of strategic opportunities. Satellite communications, portable personal computers, facsimilies, electronic mail, computer spreadsheets, fourth-generation computer languages (4GLs) and automated materials handling systems are but a few of the technological advances available to progressive organizations in the 1990s.

Rapid globalization of markets, together with increasing intensity of global competition, has created an environment whereby organizations must either take advantage of the strategic opportunities afforded by technology or fall behind. In this chapter we will examine some of the strategic opportunities available to progressive logistics managers.

Strategic implications of technology

Adoption of any form of technology without a clear understanding of where it fits in the organization's overall strategic plan will, at best, result in a sub-optimal utilization of resources, or in the worst possible case cause the organization to lose focus as it tries to come to terms with the technology. Progressive organizations which have successfully utilized technology to create competitive advantage, actively

- seek to identify opportunities where technology can provide a strategic advantage; and
- look out for threats created by competitors using technology strategically.

These organizations tend not to develop proprietary technology, rather they focus on innovative ways of using technology developed elsewhere.

Utilizing technology to differentiate their products and services from those of competitors, these progressive organizations have:

1 created a perception of 'added value' in the minds of their customers;
2 replaced an adversarial relationship with one of partnership;
3 created significant switching costs for their customers by raising their levels of expectation as to what constitutes good service;
4 reduced the overall cost of service delivery; and
5 developed effective barriers to entry by competitors.

This position of competitive advantage is depicted in Figure 27.1. Clearly, the favoured position is in the top right-hand corner – that is, high product differentiation combined with low delivered cost.

Information technology and competitive advantage

History provides us with myriad examples of the decisive role information has played in the fortunes of both individuals and nations. Thus it is not surprising that information technology is now seen as one of the keys to achieving sustainable competitive advantage in modern organizations. Whilst other forms of techno-

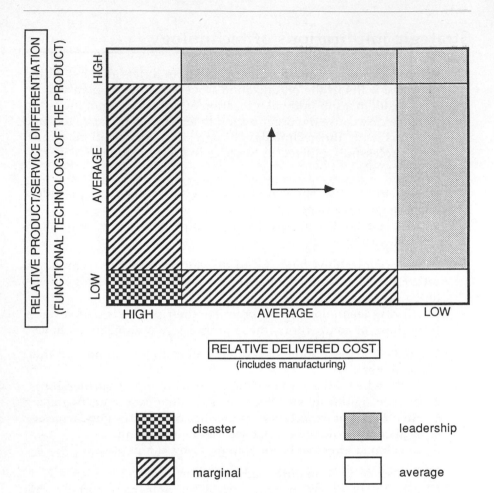

Figure 27.1   **Technology and competitive advantage**

logy play important roles, information technology in its various forms is all-pervasive.

Too often, an organization seizes an opportunity to use technology to improve one aspect of its operation without considering the overall effect. Effective utilization of technology is only achieved when there is a net positive effect. When considering the implementation of technology, the positive and negative effects on various parts of the organization, its distribution channels and customers must be aggregated to ensure a net positive outcome.

One of the best examples of gaining competitive advantage

through use of information technology-based logistics systems, is the US–based organization, American Hospital Supply (AHS). AHS's move into electronic ordering was started by a regional distribution manager working to fill the needs of a single customer. AHS senior management saw the potential of the scheme and provided support and development funds.

The resultant order entry distribution system, code-named ASAP, features computer terminals in over 4,000 customer sites (mainly hospital pharmacies). The system allows customers access to AHS's order entry distribution system and also allows them to perform their own inventory control using the AHS system. AHS found that their average order size grew to 5.8 items versus an industry average of 2.7 items per order. Further, AHS found that the average dollar value of customer orders was three times greater using ASAP than under the previous manual system.

AHS considered the major benefits of their ASAP system to be:

- a substantially simplified ordering process;
- reduced costs to both parties;
- the ability to manage pricing incentives across broad product lines;
- the creation of high customer loyalty and increased market share;
- the creation of significant switching costs for customers; and
- the creation of high entry barriers for competitors.

Similar benefits are being achieved by European automotive paint manufacturer AKZO Coatings. In this case the company provides terminals in the repairers' workshops to facilitate ordering of paints, whilst at the same time allowing repairers to prepare computerized repair estimates using AKZO-provided software. AKZO's increased market share and lower overall costs can be substantially attributed to their innovative use of established technology.

Electronic data interchange (EDI)

Unlike the telex and the facsimile, there is no single internationally accepted standard for communication between different types of computer. Nevertheless an increasing number of organizations are communicating electronically. EDI involves the transfer of data from files on one computer to another using telephone lines. There are potential strategic benefits for organizations who learn not only what EDI can achieve, but also how to use this newly emerging technology effectively.

A major benefit of EDI is service differentiation – using information to provide superior service. Amongst its potential advantages are:

- a reduction in labour-intensive activities;
- a reduction in labour costs;
- a reduction in mundane tasks prone to error;
- a reduction in working capital;
- an increase in customer service (both actual and perceived); and
- a move to one-time data entry – elimination of superfluous paperwork.

EDI is not without its risks, which include:

- a reduction in personal contact between sales staff and customers;
- resistance to change – lack of understanding; and
- the need for cooperative suppliers, customers, carriers and so on.

Further, there is a definite feeling in some organizations that an 'organization' that communicates by computer could be perceived as less customer service-oriented.

Whilst the risks are real and should not be underestimated, EDI provides many strategic opportunities for organizations, especially in the area of logistics operations. For example, EDI can provide an organization with the ability to maintain control over the inbound movement of raw material, thereby enhancing its ability to implement JIT manufacturing.

Similarly, retailers can use EDI's more timely communication to control the flow of goods in-transit. The US-based express freight carrier, Federal Express has used its extensive electronic parcel tracking system to provide their customers with a concept which they term the 'moving warehouse'.

The US Department of Defence used to process manually in excess of 1.4 billion Bills of Lading each year. Following trials of a system using EDI to process this information, the Department adopted EDI as the sole method for processing Bills of Lading, estimating savings to be between US $10–17 million per annum.

Since adopting EDI to control the flow of merchandise from suppliers, the US chain store Walmart has achieved a reduction from 21 days to nine days in its order cycle time with a corresponding 17 per cent reduction in inventory. This clearly demonstrates the benefits available from effective utilization of technology.

One trend emerging as more retailers adopt EDI to control the inward movement of merchandise, is their demand that manufacturers communicate with them electronically. However, retailers are reluctant to reciprocate, continuing to demand their previously liberal payment terms. The tendency for retailers to try to keep all the benefits derived from EDI for themselves reflects the changing retailer – manufacturer channel relationships referred to in Chapter 7. Consequently, manufacturers must look for internal savings to offset the costs of adopting EDI technology.

Integration using information technology

Many organizations store vast amounts of data, often duplicated, and rarely accessible in the time or format required to enable business decisions to be made, based on the best available information. Lack of appropriate data is usually not the problem, rather it is the inability to make cost-effective and timely use of the data which sees many opportunities lost.

The ability of functional groups within organizations to utilize shared data is one of the greatest potential benefits to result from advances in information technology. In this context, integration is defined as 'the ability to bring together information needed to make good business decisions'.

In developing a cost-effective information integration strategy, it is important to realize that, irrespective of organizational structure, all departments and functions are to some extent interdependent and cannot stand alone. As a minimum requirement, any integration strategy should:

- identify departments that use common information;
- determine the logical point(s) at which common data should be entered, thereby reducing to a minimum the number of times data must be entered;
- define business and processing policies across applications to be integrated;

- define common terms and coding schemes;
- wherever possible, consider using shared databases;
- classify data elements as either 'action data' (for example, order processing, distribution, purchasing, inventory control, accounts receivable and payable) or 'planning data' (for example, MRP, DRP, sales forecasts and so on).

By adopting this approach, organizations can ensure that systems are developed that provide real time availability of 'action data' to all who need this information to make good business decisions.

Whilst internal savings may be achieved by reducing data redundancy, the real benefits to the organization are realized through more timely and informed decision-making and its effect on customer service.

The path to integrated information systems is not easy. The Japanese computer manufacturer Hitachi has found that the difficulty arises not from integrating the machines, but rather the people. Hitachi's worldwide computer integrated manufacturing system, depicted in Figure 27.2 involves the linking of large mainframe computers with a number of mini-computers. These in turn are linked to a large number of micro-computer-controlled manufacturing stations, many of which involve robots.

ʻ Hitachi's difficulty arises in having traditional mainframe EDP personnel think about the process of integration in the same way as technical and engineering personnel closer to the manufacturing process. Hitachi's commitment to achieving a common level of understanding throughout the organization is highlighted by the presence of a small group headed by a senior manager with the title 'Computer Integrated Manufacturing Promotions Manager'. This group's role is to promote understanding of the CIM philosophy throughout the organization.

Technology and primary industry

Strategic opportunities for innovative use of technology is not confined to manufacturing and service industries. Primary producers and rural industries are increasingly turning to technology to provide them with a competitive advantage. The use of computer-based systems to help small farmers is depicted in Figure 27.3 which highlights a system developed in the USA by Agway Cooperative, a rural-based organization.

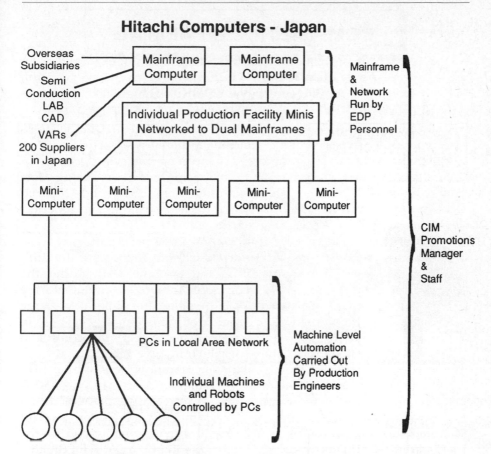

Hitachi Computers - Japan

Overseas Subsidiaries
Semi Conduction
LAB
CAD
VARs
200 Suppliers in Japan

Mainframe Computer — Mainframe Computer

Individual Production Facility Minis Networked to Dual Mainframes

Mainframe & Network Run by EDP Personnel

Mini-Computer   Mini-Computer   Mini-Computer   Mini-Computer   Mini-Computer

CIM Promotions Manager & Staff

PCs in Local Area Network

Individual Machines and Robots Controlled by PCs

Machine Level Automation Carried Out By Production Engineers

Technical integration is relatively straightforward.
Achieving an integrated outlook between EDP and production engineering staff is more difficult.
This is the role of the CIM Promotions Manager.

Figure 27.2   A computer-integrated manufacturing system

In Australia, cotton growers utilize the services of a dial-up computer-based tactical crop management expert system called SIRATAC. Cotton cannot be grown with commercial success in Australia without chemical control of pests costing from $100 to $300 per hectare. Excessive spraying is costly, may cause outbreaks of secondary pests, increases the risks of pests becoming resistant to insecticides and causes public concern about pollution. The

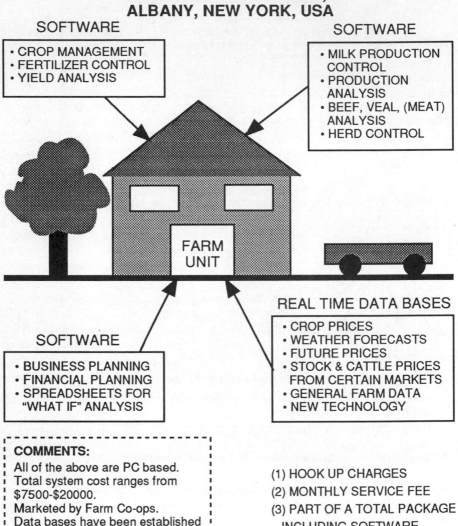

COMPUTERISED FARMING

**AGWAY CO-OPERATIVE,
ALBANY, NEW YORK, USA**

SOFTWARE
- CROP MANAGEMENT
- FERTILIZER CONTROL
- YIELD ANALYSIS

SOFTWARE
- MILK PRODUCTION CONTROL
- PRODUCTION ANALYSIS
- BEEF, VEAL, (MEAT) ANALYSIS
- HERD CONTROL

FARM UNIT

SOFTWARE
- BUSINESS PLANNING
- FINANCIAL PLANNING
- SPREADSHEETS FOR "WHAT IF" ANALYSIS

REAL TIME DATA BASES
- CROP PRICES
- WEATHER FORECASTS
- FUTURE PRICES
- STOCK & CATTLE PRICES FROM CERTAIN MARKETS
- GENERAL FARM DATA
- NEW TECHNOLOGY

COMMENTS:
All of the above are PC based.
Total system cost ranges from $7500-$20000.
Marketed by Farm Co-ops.
Data bases have been established by Universities, Banks and Co-ops.

(1) HOOK UP CHARGES
(2) MONTHLY SERVICE FEE
(3) PART OF A TOTAL PACKAGE INCLUDING SOFTWARE PACKAGES OR SEPARATE

Figure 27.3   An example of a computer-based tactical farm management system

SIRATAC system was developed to assist growers to reduce these risks by making good tactical decisions on the use of insecticides. Over 30 per cent of the national cotton crop is now managed using this system.

Materials handling technology

Surveys conducted over several years in the UK, Australia, the USA and Europe have found that customers rate reliability and consistency of delivery as more important than price. These surveys have also generally found that few suppliers meet their customers expectations. Late deliveries, part deliveries, short- or over-shipments and shipments of incorrect items are the greatest causes of customer dissatisfaction.

The resulting loss of customer goodwill is not the only cost for the supplier. Studies have found that the administrative cost of filling a customer's order triples if back-orders are involved and increases by a factor of 10 if returns and redeliveries are involved. With distribution cost accounting for between 12 and 25 per cent of every sales dollar, major opportunities exist for progressive organizations to reduce distribution costs and at the same time improve their actual and perceived level of customer service through strategic use of materials handling technology.

Order picking systems range from sophisticated paperless systems incorporating indicators and confirmation stations at each picking face, to computer-generated adhesive labels incorporating barcodes and delivery detail. Yet other systems utilize computer terminals mounted on picking trolleys and radio-linked direct to the organization's computer. All these systems increase productivity and reduce the risk of error.

The almost universal use of barcodes for product identification together with improvements in scanning technology has paved the way for a new generation of conveyor systems. Incorporating computer-controlled sorters, scanners and accumulators, these systems facilitate the simultaneous assembly of multiple orders accurately with minimum human intervention.

Whilst distribution centres incorporating the types of technology outlined are increasing, not all organizations which have made the substantial financial commitment necessary to commission such systems are reaping the benefits. Too often, decisions are taken for non-strategic reasons – for example, to reduce labour costs. Unless the use of sophisticated technology forms part of the organization's overall vision, the likelihood of failing to achieve a net positive outcome is very real.

Logistics managers have the opportunity to ensure that their organizations use information and materials technology strategically. Only in this way can organizations develop a competitive advantage upon which to build in the 1990s and beyond.

28 Reverse Logistics: the New Distribution Structure for the 1990s and Beyond

Richard A. Lancioni

The state of the world energy situation has stabilized since 1980. Crude oil supplies have stabilized, and the oil-consuming countries have reached a consensus that efficiency is an essential ingredient in all aspects of transportation and distribution. With this realization has come a new dilemma in the environmental movement – how to handle the huge amounts of solid waste that is generated from industrial and consumer consumption systems and what is the most efficient way of transporting and handling it.

Also, the increase in the number of laws requiring that firms recall products that are defective has resulted in the realization that companies must now begin to develop reverse distribution systems to handle the flow of recycled and defective products. Product recalls are no longer in the realm of theoretical possibilities: it is a regular fact of business life among manufacturers of both industrial and consumer products. Machine tools, automobiles, television sets, appliances, cosmetics, clothes – no product is immune and the list is virtually endless. The actual value of product units recalled and solid recycled waste needed to be transported runs into billions of dollars. Moreover, the prognostication from the evidence so far is that the trend will continue principally for the following reasons:

1 fast-changing technology necessitating frequent changes in product design;
2 new laws being enacted worldwide, requiring the recall of defective products and the recycling of solid waste.

Despite the gravity of the problem, most logisticians in both large and small companies have been lax in developing systematic plans to recall defective products and recycle solid wastes. Their reactions when faced with recall decisions or recycling decisions have been shortsighted. What is needed is for the logistician to take a strategic view of product recall and develop a plan of action to deal with the issue.

The concept of backward distribution

In designing a total system of distribution logisticians have traditionally examined the distribution process starting with the producer and the flow of goods from the producer to the consumer.

However, today, for a variety of reasons other than just defective products, logisticians should start thinking of reverse distribution systems – that is, consumer to producer – and the economics and efficiency of building good reverse distribution systems. For example, recycling of wastes is now a major goal of many ecologists, environmentalists and conservationists. One of the major obstacles in the recycling process is the lack of an orderly reverse distribution system and the enormous cost of collection and transportation. The American Paper Institute reckons that a major portion of the cost of recycling paper (90 per cent) is the cost of distribution.[1] The Glass and Aluminium industry also constantly evaluates the economics of reverse physical distribution and searches for efficient methods of reverse distribution systems.[2]

The crucial area where the concept of reverse physical distribution applies is, of course, the product recall area. It is logical that product recall be treated as a reverse distribution problem because here, too, as in the cases cited above, the traditional physical flow of products is reversed. While conceptually it may sound easy, logisticians should be forewarned about underestimating the difficulty of reversing the distribution process. This is because, for most companies and products, the distribution system has evolved gradually over time, rather than as a result of some systematic planning. And to devise a reverse distribution process for a company or a product, where in many cases no systematic forward distribution plan exists, is indeed difficult.[3] Further, many products pass into the hands of retailers and consumers without any record of the identity of the product or the purchaser. Locating these products and sending back and upward into the hands of the manufacturer is a very costly process. For example, one can hardly underestimate the problem and cost involved in locating and recalling thousands of cases of soup from many distribution centres, hundreds of supermarkets and thousands of small grocery stores. Very few studies have been carried out on improving the economics and efficiency of the reverse distribution problem.

Urgency, scope and effectiveness of the recall process

Products could be recalled by a company for a variety of reasons. They could, for example, be recalled because of poor packaging, improper labelling or improper distribution methods resulting in loss of temperature control, contamination and the like. The urgency of a recall depends on certain factors, the most important of which of course is the seriousness of the product hazard. In this connection, generally three classes of recalls can be cited.[4]

- *Class I.* Products in this class are recalled because they are declared to be imminently hazardous by the Food and Drug Administration or Consumer Product Safety Commission, and as such pose an immediate danger of death or serious injury to the consumers of the product. In such cases, the products involved have to be recalled in the shortest possible time. Efforts are made to trace each and every item (100 per cent recall) in the distribution system. Bon Vivant soups with the deadly botulism toxin exemplifies this class of products. For logisticians this class of recall presents the greatest problems.
- *Class II.* Products in this class, while not imminently hazardous, might still be of a dangerous nature and have the potential to cause injury and possibly be life-threatening as well. Tris-treated clothes and other such products would exemplify this class of recall. Such products also have to be cleared as quickly as possible, but the time urgency is of a slightly lesser order.
- *Class III.* Products in this class are recalled for a variety of reasons. Some of them may be recalled because of some conscious or unconscious violation of federal regulations. Mislabelled, mis-branded products come into this category. They may have only a remote chance of threatening life or limb and yet they have to be recalled. Recalls of a 'defensive type' involving quality failures

would also fall into this class. Many companies, especially the automobile companies, take a conservative posture and recall products voluntarily even though there are no complaints. Their reasoning in such cases is that it is better to be safe than sorry. For logisticians this class of recall is relatively easier to carry out.

The scope of the recall process depends on the nature of the product and the level of penetration in the distribution system. Industrial products with direct or short channels of distribution are easier to recall than consumer products with longer or indirect channels of distribution. Other variables that affect the recall process are: fewer units manufactured, fewer units in consumers' hands and longer product life. The scope and effectiveness of the recall process also depends upon certain other factors. For example, the ability to locate and notify consumers directly, requiring no initiative from consumers, and replacing or repairing the product at their homes increases the effectiveness of the recall.[5] Likewise decisions to limit the recall and correct the problem by methods other than recall also affect the scope and effectiveness of the recall process.

The challenge, however, exists for a logistician to design a reverse system of distribution and to get it to work at a desired performance level at the lowest possible total cost.

Locating the product

Since locating a product in a distribution system is the primary step in a recall process, the first task for a logistician would be to see if a product can be located anywhere within the existing distribution system with ease. Three distinct levels of difficulty associated with the penetration of the product in the system can be isolated.[6] At the first level the product is still under the control of the manufacturer in company-controlled warehouses or primary distributor-controlled warehouses. At this level locating the product and recovering and recalling the product is a simple matter of stock recovery for a logistician. At the second level the product would have to be located and withdrawn from the middlemen involved in the distribution of the product, namely wholesalers and retailers. The recall in this case becomes slightly more difficult. At the third level the product is in the hands of consumers. Locating and recovering products at this level is the most difficult of all. Needless to add that the movement of the product into each successive level not only complicates the recall for the logistician but adds to the cost of the operation as well.

Mechanism for locating products in the channel

Locating durable products with a direct distribution link, that is manufacturer to consumer – is perhaps the easiest of all. For many products, especially industrial products, a direct forward or backward link can be established for repair, replacement or refund of the product through bills, invoices or other such devices. In the case of most consumer durable products, a logistician can locate these products through a good warranty card system. A computerized warranty card can be precoded with all the critical information necessary for tracking the product in the distribution system. The kinds of information that can be coded are: product description, manufacturing plans, lot, batch number and dates with quantities manufactured, forward order number, shipping dates, rail or truck number, geographic areas of distribution, scheduled arrival dates, shelf life and estimated rate of use. Customer name and address obtained after the sale can then be coded into the card and stored for fast retrieval whenever necessary. Warranty cards are, however, not always returned by consumers and this is a weak link in the system. The reasons for warranty cards not being returned are that:

a) they are perceived as information-gathering devices, with the name and addresses being used for unsolicited mailings later on; and

b) other documentary evidence like receipts and cheques can be used to show proof of purchase, should the need to repair or return the product occur later on.

However the return of warranty cards can be improved by:

a) designing them attractively and stressing boldly in front the importance of returning them for tracing ownerships in the case of a recall;

b) providing postage-paid warranty cards; and

c) negotiating contractual agreements with retailers wherein they agree to retain records of the identity of the owner of warranty cards.

Such methods have achieved a fair amount of success in many cases.

Locating consumers and notifying them directly are prime factors in a recall success.

In the case of consumer non-durables, the problem of location is relatively more difficult because the distribution system is much more complex and indirect. First, a product is likely to be produced in several geographically dispersed manufacturing locations and follow many different routes in reaching an ultimate destination. There may be multiple primary distributors, intermediate sellers and retail organizations made up of hundreds of independent units. The product is therefore likely to rest in public warehouses, cooperative warehouses, distribution centres and a variety of other such places before reaching its ultimate destination. Record-keeping is therefore of vital importance. Good systems provide adequate information about the products' manufacturing locations and, in addition, also provide computerized tear-off or tag cards to show each critical move of a product within the distribution system up to the last transfer point before being sold to a consumer. Most logistics departments maintain a tracing section to locate a product in the distribution system. In conjunction with a carrier they provide a 'pro' number which allows rapid location to transfer points and destinations. Once the logistician traces the product to the last retailing point he can get the retailers to take the defective product off the shelves and hold for further instructions. However, if the product has been sold to consumers a media blitz in the vicinity of the stores that sold the defective product, requesting the return of the product, is the best method of locating it. The recall advertisement should also be displayed prominently in all the stores.

Retrieval of products

After the product is located, logisticians can coordinate the process of retrieving the product in the field either through:

a)   the company's field salesforce;
b)   the retailer or other middlemen;
c)   outside collection specialists.

This new breed of specialists, specialising in recall, not only help locate suspect products with their own field representatives, but also monitor and audit the whole process as well. However in many cases the manufacturers and their logistics staff take direct control of the recall, isolating all others in the process.

Effective retrievals require that:

- the customer be motivated to return defective products for repair, replacement or refund; and
- good relationships be established among carriers and other participants in the distribution process such as channel members.

The biggest obstacle in recalling products however is the consumer. The experience of many firms indicate that consumers are unwilling or lax in returning hazardous products even if notified, especially if the product cost less than 20 or 30 dollars. Motivating consumers to return such products is a difficult task. Financial incentives and education of consumers through instruction manuals including warnings that buyers may be liable in civil contributory negligence if they fail to return the hazardous products has been suggested as an answer.[7] Legislation, forcing consumers to return recalled products has also been suggested, although such legislation is unlikely. Even if enacted, such legislation would not change the situation drastically.

Retailers, carriers and others involved in the distribution process must be willing to cooperate with the manufacturers if the reverse distribution process is to work properly. More often than not, members of the distribution process are not prepared to cope with the problems and responsibilities of reverse distribution because they do not receive specific guidelines from the logisticians in terms of quality or quantity. The failure of logisticians to reimburse the distribution members for certain out-of-pocket expenses involved in the recall of hazardous products is also a contributory factor. The problems associated with the recall of Tris-treated sleepwear for children exemplifies the above mentioned points clearly. Thousands of garments are piled up at retailers' warehouses with no instruction whatsoever. This lack of communication can be a major source of conflict for participants in the distribution process if not handled properly.

Reverse distribution as a part of logistics strategy

From the company viewpoint, the reverse distribution process for product recall should be treated as an integral part of logistics strategy. The success of a firms' recall will to a large extent be contingent upon prior planning and the clear assignment of responsibilities. Accordingly, the concern of logistics managers must be to determine in advance what, if any, modifications are needed in the existing distribution system to handle recalls. Management of the logistics aspects of the reverse distribution system should be assigned to a senior coordinator who will be responsible for interfacing and preplanning with all the other departments involved. All subsystems within the logistics network should be tested to see if they perform easily in reverse in an emergency. Logisticians should also take care to look at existing systems in companies that have had some experience in this area, before modifying their internal distribution system for recall purposes. Some automobile, aluminium and food companies have developed good reverse distribution systems. All possible alternatives should be studied.

Facility network

The existing geographical distribution of manufacturing locations, warehouses, retail outlets and all other such facilities utilized by the company for the physical flow of goods should be pinpointed. In the event of a recall it is essential that production and flow data be traced back to certain specific locations in the total facilities network. Also, logisticians must be able to determine at short notice the number of defective products anywhere in the distribution system, be they in company warehouses or public warehouses. Establishing inventory and identifying locations in a hurry, especially where brokers, drop shipments or transhipments are involved can be complicated. In a recall, it is a primary function whose importance cannot be overstated.

Communications and order processing

The order processing systems and procedures should be reviewed. In fact, a review of all the communications system should be undertaken. Invoice handling and warranty card administration should be checked with special care. In a recall they perform a vital function. A good communications system will allow the logisticians substantially to reduce the time and manpower required for a recall and limit geographical area of involvement.

Transportation and traffic management

Transportation and traffic management systems should be reviewed with special emphasis on pinpointing shipping dates, orders, destinations and vehicle identifications, and stoppage of further movement. Documentation of product movement is crucial for the reverse distribution process. Carriers in a recall must receive clear instructions about pick-up and return procedures. Carriers must be evaluated for speed, capability, availability and dependability. Collection points for the return of the products should be designed along with instructions for their disposal or salvage if possible. Policies for returned merchandise and arrangements for replacements should also be made.

Logistics costing

An accounting and cost review of expenditures for the performance of activities involved in recall must also be made. Table 28.1 gives some of the cost elements involved in a recall.[8]

The costs of recall and reverse distribution are two or three times higher than the costs of forward distribution because of the small quantities involved and the urgency of the problem.

A reverse distribution model

The stages in a reverse distribution system are shown in Figure 28.1 and end at the production source. What is required is that a firm views the system in the same way that it operates its outbound or forward distribution system and that these activities be integrated with the reverse distribution tasks that may arise at different times. A reverse distribution system, like a forward or outbound system, has multi-level inventory retrieval activities, transportation gap problems, a requirement for communications and other processing, the need for materials handling, and storage. Each activity involves the same type of management decisions involved in outbound product distribution. Figure 28.2 presents a recall distribution

Table 28.1
Cost elements involved in a product recall

Communication Costs

Registered and certified mail
Return receipts
Employee visits
Telephone, telegrams
Messenger service

Documentation Costs

Filing of receipts of notices for
  recall
Estimates for disposition and
  replacement
Plans of item recalled
Plans for replacement item
Instructions for replacement/repair
Authorisations for work to be
  performed
Receipts for items replaced/
  repaired

Replacement Costs
Manufacture and installation
Label
Instructions
Shipping, packing and warehousing
Testing and retesting
Identification of product
Identification of carton
Identification of shipping carton
Temporary personnel
Invoicing
Overtime of employees

Disposition Costs
Locating all items
Inventory of items
Removal from customer's property
Packaging and unpacking
Labelling
Shipping
Inspection
Repair or replace
Discard or salvage
Instruction pamphlet
Refunding
Allowances for time used
Repurchase of item
Compensation for loss of use
Warehousing – storage

decision model detailing the system objectives in each decision area
and the overall system objectives.

As shown in Figure 28.2 the objective of each logistics area in
handling the product recall are focused in speeding up withdrawal of
the product(s) from the marketplace at a reduced cost. In the
transportation area, the distribution manager has the task of the
selection of the proper mode of transport for return of the goods,

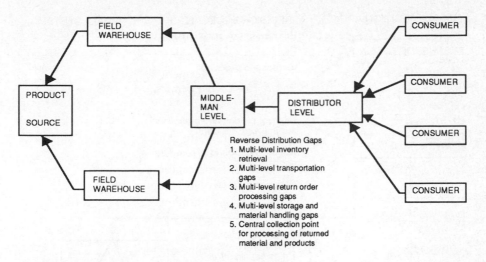

Figure 28.1   Stages in a reverse distribution flow system

while at the same time ensuring that the return haul is utilized to the fullest extent. TL or CL returns are the most efficient, for freight costs can be kept at a minimum. The warehousing of returned goods must be combined with the routine storage of products destined for final consumption. Here, the space allotted to returned goods should be kept at a minimum and the handling and repackaging time also reduced. The reverse distribution flow of goods through field warehouses will be small, and internal efficiences can only be maintained if this flow is integrated into the normal operational routine of the system.

The inventory of returned goods should be integrated into the same master inventory system utilized to handle the outbound products. Here, special product codes should be assigned to the returned flow items to identify and segregate them from the normal inventory items. The expeditious removal of the product from the marketplace and possible salvaging, reprocessing or refabrication of the returned goods into new inventory which can later be remarketed, are necessary tasks. In one consumer products firm where the problem of reverse distribution has arisen numerous times in the past, the company has established a returned goods inventory group that traces, locates, handles the removal of the good from the marketplace, and explores ways of reprocessing the product for possible resale.

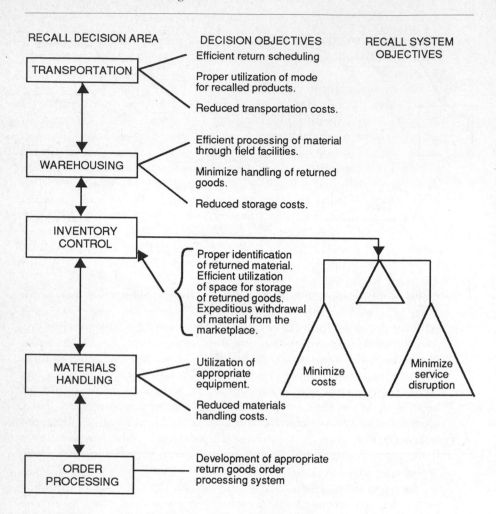

Figure 28.2   A recall distribution decision model

As Figure 28.2 shows the materials handling component of a distribution recall system stresses the objectives of proper equipment utilization and reduced costs. Since materials handling is an activity which occurs throughout a logistics system, distribution costs can be minimized if this activity is properly handled. For example, the stacking of returned goods, while at the same time retrieving outbound products, is an activity that could occur in every level of the distribution system (Figure 28.1). Materials handling costs could also be reduced, if the returned goods are loaded on vehicles normally scheduled to make return trips to a central warehousing facility. Truck or car utilization will be improved and transportation costs lowered.

The final activity important in a recall distribution system is order processing. Proper documentation of the returned merchandise is important to expedite its handling and inventory processing. In effect, a return product document system is necessary. This was implemented in one major US automobile firm, where cars that were recalled were assigned an identifying code and a document set. The documents included a recall activity report; *a maintenance completion form* which detailed the repairs performed on the vehicle; *a dealer assigned form* indicating the dealership where the repairs were made; and *a warranty completion form* detailing the owner's name, warranty coverage, and manufacturer's liability. Each of these documents was computer-generated, and an accurate record was kept of all vehicles involved in a recall.

The distribution activities involved in the returned product flow are integrated and are interdependent. The efficient performance of each activity depends upon the other. The overall system objectives in the recall distribution process are cost minimization and minimal service disruption. If these objectives can be achieved in each reverse logistics situation, then the task that is becoming more frequent in the marketplace will be easier for firms to perform.

Conclusion

Reverse logistics systems will be important in the future. The need to understand how such systems can be adapted to a company's operation are important if a firm is to deal effectively with the challenge of product recall and waste disposal in the 1990s.

References

1 Margulies, W. P., "Steel and Paper Industries Look to Recycling as an Answer to Pollution", Advertising Age, Vol 41, October 19, 1970, p.63.
2 Margulies, W. P. "Glass, Paper Makers Tackle our Package Pollution Woes," Advertising Age, Vol 41, September 1970, page 43.

3   James, D. E., "Distribution Channel Consideration," in Managing Product Recalls, Ed. E. P. McGuire, New York, The Conference Board, 1974, p. 77–81.

4   Healand, J., "Product Recall Problems and Options-Non Durable Products", in Managing Product Recalls. Ed. E. P. McGuire, New York, The Conference Board, 1974, page 57–65.

5   Product Safety Letter, Washington DC, 17 January 1977, page 1.

6   Ibid, citation 4 above.

7   McGuire, E. P., "What is Ahead in Product Safety?", The Conference Board Record, August 1976, p. 33–34.

8   Hammer, W., "Handbook of System and Product Safety". Englewood Cliffs, NJ. Prentice Hall, 1972, page 7.

29 The Human Resource Factor in Logistics

Norman Chorn

Human resources: the 'forgotten factor'

It is perhaps symptomatic of some of the issues in this chapter that the human resources issue is considered in the concluding part of this book. That it is part of the so-called 'New Wave' of logistics further illustrates how our thinking and research has failed to keep pace with the realities of our workplace.

The purpose of this chapter is twofold. First, it illustrates the importance and potential impact of the human resource factor in logistics. Second, it suggests avenues for improving the logistics function by considering aspects of human resource management in organizations.

An implicit assumption which underpins most of the preceding chapters is the desire to increase effectiveness and efficiency in organizational logistics. This chapter will point out that, in a changing social and work environment, the achievement of this goal is greatly enhanced by focusing on human resource issues in the organization.

The traditional view of logistics

Logistics is generally defined as the process of strategically managing the acquisition, movement and storage of materials, parts and finished inventory (and related information flows) through an organization and its marketing channels to fulfil orders most cost-effectively. In an analysis of this function, Pfohl and Zollner (1988) summarize the major factors that impact upon the design and operation of this function within organizations. These factors include the nature of the environment within which the organization oper-

475

ates, the types of products supplied, the technology used and the size of the organization.

No specific mention is made of the impact and contribution made by the organization's human resources. It is generally believed that these (human) resources can simply be slotted into the appropriate jobs inside the requisite structure. However, there is much evidence to suggest that this approach will not optimize the productivity of the whole system – indeed, it may even result in situations where the organization's human resources hinder the overall functioning of the system (Koehn, 1983). As organizations have changed in response to their new environments (see Chapter 30), the human resource factor has emerged as a critical component in the overall productivity equation for logistics. Changes in organization design and structure, as well as fundamental shifts in the basic value systems of our workforce, suggest a more complete view of performance and productivity in our logistics systems.

A human resources view of logistics

The performance of the logistics function might be viewed as the interplay between the key factors of organizational characteristics, group dynamics and the individual's attributes.

The model in Figure 29.1 reflects the various factors that contribute to performance in the logistics function. As many of these have been discussed in preceding chapters, the discussion which follows will focus only on those human resource factors that impact upon the performance of the logistics function (all the factors in bold type).

The human resource factors in logistics

Ability
Ability refers to an individual's capacity to perform the various tasks in a job. It is an assessment of what he or she can do. An individual's overall abilities are essentially made up of his or her intellectual and physical skills.

Intellectual ability
Four important intellectual dimensions may be identified (see Table 29.1), and the individual's abilities in each should be assessed against

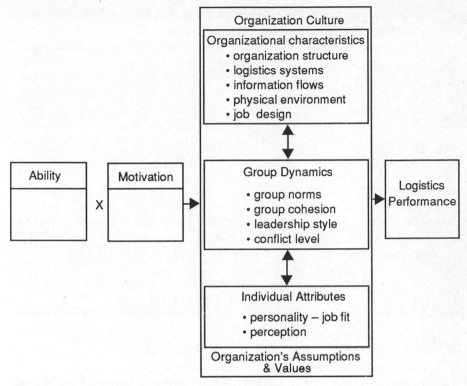

Figure 29.1   Human resources view of logistics

Table 29.1
Dimensions of intellectual ability

Dimension	Description
Number aptitude	Ability to do fast and accurate arithmetic computation
Verbal comprehension	Ability to understand what is read and heard
Perceptual speed	Ability to identify visually similarities and differences between items
Inductive reasoning	Ability to identify a logical sequence in a problem and then to solve the problem

Table 29.2
Nine basic physical abilities

Strength Factors:

Dynamic strength	Ability to exert muscular force repeatedly or continuously over time
Trunk strength	Ability to exert muscular strength using the trunk
Static strength	Ability to exert force against external objects
Explosive strength	Ability to expend a maximum of energy in one or more explosive bursts

Flexibility Factors:

Extent flexibility	Ability to move the trunk and back muscles as far as possible
Dynamic flexibility	Ability to make rapid, repeated flexing movements

Other factors:

Body Coordination	Ability to coordinate simultaneous actions of different parts of the body
Balance	Ability to retain bodily balance over uneven terrain

the requirements of the job. Generally speaking, the more senior the job, the higher the level of intellectual ability that may be required.

Most jobs in the logistics function will consist of all four dimensions, but their relative importance will differ according to the type of job and level of seniority within the organization.

Physical ability

In many parts of the logistics function, individuals will be called upon to perform tasks and jobs that require physical abilities. Research has revealed nine basic abilities which are found in varying degrees in jobs (Fleishman, 1979).

The better the ability–job fit, the better the likely performance of an individual in the job. Clearly, where abilities do not meet job requirements, the individual is likely to fail. Where abilities exceed job requirements, the individual will probably perform satisfactorily in the short to medium term. In the longer term, however, dissatisfaction and boredom will reduce overall performance and organizational efficiencies.

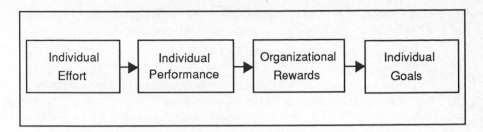

Figure 29.2 Simplified expectancy model of motivation

The best fit is one in which the individual not only has adequate ability to meet the immediate requirements of the job, but also where an opportunity to "grow into the job" exists.

Motivation

Motivation is the willingness to exert high levels of effort towards organizational goals, conditioned by the effort's ability to satisfy some individual need. Motivation is usually viewed as a result of the interaction between the individual and a situation (Robbins, 1986).

In an effort to explain and predict levels of motivation amongst individuals, a large number of theories have been developed over the years. These include the well known hierarchy of needs theory (Maslow, 1954), Theory x and Theory y (McGregor, 1960) and the motivation-hygiene theory (House and Wigdor, 1967). Currently, however, the expectancy theory is the most widely accepted explanation of motivation (Vroom, 1964; Porter and Lawler, 1968; Arnold, 1981).

The expectancy theory argues that the tendency to act in a certain way depends on the expectation of a given outcome, and of the attractiveness of that outcome to the individual. A simplified version of this model appears as Figure 29.2.

There are three key variables in this model:

1 attractiveness of the outcome – how desirable the potential outcome is to the individual.
2 performance–reward linkage – the degree to which the individual believes that performing at a particular level will result in the desired outcome;
3 effort–performance linkage – the individual's perceived probability that exerting a given amount of effort will lead to performance.

The four steps inherent in this theory are as follows:

a) *What perceived outcomes does the job offer to employees?* These may be positive (pay, a chance to use skills, security) or negative (fatigue, frustration, dismissal). Remember, it is the *perception* of what the outcomes are, regardless of whether or not they are accurate.

b) *How attractive or desirable are the outcomes to the individual?* This is an internal issue for individuals and considers their personal values, personality and needs.

c) *What kind of behaviour is necessary to produce these outcomes?* Unless the individual understands clearly what behaviours are required, the outcomes are unlikely to have much effect on performance.

d) *How does the individual view his/her chances of doing what is asked of him/her?* This obviously depends on an assessment of personal competences and the ability to control those variables that determine success.

There are thus four key implications of the expectancy theory of motivation:

- It emphasizes pay-offs and rewards. Therefore, the rewards offered by organizations should align with individual wants.
- It requires an understanding of what value the individual places on organizational pay-offs. In other words, how important are organizational pay-offs relative to other aspirations that the individual might have?
- It focuses on expected behaviours. Therefore, it is essential that the individual understands clearly what behaviours are expected and how they are likely to be appraised.
- It concerns expectations. Thus, an individual's own *expectations* of performance and outcomes will determine the level of effort, not the *actual* outcomes themselves.

Organizational culture

The organizational culture may be referred to as a collective frame of reference shared by the personnel in an organization (Berger and Luckman, 1966). This frame of reference produces the shared meaning and understanding amongst these personnel, and serves to distinguish the organization from other organizations (Becker, 1982).

The organization's culture is made up of the organization's underlying assumptions which reflect the taken-for-granted 'truths'; values and beliefs about the organization's means and ends; and the various

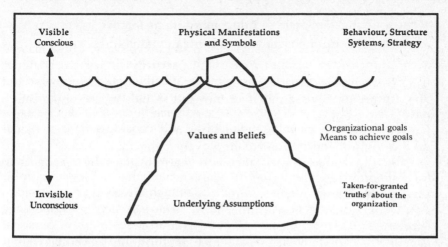

Figure 29.3   The organizational iceberg

physical manifestations and symbols of these assumptions, values and beliefs (Pondy and Mitroff, 1979; Schein, 1981; Schein, 1985). A convenient representation of organization culture is the iceberg (Chorn, 1987).

The implications of this model are threefold:

1   The bulk of the organization lies 'below the surface'. The visible and conscious elements of an organization are a small part of the total.

2   The values, beliefs and underlying assumptions held by personnel make up the organization's collective frame of reference. This influences and shapes its physical manifestations and symbols. Behaviour, systems, structure and strategy are therefore *reflections* of these organizations' values, beliefs and underlying assumptions.

3   Programmes and plans to change the organization's strategies should have a major focus on the elements below the surface. Attempts to shift strategy without a concomitant shift in values, beliefs and assumptions will only produce a partial or short-lived change in the way the strategy is actually implemented.

Dimensions of culture

The shape of the organization's physical manifestations is largely influenced by the nature of the values, beliefs and assumptions with regard to eight important dimensions, which are summarized in table 29.3 below. It follows, therefore, that changes in strategy or any

Table 29.3
Eight dimensions of organizational culture

- *Individual autonomy:* the degree of responsibility, independence and opportunity to exercise initiative that individuals in the organization have.
- *Control:* the degree of rules, regulations and direct supervision that is used to control and coordinate employees behaviour.
- *Support:* the degree of assistance and warmth given by managers to their subordinates.
- *Identity:* the degree to which employees identify with the organization as a whole rather than with their work group or field of professional expertise.
- *Performance–reward:* the degree to which organizational rewards (wages, promotion) are based on employee performance criteria.
- *Conflict tolerance:* the degree of conflict present in work relationships between peers and groups, and the willingness to be open and honest about these.
- *Communication:* the nature and extent of the patterns of communication within the organisation.
- *Risk tolerance:* the degree to which employees are encouraged to be aggressive, innovative and risk-seeking.

Source: Adapted from Campbell, Dunnette, Lawler and Weick, 1970.

organizational arrangements should be accompanied by changes in the eight cultural dimensions.

Impact of culture

By producing a sense of shared meaning and understanding, the culture impacts on the organization in very specific ways. It creates cohesion and cooperation within the organization, is responsible for shaping the distinctive 'style' that distinguishes one organization from another, and engenders the loyalty and commitment to the organization and its vision. The effects of culture are summarized in Table 29.4 below.

The phenomenon of culture in organizations produces a number of implications for the management of the logistics function. These are as follows.

1   In order to fully understand the organization and its logistics capabilities, the culture has to be defined and diagnosed.

Table 29.4
The effect of culture on the organization

- *Communication:* Culture improves communication within the organization by providing members with a common language. Language is a symbol of culture.
- *Style:* Culture defines the psychological contract between an individual and the organization. This identifies the role structure and behavioural expectations from individuals, and so produces the organization's distinctive style.
- *Status:* Culture produces the different status levels in the organization by allocating power, influence and authority. This acts as an incentive to employees and sets the patterns of work.
- *Membership:* Culture identifies the membership attributes that the organization considers valuable. This guides newcomers and existing employees to act in the appropriate manner to retain their membership.
- *Behaviour:* Culture produces a common frame of reference for the individuals in the organization. This guides decision-making and behaviour, particularly in unusual circumstances or decentralized location.
- *Commitment:* Culture assimilates and embodies the vision for the future of the organization. By sharing the organization's values and beliefs, commitment to this vision is induced.

Source: Chorn, 1987

2   Strategy and logistics capabilities 'emerge' from the organization's culture. Culture therefore shapes a large part of the organization's strategic agenda, rather than the other way around.

3   Culture is an important component in the *implementation* of a specific strategy. Where the strategy runs counter to some of the dimensions of the organization's culture, its chances of successful implementation are diminished.

4   Culture represents a powerful source of control over the implementation of strategy. A vital part of management's role, therefore, is the active shaping and influencing of organizational culture.

Job design
The manner in which jobs are designed will influence individual performance and satisfaction. As discussed above, motivation is

Table 29.5
Five core job dimensions

- *Skill variety:* the degree to which a job requires a variety of different activities so that the worker can use a variety of skills and talents.
- *Task identity:* the degree to which a job requires completion of a whole and identifiable piece of work.
- *Task significance:* the degree to which a job has substantial impact on the lives or work of other people.
- *Autonomy:* the degree to which the job provides freedom, independence and discretion to the individual in scheduling the work and in determining the procedures to be used in carrying it out.
- *Feedback:* the degree to which carrying out the work activities results in the individual getting direct and clear information about the effectiveness of his or her performance.

viewed as the interaction between the individual and a given situation. In this case, the situation is the design of the job, which refers to the way in which the various tasks are combined to form the complete job.

The Job Characteristics Model (Hackman *and* Oldham, 1975) suggests that jobs which are high on *motivating potential* are more likely to produce consistently high levels of performance. Jobs may be defined in terms of five core dimensions, and the combination of these produce the overall level of motivating potential. Table 29.5 describes these core dimensions, and Figure 29.4 shows how they combine to impact ultimately on performance.

Group norms

Within organizations, departments and work groups often form subsets of the overall organizational culture. These 'sub-cultures' usually manifest themselves in different standards of behaviour that are shared by the group members.

Most groups have established norms which 'tell' members what they ought or ought not to do under certain circumstances. When agreed to and accepted by the group, norms act as a means of influencing the behaviour of group members with a minimum of external controls. Formalized norms are written up in organizational manuals, setting out the rules and procedures for employees to follow. However, the majority of norms in groups and organizations are informal.

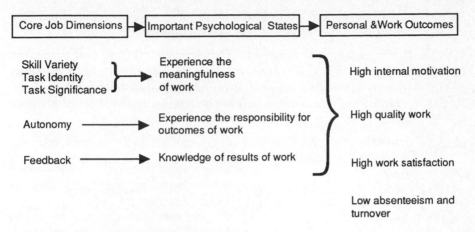

Figure 29.4   The Job Characteristics Model
Source: Hackman 1979

Common Group Norms
Although a group's norms are unique, there are still some common classes of norms that appear in many organizations:

- Effort and performance – work norms that provide members with explicit cues on how hard they should work and their overall output quantity and quality.
- Dress codes – indications on what the acceptable style and class of dress should be. These are often influenced by the preferred lifestyle of members as well as the prevailing working conditions.
- Loyalty – the nature of the psychological attachment and commitment to an organization. Loyalty norms generally result in certain required behaviours when dealing with the public or being asked to perform an unpleasant duty.

How group norms develop
Most group norms develop in one or more of the following ways (Feldman, 1984):

- from explicit statements or rulings by a powerful member of the group – often a supervisor or informal leader;
- from important events which occurred in the group's history and set precedents;
- from primacy – the first or early events that occur in a group often sets the pattern for the future;

- from carry-over from past situations – where group members bring certain behaviours from past experience into the group.

Only important norms are established. Generally, not all situations are covered by agreed upon norms and standards of behaviour. Groups will usually establish and enforce group norms when these are 'important' to it. Important norms are generally those that:

- facilitate group survival;
- increase the predictability of group member's behaviour, and allow them to anticipate each other's actions and responses in given situations;
- reduce embarrassing interpersonal problems amongst members;
- allow the members to express the central values and distinctive identity of the group.

There is much evidence to suggest that groups exert significant pressure on individuals to get them to conform to the accepted norms (Kiesler and Kiesler, 1969). Some groups have more potential to achieve conformity from individuals than others, and these are generally referred to as *reference groups*. In general, reference groups are those that the individual would like to join, or considers to be relevant in a given situation (Kiesler and Kiesler, 1969).

The existence of group norms has specific implications for performance in organizations:

1 Group norms generally press individuals towards conformity.
2 Group norms can, and sometimes do, develop contrary to the organization's performance expectations.
3 Overall organizational performance can be detrimentally affected by the presence of counter-group norms.

Group cohesion
Group cohesion refers to the degree to which individual members are attracted to one another and share the group's goals.

Determinants of cohesion
Group cohesion is brought about by a number of factors which influence individual members and the group as a whole. These include:

- *Time spent together*: the amount of time spent together has a positive effect on cohesion amongst individuals. Often, this factor

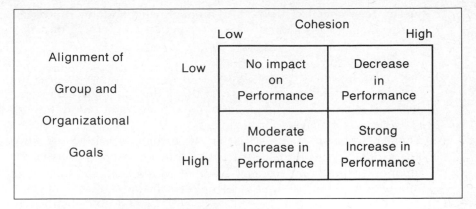

Figure 29.5 Relationship of cohesion and performance
Source: Adapted from Robbins, 1986

is influenced by geographical proximity where people, who are physically close to one another, are able to spend more time together.

- *Initiation process*: how difficult it is to gain and retain membership of a group. Where initiation processes are severe, cohesion amongst members will increase.
- *Group size*: the number of members. Where groups are large, cohesion is reduced as it becomes more difficult for individuals to interact with all the members. The situation is reversed for smaller groups.
- *External threats*: where the group is under threat from an external source, the level of cohesion will generally rise (Stein, 1976).
- *Previous successes*: successful groups develop 'winner attitudes' and generally experience an increase in cohesion.

Impact on performance

In general terms, increased cohesion is usually associated with improved group performance (Berkowitz, 1954). However, the final performance of the group also depends on the alignment of the group's goals with those of the organization.

As Figure 29.5 suggests, high cohesion will result in good performance, provided that the group's goals are compatible with those of the organization. On the other hand, cohesive groups with goals that are contrary to the organization's will result in a decrease in the overall level of performance. Alignment of goals, therefore, becomes the key determinant as to whether or not group cohesion will increase organizational performance.

Leadership style

Leadership is viewed as the ability to influence a group towards the achievement of goals. The source of this influence might be formal, such as that provided by managerial rank in an organization. But not all leaders are managers, or vice versa.

Non-sanctioned leaders – that is, those that are able to influence others outside the formal structure – are as important, or more important, than formal leaders. In other words, leaders can emerge from within a group as well as being formally appointed.

Leadership theories

The research and theory in this area is vast. Unfortunately, much of it is confusing and contradictory. Many of the theories that are intuitively appealing and practically useful are not supported by research, while many of the more academically rigorous approaches are only good for guiding future research. Consequently, we will review one of the most widely practised leadership approaches, the Situational Leadership Model (Hersey and Blanchard, 1982).

Situational leadership

According to this approach, successful leadership is achieved by selecting the correct leadership style for a given situation. The correct leadership style is achieved by regarding the maturity level of one's followers.

This emphasizes the role of the followers and, in particular, the extent to which they accept or reject the leader. It also focuses on the followers' level of maturity, which is a composite of job maturity and psychological maturity (Figure 29.6).

The model suggests that leadership style is made up of two components – namely, relationship behaviour and task behaviour. Relationship behaviour refers to the support and encouragement given to subordinates, while task behaviour refers to issues concerning the work itself and productivity levels.

As the maturity of followers increase, so the leader is expected to modify his or her style by moving through telling, selling, participating and delegating. In each case, the appropriate combination of relationship and task behaviour is combined to produce the requisite style of leadership.

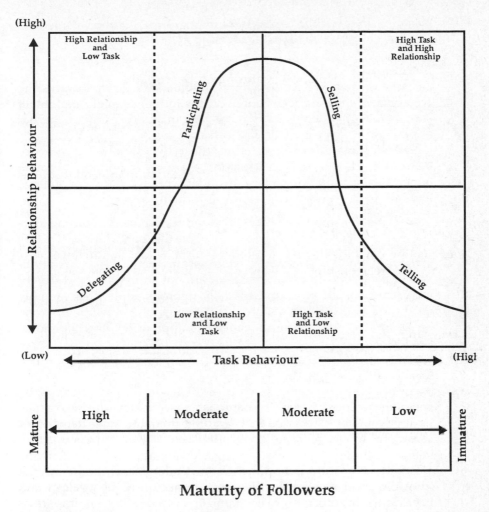

Maturity of Followers

Figure 29.6   Situational leadership
   Source: Hersey and Blanchard, 1982

Table 29.6 below summarizes the relevant four leadership styles.

The major implication of this model is that the effective manager will modify his or her style as circumstances change. This assumes, of course, that the individual is capable of a reasonable amount of flexibility in leadership style, and can make the necessary adjustments in the levels of task and relationship behaviour.

Although there is contradictory evidence on this point, it is

Table 29.6
Situational leadership styles

Style	Components	Maturing of Followers	Description
Telling	High task–low relationship	Low	The leader defines roles, and tells people what, how, when and where to do tasks. Emphasis on directive behaviour
Selling	High task–high relationship	Moderate–Low	The leader provides both directive behaviour and supportive behaviour
Participating	Low task–high relationship	Moderate–High	The leader and follower share in decision-making. The main role of the leader is facilitating and communicating
Delegating	Low task–low relationship	High	The leader provides little direction or support

Source: Adapted from Hersey and Blanchard, 1982.

generally accepted, however, that most managers are capable of some flexibility in their repertoire of leadership skills, and that greater sensitivity to the requisite style often comes with experience in a managerial role.

Finally, it is worth noting that an impending crisis, or a matter of great importance, will have the effect of increasing the levels of task behaviour. In other words, managers faced with an important decision in a crisis situation will often resort to a 'selling' or even 'telling' style until the crisis is over. In these cases, managers should evaluate whether the possible resentment caused by treating followers as 'immature' is worth the benefits of averting the crisis.

Conflict Level

Conflict is defined as the process whereby an effort is made to offset the efforts of others in a form of blocking behaviour which is likely to produce frustration and anxiety. Some of the key underlying assumptions of this definiton include the following:

- Conflict exists if the different parties perceive it to exist.
- The different parties have different interests or goals.
- One, or more, of the parties acts deliberately to block and frustrate the effort of the other(s).

Is conflict good or bad?
Our views on conflict have evolved steadily as organizations and group behaviour have been studied. The traditional view held that most conflict in groups was bad, and that managers should attempt to eliminate it entirely. Although we readily acknowledge that this view is inappropriate in modern organizations, many of us still evaluate conflict using this outmoded standard.

The behavioural view, which dominated theory from 1950 until the mid-1970s, holds that conflict is inevitable and cannot be eliminated. Consequently, it should be managed and even institutionalized. Much of our industrial relations legislation is based on this premise.

Finally, the interactionist view (Robbins, 1986) argues that an optimum level of conflict exists in groups and organizations. Too little conflicts results in groups becoming static, apathetic and non-responsive, while too much conflict results in dysfunctional behaviour and high levels of energy being directed towards unproductive activities. Figure 29.7 summarizes this situation.

- *Stage one – potential opposition*: This describes the condition that creates the opportunities for conflict to arise. Factors include poor communication (although it is a major myth that poor communication is the cause of most conflict), organization structure (particularly those that create separate groups of specialists) and personal variables (such as personal values and beliefs).
- *Stage two – cognition and personalization*: This is the stage at which individuals actually feel and/or perceive the conflict. At this point individuals become emotionally involved and experience anxiety, tension, frustration or hostility.
- *Stage three – behaviour*: At this stage, individuals take action to either prevent others from achieving their goals, or to handle the conflict situation in which they find themselves.

In conflict–inducing behaviour, we are able to identify a broad spectrum from subtle, indirect, and highly controlled forms of interference to direct, aggressive, violent and uncontrolled struggle. At the low range, this behaviour is illustrated by a student who raises his or her hand in class to question a point made by the

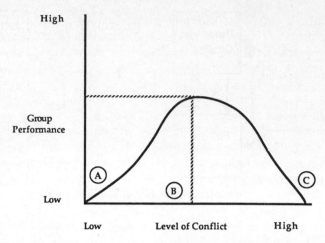

Situation	Conflict Level	Type of Conflict	Group's Internal Characteristics	Group's Performance Outcome
A	Low, or none	Dysfunctional	Apathetic Stagnant Non-responsive to change	Low
B	Optimal	Functional	Viable Self Critical Innovative	High
C	High	Dysfunctional	Disruptive Chaotic Uncooperative	Low

Figure 29.7   Conflict and group performance

instructor. At the high range, strikes, riots and warfare are an example.

Conflict–handling behaviour also occurs at the behaviour stage. A range of behaviours are used by individuals for dealing with their conflict. These may be explained by considering the factors of cooperativeness and assertiveness (Thomas, 1976). Cooperativeness measures the extent to which one party attempts to satisfy

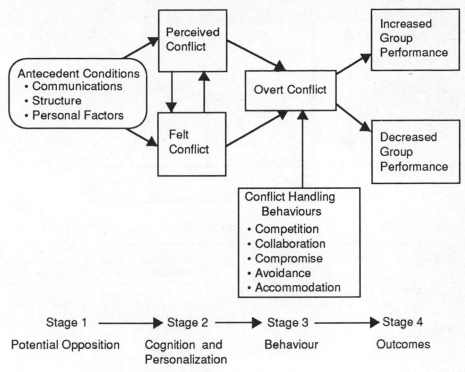

Figure 29.8 The conflict process
Source: Robbins, 1986

the other party's concerns, while assertiveness refers to the degree to which a party attempts to satisfy his or her own concerns. The likely conflict–handling behaviours are depicted in Figure 29.9.

- *Stage four – outcomes:* the interplay between the conflict–inducing and conflict–handling behaviours result in certain outcomes and consequences. As discussed earlier, these may be functional (positive) or dysfunctional (negative). Functional outcomes result when the conflict stimulates thought, debate and constructive criticism, while dysfunctional outcomes result from apathy and laziness (low conflict) or disruptive behaviour (high conflict).

Personality – job fit
Personality describes the sum total of ways in which an individual reacts and interacts with others. Personality therefore describes the overall pattern of actions, behaviours and communication which an individual displays over a period of time.

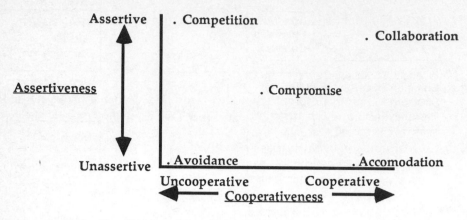

Figure 29.9   Conflict-handling behaviour
  Source: Thomas, 1976

How is personality determined?
An adult's personality is generally considered to be made up of both hereditary and environmental factors, moderated by situational conditions:

Heredity
These are factors determined at conception. Physical and physiological characteristics are generally considered to be either completely or substantially influenced by one's parents, but this is not the case with personality. Although the heredity approach argues that personality is determined by the molecular structure of one's genes (Kelly, 1974), this viewpoint is generally not supported by research. While this approach may be appealing to the bigots of the world, it remains an inadequate explanation of personality.

Environment
Environmental factors play a critical role in shaping our personalities. In particular, we are largely influenced by the culture in which we are raised, the norms of our family, friends and social groups, and other influences and experiences that we are exposed to.
   Although heredity may set some of the outer limits of an individuals potential, the full potential will be determined by how he or she

adjusts to the demands and opportunities presented by the environment.

Situation
An individual's personality, while generally stable and consistent, does change in different situations. Different demands in different situations bring out different aspects of one's personality (Sechrest, 1976). In particular, we know that certain situations impose more constraints on behaviour than others. An employment interview, for example, would probably constrain behaviour, while a picnic in a park would impose far fewer constraints.

Matching personality and jobs
In attempting to match individuals (with different personalities) with jobs, we make three important assumptions:

1   Different people appear to have different personalities.
2   Certain personalities are suited to certain kinds of jobs and roles.
3   Improving the personality–job fit will improve the ultimate performance of the individual in the job

Figure 29.10 identifies six basic personality types. Each has a set of key characteristics and can therefore be matched with certain types of jobs. Table 29.7 lists these characteristics and job types.

Figure 29.10 also identifies that the closer two personality types are to one another on the hexagon, the more compatible they are. Opposites indicate the greatest degree of incompatibility. The obvious implication of this theory is that one should attempt to match an individual with a compatible job type. The greater the incompatibility, the greater the tendency for poor job performance and dissatisfaction.

Perception
Perception is the final factor which determines performance in the logistics function. It is the process whereby individuals organize and interpret their sensory impressions in order to give meaning to their environment. It is therefore the process that allows them to understand their environment.

We are interested in perceptions because people's behaviour is based on their *perceptions* of what reality is, not reality itself. In an organization, therefore, people will behave and make decisions on the basis of the way that they understand (perceive) the organization

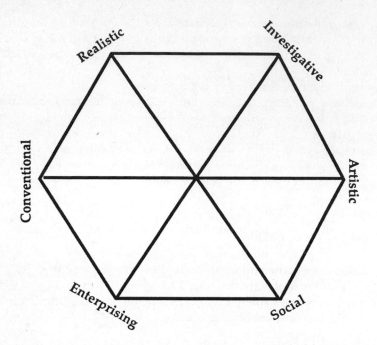

Figure 29.10   Personality type
        Source: Holland, 1973

and its goals, and this has obvious implications for overall performance.

What influences perception?

Why do different people perceive the same thing differently? A number of factors operate to shape and sometimes distort perceptions. These include:

- The perceiver: the personal characteristics of the individual influences what he or she perceives. Among the more relevant personal characteristics affecting perception are attitudes, motives, interests, past experience and expectations of the future.
- The target: characteristics of the target being observed also affect what is observed. For example, loud people are more likely to be noticed than quiet, reserved people. Motion, sound, size and other attributes of a target also shape the way we see it.

    In addition, targets are not looked at in isolation. The relationship of a target to its background influences perception, as does

Table 29.7
Matching personality types with jobs

Personality Type	Personality Characteristics	Job types suited to the personality
Realistic	Involves aggressive behaviour, physical activities requiring skill, strength and co-ordination	forestry, farming, architecture, factory work, building
Investigative	Involves activities requiring thinking, organizing and understanding rather than feeling or emotion	biology, mathematics. news reporting
Social	Involves interpersonal activities rather than intellectual or physical activities	social work, clinical psychology
Conventional	Involves rule-regulated activities and sublimination of personal needs to an organization or person of power and status	accounting, finance, corporate management
Enterprising	Involves verbal activities to influence others in order to attain power and status	law, public relations small-business management
Artistic	Involves self-expression, artistic creation or emotional activities	art, music, writing

our tendency to group close things and similar things together. Because of this, we tend to think of people in a department as a group who hold similar views and opinions. Women, blacks or any other group that has clearly distinguishable characteristics in terms of features or colour will tend to be perceived as alike in other, unrelated, characteristics as well.

Thus, perceptions will often distort reality significantly, causing us to make generalizations too hastily and often failing to recognize significant differences in people and situations.

- The situation: The context in which we see objects or events is important. Elements in the surrounding environment influence our perceptions, and allow us to notice or miss features of significance.

Characteristics of the perceiver, the target and the situation will therefore influence the manner in which individuals perceive and understand their organizational environment. Understanding these influences is important, as it can help us to better understand the reality faced by the individual, and therefore, to better manage performance.

Conclusions

The human resource factors outlined in this chapter allow us to 'fill in' the all-important contribution to performance that is made by the people in our organizations. However, instead of considering them *after* the more traditional factors in logistics management, they should be viewed at least as equal in importance.

As the research in the chapter has revealed, the human resource factor makes a significant contribution to performance where it is neglected or nurtured. The most sophisticated logistics and distribution systems can be rendered inoperable by an uncooperative and unwilling workforce. On the other hand, as a vital resource in the organization, it is one of the few assets that, if correctly nurtured and developed, can appreciate significantly in value over time.

References

1   Arnold, H. J., 'A Test of the Multiplicative Hypothesis of Expectancy' – Valence Theories of Work Motivation, *Academy of Management Journal*, April, 1981.

2   Ballou, R. H. *Business Logistics Management*. Prentice Hall, Englewood Cliffs, New Jersey, 1973.

3   Becker, H.S., 'Culture: A Sociological View', *Yale Review*, Summer 1982.

4   Berger, P. L. and Luckman T., *'The Social Construction of Reality'*, Anchor Books, New York, 1966.

5   Berkowitz, L., 'Group Standards, Cohesiveness and Productivity Human Relations', Human Relations, November, 1954.

6   Campbell, J. P., Dunnette, M. D., Lawler, E. E. and Weick, K. E.,

Managerial Behaviour, Performance and Effectiveness, New York: McGraw-Hill, 1970.

7　Chorn, N. H., The Relationship between Business-Level Strategy and Organisational Culture, Unpublished Ph.D. thesis, University of Witwatersrand, 1987.

8　Feldman, D. C., 'The Development and Enforcement of Group Norms,' Academy of Management Journal, January, 1984.

9　Fleishman, E. A., 'Evaluating Physical Abilities Required by Jobs', *Personnel Administrator*, June, 1979.

10　Hackman, J. R. and Oldham, G. R., 'Development of the Job Diagnostic Survey', Journal of Applied Psychology, April 1975.

11　Hersey, P. and Blanchard, K. H., Management of Organisational Behaviour: Utilizing Human Resources, London: Prentice Hall, 1982.

12　House, R. J. and Wigdor, L. A., 'Herzberg's Dual-Factor Theory of Job Satisfaction and Motivations: A Review of the Evidence and Criticisms', *Personnel Psychology*, Winter 1967.

13　Kelly, J., Organization Behaviour, Homewood Ill: Richard Irwin, 1974.

14　Kiesler, C. A. and Kiesler, S. B., *Conformity*, New York: Addision-Wesley, 1969.

15　Koehn, H. E., 'The Post-Industrial Worker', *Public Personnel Management Journal*, Fall 1983.

16　McGregor, D., *The Human Side of Enterprise*, McGraw Hill, New York: 1960.

17　Maslow, A., *Motivation and Personality*, Harper and Row, New York: 1954.

18　Pondy, L. R. and Mitroff, I. I., *Beyond Open Systems Models of Organizations*, JAI Press, New York, 1979.

19　Porter, L. W. and Lawler, E. E., *Managerial Attitudes and Performance*. Homewood, Illinois, Richard Irwin, 1968.

20　Pfohl, H. C. and Zollner, W., 'Organisation for Logistics', *International Journal of Physical Distribution and Materials Management*, 17 January, 1988.

21　Robbins, S., Organization Theory: The Structure and Design of Organizations, Prentice Hall, Englewood Cliffs, NJ: 1986.

22　Robbins, S., *Organization Behaviour: Concepts, Controversies and Applications*. Prentice Hall, Englewood Cliffs, NJ: 1986.

23　Schein, E. H., 'Does Japanese Style have a message for American Managers?,' Sloan Management Review, Fall 1981.

24 Schein, E. H., *Organization Culture and Leadership*, Jossey-Bass, California: 1985.

25 Sechrest, L., 'Personality', *Annual Review of Psychology*, Vol. 27, 1976.

26 Stein, A., 'Conflict and Cohesion. A Review of the Literature', *Journal of Conflict Resolution*, March, 1976.

27 Thomas, K. W. (1976) 'Conflict and Conflict Management' in M. Dunelle (ed), *Handbook of Industrial and Organizational Psychology*, Rand McNally, Chicago, 1976.

28 Vroom, V. H., *Work and Motivation*, John Wiley, New York: 1964.

30 The New Logistics Organization

Norman Chorn

Introduction

In understanding the logistics function of the future, we need to understand something of the organization of the future. Since the organization provides a framework within which the logistics function takes place, a knowledge of this will provide useful pointers as to the future shape of logistics.

Shifting organizations

The last 40 years has revealed a number of significant changes inside Western organizations. In general, we have shifted away from organizations dominated by simple, physical tasks and mechanical technology to those characterized by increasingly complex, intellectual tasks and electronic (even biological) technology. Problems and decisions which were characterized by direct cause and effect relationships are increasingly replaced by situations in which multiple cause and effect links are evident. Stable markets and suppliers are gradually giving way to more fluid, dynamic market environments, and the clear distinctions which existed between management and workers no longer apply (Kanter, 1983).

As these changes continue to confront organizations, managers and leaders seek better understanding of the trends and issues that these changes represent. To this end, it is useful to briefly review the key features of the different phases in the development of our modern organization. In doing this, it is hoped that we will arrive at a better understanding of the organizational environment of the future, and consequently, the logistics function within.

Models of organization

Since the 1940s, each decade has been marked by a series of characteristics which have distinguished organizations. These may be summarized as follows:

- 1940s:
  - traditional approach to organisations,
  - focus on core activities of making the product, selling it, and collecting the money
  - management seen as the 'brain' of the organization,
  - paternalistic approach to employees.
- 1950s:
  - focus on work study and improving the organization's efficiency,
  - recognition that a contented workforce is likely to be more productive,
  - management viewed as a gentlemanly activity.
- 1960s:
  - focus on acquisition and expanding markets,
  - autocratic and technocratic approaches to management,
  - a planned approach to organizational growth.
- 1970s:
  - inflation, credit squeezes and the rationalizing of business,
  - growth and increasing importance of technology, particularly electronic,
  - management focus on the development of the organization's human resources,
  - growth of rational, logical approaches to management, such as MBO.

In analysing these characteristics, it is possible to identify a number of relatively distinct organizational models. By models, we mean the templates that managers use in their decisions about the nature of organizations. These are the frames of reference, the sets of assumptions about the way organisations are and should be managed (Limerick, 1987).

Essentially, three models of organization dominate our thinking up to the present. These are:

1 *The traditional/classical model*: the period up to the 1940s which was characterized by a concern for the basic functions of business and organization.

2   *The human relations model*: the period during the 1950s which saw the surge in interest in the contribution made by the organization's human resources.
3   *The systems model*: the period between the 1960s and 1970s which saw a renewed interest in improving organizational efficiency and effectiveness through an application of systems theory.

In many respects, the development of the organization of the future is a reaction to the models of the past. In particular, the systems model has produced a series of reactions which has contributed to a new form with far-reaching implications for the logistics function. For this reason, it is useful to review a number of assumptions which underpin the systems model and to consider some of the implications for organizations.

The systems model

The core assumptions which underpin systems theory in organizations are:

1   *Interdependence*: Organizations should be tightly coupled internally. Everything should be interrelated.
2   *Alignment*: Organizations should be aligned to the needs of the environment, reflecting the environmental needs in structural characteristics.
3   *Holism*: Organizations should be viewed as a whole – this allows us to understand the parts more completely.
4   *Rationality*: Organizations may be understood and designed by applying high levels of rationality and logic.
5   *Teamwork*: Organizations will operate effectively when they are made up of tightly coupled, interlocking groups of people (Limerick and Cunnington, 1987).

Increasingly, the systems model has proved unsuccessful in dealing with rapidly changing, turbulent environments.

Interdependence has produced clumsiness and created large, cumbersome organizations which are unable to respond to changes swiftly because of the need to consider all the linkage points and dependencies.

The concept of alignment has led to organizations studying the environment to identify trends and indications which suggest new patterns of alignment and internal configurational. This has resulted in reactive, 'after-the-event' changes which are inevitably too late to capitalize on environmental opportunities. Indeed, the concept of adjusting to environmental change is the antithesis of entrepreneurial behaviour which we continually cry out for.

Holism implies that the individual parts or units within the organization are part of some larger whole. This largely negates the concept that the organization might be made up of business units which are dominated by different sets of strategic logic.

The dominance of rationality and logic in organizations has resulted in the suppression of the *feeling* and *creative* dimensions of thinking and planning. The 'big idea' and the ability to 'create' has consequently been underplayed in favour of analysis and optimization.

Finally, the focus on teamwork has suppressed the contribution of the *individual* and the resultant maverick-type behaviour which is needed to challenge traditional assumptions. Organizations have found it more difficult to shift out of their well accepted styles and approaches.

A new model of organization

Largely as a result of the deficiencies of the systems model in a changing, turbulent environment, a new model of organization has emerged (Peters and Waterman, 1982: Limerick and Cunnington, 1987: Drucker, 1985). This new model appears to be characterized by five key features which reflect the changing assumptions of organizations and their environments. These are described below.

Vision before analysis

In a deliberate attempt to be pro-active in a changing and turbulent environment, organizations are articulating their overall purpose and direction prior to undertaking more detailed analysis of the environment. Instead of reacting to the environment by selecting options after an analysis of various opportunities, they act as 'path-finders' by imagining and creating future scenarios for themselves.

The analysis that follows is *not* of lesser importance, however. It takes place *after* the overall vision has been articulated, and in this way, is clearly *focused* around the specific needs of the organization's future direction. Perhaps more importantly, the analysis is now viewed as a tool to enable the organization to achieve its strategic purposes, rather than a framework which reactively determines the vision.

Individual oriented

As opposed to the obsession of developing effective teamwork which dominated management thinking in the 1970s, managers now recognize that *individuals* will play an increasingly important role in making organizations effective. It is individuals that are at the core of creative, innovative ideas and the delivery of good customer service. Limerick (1987) has coined the term 'collaborative individualism' to describe the phenomenon of individuals who are not imprisoned by the boundaries of the group, and who can act with self-driven capacity to transform organizations. At the same time, however, these individuals understand the need to act in concert with respect to a broadly defined common agenda.

Collaborative individualism therefore differs radically from the systems concept of cohesive teamwork. In many ways, it may be considered as the opposite end of the spectrum, and views the contribution made by individuals as paramount in the alignment of organizations with their environments.

Fluid teams

With respect to the *collaborative* component of individualism, organizations are developing a fluid approach to the concept of teams. By and large, individuals are combining their efforts to work collectively on projects or assignments for shorter periods of time. The task at hand, rather than the organization structure, becomes the primary logic for the team's make up. In addition, three other characteristics distinguish these teams from those found in more traditional, systems-oriented organizations.

First, the teams are semi-autonomous and only loosely coupled with one another (Meddings, 1989). As Limerick (1987) points out, this usually results in fewer, rather than more, relationships amongst people in the organization. Second, the make-up of these teams changes continuously as the tasks and assignments evolve. As an individual's particular skills become more or less important to the team, he or she shifts from team to team. Finally, individuals may find themselves as members of several teams, playing different roles in each. In some, their organizing and process skills may be utilized, while in others they might be called on to contribute a particular knowledge or advisory expertise.

Decentralization and empowerment

To lead these organizations, chief executives are relying on smaller, leaner corporate headquarters, where all but the essential functions are being transferred into the operating divisions. Although the interpretation of 'essential' differs from case to case, the responsibility for many of the traditional centralized functions, such as strategic planning and industrial relations, are being transferred to line managers within the divisions.

To a large extent, this means that decision-making is taking place 'closer to the coalface' by people engaged in the organization's core activities. However, rather than being set a multitude of operational rules and regulations to follow, individuals are 'empowered' by the organization's leaders, which means, quite simply, that they create widespread understanding of the organization's strategic vision, and allow individuals to operate relatively independently within this strategic framework. This results in a high level of creative, market-oriented behaviour throughout the organization.

Indirect control

Whereas the systems-oriented organization is characterized by 'direct' forms of control such as objective standards, explicit job descriptions and standard operating procedures, more modern organizations increasingly rely on a range of more implicit and subjective means of control. These include a common understanding of a strategic vision, a core set of values and self-motivated individuals in key leadership positions (Chorn, 1987). This creates what Waterman (1987) refers to as 'stability in motion', and provides a series of indications to personnel about the required behaviours and approaches.

In many respects, the use of indirect means of control may be likened to the provision of a 'compass' which suggests broad directions, rather than the direct-control approach of providing a series of 'road maps'.

Guidelines for organizational architects

Given these observations about the new model of organizations, what guidelines may be offered to the architect of tomorrow's organization and logistics function?

1   *Challenge your old assumptions about how organizations function.* Recognize that the way you think about an organization is dependent upon the prevailing set of assumptions you hold about people, management and technology. This 'model' of organization may well be inappropriate in the light of today's realities and tomorrow's environment. Try to forget what you knew in the past, and visualize the world you may work in tomorrow.

　　Imagine yourself already there, and think about the conditions that your organization may have to contend with (Manning, 1988).

2   *Design an organization to fit the New World.* As Manning (1988) argues, do not be constrained by the familiar organization chart. Instead, consider the information flows and work relationships that may take place, and build networks between individuals and groups accordingly.

　　In most cases, the resultant form may look radically different to the conventional pyramid-type structures we are familiar with, but do not be concerned about this. Remember, you are purpose-building the new organization and logistics function.

3   *Consider all possible stakeholder relationships.* Stakeholders exert considerable influence over the shape and form of organizations (Freeman, 1980). In turbulent, changing environments, these stakeholder forces may shift and alter the form of the ideal organization. Consequently, all stakeholder relationships should be reviewed and assessed. Consider customers, suppliers, employees, government and any strategic alliances that might emerge. All of these factors should be accounted for in designing optimum organizations and logistic functions.

4   *Test the water: don't risk the whole organization.* Formally prepared designs which are introduced through the whole organization are unnecessary and too risky. First, they give those who are opposed to the changes the opportunity to plan their resistance (Quinn, 1985) and, second, they place the *entire* organization at risk if the design has flaws (Manning, 1988).

　　Consequently, be prepared to try out new ideas before they

have been fully formalized. Expose small parts of the organization to the changes to minimize the overall risk. This approach will give you the opportunity to learn as you go along, and also avoid disruption to the total organization.

Conclusions

Modern organizations will require new mind-sets from their leaders and managers. These will be characterized by new assumptions about people, groups, technology, leadership and the environment. By understanding these assumptions and their implications, we should be able to design a more effective and efficient logistics function.

References

Chorn, N. H., 'The Relationship between Business-Level Strategy and Organisational Culture', Unpublished Ph.D. thesis, University of Witwatersrand, 1987.

Drucker, D. F., *Innovation and Entrepreneurship*, London, Heinemann, 1985.

Freeman, M., *Managing in a Turbulent Environment*, New York, JAI Press, 1980.

Kanter, R. M., *The Change Masters: Corporate Entrepreneurs at Work*, London: George Allen and Unwin, 1983.

Limerick, D., *The Wizards of Aus: The Changing Role of Australian Chief Executives*, Australia: Griffith University, 1987.

Limerick, D. and Cunnington, 'Management Development: The Fourth Blueprint', *Journal of Management Development*, Vol.6, 1987.

Manning, A. D., *The New Age Strategist*, Johannesburg Southern, 1988.

Meddings, P., 'The Future Business Environment', *The Executive Connection*, Occasional Publication, March 1989.

Peters, T. J. and Waterman, R. H., *In Search of Excellence*, New York: Harper and Row, 1982.

Quinn, J. B., 'Innovation and Corporate Strategy; Managed Chaos, *Technology in Society*, Vol. 7.

Waterman, R. H., *The Renewal Factor*, New York, Bantam, 1987.

Index